Mito and the Politics of Reform in Early Modern Japan

NEW STUDIES IN MODERN JAPAN

Series Editors: Doug Slaymaker and William M. Tsutsui

New Studies in Modern Japan is a multidisciplinary series that consists primarily of original studies on a broad spectrum of topics dealing with Japan since the mid-nineteenth century. Additionally, the series aims to bring back into print classic works that shed new light on contemporary Japan. The series speaks to cultural studies (literature, translations, film), history, and social sciences audiences. We publish compelling works of scholarship, by both established and rising scholars in the field, on a broad arena of topics, in order to nuance our understandings of Japan and the Japanese.

Advisory Board

Michael Bourdaghs, University of Chicago
Rebecca Copeland, Washington University in St. Louis
Aaron Gerow, Yale University
Yoshikuni Igarashi, Vanderbilt University
Koichi Iwabuchi, Monash University
T. J. Pempel, University of California, Berkeley
Julia Adeney Thomas, University of Notre Dame
Dennis Washburn, Dartmouth College
Merry White, Boston University

Recent Titles in the Series

Mito and the Politics of Reform in Early Modern Japan, by Michael Alan Thornton

Wild Lines and Poetic Travels: A Keijiro Suga Reader, edited by Doug Slaymaker

A Transnational Critique of Japaneseness: Cultural Nationalism, Racism, and Multiculturalism in Japan, by Yuko Kawai

Literature among the Ruins, 1945–1955: Postwar Japanese Literary Criticism, edited by Atsuko Ueda, Michael K. Bourdaghs, Richi Sakakibara, and Hirokazu Toeda

Living Transnationally between Japan and Brazil: Routes beyond Roots, by Sarah A. LeBaron von Baeyer

Tawada Yōko: On Writing and Rewriting, edited by Doug Slaymaker

The Unfinished Atomic Bomb: Shadows and Reflections, edited by David Lowe, Cassandra Atherton, and Alyson Miller

Mito and the Politics of Reform in Early Modern Japan

Michael Alan Thornton

LEXINGTON BOOKS
Lanham • Boulder • New York • London

Published by Lexington Books
An imprint of The Rowman & Littlefield Publishing Group, Inc.
4501 Forbes Boulevard, Suite 200, Lanham, Maryland 20706
www.rowman.com

86-90 Paul Street, London EC2A 4NE

British Library Cataloguing in Publication Information Available

Library of Congress Cataloging-in-Publication Data

Names: Thornton, Michael Alan, author.
Title: Mito and the politics of reform in early modern Japan / Michael Alan
    Thornton.
Description: Lanham : Lexington Books, [2021] | Series: New studies in
    modern Japan | Includes bibliographical references and index. | Summary:
    "This book takes the perspective of Mito Domain, one of three branches
    of Japan's ruling Tokugawa shogunate, to explore the dynamic history of
    political reform in early modern Japan. This book, while grounded in
    Mito, examines the role that this domain and its people played in the
    birth of the modern Japanese nation-state in the nineteenth century"—
    Provided by publisher.
Identifiers: LCCN 2021046911 (print) | LCCN 2021046912 (ebook) | ISBN
    9781793641892 (cloth) | ISBN 9781793641908 (epub)
Subjects: LCSH: Mito-han (Japan)—Politics and government. | Mitogaku. |
    Mito-han—History. | Japan—History—1787-1868.
Classification: LCC DS894.49.I229 T46 2021 (print) | LCC DS894.49.I229
    (ebook) | DDC 952/.131025—dc23
LC record available at https://lccn.loc.gov/2021046911
LC ebook record available at https://lccn.loc.gov/2021046912

Contents

Foreword

The origins of this book date to the start of the "Project to Revitalize the Heart of Mito" (*Mito domannaka saisei project*) in February 2016, which in turn had much more personal roots. I grew up in places with deep ties to Mito's history. My elementary school, Sannomaru Elementary, was built on the grounds of the Kōdōkan, the academy founded by Tokugawa Nariaki and Fujita Tōko. My middle school, Mito Second Junior High, is on the site of the Shōkōkan, built by Tokugawa Mitsukuni to house the *Dai Nihon shi* history project. And my high school, Mito First High, is in what used to be the main compound of Mito Castle. These sites were the birthplace of Mito's famous "revere the emperor, expel the barbarian" ideology. As a teenager, I studied hard at school and trained hard on my swim team, following traditional Mito maxims: "academic and military arts should not be separated" and "balance hard work with relaxation." Incidentally, even my first kiss happened in a place with ties to Mito's past: the Kairakuen, overlooking Lake Senba.

But after graduating from high school and entering Kyoto University in 1981, my parents moved to Tokyo, and for the next thirty-four years, I drifted far from Mito. I joined a trading company, got a degree at Harvard, started a business school and a venture capital firm, GLOBIS, raised five children, and founded G1, a think tank to "improve Japan."

I returned to Mito in August 2015 to attend an alumni reunion for my old swim team. I was shocked at what I saw in Mito: there were few people walking the streets, and downtown was full of abandoned department stores and shuttered shops. I felt terrible that I'd done nothing to contribute to Mito since I left there. After talking with Mayor Takahashi Yasushi, I founded the revitalization project. My goal was simple: to raise the spirits of my hometown to the bring back prosperity to Mito, which is the capital city of Ibaraki Prefecture (Mito has 270,000 people, and Ibaraki's population is 2.8 million).

The first step in the revitalization project was to take over the local professional basketball team, the Ibaraki Robots. We then quickly established a special campus of GLOBIS and transformed an empty lot in central Mito with an arena, café, studio, and park. We bought land near the Kairakuen and on the shores of Lake Senba, and we drafted plans to boost their tourism appeal. We even acquired Ibaraki's only broadcasting station and began reforming it.

Throughout all of this, I always wanted to highlight Mito's history, and particularly its central role in the Meiji Restoration, and share that history with people across Japan and around the world. A friend introduced me to Dr. Michael Thornton, whom I immediately asked to write this book. Happily, he agreed.

To make this book a reality, I worked with Kawasaki Atsushi, the leader of the GLOBIS Mito campus, to assemble a team. I asked one of my former swim team *kōhai*, Inaba Jurō, to work with Michael on the Japanese version of this book. He supervised the translation, fact checked, and helped identify local research materials. He also wrote the Japanese appendix, a historical travel guide to Mito. His tireless support was invaluable. I'd like to express my appreciation to both Jurō and Michael for bringing this project to light. Good job, and thank you!

In 2018, we raised six million yen via crowdfunding to support the project. In 2020, we raised another three million yen to cover publication costs. I want to express my deep thanks to all those who donated to the project.

Finally, I want to offer my view of the key themes of this book. This book highlights the lives of several influential individuals in Mito's history, showing how their actions and ideas led to the Meiji Restoration. As I see it, there were four stages in this history. First, Tokugawa Mitsukuni started the *Dai Nihon shi*, which formed the basis of Mito's "revere the emperor, expel the barbarian" philosophy; under Tachihara Suiken, these ideas matured. Second, Aizawa Seishisai and Fujita Tōko helped spread Mito's ideas to people across Japan, particularly the samurai in Satsuma, Chōshū, Tosa, and Hizen domains who went on to topple the Tokugawa shogunate in 1868. Third, at the end of Tokugawa Nariaki's reign, a group of Mito samurai assassinated Ii Naosuke at Sakurada Gate, which decisively weakened the shogunate. Finally, Tokugawa Yoshinobu decided to return the Tokugawa ruling mandate to the imperial throne in late 1867, formally restoring power to the emperor. Seen this way, Mito played a role at every stage of the Restoration.

It is often said that history is written by the victors. In the Meiji period, when the national government was dominated by a clique of Satsuma and Chōshū men, Mito faded out of sight. As a Mitoite, this fact makes me sad. I really believe that Mito laid the foundation for modern Japan. The impact Mito's leaders and their ideas had on men like Shibusawa Eiichi and Matsushita Kōnosuke are proof of Mito's lasting impact. Mito's values, developed over two hundred years, inspired *shishi* across Japan to build a new era. This book shows how this happened.

Now it is up to readers to determine how it all turned out. I hope that many people will read this book, visit Mito, and discover how Mito's past shaped the birth of modern Japan.

Finally, I offer a word of thanks to Ōyama Kōsuke at PHP kenkyūjo, for his support in publishing the Japanese version of this book, and to Lexington Books for publishing this English version.

Yoshito Hori
Founder and Chair, Project to Revitalize the Heart of Mito

Acknowledgments

This project began as a short exercise in public history in the city of Mito, where locals are working hard to reinvigorate the city center and inspire locals and visitors to take interest in Mito's remarkable history. As the project developed, it turned into something much larger. The debts I owe to friends, colleagues, and supporters have correspondingly grown, too.

First, thanks are due to Yoshi Hori for inviting me to write this short history of Mito. His enthusiasm for local history is admirable. He and his colleagues in the Mito Domannaka Saisei Project have generously hosted me in Tokyo and Mito. I am also grateful to the staff at GLOBIS in Tokyo for hosting several stimulating seminars about Mito's history. Jesper Koll deserves thanks for connecting me to Yoshi and the Mito project.

A number of people in Mito have turned this project from a brief set of notes into a book. I have enjoyed the support of local officials in Mito, including Kikkawa Eisaku at the Ibaraki Prefectural Government's Tourism and Local Products Association. Kawasaki Atsushi has coordinated my visits to Mito and has been instrumental in driving this project forward.

I have worked on this project mostly while based in New Haven and New York. I have been fortunate to spend the last three years on a postdoctoral fellowship at the Council on East Asian Studies at Yale University, which has afforded me time to research and write about Mito. Special thanks are due to Professor Fabian Drixler, who convened a Japanese history workshop in which I presented early drafts of this work, and to my colleagues in that workshop. Fabian also kindly made the maps in this book. I must also thank Yale's wonderful Japanese Studies librarian, Haruko Nakamura, who helped me obtain library materials, especially during the disruption of COVID-19 in the spring of 2020. Professor Dani Botsman has also been a generous and insightful interlocutor and a patient supervisor as this project overwhelmed some of my other responsibilities.

I owe deeper debts to mentors and family. Professors Andy Gordon, David Howell, and Ian Miller trained me in Japanese history during my PhD years at Harvard, and while this book is a departure from my doctoral studies, their influence has nevertheless shaped the way I think about Mito's history, too. Kathy Krauth introduced me to Japanese history during my high school years at the American School in Japan, in Tokyo, and she remains an inspiration for putting history to use in the present. More recently, my parents offered incisive comments on every chapter of an earlier version of this manuscript via Zoom from rural Devon, England. My partner Jon patiently listened to my constant ramblings about this far-off city. He has offered steady support for a project that was meant to last for three months and, instead, has taken three years.

Many of the funds for this project have come from the people of Mito themselves, and I am enormously grateful for and humbled by the outpouring of interest and support for this project. It has been quite daunting to tackle local history, particularly in a place that takes that history so seriously, but the encouragement of people in Mito has inspired me to keep writing. I hope that I have been able to address at least a few of the many questions and suggestions raised at the many talks and seminars in Mito.

I am also grateful to the various museums and libraries that have generously allowed me to reproduce materials. These include the Ibaraki Prefectural Library, Ibaraki Prefectural Archives and Museum, Mito City, the Kōdōkan Office, the Mito Tourism and Convention Office, Tokiwa Shrine, Mito Tōshōgū, Tawara City Museum, Hokkaido University Library, Tokugawa Museum, the University of Tokyo Historiographic Institute, and the U.S. Library of Congress.

A Japanese version of this text was published in early 2021 by PHP kenkyūjo. I am grateful for the skillful editing of Ōyama Kōsuke, who turned clunky academic prose into something much more readable for a popular audience in Japan.

My thanks are also due to the editorial team at Lexington Books, who have been beyond patient as I revised and re-revised this manuscript into something more suitable for an academic press. I am grateful to the two anonymous reviewers for the press, both of whom saw promise in the manuscript and pushed me to rework it in more fruitful directions.

Finally, I reserve my most heartfelt appreciation for Inaba Jurō. Inaba-san has been a tireless advocate for this project, and his seemingly limitless knowledge about Mito's past has proven indispensable. His thorough and exacting comments have helped me avoid many errors of both fact and interpretation, and have made this book stronger. (The errors that remain, of course, are all mine!) I hope that I will be able to count him among my colleagues for years to come.

A Note on Names and Dates

Individuals in Tokugawa Japan often took on multiple names over the course of their lives; this was particularly true for daimyo and scholars. In this book, I have opted to use the name most commonly associated with each person today, even though this leads to many anachronistic usages. Furthermore, I have referred to many individuals by their first name, or pen name, rather than their family name. Given the many generations of Tokugawas, Aizawas, and Fujitas that populate the text, I hope that this will help the reader keep things straight. In Mito, it is common today to append the honorific title *kō* to the names of Mito's historical daimyo; I have not done so here.

Most dates are given in year/month/day format or written out ("the third day of the fifth month"). Following historiographical convention, I have converted the years to the Gregorian calendar but left the months and dates in the traditional lunar-solar calendar used in Japan until 1873. Intercalary months, inserted from time to time to keep the lunar calendar in line with the solar year, are indicated in the text. Dates with English month names are in the Gregorian calendar. The Japanese and Gregorian calendars were offset by three to six weeks, depending on the year; Japanese New Year fell in late January or early February. As a result, some dates at the end of the year will include a Gregorian year that is, strictly speaking, incorrect (e.g., the rump band of the Tengutō surrendered on 1864/12/16, which works out to January 13, 1865). I hope that the convenience of Gregorian dates for the non-Japanese reader is worth the small sacrifice in historical accuracy.

Place names mentioned in this book

◎ major cities

○ castle towns

⏬ ports

tozama domains

Karafuto (Sakhalin)

Chishima (Kurils)

Etorofu

Ezochi

Ishikari

Matsumae ○

Mt Tsukuba ○ Mito

Edo ◎

Kanagawa ⏬ (Yokohama)

Fukui ○

Tsuruga ⏬ Nagoya ○

Sunpu (Shizuoka) ○

Kyoto ◎ Hikone ○

Hyōgo (Kōbe) ⏬ ◎ Osaka

Wakayama ○

Chōshū

Hagi ○ Kōchi ○

Shimonoseki ⏬ *Tosa*

Uwajima ○

Kurume ○

⏬ Nagasaki

Kagoshima ○

Satsuma

c Fabian Drixler

Japan
(Created by Fabian Drixler)

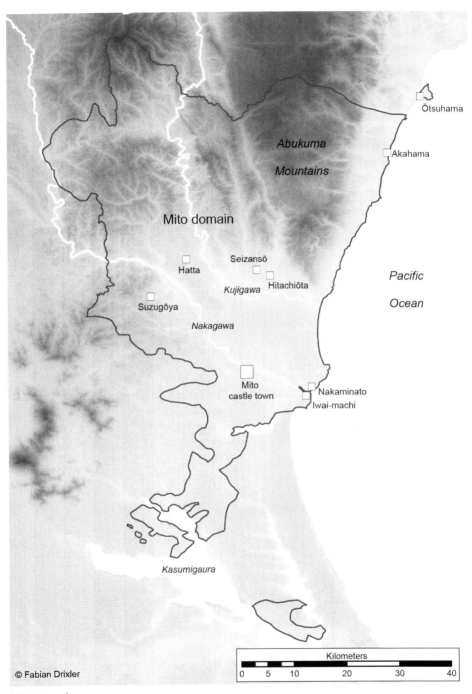

Mito Domain
(Created by Fabian Drixler)

Introduction

Modern Mito, with its busy train station, high-rise apartment blocks, and suburban sprawl, looks like an ordinary provincial city—but an extraordinary history lies just below the surface. To the first foreign visitors to Mito in the Meiji period (1868–1912), this history was apparent. Ernest Clement, a young American missionary and English teacher, called Mito the "Boston of feudal Japan." During the early modern period (1600–1868), Mito Domain was one of the "Three Houses" (*gosanke*)—the most illustrious branches of the ruling Tokugawa family. Since the late seventeenth century, it was home to some of Japan's greatest scholars. Not only did its academies resemble Boston's landscape of universities, it was also, like Boston, the birthplace of one of the world's most consequential revolutions.[1] Clement referred, in particular, to Mito's role as the "cradle of Imperialism," by which he meant an emperor-centered vision of national identity that Mito's scholars developed in the nineteenth century, in large part in response to the looming threat of Western imperialism. This ideology inspired people around Japan to strengthen their country, ultimately by toppling the Tokugawa shogunate and restoring direct imperial rule by the Meiji emperor in 1868, establishing the modern Japanese nation-state. It is this political philosophy for which Mito remains best known.

Clement noted one point, though, in which Mito "exhibited a narrow-mindedness unworthy of the Japanese Boston": a virulent xenophobia that led the ninth Mito daimyo, Tokugawa Nariaki, to militate against foreign treaties in the 1850s and inspired many of Mito's radical young samurai to embark on campaigns of assassination and terror against foreigners and their friends in the shogunate.[2] The best-known achievements of Mito's academics are strident manifestos calling on samurai to "expel the barbarians" from Japan's shores in order to "revere the emperor" through their undying

1

loyalty to the realm. The years since Clement taught English in Mito have produced much more sober assessments of imperial Japan. They have also led to much more critical assessments of Mito and its intellectual achievements, in large part because the proponents of Japan's imperialism proudly drew on Mito's teachings as they prosecuted increasingly brutal wars across Asia and the Pacific. For many postwar scholars, Mito became a place to understand what went wrong in Japan as it grew into a modern nation and empire. Today, it is ethnocentric anti-foreignism that often comes to mind when thinking about Mito's history.

Whether celebratory or critical, these views take as their starting point a broader issue in modern Japanese history, such as the achievements and failings of the 1868 Meiji Restoration, or the rise of Japanese ultranationalism, and then trace those issues back to Mito. When seen through these sorts of prisms, Mito's early modern history gets flattened into a series of developments leading inexorably to the Restoration and the rise of modern Japanese nationalism. By contrast, in this book I start with Mito's perspective to explore the politics of reform during the Tokugawa period and its role in shaping the modern nation-state that developed in the late nineteenth-century. Put differently, I am interested in what the birth of the modern Japanese nation-state looks like from the vantage point of Mito. In addition to situating my story in Mito, I also start at the beginning of Mito's history and work my way forward in time, rather than taking the mid-nineteenth century as a starting point and looking backward to understand the roots of Mito's influence. This allows me to explore the contingencies and complexities that shaped Mito's intellectual and political history, and that influenced the actions and ideas of its people.

In many respects, the resulting story is a familiar one of the spread of nationalism, particularly among radical young samurai around Japan, in the nineteenth century, but alongside this emerges a less familiar story. Mito became a respected and illustrious site of political and cultural power by the end of the seventeenth century, but just a few decades later, many structural problems—such as fiscal constraints, demographic stagnation, and the spread of a market economy—had eroded the efficacy of the political system in Mito. In response, people began to explore new standards of education and meritocracy, new forms of political organization and participation, new religious values, and nascent imperial ambitions. Mito's scholars and political leaders were key players in this movement, drawing inspiration from other domains as well as developing their own policies, which they then promoted in the shogunate. The resulting reform movements, although often couched in traditional language, contained innovative and even radical elements that challenged entrenched interests. In Mito, this confrontation became a hallmark of the domain, in part because Mito gave its forthright and debate-prone academics an unusual say in domain politics. The resulting political factionalism shaped the actions and ideas of Mito's leaders and propelled them onto the national stage in the early nineteenth century. Those ideas influenced political actors at the grassroots as well as at the highest echelons of the shogunate and court, pushing events toward the 1868 Restoration.

Ironically, however, Mito itself played little direct role in the Restoration. The powerful ideas of Mito's samurai and scholars had taken on a life of their own, spawning factional disputes, political struggle, and—in 1864—civil war within Mito. The war devastated Mito, and, in the years that followed, bitter recriminations plagued the domain. After the restoration of imperial rule in 1868, Mito Domain was abolished and its territory occupied by the imperial government, who distrusted this former Tokugawa household. The new national government, dominated by men from Satsuma, Chōshū, and other historical enemies of the Tokugawa, emphasized their victorious role in sweeping away the "backward" Tokugawa regime. They downplayed the role of Mito's leaders in creating the intellectual and political foundations of the centralized, modernized, and imperial nation-state that Japan became in the last decades of the nineteenth century. This was doubly ironic because many of these same anti-Tokugawa men—including such notable leaders as Saigō Takamori, Yoshida Shōin, and the courtier Sanjō Sanetomi—were themselves adherents to Mito's ideas and supporters of Mito's reformist scholars. Mito was a wellspring of Japan's modern political revolution, even though it ultimately failed to lead it.

ARGUMENT AND STRUCTURE

In the chapters that follow, I show how a long and contentious process of political reform and reformist politics transformed Mito over the course of the Tokugawa period. I elaborate four interrelated arguments. First, Mito's reformists sought to do far more than inculcate samurai with the "revere the emperor, expel the barbarian" political philosophy for which the domain is most famous. Mito's leaders also developed and introduced a series of reforms that anticipated the structure of the modern nation-state, including popular mobilization, national military defense, colonial expansion, and meritocratic bureaucracies. This was part of a longer sweep of reform activity in the latter half of the Tokugawa period, taking place in domains around the country. Although rooted in traditional values of "benevolent rule" and the language of "enlightened rulers" (*meikun*), particularly through an idolization of Mito's second daimyo Mitsukuni, by the nineteenth century, Mito's leaders advocated a new model of leadership: one that emphasized strength and decisiveness, rather than moral cultivation, and encouraged the development of charismatic leadership to combat a crusty and entrenched establishment. This vision of reformist leadership found a welcome audience across the country, including in the highest ranks of the shogunate and among the shogunate's strongest opponents. The reforms that Mito's leaders promoted most vigorously, particularly the domestic steps needed to strengthen Japan against the foreign threat, provided a crucial underpinning for the modernizing reforms of the Meiji period.

Second, Mito's reform movement took root in response to the particular crises facing the domain during the late eighteenth century. These included demographic decline, economic stagnation, the loss of scholarly vigor, and a series of weak political rulers. These local challenges coincided with a new shock: the arrival of Russian ships in Ezochi, and the shogunate's decision to annex the region in response to this foreign threat in 1799, marking the beginning of new understandings of Japanese territory, sovereignty, and imperialism. With a keen interest in national defense and potential commercial gain from Ezochi, Mito's leaders played an important role in Japan's early colonial ambitions. More broadly, Mito's perspective illustrates that the turn of the century marked the beginning of a new era of Japanese history, one characterized by a heightened awareness of Japan's place in the world and an urgent sense that domestic structures needed to change to accommodate changing world conditions. Mito's thinkers led the way in developing this modern political self-awareness.

Third, Mito's reformism had unusual influence not because it was unique—other domains pursued reforms and other political and academic leaders wrestled with similar challenges—but rather because the domain enjoyed unparalleled influence. In part this was because of its status as a branch house of the Tokugawa family, and the extensive kinship ties that connected it to Tokugawa allies, *tozama* lords, and the imperial court in Kyoto. It was also due to the charisma and influence of Mito's leading academic and political figures, who wrote prolifically and hosted visitors from all over Japan. Through friendship, marriage, and academic networks, Mito's leaders were able to shape the language of national politics at all levels throughout the nineteenth century.

Finally, Mito's history illustrates the power of ideas to change the world— and the tendency of such ideas to spiral out of control, with sometimes devastating consequences. The development of a reform agenda was deeply controversial, and indeed reformers explicitly framed their work as an attack on the traditional elite that had dominated power within the domain. The ideological writings of Aizawa Seishisai and Fujita Tōko functioned as manifestos, designed to excite and mobilize samurai to take action urgently. Once in power, however, reformist leaders like Tokugawa Nariaki and his son Yoshinobu realized that compromise and pragmatism were necessary to achieve any progress. Or at least some reformists did: a significant faction of them grew increasingly radicalized, sticking to their ideals and insisting that the domain leadership and the shogunate do so too. The final years of Mito Domain were marred by the tragic consequences of this idealism and the backlash against it, a good reminder that the years surrounding the Restoration were, for some parts of Japan, extremely violent and bloody.

This book is structured chronologically and thematically. Chapter 1 introduces Mito Domain, with a description of its geography, social structure, and unique political characteristics. Most of the chapter focuses on the reign of Tokugawa Mitsukuni, Mito's second daimyo, who turned the domain into one of Japan's most important academic centers, attracting scholars from around Japan and beyond. Despite his reputation as one of Tokugawa Japan's greatest daimyo, his reign was not without problems, and at the time of his death in 1700 Mito faced a number of increasingly intractable social and political challenges.

Chapter 2 traces these challenges as they developed in the early eighteenth century, before turning to a remarkable revival of Mito's academic and political fortunes in the last third of the century. One leading figure was the scholar Tachihara Suiken, who revived Mito's scholarly world by injecting a new spirit of pragmatic reform targeted at the domain's social and political issues. Out of Suiken's efforts to unite academic and political work, however, grew the seeds of a deep and corrosive factionalism, epitomized by Suiken's clash with his one-time protégé, Fujita Yūkoku.

In chapters 3 and 4, I explore the reform movement that swept Mito from the turn of the nineteenth century onward. First, I consider the birth of Mito's call to strengthen Japan against the threat of Western imperialism, a call often summed up by the slogan "revere the emperor, expel the barbarian." I focus on the importance of Ezochi (today's Hokkaido) to Mito's thinkers, especially Aizawa Seishisai, and show how plans for colonization went hand-in-hand with anti-foreign rhetoric and, increasingly, an ethnocentric understanding of Japanese identity. Chapter 4 turns to the domestic reform movement that complemented Mito's foreign policy: the so-called Tenpō Reforms. I focus in particular on the *politics* of this movement, illustrating how radical reformers, led by the daimyo Tokugawa Nariaki and his most trusted advisor, Fujita Tōko, had to negotiate with moderate reformers, such as Komiyama Fūken, and fight against their political opponents in Mito's traditional establishment.

Chapter 5 focuses on Mito's role on the national stage during the 1850s and 1860s, when first Tokugawa Nariaki and then his son, the fifteenth shogun Tokugawa Yoshinobu, dominated politics. Their efforts to reimagine the structure of Tokugawa government drew upon Mito's reform movement, although they often struggled to deal with the activism and unrest unleashed by Mito's more radical ideas. Around Japan, ordinary people and elite leaders alike read and listened to Mito's strident call for national reform and began to challenge the status quo. In 1867, Yoshinobu surrendered his authority to the imperial throne in order to unite the nation, triggering the restoration of the Meiji emperor as the head of a new imperial nation-state in 1868—a decision rooted, in part, in Mito's pro-imperial ideology, but also informed by a cold calculus of power that itself was the result of new ideas about leadership developed in nineteenth-century Mito.

The final chapter returns to focus on Mito Domain for the last dozen years of its existence. This was a time of enormous suffering and violence, and the picture of the Meiji Restoration that emerges from Mito is one of insurmountable factionalism, bitter cycles of vengeance, and repeated moments of warfare. At a broad scale, Japan's modern revolution was relatively bloodless compared to those of other countries, but the residents of Mito experienced years of terror and bloodshed.

The conclusion offers a brief study of modern Mito, focusing on several influential figures in Meiji Japan as well as trends in Mito's academic and political worlds. I touch briefly on the changing assessments of Mito's most influential ideas as Japan entered the twentieth century, and then again after the collapse of Japan's militarist empire.

I have often framed the narrative of Mito's political and social history through the stories of individual actors, and, where possible, I provide biographical information for them. I have found this valuable for two reasons. First, it contextualizes the thoughts and actions of each person, allowing us to see how the particular circumstances of the time and place in which they lived shaped their beliefs and actions. Their experience of Mito was not a representative view of all Mito's people—after all, these figures were mostly academic and political elites who spent almost all of their time in Mito castle town, Edo, or Kyoto—but their lives were deeply shaped by Mito's social, cultural, and political features. Second, by focusing on the individual rather than one or other of their texts, we start to see how compromise and contradiction characterize Mito's leaders, as much as idealistic conviction. These figures held complicated views, and they fought bitterly against their foes—or, when they compromised with those foes, elicited anger from their erstwhile allies. This goes a long way to explaining the factionalism and warfare that eventually ruined the domain. I hope that this book will complement the rich studies of Mito's ideas by bringing to life some of Mito's people.

HISTORIOGRAPHY

During the Meiji period and into the early twentieth century, Western historians were drawn to Mito's political role as a driving force in Japan's modernization. Meiji-era Anglophone historians of Japan such as William Griffis and Ernest Satow focused on Kokugaku and pro-imperial ideology as a key driver of the Meiji Restoration, connecting both those ideologies (somewhat ahistorically) to Mitsukuni and his promotion of the *Dai Nihon shi*.[3] Ernest Clement, the Mito-based missionary and English teacher, wrote several essays for the Asiatic Society of Japan, including accounts of the Ōtsuhama Incident, the Sakurada Gate Incident, and Mito's civil war. Clement also translated several important texts, such as Tokugawa Nariaki's inscriptions of the principles of the Kōdōkan School and the Kairakuen gardens. He was by no means a professional historian—he openly acknowledged using essays he assigned his students in English class as the basis for at least one of his publications—and his translation "Instructions of a Mito Prince to His Retainers" is of a text that is undoubtedly a forgery.[4] Nevertheless, he worked closely with Mito scholars of his day and did much to bring to Western audiences some of Mito's most well-known academic work. In the early twentieth century, Richard Ponsonby-Fane translated several important Mito texts, as part of his broader fascination with Shintō, ancient Japan, and the history of Japan's imperial line.[5]

More recently, studies of Mito by non-Japanese scholars have been dominated by intellectual historians who have continued the earlier focus on key texts from Mito's scholarly world.[6] Broadly speaking, this work falls into two categories. First, historians of Japanese Confucianism have explored the development of Mito's particular brand of historical scholarship, especially the massive *Dai Nihon shi* project started by Tokugawa Mitsukuni.[7] Second, and in much greater quantity, are studies of the "Late Mito School," the nineteenth-century political philosophy often described by its most famous slogan, "revere the emperor, expel the barbarian." Early work in this field focused heavily on translating and analyzing key texts from the major Late Mito thinkers, treating them as a distinct body of political philosophy within the broader sweep of Tokugawa thought.[8] Building on this early work, historians of Japanese nationalism have been particularly interested in the writings of Aizawa Seishisai and Fujita Tōko, which became especially influential in the decade or so after Commodore Matthew Perry arrived in Japan with his black ships in 1853, inspiring a wave of anti-foreign violence and helping shape Japanese national identity against Western imperialism.[9] Their focus has been to understand the strident xenophobia of Mito's thinkers. In *The*

Mito Ideology, Victor Koschmann significantly advanced our understanding of Mito's intellectual history by moving beyond the texts to demonstrate how the ideas and actions of Mito's nineteenth-century reformers functioned as ideology, mobilizing people in Mito to become political actors.[10] Most recently, scholars have started to question the distinctiveness and xenophobia of Late Mito thought, suggesting that we understand its appeal to archaic values and religious fundamentalism not as purely reactionary elements but as features common to modernity and modern nationalism in diverse parts of the world.[11] Mark McNally argues that exceptionalism, rather than nativism, is a better way to understand the work of the Late Mito School, because it drew on a universal tradition (Confucianism, in simplistic terms) to articulate a sense of Japanese uniqueness—rather than a beady-eyed rejection of anything from the outside world. McNally does admit, however, that a streak of nativism persisted in Mito, and I am not persuaded that the two concepts are mutually exclusive; the anti-foreign activism, including assassinations targeted at foreigners, of Mito's radical samurai drew both on the exceptionalist ideas articulated by Aizawa Seishisai as well as more ethnocentric, xenophobic framings of Japanese identity vis-à-vis the outside world.[12]

These studies of Mitogaku as a political philosophy, however, tend to focus on the philosophy rather than the politics. In other words, they often downplay (or ignore) the intense infighting and political tensions that characterized Mito's academic and political world.[13] At the same time, these scholars reduce Mito's significance to its most abstract expressions of national identity, the importance of imperial loyalty, and Japanese supremacy. They pay little attention to the pragmatic visions of reform (and the ensuing political fights) that also characterized Mito and shaped the shogunate's own attempts to reshape the Japanese polity. This is particularly true when considering the individual thinkers, who often get reduced to their most famous texts or ideas. In this book, I try to show the broader context in which these men acted, and the debates and compromises they encountered as they developed their ideas.

More recent work on Mito—such as that by Laura Nenzi, David Howell, and Fabian Drixler—has shifted to social and cultural history to explore parts of Mito's history rarely discussed in intellectual histories.[14] Their work complements Kate Nakai's translation of Yamakawa Kikue's *The Women of Mito Domain*, which was an early example of the shift away from intellectual history, and a rich account of the experience of samurai women during the tumultuous transition from Tokugawa to Meiji. These studies have enriched our understanding of Mito by demonstrating how political and intellectual change was not limited to Mito's samurai elite. They also remind us of the many other factors shaping life in Mito, whether religious beliefs, informal cultural exchange, or demographic trends and cultural practices around childbirth. But these works do not offer an overarching view of the domain's political history. I aim to fill some of the gaps between this work and the intellectual history work mentioned above by connecting political and intellectual change to Mito's specific social and historical context.

Finally, this book is a contribution to political histories of the late Tokugawa period that take a domain-level perspective. Until the 1980s or so, most of those energies focused on the domains that fought against the Tokugawa, such as Satsuma, Chōshū, and Tosa, to explore the causes of Tokugawa collapse and the origins of modern Japan.[15] Mito offers a different perspective: it was integral to this political revolution, but it was also part of the Tokugawa family, which made for a deeply complex set of debates and disputes within Mito and in its interactions with shogunate and court. Despite its Tokugawa ties, Mito's perspective is therefore not identical with the history of the shogunate, or of high politics in Kyoto and Edo. Although Mito features in existing studies of high politics in the late Tokugawa years, it tends to be treated as a supporting character.[16] In the meantime, a new body of domain-level studies have moved away from the teleological tendency of these older studies, recognizing that "modernity" is not the endpoint of historical progression but rather a complicated set of ideas and processes, such as capitalism, nationalism, industrialism, and so on. This group of scholars has been particularly interested in the diversity of domain-level reform efforts since the late eighteenth century to show how elements of modernity appeared in different places at different times, the result of specific historical processes that only later converged into a national form.[17] This framework helps explain Mito's own reform movements, which were intimately linked to those of reformist domains elsewhere.

At the same time, Mito's leaders were uniquely interested in influencing the shape of national politics. Unlike other reformist domains, who tended to restrict their focus to their own territories, Mito's leaders aspired to reform the shogunate and, ultimately, remodel Japan along the more centralized lines of a modern nation-state.[18] To date, Western scholars of Mito have downplayed this angle, arguing instead that Mito's thinkers cared most about "the domain as microcosm," emphasizing reforms that would make the domain an authentic representation of the natural order of the state.[19] But throughout Mito's history, its leaders took advantage of their privileged status in Edo and Kyoto to press for changes that affected the entire archipelago. The actions of Mito's radicals in the last years of the Tokugawa period also suggest a willingness to move beyond the domain as a space of political action, or even as the proper object of political loyalty. Rather, Mito men and women at all levels sought to influence national politics.

In postwar Japanese historiography on Mito, at least three trends are note-worthy. First, the traditional approach to Mito scholarship, focusing on the achievements and ideas of Mito's political leaders and academics, continued to develop. While still honoring the scholarly traditions of early modern and prewar scholars, the postwar generation delved into new sources and adopted new perspectives from intellectual history, religious studies, and literature to produce sophisticated work on these important figures and their ideas. One enduring theme, however, has been the framework of "spiritual history" (*seishinshi*), which sees a timeless, enduring set of Mito values, transmitted from the beginning of the domain through to the present.[20] Second, the de-mocratization of universities led to a boom in studies rooted in social history and critical theories such as Marxism. Academic historians focused their attention on the structures of ordinary life in Mito, researching the place of women and outcastes, as well as the role of popular protest and economic inequality. They have reinterpreted Mito's traditional intellectual and politi-cal history through new lenses, with a particular interest in showing how the ideas of the Late Mito School were historical constructs, rather than timeless ideas.[21] At times, there has been little love lost between these first two groups of scholars, with the former accusing the latter of a malicious desire to deni-grate Mito and its honor by focusing on the authoritarian elements of Mito's political philosophy and the failures of governance in early modern Mito, and the latter accusing the former of a lack of scholarly rigor, an excessively selective view of what counts as history, and a deep partisanship.[22] Finally, Mito became an important site for study of the Tokugawa family, not least because of the museum and archive established there.[23] This work has at-tracted a number of overseas scholars, particularly several from Taiwan, who have explored the legacies of Tokugawa Mitsukuni and Zhu Shunshui in the context of East Asian history.[24]

This book draws on all of these strains of existing scholarship to paint a portrait of Mito from its beginning to its end; it is the first such book in Eng-lish to do so. There is surely no professional historian of Japan who has not encountered Mito, but by and large the existing work treats Mito, its ideas, and its people in fragmented form. This has a tendency to reduce Mito to a bit of a stereotype, to focus attention on a very limited segment of Mito's popula-tion, and to emphasize certain time periods over others. The earlier parts of the Tokugawa period recede into the background in favor of the drama of the nineteenth century. Either scholars or commoners drive the action—but in isolation, it seems, depending on which book you read. By taking the domain as the subject of this book, I hope to emphasize the dynamism and complex-ity of Mito Domain, and illustrate how the specific, local conditions of this domain shaped the actions and ideas of the men and women who called it home, many of whom went on to transform Japan. Mito's exalted status, privileged academic tradition, and particular social, political, and geopolitical experiences led to new visions of overseas imperialism, reformist politics, and national leadership that reshaped the Japanese state by the mid-nineteenth century. In Mito, however, the consequences of these developments were violent and disruptive, illustrating the contentious and bloody process of forging a modern nation and empire. Nevertheless, they illustrate that the process of transforming Japan was not purely a reaction to the West, or the opportunistic seizure of power by the historical enemies of the Tokugawa. It was also the product of new visions of leadership and power generated under distinctive local conditions, and shaped by the social, economic, and political life of Mito's people.

NOTES

1. Ernest W. Clement, "The Boston of Feudal Japan," *The Open Court* 21, no. 8 (August 1907): 485. For a brief discussion of Clement and his time in Japan, see Kobayashi Noriyoshi, "Tokyo Gakuin no shiteizō: E.W. Clement to Sakata Tasuku," *Eigakushi kenkyū* 26 (1993): 137–47. My thanks to Bo Tao for pointing me to this essay.

2. Clement, "The Boston of Feudal Japan," 491.

3. Terunuma Yoshibumi, "Ihōjin no Gikō kan," in *Mito no gakufū: toku ni Kurita Hiroshi hakase wo chūshin toshite* (Mito: Mito shigakkai, 1998), 190–203.

4. Ernest Clement, "The Tokugawa Princes of Mito," *Transactions of the Asiatic Society of Japan* 18 (1889): 2–24, and Clement, "Instructions of a Mito Prince to His Retainers," *Transactions of the Asiatic Society of Japan* 26 (1898): 115–53.

5. Terunuma Yoshibumi, "Ponsonby-hakase to *Eiyaku Kōdōkanki*," in *Mito no gakufū*, 166–89.

6. In English, Klaus Kracht's 2000 bibliography of Western works on Mito's intellectual history is a good starting point to gain a sense of that particular subfield. Kracht, *Japanese Thought in the Tokugawa Era: A Bibliography of Western-language Materials* (Wiesbaden: O. Harrassowitz, 2000), 228–34.

7. Kate Wildman Nakai, "Tokugawa Confucian Historiography: The Hayashi, Early Mito School, and Arai Hakuseki," in *Confucianism in Tokugawa Culture*, ed. Peter Nosco (Princeton, NJ: Princeton University Press, 1984), 62–91; Nakai, "'The Age of the Gods' in Medieval and Early Modern Historiography," in *Writing Histories in Japan: Texts and Their Transformations from Ancient Times through the Meiji Era*, eds. James Baxter and Joshua Fogel (Kyoto: International Research Center for Japanese Studies, 2007), 11–39; Herschel Webb, "What Is the *Dai Nihon Shi*?," *Journal of Asian Studies* 19 (1960): 135–49.

8. Early works in this vein include Horst Hammitzsch, "Die Mito-Schule und ihre programmatischen Schriften Bairi Sensei Hiin, Kodokanki, Kodokangakusoku und Seiki no Uta in Übersetzung. Ein Beitrag zur Geistesgeschichte der Tokugawa-Zeit,"

MOAG 31, Teil B (1939): 1–95; Herschel Webb, "The Mito Theory of the State," in *Researches in the Social Sciences on Japan: Essays and Abstracts by Graduates of the East Asian Institute, Columbia University*, ed. John E. Lane (East Asia Institute of Columbia University, 1957), 33–52; H. D. Harootunian, *Toward Restoration: The Growth of Political Consciousness in Tokugawa Japan* (Berkeley: University of California Press, 1970); and Klaus Kracht, *Das Kōdōkanki des Fujita Tōkō (1806–1855): Ein Beitrag zum politischen Denken der Späten Mito-Schule* (Wiesbaden: Otto Harrassowitz, 1975).

9. Richard T. Chang, *From Prejudice to Tolerance: A Study of the Japanese Image of the West, 1826–1864* (Tokyo: Sophia University, 1970), H. D. Harootunian, *Toward Restoration*, and Bob Tadashi Wakabayashi, *Anti-Foreignism and Western Learning in Early-Modern Japan: The "New Theses" of 1825* (Cambridge, MA: Council on East Asian Studies, Harvard University, 1986).

10. J. Victor Koschmann, *The Mito Ideology: Discourse, Reform, and Insurrection in Late Tokugawa Japan* (Berkeley: University of California Press, 1987).

11. Kiri Paramore, "Political Modernity and Secularization: Thoughts from the Japanese Eighteenth and Nineteenth Centuries," *Journal of Religious History* 36, no. 1 (March 2012): 19–30.

12. Mark McNally, *Like No Other: Exceptionalism and Nativism in Early Modern Japan* (Honolulu: University of Hawai'i Press, 2016).

13. For a discussion of these shortcomings, see Kate Nakai's review of Koschmann's *The Mito Ideology* in *The Journal of Japanese Studies* 14, no. 2 (Summer 1988): 526–34.

14. Laura Nenzi, *The Chaos and Cosmos of Kurosawa Tokiko* (Honolulu: University of Hawai'i Press, 2015); David Howell, "Foreign Encounters and Informal Diplomacy in Early Modern Japan," *Journal of Japanese Studies* 29, no. 1 (2009): 65–80; and Fabian Drixler, *Mabiki: Infanticide and Population Growth in Eastern Japan, 1660–1950* (Berkeley: University of California Press, 2013).

15. Many of these studies are now classics in the field, including Albert Craig, *Choshu in the Meiji Restoration* (Cambridge, MA: Harvard University Press, 1961) and Marius Jansen, *Sakamoto Ryōma and the Meiji Restoration* (Princeton, NJ: Princeton University Press, 1961).

16. As in, for example, Conrad Totman's classic study of late shogunal politics: *The Collapse of the Tokugawa Bakufu, 1862–1868* (Honolulu: University of Hawai'i Press, 1980). More recently, Mark Ravina's *To Stand with the Nations of the World* (Oxford: Oxford University Press, 2017) similarly focuses on Satsuma and Chōshū, with Mito's thinkers and politicians playing only intermittent roles.

17. For a discussion of these recent trends, see Mark Ravina, "Kindaika, kindaisei to meikunzō no saikentō," *Rekishi hyōron* 717 (January 2010): 37–50. See also the introduction to Koseki Yūichirō, *"Meikun" no kinsei* (Tokyo: Yoshikawa kōbunkan, 2011), 1–9. Notable examples include Mark Ravina, *Land and Lordship in Early Modern Japan* (Stanford, CA: Stanford University Press, 1999) and Luke Roberts, *Mercantilism in a Japanese Domain: The Merchant Origins of Economic Nationalism in 18th-Century Tosa* (Cambridge: Cambridge University Press, 1998). In Mito's case, Isoda Michinori has done interesting work on the relationship between Mito's

reforms and those elsewhere, and the effect of this interchange on Mito's leaders. See, for example, Isoda Michinori, "Mito-han Tenpō kaikaku no dōjidaiteki hyōka to eikyō: shin shiryō 'Mito kenbunroku ron' no bunseki," *Ibaraki kenshi kenkyū* 95 (March 2011): 31–50.

18. For example, the domains that Mark Ravina studies—Yonezawa, Hirosaki, and Tokushima—had little interest in national affairs, which Ravina uses to suggest that "domain politics" was paramount for many domains across Japan.

19. Koschmann, *The Mito Ideology*, 125–29.

20. The local history society, Mito shigakkai, hosts many of these scholars and publishes their work in partnership with Kinseisha publishers. The quality of this work varies considerably, with the worst veering into political screeds. The best, however, are invaluable contributions. Notable examples include Nagoya Tokimasa's wide-ranging studies on Mito's political and intellectual history, Kajiyama Takao's work on the place of Kokugaku within Mitogaku, and Nakata Shōichi's work on lesser known Mito officials. Representative works can be found in the bibliography.

21. The single greatest accomplishment in this vein is probably the nine-volume city-sponsored history of Mito, one of the finer examples of this style of local scholarship. Mito shishi hensan iinkai, ed., *Mito shishi*, 9 vols. (Mito: Mito Shiyakusho, 1963–1998). Seya Yoshihiko, one of the leaders of that project, represents the liberalizing trends of postwar scholarship. Other important academic historians include Inui Hiromi, Suzuki Eiichi, Takahashi Hirofumi, Yamakawa Kikue, and Yoshida Toshizumi. The prominent Tokugawa intellectual historian Bitō Masahide joined Seya to oversee the *Mitogaku* volume of the Nihon shisō taikei, which remains a gold standard in critical intellectual history of the Late Mito School. Imai Usaburō, Seya Yoshihiko, and Bitō Masahide, eds., *Mitogaku*, Nihon shisō taikei 53 (Tokyo: Iwanami shoten, 1973).

22. Haga Noboru offers perhaps the most thorough historiography of modern Mito scholarship, but it is unabashedly critical (and frustratingly disorganized). Haga, *Kindai Mitogaku kenkyū shi* (Tokyo: Kyōiku shuppan sentā, 1996). In response, Kajiyama Takao offered a more sympathetic view of postwar Mito scholarship, pushing back against the arguments of Haga and other critical scholars. Kajiyama, *Gendai Mitogakuron hihan* (Tokyo: Kinseisha, 2007).

23. The Tokugawa Museum inherited much of Mito Domain's academic library, as well as materials related to the main Tokugawa household.

24. See, for example, the special issue of *Nihon shisō shi* 81 (2014), which includes eight articles on Zhu Shunshui's work in Mito.

Chapter One

The Origins of Mito Domain and Tokugawa Mitsukuni's "Golden Age"

In 1609, Tokugawa Ieyasu granted his eleventh son, Yorifusa (1603–1661), the lordship of Mito Castle and its surrounding territory, a sizeable domain valued at two hundred and fifty thousand *koku* and strategically placed upon the coastal highways to northern Japan.[1] Yorifusa was not the first of Ieyasu's sons to hold Mito Castle: after seizing Mito from the Satake clan in 1602, as punishment for their ambivalent stance during the Battle of Sekigahara, Ieyasu had initially placed it under control of his fifth son, Nobuyoshi. Nobuyoshi died young just a year later, and the title passed to Ieyasu's tenth son, Yorinobu, until his reappointment as lord of Sunpu Domain in 1609, at which point Mito finally passed to Yorifusa. At the time he received his new title, Yorifusa was only six years old, and it would be another decade before he first set foot in his new territory during a short, two-month jaunt from Edo, where he maintained his permanent home. Despite this unpromising start, Yorifusa remained the lord of Mito for the rest of his life. In 1636, he was granted the use of the Tokugawa surname, and his family line became one of the three senior branches (*gosanke*) of the Tokugawa family. The Mito Tokugawa ruled Mito until the abolishment of the domain in 1869.

As the home of the Mito Tokugawa branch family, Mito enjoyed enormous status and influence. Yorifusa's son, the second daimyo Mitsukuni (1636–1700; r. 1661–1690), elevated Mito's stature even further by cultivating a reputation of an enlightened ruler through political, commercial, and cultural projects, most famously the massive history project, the *Dai Nihon shi* (*History of Great Japan*). Mito's place within the political hierarchy of Tokugawa Japan and the efforts of Mitsukuni to turn Mito into a beacon of moral government shaped the domain's self-image for the rest of its tenure: this was Mito's Golden Age. Economic prosperity and population growth helped Mito's castle town flourish. In this same era, however, serious political and economic challenges started to grow clearer. As a new household created by Ieyasu, the Mito Tokugawa did not have a retainer band with deep ties of loyalty to the family, leading to factionalism and morale problems. The domain's government was divided between Mito and its lavish estates in Edo. Although the domain enjoyed high status, its economic base was comparatively small, leading to chronic fiscal problems—and high tax rates for an increasingly restive commoner population. The cost of Mitsukuni's grand projects compounded these underlying strains.

At the time of Mitsukuni's death in 1700, therefore, Mito had developed a deeply contradictory character: a domain that enjoyed high status and an exalted reputation, but one whose internal political, social, and economic challenges threatened to overwhelm its people. This tension would characterize the domain for the rest of its history, and subsequent generations of Mito's leaders looked back to this time often as they tried to solve these various problems. The development of Mito in the seventeenth century is crucial context for understanding the historical developments that unfolded in the eighteenth century, as well as the intellectual ferment, social tensions, and political drama of the last decades of the Tokugawa period.

AN OVERVIEW OF MITO DOMAIN

"The name 'Mito,'" written with the characters for 'water' and 'door,' "might originate in the strange springs within the grounds of the castle, but it's doubtful." So begins a meticulous, neighborhood-by-neighborhood guide to the castle town of Mito, written between 1783 and 1786 by Takakura Taneaki, a prominent local historian. Takakura goes on to wonder whether perhaps Mito is short for *Minato*, or "port," referring to an ancient ferry landing on the Naka River. Modern scholars prefer a different explanation: Mito refers to the place where freshwater from Lake Senba meets the brackish water of the Naka.[2] Whatever the case, Mito is defined by water. Wedged on a narrow bluff between the Naka to the north and Lake Senba to the south, Mito dominates the northeastern edge of the Kantō Plain. The Pacific lies ten kilometers to the east, while the foothills of the Abukuma Mountains rise about twenty kilometers to the north and west, along the Naka and Kuji Rivers. To the southwest stands Mount Tsukuba, the most prominent mountain in the Kantō, while the lowlands south of Mito lead to Kasumigaura, Japan's second largest lake.

Mito Domain stretched northward from the castle town, covering the northern half of Hitachi Province. Despite being a branch household of the Tokugawa family, Mito was not ruled directly by the shogunate. Instead, like all of the 260-odd domains in Tokugawa Japan, Mito had almost total autonomy over its internal affairs. Mito was one of the largest domains: initially assessed at two hundred and fifty thousand *koku*, it was reassessed to two hundred and eighty thousand *koku* in 1622. In 1701, this figure rose to three hundred and fifty thousand *koku*, although the actual yield (*uchidaka*) of Mito's agricultural land probably never reached this figure. This is curious: in many domains, actual yield was greater than the official assessments. In Mito's case, however, it seems that the domain's rulers wanted to inflate their prestige by claiming a greater size and strength. This was especially true vis-à-vis the other two *gosanke* branches, Owari (Nagoya) and Kii (Wakayama). Both Owari and Kii were slightly higher in rank, and each was about twice the size of Mito. Mito's relative poverty compared to the other Tokugawa branches became a recurrent complaint among the domain's leadership.

The Mito Tokugawa family was a warrior organization, comprising the daimyo (or lord), his family, and their band of samurai retainers. Mito, like most domains, required all of its retainers to live in the castle town (or in Edo) rather than in rural areas. By the 1660s, there were six hundred samurai households in the castle town. This grew to eight hundred and thirty households by the 1690s, home to perhaps three thousand retainers, male samurai who worked directly for the lord. Including their wives, families, and servants, there were probably twenty thousand people living in Mito's samurai households around 1700, with several thousand more Mito samurai living in Edo.[3] The size of the retainer band stayed relatively consistent for the remainder of the domain's history.

The majority of Mito's samurai households had relatively small stipends, forcing them to engage in side-businesses to make ends meet. Scholarly types ran private academies. Others did piecework for local cottage industries or grew vegetable gardens. Men travelled freely to and from the castle or other places of work, but women were, by and large, restricted to the home, managing the household and raising children. The eldest son usually inherited the household. Second and third sons often became retainers for other samurai families, where they ran errands, delivered messages, and did the shopping. Few samurai had maids, however, leaving much of the housework to the wife and daughters. Daughters usually married into other families, although sometimes a family with no sons would adopt the son of another family to marry into their family and inherit the family line.[4]

At the center of the castle town lay Mito Castle, the focal point of samurai society. Mito's natural bluff and vantage over the coastal plain made it an obvious site for a defensive stronghold; the first recorded fort dates to the twelfth century. A warlord family named the Edo (no relation to the city) seized this fort around 1400 and replaced it with a larger castle. The Satake expanded the castle again in the 1590s, before surrendering it to Tokugawa Ieyasu in 1602. Between 1625 and 1639, Tokugawa Yorifusa completely reconstructed the castle. Its unique location on a natural bluff meant that the walls of the castle were simply escarpments shaped out of the earth, with dry moats dug or enlarged in natural valleys. Unlike most Japanese castles, Mito Castle has no stone walls. Atop these escarpments, the castle spread across three compounds, each containing simple, low-slung buildings with wooden or thatched roofs. Roof tiles did not become common until the late eighteenth century.[5] Like other castles near Edo, Mito Castle did not feature a fortified keep, although it did have a wooden watchtower.

The castle marked the divide between Mito's Upper Town and Lower Town, and until a causeway was built along the shore of Lake Senba in 1651, residents had to pass through the castle to get from one side to the other—or ferry themselves across the lake. Immediately outside the castle in the Upper Town, neighborhoods like Sannomaru and Sakumachi hosted the estates of the highest-ranked retainers. Samurai inhabited the blocks stretching west of the castle, with their household rank determining how close they lived to the castle gates. These residences also functioned as offices for those retainers with specific roles: the domain's inspectors (*metsuke*) lived in Tamikōji and Ōmachi, for instance, while the lower-ranked *yoriki*, who supervised police and other patrols in the castle town, lived further away, in Nishimachi and Yorikimachi. At the base of the hill below Tamikōji was a row of inns on the road to the Aoyagi ferry crossing on the Naka River. Just beyond the borders of the town, these inns marked the start of the highways to northern parts of Mito Domain and beyond. This was also a popular spot for fishing and was known for its stud farms, which provided horses for samurai. It was also a spot for stag parties, where young men would gather and throw water on a groom-to-be. They apparently got a little too rowdy, too often, because before long the town authorities had started regulating the celebrations, and by the 1750s they had died out.[6]

During the first part of the seventeenth century, the Upper Town grew quickly, stretching along the main roads toward the west with new districts for townspeople: the merchants, carpenters, masons, brewers, innkeepers, waste collectors, and others who provided their goods and services to the castle and samurai society. Under the Tokugawa status system, samurai and townspeople were governed by different sets of laws. In the castle town, this meant they lived in different neighborhoods and had different responsibilities to the domain. Life as a townsperson in Mito revolved around the neighborhood (*chō*), which, like samurai society, was made up of households. Most households were headed by the eldest male, although women occasionally served as household head. Household heads were eligible to serve at various levels of the municipal government. In return, they were expected to fulfill a range of duties, such as neighborhood security and firefighting, and pay

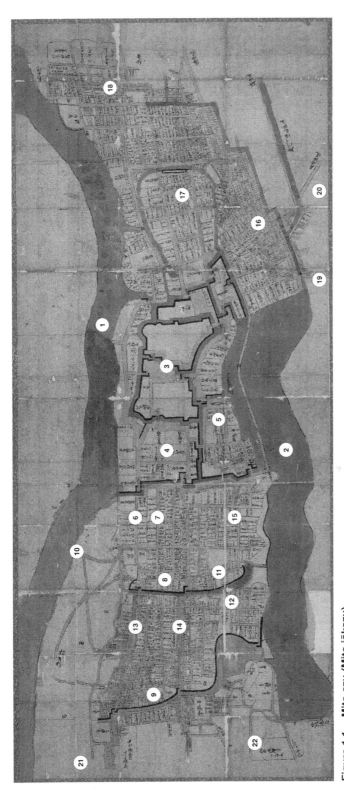

Figure 1.1.   Mito ezu (Mito jōkazu)
1. Naka River, 2. Lake Senba, 3. Mito Castle, *The Upper Town*, 4. Sannomaru and the Kōdōkan, 5. Sakumachi, 6. Tamikōji, 7. Ōmachi, 8. Nishimachi, 9. Yorikimachi, 10. Aoyagi Ferry, 11. Saiwai-chō and Takajō-chō, 12. Bizenmachi, 13. Kanemachi, 14. Izumi-chō, 15. Baikō, *The Lower Town*, 16. Hon-chō, 17. Daikan-chō, 18. Hosoya, 19. Fujigara-chō and Yoshida Shrine, *On the Edge of Town*, 20. Sakado Common Cemetery, 21. Tokiwa Common Cemetery, 22. Kairakuen and Tokiwa Shrine.

any fees levied by the domain. Mito did not assess a property tax on urban households, but expected neighborhoods to provide packhorses, messengers, delivery service, and other labor. Overseeing the semi-autonomous neighborhoods were the town elders, who reported to the domain government and were ultimately responsible for all townspeople affairs. Townspeople lived and worked in the same buildings, with the entire household working in the family business. In 1665, roughly two hundred households were sake brewers, by far the largest occupation in town. Other common businesses included fabric sellers, used clothing shops, dyers, carpenters, sawyers, and blacksmiths. These occupations tended to cluster in certain neighborhoods, and the households of a given occupation often formed a guild or association that imposed another layer of self-governance on its members.[7]

In Kanemachi, the core of the commoner section of the Upper Town, a large notice board proclaimed the various rules and regulations governing the behavior of the townspeople.[8] Some, like the proscription of Christianity, were laws issued by the Tokugawa shogunate. Others, such as rules for preventing fire, organizing commerce, and ensuring safety, were common sense ways to manage life in the crowded town. The largest number of rules, though, set out restrictions on the lifestyle of commoners. Townspeople could not gamble, take naps in the entrance to their shops, or bathe in the river. Friends or bystanders who joined in on a fight or argument would be punished more harshly than the original combatants. Commoners could only wear cotton or rough silk garments. At New Year's, the decorative pine boughs placed in front of homes could not be too large. Rules like these carefully constrained daily life in the castle town.[9]

In addition to controlling behavior, Mito's authorities occasionally intervened in the castle town to try to address problems like population decline, or the loss of economic vitality. Nowhere was that more the case than on the southeastern side of Mito: the Lower Town. In 1625, the domain relocated a number of merchants to the flat, marshy ground to the east of the castle, part of a conscious policy to promote economic growth. Highways to Edo and northward along the Pacific Coast converged here, encouraging traders and shippers to concentrate in the area. Workers had to reclaim the marshy ground, and flooding would continue to be a problem, but the resulting network of canals also connected the Lower Town to the river trade along the Naka River. Plenty of samurai lived in the Lower Town, too, tucked under the southeastern flanks of the castle. The extra space (and flat land) made it a good area for horse stables. Mito's district administrators also kept their offices here, with easy access to the roads out of town and to the horses and travel supplies that the townspeople of the Lower Town were required to provide to the domain. The economic life of the Lower Town centered on Honchō, which for a time was Mito's liveliest neighborhood.[10] Rice merchants and fish wholesalers, doll makers and sake brewers, sellers of used clothes and innkeepers all maintained their businesses here, taking advantage of the good transportation links. Traders and merchants from other domains set up shop in this part of town, staying for just a few days or sometimes longer, like Dōmei Sakubei, a merchant from Kii Domain in western Japan, who opened a large bar in Hon-chō with a giant wooden orangutan-like creature above the door to welcome guests. He sadly left after a few years when business dried up, but he lived on in local lore for years.[11]

Samurai and townspeople were not the only residents of Mito: the status system carved out separate categories for outcastes, priests, and other marginal groups. Mito was unusual in that its outcastes were not subject to the rule of Danzaemon, the Edo-based head of outcaste groups in eastern Japan. Instead, the hereditary leader of Mito's outcastes, Gohei, governed outcastes living throughout Mito Domain from his home in a village just south of the castle town. Outcastes made a living through agriculture and leatherwork, and their primary responsibilities to the domain included the supply of leather as well as various police roles, ensuring security throughout Mito.[12] In the castle town itself, a group of outcastes lived on the eastern edges of the town. Priests, monks, nuns, and other religious figures also fell into a marginal group. Parts of town, especially in the Lower Town, fell under the administration of Yoshida Shrine, one of the most important Shintō sites in Mito. The shrine collected its own taxes and issued its own rules for those areas, adding yet another layer to Mito's urban fabric.[13] Mito, however, controlled religion more than many other places did. As we will see, Mitsukuni restricted the number of temples and shrines in the domain and forced his retainers to use non-sectarian cemeteries, undercutting the power of religious institutions.

Mito stood out in another way: for most of its history, it had no licensed brothel quarter. Yorifusa had ordered brothels built in Fujigara-chō, in the Lower Town, and townspeople and villagers would dress up, wear swords, and stroll around the neighborhood for nights out on the town. Samurai would also visit the area, mixing in with the commoners, forming rowdy crowds and frequently getting into fights. In the 1680s, the domain relocated the brothel district to Iwai, on the coast about ten kilometers away, formally banning the sex trade within the castle town.[14] Over time restaurants, inns, and playhouses in places like Izumi-chō in the Upper Town came to fulfill similar roles in an informal way. Nevertheless, Mito developed a reputation as an austere, somewhat puritanical place.

Mito Domain was much more than its castle town. A series of rural market towns functioned as important regional centers in the castle town's hinterland. Ōta, to the north, was home to the Mito Tokugawa family mausoleum, and also an important minting industry. To the east, the port of Nakaminato at the mouth of the Naka River was a major transshipment hub. Ships plying Japan's pacific coast and smaller barges traversing the inland waterways of the Kanto region converged there, ensuring Mito Domain's dominance in regional transportation. Most of Mito's subjects lived in the 462 small villages scattered across the domain. In 1644, there were probably close to two hundred thousand rural commoners in Mito Domain. This figure surpassed three hundred thousand people by the end of the century.[15] This rise reflects general trends of demographic and economic growth in seventeenth-century Japan, as well as specific attempts to open new land for cultivation in Mito.

The vast majority of these commoners were farmers living in semi-autonomous and self-governing villages. In exchange for submitting annual taxes, usually paid in rice, the villages largely regulated themselves, at least initially. Over time Mito's rulers began to intervene more aggressively in rural life, dispatching administrators to regional offices and embarking on tours of the countryside to improve rural lifestyles and increase agricultural production. They often discovered that villages had drifted far from their origins as self-sufficient agricultural communities, as commercialization had reached the countryside. Cash crops, such as tobacco, were commonly grown and commercial products, such as sake, paper, and lacquer ware, had turned many farmers into manufacturers and merchants. While commercialization brought prosperity to some villagers, it increased inequality. Wealthier farmers used their capital to buy land or invest in new ventures, while poorer farmers gradually became tenants of these wealthier landholders. Meanwhile, shrinking family size and migration to cities like Edo caused rural depopulation. These trends unfolded across Japan, particularly from the late seventeenth century, and like in other domains, Mito's rulers struggled to adapt the organization of their government—and particularly their tax code—to cope with them.

Finally, Mito sat at the intersection of several highways, linking it to northeastern Japan, the northern Kantō, and—most importantly—Edo, the shogun's capital. It took three days and two nights to travel to Edo by foot, stopping at post stations along the way. Domain officials, merchants, and pilgrims traversed this route regularly, as did packhorses and speedy letter carriers. Takakura complained that Edo's proximity distorted Mito's economy, but it also meant that Mito enjoyed unparalleled access to the center of Tokugawa power.

Ironically, this proximity enabled another unusual feature of Mito Domain: the domain's true center of power and authority was not, in fact, Mito Castle. Mito's daimyo spent most of their lives, instead, at lavish estates in the center of Edo. Some Mito daimyo never spent time in their domain at all. The "permanent residence" (*jōfu*) of Mito's rulers in Edo exempted the domain from the "alternate attendance" (*sankin kōtai*) system, under which most daimyo were required to travel back and forth between Edo and their home domains on a regular cycle, while leaving their wives and heirs in Edo, essentially as hostages. Through this system, the Tokugawa could keep close tabs on their allies and former enemies, while the enormous expense of moving a daimyo and his retinue to and from the capital limited the daimyo's ability to invest in his own military forces. It is not clear why Mito was exempt from this system; Mito was one of just a handful of domains, and by far the largest of such domains, granted this privilege.[16]

As a large domain, Mito maintained several estates in the capital. The first was completed in 1616 and lay within the Edo castle grounds. In 1622, the shogunate granted Mito a second estate, at Komagome in the northeast of the city, and in 1624 Mito also gained a complex of warehouses near Asakusa on the Sumida River. In 1629, Yorifusa moved into a new estate at Koishikawa, on the northern fringe of the shogun's castle, which became the domain's primary estate in 1657 after fire destroyed the buildings within the castle grounds. In 1693, the Asakusa warehouse complex was traded for a large estate on the opposite bank of the Sumida River at Koume. Mito would control these three estates—Koishikawa, Komagome, and Koume—until 1869. The daimyo and his family lived primarily at Koishikawa, along with his principal retainers and their families. Koishikawa was the Edo headquarters of domain administration: the daimyo met with his advisors, discipline and justice were meted out to retainers, and prison cells held offenders. The sprawling complex also contained the sumptuous (and still extant) Kōrakuen gardens. Komagome had the air of a second home, functioning as both a respite from the city and a refuge from fire, a frequent scourge. Komagome also hosted the domain's research institute and library, as well as scholars' homes.[17] Koume contained the domain's warehouses, workshops, and vegetable gardens. The domain would often ship supplies from Mito along the rivers and canals across the northern Kantō to the Sumida before storing them at Koume.

Life on Mito's Edo estates was a world removed from that in Mito itself. By the end of the seventeenth century, Edo had ballooned into a massive city of one million people. Samurai from all over Japan mingled, both through their official work at the shogun's castle and informally, at playhouses and study groups. Edo's commoners had built a vibrant commercial economy, which in turn spawned a rich literary and visual culture. Mito's daimyo and his retainers enjoyed a range of goods and services that would be unmatched in Mito for decades. Further, living permanently in Edo gave Mito's rulers unparalleled access to the shogunate. Officially, Mito's daimyo did not have formal roles within the shogunate, but their status and constant presence in

the city gave them an outside position of influence. Edo residents even referred to the Mito daimyo as the "vice shogun."[18]

Over time, however, several drawbacks of permanent residence in Edo
became clear. First, the cost of living in Edo rose faster than Mito Domain's
tax revenues, making the lavish Edo lifestyle of the daimyo and his advisors
an increasingly serious burden on the domain's finances. Second, from the
perspective of officials in Mito castle town, Mito's daimyo was remote and
inattentive. Finally, permanent residence also meant, in effect, duplicating
the structure of governance, maintaining large bureaucracies in both Edo
and Mito. By the late seventeenth century, there were roughly five thousand
retainer families in the domain. Of these, two thousand or so lived in the Edo
estates. This division contributed to a constant tension between Edo and Mito,
with Mito-based samurai envious of their Edo counterparts and Edo-based retainers disparaging their provincial fellows.[19] By the eighteenth century, these
fiscal, political, and cultural drawbacks of Mito's rulers' permanent residence
in Edo grew into serious structural problems for the domain, straining its budget and system of governance. These issues became one of the main targets
of the reform movement that dominated Mito in the nineteenth century and
defined the political philosophy of its leaders. Ultimately, the lack of trust between Edo and Mito exacerbated the political and ideological differences that
accompanied this movement. It would prove impossible for any one leader
to overcome the centuries of division at the heart of Mito represented by the
permanent residence system.

THE "ENLIGHTENED RULE" OF TOKUGAWA MITSUKUNI

Mention Mito to a friend in Japan, and you will likely hear about *Mito
Kōmon*, a popular historical drama that has run on television more or less
uninterrupted since 1954. The series follows a fictionalized Tokugawa Mitsukuni as he travels around Japan in disguise, exposing corrupt officials and
righting the wrongs of Tokugawa society. *Mito Kōmon* is only the latest in
several generations of fictional accounts of Mitsukuni's virtuous exploits,
which have enshrined him as a paragon of lordly valor and benevolent samurai rule. Under his rule, Mito flourished as a cultural and academic center. He
embarked on one of Japan's most important historical projects, the *Dai Nihon shi*, or *History of Great Japan*. His interest in the history of the imperial
court and Shintō religious traditions earned him the acclaim of pro-imperial
thinkers in later decades. His devotion to Confucian values of filial piety and
primogeniture reinforced his reputation as a moral leader, a model for subsequent generations. Since his death in 1700, generations of Mito's samurai and
scholars have regarded him as Mito's greatest daimyo.

Figure 1.2.   Tokugawa Mitsukuni
(Ibaraki Prefectural Archives and Museum)

Mitsukuni's achievements and ambitions shaped his reputation as an "enlightened ruler" (*meikun*). In Tokugawa Japan, this term described daimyo who embodied the virtuous ideals of rulership as laid out in the Chinese classics. Daimyo who exhibited "benevolent rule" (*jinsei*), helping their subjects and cultivating moral behavior, were paragons of this model. In part as a result of his own efforts to portray himself as a benevolent lord, historical accounts of Mitsukuni's life and times verge more often than not into the realm of hagiography. Mitsukuni left few papers, forcing us to rely on the accounts of his aides and acolytes, many of whom recorded their accounts after his death. For centuries, Mito's scholars have treated Mitsukuni reverently, focusing on the strength of his moral "spirit" and the transmission of his "deep wish" to reveal the centrality of the imperial line to Japanese history.[20] Critics of these views have focused on the plight of commoners in Mito's villages to illustrate the shortcomings of such accounts.[21] Intellectual historians have focused their energies on Mitsukuni's political philosophy, focusing on the *Dai Nihon shi* in particular.[22] Western scholars have largely fallen into this camp, too, with particular interest on the relationship between Confucian thought and exceptionalist ideas in the *Dai Nihon shi*.[23] Over the last two or three decades, however, historians have demonstrated that the creation of "enlightened rule" depended on a wide range of social contracts between lord and subject, and rested upon a political culture that was less authoritarian and moralistic than in previous portrayals of the Tokugawa period.[24] Mitsukuni's efforts, too, were driven by practical political considerations as much as moral idealism. His administrative achievements, commercial projects, and religious reforms all reflected a pragmatic desire to consolidate political power and authority. Mitsukuni's early years, however, gave little indication that he would become one of Mito's most influential rulers.

Mitsukuni's birth, childhood, and rise to power rested upon complex family politics and the close relationship between the Mito Tokugawa clan and the shogun's family. Mitsukuni's father, Yorifusa, fell in love with a woman named Hisako (1604–1662), whose mother was the senior lady-in-waiting of the Mito household. In 1622, he got Hisako pregnant with his first child, Mitsukuni's elder brother Yorishige. Yorifusa's first wife, Okatsu, was not pleased. She demanded that Yorifusa order Hisako to abort the child. Miki Musa, also a senior lady-in-waiting and the wife of one of Yorifusa's most trusted retainers, consulted Yorifusa's adoptive mother, Eishōin, a powerful and well-connected widow of Tokugawa Ieyasu. At Eishōin's suggestion, Hisako went to live with the Miki family at their Edo mansion. There, Hisako gave birth to Yorishige, who was later spirited away to Kyoto, courtesy of the Miki family's connections to the imperial court. Yorifusa was, at least on paper, kept in the dark about his eldest son's existence and thereby avoided a nasty spat with Okatsu. Yet, Yorifusa's affection for Hisako did not abate, and, just six years later, he impregnated her again. This time, Yorifusa asked the Miki family to take in Hisako and make arrangements for a secret birth, while publicly ordering her to abort the fetus. The Mikis took Hisako to their estate in Mito, several days' journey from the Edo mansion where Yorifusa lived with Okatsu. In 1628, Mitsukuni was born in Mito castle town, with little fanfare and no formal recognition from his father.

Over the next few years, Yorifusa, Eishōin, Okatsu, Hisako, and the Mikis engaged in intricate palace intrigue to determine who would become Yorifusa's heir. Okatsu gave birth to a son just a year after Mitsukuni, and as Yorifusa's first wife had legitimate reason to have him named heir. The Mikis and Hisako, of course, supported Mitsukuni, and it seems that Yorifusa, too, preferred him, perhaps because of his love for Hisako. Yet, publicly announcing this would upset Okatsu. To avoid this, Yorifusa, the Mikis, and Eishōin secretly arranged for the shogun, Iemitsu, to declare Mitsukuni as Yorifusa's rightful heir, thus forcing Okatsu to give up her case. In 1633 they succeeded, and Mitsukuni was officially announced as heir. He moved to Edo in 1634, where he began training to succeed his father as ruler of Mito Domain.[25]

The young Mitsukuni was a troublemaker. At the age of seven, he supposedly snuck out at night to the Mito estate's riding grounds, where he stole the severed head of an executed criminal and dragged it back to the house. At age twelve, he swam across the Sumida River during heavy floods, pushing away the bloated corpses of famine victims that were floating downstream. Alongside these acts of bravado, he was a lazy student, and became increasingly rambunctious and badly behaved as a teenager. Falling into the fads of 1640s Edo, he took on the swagger of a *kabukimono*, wearing garish clothes, playing *shamisen* and *koto*, hanging out in the quarters of low-ranking retainers, talking in lowbrow slang, and loudly discussing sex and other lewd topics in front of his impressionable younger brothers. He visited prostitutes and became a heavy sake drinker. This was, in his tutor's view, entirely unbecoming for a descendant of Ieyasu.[26]

But within just a couple of years, Mitsukuni snapped out of these bawdy ways. Ostensibly this change of heart came about when Mitsukuni read a passage from Sima Qian's *Shiji*, the first-century BCE classic of Chinese historical scholarship. The passage relates the story of two brothers, Bo Yi and Shu Qi, who were the sons of the ruler of a small state in northern China during the second millennium BCE. The younger Shu Qi was named heir, but he fled with his brother rather than cause disharmony by upsetting the natural order of primogeniture. In a further sign of their moral purity, the two brothers starved themselves to death rather than support the immoral rulers of the neighboring state of Zhou. For Mitsukuni, this story hit close to home:

he started feeling guilty about succeeding to the head of the family over his elder brother, Yorishige. His guilt was made worse by the fact that he was tarnishing this position of responsibility and honor with rowdy and raunchy behavior. He decided to devote himself to his studies, especially the study of history. Through history, he realized, he could learn the moral precepts necessary to be a good ruler—and a good brother. In fact, he tried to give up his position as heir to Yorishige, to no avail. In later years, though, he adopted Yorishige's son in order to return the main family line to its rightful position at the head of the Mito household.[27]

It is perhaps unsurprising that historians have grown so attached to this account of Mitsukuni's conversion to sober adulthood by reading a history book. It seems more likely that Yorifusa's growing impatience with Mitsukuni's bad behavior, the swirling rumors about Mitsukuni's excesses, and, perhaps, a growing chorus of critical voices among his advisors, teachers, and friends, helped him tame his wilder side. Whatever the truth of the matter, Mitsukuni's behavior did take a sharp turn after his eighteenth birthday. As he trained to become daimyo, he devoted himself to the study of Confucian ethics and history, as well as Japanese literature and Shintō. Over time, Mitsukuni's zeal for scholarship distinguished him from his fellow daimyo as a model of a Confucian scholar-ruler in seventeenth-century Japan.[28]

THE *DAI NIHON SHI* AND THE
BIRTH OF THE MITO SCHOOL

Mitsukuni claimed that the story of Bo Yi inspired his passion for moral governance. It also inspired a lifelong belief in the value of academic scholarship. Mitsukuni was not unique in this belief, but his zeal for promoting scholarship went far beyond most other daimyo in Tokugawa Japan. In particular, his passion for history led to the rise of Mito as one of the foremost academic centers in early modern Japan. The work of the so-called Early Mito School centered on the production of the *Dai Nihon shi*, a massive, Chinese-style history of Japan that focused on the Japanese imperial lineage from ancient times to the end of the fourteenth century.[29] The philosophical implications of this project, particularly relating to the history and legitimacy of imperial rule in Japan, caused debate almost from the very beginning, and sowed the seeds of academic factionalism in Mito. The immense scale of the project swallowed up a significant amount of money in Mito, straining the domain's finances. Finally, Mitsukuni's emphasis on scholarship gave academics a privileged position in the domain and created a path for low-ranking samurai and non-samurai families to reach important and influential political positions, setting the stage for conflicts with traditional elites. In these ways, Mitsukuni's scholarly contributions undeniably raised Mito's stature and commanded enormous respect, but they also placed strains on the domain's ruling class and laid fertile ground for intense debates that spilled over into political conflict in later years.

In 1657, four years before becoming daimyo, Mitsukuni established a small history research institute on one of Mito's Edo estates, which soon grew into one of the major academic centers of Tokugawa Japan. By 1672 he had renamed this institute the Shōkōkan, a term drawn from the *Zuozhuan*, an ancient Chinese history. The term exhorted students to "explicate the past (*shōō*) to consider the future (*kōrai*)," a statement of purpose that encapsulates Mitsukuni's vision for his institute, and for the role of scholarship more generally. The Shōkōkan workforce increased to fifty scholars in the 1690s, not counting many visiting academics. Mitsukuni recruited these scholars from across Japan and even further afield: Zhu Shunshui, an exile from Ming China, found a home in Mito, and served as an important conduit of contemporary Chinese scholarship into the Early Mito School (see below). These scholars included a number of low-ranking samurai and *rōnin* and came from a variety of scholarly lineages. Adherents of the Edo-based Hayashi School of Zhu Xi-style Neo-Confucianism were greatest in number, but there were also students of Itō Jinsai's "ancient learning," critical of Zhu Xi thought, and of Yamazaki Ansai, who pioneered the incorporation of Shintō ideas into Confucian teachings.[30] These academics scoured the archipelago for historical documents, drafted sections of the *Dai Nihon shi*, worked on other scholarly projects, and lectured publicly to students from other domain estates in Edo.

The preponderance of Zhu Xi adherents among the Shōkōkan workforce underscores the centrality of that strain of Neo-Confucian thought to Mitsukuni's academic pursuits. Zhu Xi, a twelfth-century Chinese philosopher, emphasized rational, humanistic learning and the practical application of those skills to moral improvement. Zhu Xi also reaffirmed the use of history as a didactic tool, a mirror that enabled one to identify "the basic patterns of social and political conduct" and, at least implicitly, evaluate the moral behavior of the present. Mitsukuni, like the other Confucian historians of the early Tokugawa period, saw history as a way to establish the legitimacy of the social order—a useful task for a regime that was still, in historical terms, young.[31] The production of a major history of Japan would also mark Mitsukuni as a devoted, moral servant of the Japanese imperial court, a useful attribute for a man seeking a reputation as a benevolent ruler.

The particular circumstances surrounding the start of the *Dai Nihon shi* suggest that Mitsukuni was driven by practical considerations in addition to moral ones: in particular, the desire to boost Mito's prestige vis-à-vis the shogunate and the other high-ranking Tokugawa branch households. Mitsukuni's decision to establish a historical institute in 1657 came just one month after the Meireki fire destroyed the copy of the *Honchō hennenroku*, an official history of Japan produced by the Confucian scholar Hayashi Razan on the orders of the shogunate. The decision to rename the institute the "Shōkōkan" and accelerate the *Dai Nihon shi* project in 1672 came just two years after Razan's son Gahō revised and extended his father's work into the *Honchō tsūgan*.[32] Meanwhile, the lords of Owari and Kii had produced their own histories (albeit ones more narrowly focused on the Tokugawa family) during the 1640s and 1650s.[33] Mitsukuni admired these efforts, but they also inspired him to make sure Mito was not left behind in the competition to produce major works of historical scholarship.

The resulting *Dai Nihon shi* was a more ambitious project than the Hayashi's works, or the smaller histories written in Owari and Kii. Mitsukuni was the first Japanese historian to adopt the *kidentai* format of history writing common to China's formal dynastic histories. This form went beyond the straightforward chronological annals common to existing histories, additionally offering moral assessments of figures in the past in the form of biographical essays and other information. Mitsukuni also enjoyed much greater access to the records of courtiers and temples related to the court: he was of much higher status than either of the Hayashis and did not claim to represent the shogunate—rather, he intended to put the court front and center in his history. Finally, he insisted on a very high degree of historical documentation: unlike most other histories, every entry of the *Dai Nihon shi* included citations of primary sources, and Shōkōkan scholars carefully scrutinized their sources for myths, forgeries, and inconsistencies. For all these reasons, the *Dai Nihon shi* became perhaps the greatest work of empirical history in premodern Japan.[34] Certainly it surpassed its peers in terms of its scope and attention to historical detail.

The *Dai Nihon shi* was also significant because it reflected a new strain of political philosophy that sought to reconcile Confucian ethical values, the actual sociopolitical structure of the Tokugawa shogunate, and imperial loyalism. This complex set of ideas inspired debate from the very beginning, and the tensions between them allowed different scholars and political leaders to interpret Mitsukuni's intentions in different ways. Without getting too sidetracked by the intricacies of these debates, it is worth noting a few of the most important and controversial characteristics of the *Dai Nihon shi*. These elements would become crucial referents for the Early Mito School's scholarly descendants and would be the source of many of the factional disputes that eventually tore Mito apart.

First, the *Dai Nihon shi* treated Japan's imperial dynasty as the proper object of Confucian historical study and assessment, elevating the emperor's role as the legitimate source of political authority and ultimate object of samurai loyalty. However, Mitsukuni's choice to focus on the lineage of emperors required several difficult historiographical decisions. The most significant questions related to several moments of ambiguity about the legitimacy of the reigning monarch. Of the *Dai Nihon shi*'s "three special features" (*san dai tokuhitsu*), the most famous was Mitsukuni's decision to ascribe legitimacy to the Southern (Yoshino) Court during the fourteenth-century court schism. Debate continues about why precisely Mitsukuni made this decision: after all, the Southern Court was the junior branch of the imperial line, and therefore less deserving than the claims via primogeniture of the senior Northern branch. Given Mitsukuni's commitment to restoring his own family line to the son of his elder brother, this seems to be a striking contradiction. The Southern Court lineage also ultimately failed to survive, ceding power to the Northern Court, from whom all subsequent Japanese emperors descended. The legitimacy of the Tokugawa shoguns depended upon emperors of the Northern Court lineage. In fact the early Mito scholars even criticized the Southern Court emperors on moral grounds, in part, because they failed to secure their own restoration: surely this was a sign that the mandate of heaven had abandoned the dynasty.[35]

Yet, despite all of these factors, Mitsukuni regarded the Northern Court as an illegitimate dynasty. This view was rooted in his assessment of the schism as an act of rebellion by Ashikaga Takauji, founder of the Ashikaga (Muromachi) shogunate, against the Emperor Go-Daigo, who had tried to restore direct imperial rule during the Kenmu Restoration of 1333–1336. Takauji, frustrated with Go-Daigo, unilaterally declared himself shogun and thereby subverted Go-Daigo's will, most dramatically in the Battle of Minatogawa when he defeated and killed Kusunoki Masashige, one of Go-Daigo's most loyal warriors. In the minds of many warriors in medieval and early Tokugawa Japan, Kusunoki's selflessness and devotion to the emperor made him a perfect example of the warrior's willingness to die for his lord, a symbol of absolute loyalty. The Ashikaga, by contrast, were willing to disregard and overturn the imperial will, claiming greater authority and power by establishing a puppet dynasty to legitimize their actions. This disobedience was seen as a rejection of the code of loyalty central to the ideals of medieval warrior society, and by extension tainted the Northern Court.

Mitsukuni's loyalist devotion to the Southern Court, interpreted in part through the sacrifice of the warrior Kusunoki, sat in tension with the moral assessment of the failures of the Southern Court that stemmed from more orthodox Confucian historiographical practice. In other words, two distinct moral systems were at play in Mitsukuni's approach to the *Dai Nihon shi*. The first was the orthodox Confucian emphasis on historiography as a way to assess and pass judgment on previous rulers, especially rulers whose dynasties collapsed when they lost heaven's mandate to rule. The second was the ideal of absolute and unswerving loyalty, represented by Kusunoki's devotion to the Southern Court. Although the subordination of subject to ruler was a traditional and familiar part of Confucian ethics, it took on a more extreme cast in the warrior society of Japan's medieval period. A subject's role was to obey no matter what—that is, even if his lord was wrong or immoral.

A second important feature of the *Dai Nihon shi* that stemmed from the tension between loyalty and legitimacy was a focus on social status rather than individual behavior. In the language of Mito scholarship (and scholarship on Mito), this distinction has sometimes been framed as a shift in emphasis from "rectification of names" (*seimei*) toward a focus on "names and statuses" (*meibun*).[36] To simplify considerably, the former approach drew on the *Analects* to argue that people (or things) should be named in ways appropriate to their content or substance. That is, lords should behave in ways appropriate to being a lord, and subjects in ways appropriate to their role as subjects. For lords who behaved inappropriately, there were two options: either to rename that person to better describe their substance, or to change their behavior to accord with their name. A disobedient or immoral advisor might be renamed a traitor, for example, or a wayward heir to the throne might be induced to change his behavior to fit the moral standards required of his role.

The latter approach focused on "names and statuses" that rarely appeared in the Confucian canon. This approach emphasized the importance of names over substance: that is, one's status was paramount, even if it did not accord with one's behavior or actions. A lord was a lord, even if they were immoral or inept, and a subject should subordinate oneself to their lord, even if it meant a tragic death for a wrongful cause.[37] This interpretation of social hierarchy and its ethical implications fit naturally with Japan's medieval and post-medieval warrior society, with its idealized emphasis on unswerving obedience to one's master and a political structure based on military hierarchy and personal political loyalties. In this way, the *Dai Nihon shi* reflected an important shift in political philosophy from purely Chinese Confucian models toward one that incorporated distinctive features of Japan's own history.

Third, the *Dai Nihon shi*'s emphasis on the centrality of imperial rule raised another important distinction from Chinese history: the lack of dynastic change in Japan's imperial line. Mito scholars in the nineteenth and twentieth centuries came to revere Mitsukuni's belief in the "unbroken" nature of Japan's imperial line as the fundamental characteristic of the Japanese nation.[38] However, here too there was considerable ambiguity in the relationship between court and shogunate. If the emperor had lost functional power during the Kamakura, Ashikaga, and now Tokugawa shogunates, surely they had lost Heaven's mandate to rule? And if the "legitimate" Southern Court had died out in 1392, did that not also mark the end of a dynasty? Mito's historians wrestled with these thorny questions long after Mitsukuni's death, and we do not know whether Mitsukuni had a clear opinion of the specifics of these questions. But we do know that he developed a strong sense of national pride, centered on the imperial court. He rejected the theory that the Japanese imperial line descended from an exile from China. He argued that "the Middle Kingdom" was an inappropriate name for China, as it implied that country's superiority over Japan. In these ways, Mitsukuni's vision for the *Dai Nihon shi* created an opening for Mito's Confucian scholars to adapt and absorb ideas from later Kokugaku scholars who believed that Japan's sacred and unbroken imperial lineage made Japan not only distinct but also superior to other nations. Many years later, this syncretism became a defining feature of Mitsukuni's successors in the Late Mito School.

Finally, the choice to focus on emperors, rather than the shoguns and warrior lords who had held real power since the medieval period, could be interpreted as a quiet attack on the legitimacy of the ruling Tokugawa shogunate. Yet, there is no evidence that Mitsukuni sought to subvert the Tokugawa shogunate. Rather, he saw the telling of Japan's imperial history as a way to explore the nature of virtuous leadership, based on Confucian and native ideals. In contrast to the duplicitous Ashikaga Takauji, for example, the Tokugawa shogunate appeared to the reader as a model of loyalty to the court. The shogunate blessed the *Dai Nihon shi* project, which earned Mitsukuni and Mito enormous respect across Japan. Nevertheless, by articulating an overarching respect for the imperial line, it left open a door for criticism of the shogunate, especially if shogun and emperor were to clash. At the turn of the eighteenth century, such a clash was nowhere on the horizon. In later years, when Tokugawa power began to fray, the centrality of the imperial household in Mito's political philosophy became increasingly attractive to opponents of the shogunate.

Aside from the philosophical implications of the *Dai Nihon shi*, the project also elevated Mitsukuni's stature and legacy within Mito. By and large the structure and editorial decisions of the *Dai Nihon shi* have been interpreted as a reflection of Mitsukuni's personal beliefs, and he regularly and carefully oversaw the editorial process, weighing in on important debates until his death. But the project continued for two centuries after his death, and subsequent scholars revisited, revised, and rehashed many of the decisions made early on—often by claiming that Mitsukuni's "true" vision had been forgotten or misinterpreted.[39] Later scholars argued for their own interpretations and claims by appealing to Mitsukuni's intentions. Mitsukuni became a larger-than-life figure, the progenitor of a scholarly tradition that reinforced

**Figure 1.3. Tachihara
Kyōsho (1785–1840),
Portrait of Zhu Shunshui**
(Ibaraki Prefectural Archives
and Museum)

his reputation as an enlightened ruler. In practical terms, Mitsukuni's promotion of the *Dai Nihon shi* established academics as a major social and political force within Mito Domain. In addition to historical research, Shōkōkan scholars explored native traditions, whether early examples of Japanese poetry from the *Man'yōshū*, ritual practices from the imperial court, or records of various Shintō rites. They collected examples of both Chinese poetry and Japanese prose and produced research guides for old documents and handwriting. Mitsukuni also encouraged the spread of medical science, astronomy, and Japanese mathematics. He also sought out expertise from further afield, most famously in the person of Zhu Shunshui (1600–1682).

Shunshui was born to a line of local officials in Yuyao, a small city not far from the major port of Ningbo on China's eastern seaboard. He halfheartedly pursued a civil service career, but the collapse of the Ming dynasty in 1644 threw his life into turmoil. From 1645 to 1659, he became a peripatetic exile, travelling back and forth between Nagasaki, Annam (in present-day Vietnam), and towns along the southern Chinese coast. He reviled the Manchu forces that were taking over China, but also refused to serve the weak remnants of the Ming. His calling, he believed, was to spread the ideal of a peaceful and ordered society (*datong*), as exemplified by the virtuous rule of various ancient Chinese rulers, and characterized by careful hierarchies of gender, age, and education. With the Qing unreceptive to these teachings, in his view, he decided Japan would have to inherit these ideals. He requested permission to settle in Japan, which he was granted in 1659. After several years in the cosmopolitan trading port of Nagasaki, where he taught local scholars and wrote essays about the collapse of the Ming, Shunshui came to the attention of Mitsukuni.

Mitsukuni invited Shunshui to Edo, where he became Mitsukuni's personal advisor. Dividing his time between Edo and Mito, Shunshui lectured publicly on political economy and other practical skills of government, such as agricultural policy and even how to encourage women to produce textiles. Shunshui did not speak Japanese, so his devoted students tried to learn some of his native language, while others listened to his lectures through interpreters or relied on "brush talk" to communicate via their shared written language of classical Chinese. Shunshui advised Mitsukuni on the design of Kōrakuen, the grand garden at Mito's main Edo estate, which replicated, in miniature, famous features of the Chinese landscape. He wrote accolades for Japanese historical figures, most notably Kusunoki Masashige. Shunshui encouraged Mitsukuni to introduce Confucian rites into Mito's ritual calendar, taught Mito's scholars how to celebrate the cult of Confucius in 1672, and produced Ming-style clothing.[40] He even drew up plans and built a wooden model of a Confucian temple and school for Mito castle town, although budget constraints meant this was never constructed. Nevertheless, he helped Mitsukuni define and articulate a vision of benevolent rule, deeply rooted in the precepts of the Confucian classics.[41] After his death in 1682, Shunshui was laid to rest at the Mito Tokugawa family temple at Zuiryūzan, north of Mito, testament to his influential position in the domain.[42]

Mitsukuni's sponsorship of Shunshui illustrates his cosmopolitan academic interests and his ambitions for Mito's academic life. After Shunshui's death, Mitsukuni continued his efforts to turn Mito's Edo estates, and then Mito itself, into major academic centers.[43] This vision was not cheap: hiring dozens of scholars from across Japan and the numerous research trips to temples and other document repositories drove up the costs of the *Dai Nihon shi*. No precise records remain, but contemporary rumors claimed a third of Mito's expenditures went to the Shōkōkan's projects.[44] Nevertheless, the domain continued to invest in its academic reputation, even after Mitsukuni's death. Over time, academic success offered low-ranking samurai and even commoners a path into Mito's political establishment. Daimyo after Mitsukuni relied on academics as advisors and administrators. Mito's elites took ideas seriously and recognized the power of those ideas to shape society and history.

THE REALITIES OF ENLIGHTENED RULE

While Mitsukuni's scholarly achievements are his most famous legacy, his approach to government also reflected his efforts to become an "enlightened ruler," as well as the practical reality of that project. He became daimyo upon the death of his father in 1661, four years after founding the Shōkōkan. His thirty-year reign in Mito overlapped with an age of political stability, economic growth, and cultural flourishing across Tokugawa Japan. Mitsukuni, benefitting from this context and his father's efforts to establish and stabilize Mito's administrative institutions, had a free hand to pursue benevolent rule, drawing on his study of Confucian political philosophy and focused on the pragmatic needs of a society undergoing economic and social change. Mitsukuni's vision of benevolent rule was not unique: it was the dominant model of "enlightened despotism" among domains across Japan during the Tokugawa period, influencing domain administration, tax policy, economic interventions, and poor relief.[45] But as the *Dai Nihon shi* demonstrated, Mitsukuni aimed to become an "enlightened lord" with a reputation far beyond Mito's borders. His ambitions, including the establishment of trade links with Ezochi, were designed to reinforce Mito's high rank among Tokugawa domains. They also left an important legacy for later generations of leaders: a willingness to make big plans and take big risks in order to improve society at home in Mito and across Japan.

Mitsukuni made his first trip to Mito as daimyo three years after his father's death, with a goal of improving the quality of his retainer band. The trip was only a few months long, but while he was there he appointed two dozen retainers to his administration. Over the course of his reign, he successfully oversaw the expansion of his retainer band to roughly five thousand samurai, which helped stabilize government of the domain. He believed strongly in the importance of focusing on his retainers' strengths, rather than excessively criticizing their weaknesses, and he urged his retainers to freely speak their minds in offering him advice. Of course, he could also be capricious and willful, and in later years his closest advisors would remember that it was often difficult to tell what he was really thinking. He was a generous lord, but an exacting one.

Enlightened leadership applied not only to samurai retainers: Mitsukuni also demonstrated his benevolence by attending to matters affecting Mito's commoner population. He visited the domain frequently over the course of his reign and took an interest in local affairs. One pressing issue at the start of his reign was the issue of water supply in the growing castle town. In the Upper Town, wells needed to be dug so deep to reach the water table that they were impractical. In the Lower Town, the water table was shallow, but the quality of the water was poor. To solve these issues, Mitsukuni ordered the construction of the Kasahara Aqueduct in 1662, over the protests of local farmers concerned about a loss of water. This aqueduct carried water from the village of Kasahara, a few kilometers south of Mito, into the Lower Town, enabling the area to flourish.[46] Mitsukuni also oversaw the introduction of various policies to promote the commercial economy, while simultaneously trying to shield rural villages from the negative effects of rapidly expanding national commercial networks. He carefully controlled rice imports and exports, and also limited sales of Mito's main commercial products: sake, cotton, and paper. Mining ventures, commercial forestry, and fishing along the Naka River all expanded, bolstering the domain's revenue. The castle town flourished, growing in size and economic clout. Markets gave way to permanent shops in town, concentrating merchant and artisanal activity.

In response to competitive pressure from Edo- and Kansai-based merchants, the domain government gave many local industries special rights and privileges. Mito's paper industry in particular began to suffer severe competition from better-financed Edo papermakers by the 1680s. In addition to directly undercutting local papermakers, many Edo merchants offered predatory loans for Mito papermakers trying to sell their product in Edo, a practice that had indebted many local people. In response, Mitsukuni's administration introduced various monopoly rights and banned the sale of Mito paper outside the domain in order to control prices and limit the spread of indebtedness. They also introduced a system of cheap loans for Mito's papermakers.[47] Sadly we do not know how effective these protections were in the long term, although in the short term they did help shore up the reputation of Mito's papermakers in Edo. Regardless, the scale of the domain's efforts hints at the challenges that accompanied commercial growth around the turn of the eighteenth century.

In rural areas, Mitsukuni introduced new administrative systems to promote the agricultural economy—and improve the efficiency of tax collection. From the 1670s, rural magistrates and intendants took greater responsibility for appointing village officials, interfering more directly in rural affairs. This replaced older customs whereby villagers tended to select their own leaders. In Mitsukuni's era, tax rates were also high: in many areas, they were 50 percent or more of rice yields (paid in kind), with additional cash levies on dry-field crops and a variety of miscellaneous assessments in kind, cash, or labor. On the other hand, Mitsukuni oversaw a shift toward a decentralized tax assessment system toward the end of his reign, allowing a degree of self-administration. This system tacitly expected a degree of self-interested underassessment by local farmers, which created enough slack in the tax collection system to allow for lean harvest years without needing to rely as heavily on tax relief.[48] Not all villages adopted this system, and in some areas such a system predated Mitsukuni's era, but nevertheless the measure has been held up as a symbol of Mitsukuni's benevolent efforts in rural administration.

Unfortunately, this approach failed to address one of Mito's core problems: a persistent inability to restrain the domain's spending to match available agricultural tax revenue. Mitsukuni tried to promote rural industry to increase non-agricultural revenue, but many of these ventures struggled. Farmers who turned to commercial activities often overextended themselves or abandoned farming in favor of manufacturing goods for commercial markets. In bad harvest years or if the market for their good weakened, these farmers often found themselves bankrupt, in debt to moneylenders, and without their own food supplies. These dynamics destabilized village society and contributed to widening wealth inequality in rural Mito by the end of the seventeenth century.[49]

Mitsukuni's mercantilist efforts in Mito resembled those of other domains across Japan confronting the same challenges.[50] But unlike most other domains, Mitsukuni's interest in promoting economic growth stretched far beyond Mito's borders. From the start of his reign, he pursued plans to develop the coastal shipping routes that used Nakaminato as a transfer point between ocean vessels and barges that carried goods through the river system of the

Kantō to Edo. The prize at the end of these routes was Ezochi, whose natural resources—salmon, pelts, seaweed, and other marine products—were quickly becoming a hot commodity across Japan. The indigenous Ainu and, increasingly, Japanese (*wajin*) merchants and fishers, extracted these resources and traded them at posts scattered along the Ezochi coastline. Unfortunately for Mitsukuni, however, the Ezochi trade was monopolized by Matsumae Domain, located on the southern tip of the island today known as Hokkaido.[51]

In the seventeenth century, Matsumae was quite literally the edge of Japan. Matsumae's leaders were treated like daimyo of other domains, but they governed an unusual territory. Unlike most other domains, Matsumae's tax revenue came not from agricultural products but rather from levies assessed on trade with the indigenous Ainu people, who lived across Ezochi and the islands to its north and east (today's Sakhalin and Kuril Archipelago). The Tokugawa shogunate delegated responsibility for maintaining trade and diplomatic ties with the Ainu to Matsumae's leaders, giving them monopoly access to a vast area. In 1669, several Ainu groups launched the Shakushain War against the increasingly predatory actions of Japanese merchants. The war ultimately ended in Ainu defeat, cementing Matsumae's military and economic supremacy over Ainu lands.[52] By the end of the seventeenth century, the Ezochi trade had become increasingly lucrative, especially the trade in fish and other marine products harvested along the region's coastline. Japanese merchants clamored to gain direct access to these fishing grounds, and Matsumae gradually turned over control of this trade to large merchant concerns. Wealthy merchants, many based in Osaka and elsewhere in western Japan, created profitable trade routes that stretched up and down the western coast of the archipelago, connecting Matsumae to Hokuriku, Nagasaki, and Osaka. At Nagasaki, Ezochi's products were a growing component of Japan's foreign trade with China, reinforcing the region's value to Japanese interests.[53]

Shortly after assuming his position as daimyo, Mitsukuni had begun exploring how to build a large, oceangoing ship to reach this increasingly valuable market. Normally, the Tokugawa shogunate banned the construction of large vessels, but Mitsukuni was able to secure a dispensation for this project, probably because of Mito's close ties to the shogunal government. Several prototype vessels foundered or got lost in the treacherous Pacific currents off eastern Japan, so Mitsukuni ordered Western nautical instruments and charts, imported via Nagasaki, to improve navigation. Finally, in 1687, these efforts paid off, and a ship named the Kaifūmaru made its maiden voyage to Ezochi.[54] By dispatching the Kaifūmaru, Mitsukuni hoped to tap into the lucrative Ezochi trade and create an alternative route along Japan's eastern seaboard, connecting Ezochi to Edo via Mito. This would give Mito a source of wealth to augment its relatively small agricultural base, and a position of influence in the increasingly national, increasingly commercialized economy. Yet, Matsumae's officials, jealously protective of their monopoly rights to Ezochi, refused to let the Kaifūmaru travel any further than Matsumae castle town on either its first or its second trip, which took place in 1688. Finally, though, Matsumae's leaders relented, agreeing to let the Kaifūmaru travel beyond Matsumae on its third trip, in 1689. The Kaifūmaru travelled up the west coast of Ezochi as far as Ishikari, site of the most profitable trading posts and fishing grounds in the region. The Mito sailors spent forty days there, exploring the Ishikari River and mapping the region. They spoke to local Ainu people and gathered samples of trade items such as salted salmon and sea otter pelts.[55] Although Shakushain's War had only ended seventeen years earlier, the Mito reports from the journey recorded warm welcomes and good cheer from their Ainu hosts, who accompanied them along the Ishikari River valley and showed them the wealth of the region's salmon runs.

The success of their mission demonstrated the economic potential of Ainu lands, creating a strong precedent for Japan's ultimate colonization of the region. Mitsukuni shrewdly realized that exploitation of Ezochi's natural resources would accrue to the benefit of mainland powers, whether individual domains or the shogunate. There is no evidence that he was interested in a military expedition or colonial settlement, but he nevertheless envisaged for Mito a role in the economic penetration of Ezochi. Mitsukuni did not pursue his plans for Ezochi after the Kaifūmaru's journey to Ishikari. The ship was eventually dismantled, and Mitsukuni and his successors shifted their attention to domestic economic and social issues. Nevertheless, the Kaifūmaru's journey had an important legacy: Mito's nineteenth-century leaders used Mitsukuni's example to justify their own, much more aggressive plans to colonize Ezochi. In this regard, his efforts formed an important moment in the formation of Japanese colonial ambitions during the early Tokugawa period. The intensification of Japanese economic activity in Ezochi precipitated widespread ecological and social disruption among the Ainu, reducing their autonomy and paving the way for formal political conquest of the region in the nineteenth century.[56] From the perspective of the end of the seventeenth century, however, Mitsukuni's ambitions are better understood as part of his efforts to be an enlightened, benevolent ruler, one committed to the economic flourishing of his realm. Thanks in no small part to his status as head of a branch family of the Tokugawa, he was able to make far-reaching plans that exceeded those of most other domains. This, too, formed an important precedent for Mito's later leaders: the willingness to be ambitious in their pursuits of social, political, and moral transformation, both at home in Mito and across the archipelago.

In Mito itself, the most dramatic changes to daily life came from a series of religious reforms that saw the destruction or expulsion of many Buddhist temples in the castle town, particularly those from newer sects, and the rationalization of many village Shintō shrines. Like his Ezochi ambitions and scholarly accomplishments, Mitsukuni's religious reforms set an important precedent for future generations keen to promote Shintō and reduce the influence of Buddhism. In part due to Mitsukuni's reforms, Mito gained a reputation as a staunchly anti-Buddhist domain, but rather than an ideological program targeting Buddhism, his reform program is better understood as an effort to consolidate the authority of domain government over religious institutions.[57] Like Mitsukuni's imposition of new governing structures in rural villages, Mitsukuni's religious reforms were a pragmatic effort to centralize and strengthen political authority.

Mitsukuni's religious reforms reflected the extension of the domain's power over the religious realm. In 1663, Mitsukuni ordered a census of all temples in the domain. Of the 2,377 identified, he ordered nearly half destroyed, citing a failure to offer religious services, a lack of parishioners, refusal to offer funerals, or the occupation of taxable land. In addition to destroying Buddhist temples, Mitsukuni also removed Buddhist elements from syncretic shrine compounds in an effort to create "pure" Shintō sites of worship. He also demanded that villages consolidate their Shintō shrines to one site, and in 1665 he established a magistrate's office to oversee this process. By simplifying village worship practices, the domain could intervene more directly in local religion, controlling priests, their shrines, and their teachings. In 1666, Mitsukuni established samurai cemeteries that were not attached to any temple and urged samurai to adopt Confucian or Shintō burials. This practice did not linger past his death but use of the non-sectarian cemeteries continued until modern times. Today, the graves of many of Mito's most famous scholars and samurai can be found in the city's Tokiwa and Sakado common cemeteries.

Mitsukuni's interest in religious reform has often been attributed to his intellectual background: his respect for contemporary Neo-Confucian scholars such as Zhu Shunshui, who disapproved of Buddhism, and his belief in native Shintō practices. "Buddhism is Buddhism, Shintō is Shintō, and mountain worship is mountain worship," he argued, laying out his vision for the separation of different strands of belief.[58] His promotion of Shintō scholarship in the Shōkōkan signaled his deep interest in Japan's native religious traditions. He rejected the theory that Japan's emperors descended from Chinese migrants and recognized Emperor Jinmu as the founder of the country.[59] In later years, religious reformers in Mito would look to Mitsukuni as inspiration for their own attacks on Buddhism, and their efforts to bolster Shintō as the "true religion" of Japan.

But Mitsukuni's approach to religion was not as consistent as later reformers might have liked. He admired the imperial court but regarded the accounts of its divine origins during the prehistoric Age of the Gods skeptically. In the *Dai Nihon shi* and other scholarly works, he and other Mito scholars avoided the stranger stories from this era and sought to assess the early imperial age within the empirical framework of Confucian historiography.[60] He also criticized samurai who hung charms around their house or partook in annual rituals to update and replace those charms as superstitious and illogical.[61] Moreover, even his temple reforms were limited in scope. Despite drastically reducing the number of Buddhist temples, Mitsukuni spared almost all temples with roots in the Heian and medieval eras, and in fact built new temples, including one in honor of his mother.

These factors suggest that ideological concerns about religious purity mattered somewhat less than practical concerns with asserting daimyo authority over religious institutions. Religious sects, whether Christian, Buddhist, or otherwise, had long been a source of political rebellion and social unrest. Earlier efforts to stamp out Christianity in Mito had turned up a number of Christian relics, suggesting that hidden Christians lived in the region. The massive Christian rebellion at Shimabara in Kyushu took place when Mitsukuni was ten; the proscriptions against Christianity were not abstract for leaders of Mitsukuni's generation. Closer to home, Buddhist sects often controlled huge amounts of wealth and influence at court, and individual priests were notoriously corrupt. Mitsukuni grumbled about illiterate priests who did not know Buddhist liturgy, or those who took the tonsure not as a vocation, but merely as a way to make a living. Buddhist funerals turned into large drunken parties—completely inappropriately, in Mitsukuni's view.[62] Large swathes of land in Mito belonged to temples and shrines, who collected taxes and other duties that would otherwise go to the domain. Disestablished temples were sold off or seized by the domain government for use as samurai mansions or administrative offices.[63] By the end of the seventeenth century, Mitsukuni had strengthened secular control over religious institutions in Mito and given a narrow seal of approval to Shintō shrines that met the domain's standards and abided by the domain's ideological positions.

CLOUDS ON THE HORIZON: MITO AT THE TURN OF THE EIGHTEENTH CENTURY

In 1690, citing ill health, Mitsukuni retired from formal politics. After retiring, he spent half a year in Mito before moving to his retirement villa at Seizansō, about twenty kilometers north of the castle town. There, he focused on writing poetry, continuing his scholarly work, and overseeing religious reforms. In 1694, the shogun Tsunayoshi asked Mitsukuni to return to Edo for a year. He spent the time attending lectures, visiting the shogun and other daimyo, and hosting parties at his estate. On the twenty-third day of the eleventh month, he hosted a performance of two noh plays. He invited senior councilors of the shogunal government, several daimyo, and other shogunal retainers. Mitsukuni himself played the lead role. After the first play, Mitsukuni retired to his dressing room, where he asked two aides to summon one of Mito's senior officials, Fujii Mondayū. The aides ushered Mondayū into the dressing room, and then went back to their post at the entrance. Looking in a few minutes later, they were shocked to see Mitsukuni pinning Mondayū to the ground, sword in hand. As they watched, Mitsukuni stabbed Mondayū twice in the neck, stuffing Mondayū's robes against the wounds as he pulled out his sword to stop the blood from pouring out. Mondayū died to the roar of his blood rushing into his torso.[64]

In their official report to the shogunate, Mito's officials claimed that this was an intentional punishment for Mondayū's arrogant and intemperate behavior. Mitsukuni seems to have planned the event carefully, making an unusual inspection of the dressing rooms several days before the incident. Mitsukuni claimed that Mondayū had acted disrespectfully, and that his rule in Mito had caused unrest among officials and commoners alike. More lurid rumors swirled that Mondayū had been plotting a coup within Mito, although no evidence supports this view. Making matters more puzzling, Mitsukuni had backed Mondayū in a fast and far-reaching rise to power as a senior councilor of the domain. He trusted him with many of his reform efforts, displacing many of the traditional powerholders in Mito—who, perhaps, encouraged the rumours of discontent and disruption. Moreover, after murdering Mondayū, Mitsukuni avoided tarring Mondayū's reputation. He insisted that Mondayū's two sons be spared from punishment of death for their father's purported crime, and even included Mondayū in his prayers for the dead in later years. He immediately seized all documents from Mondayū's house, but did not make copies, and requested that they be burned immediately after his own death. One scholar speculates that Mondayū was more than a trusted advisor: perhaps he and Mitsukuni were also lovers. This would not have been unusual in seventeenth-century Japan, but no firm evidence exists. Mondayū had broken the bad news that Mitsukuni's cherished *Dai Nihon shi* project was placing an irresponsible fiscal burden on the domain. Perhaps Mitsukuni could not separate his deep disappointment about the *Dai Nihon shi* from an acute sense of personal betrayal.[65] Whatever the truth of the matter, Mitsukuni's murder of Mondayū hints at growing rifts within the Mito retainer ranks between the traditional elites of the domain and younger, lower-ranked samurai who, whether through their academic skills or political prowess, caught the attention of the daimyo.[66] These rifts grew worse over time, and ultimately destabilized Mito by pitting traditionalist, senior samurai against young reformists.

A second episode from Mitsukuni's retirement shows that Mito's problems extended beyond the factions growing in his retainer band. In the gardens of his Seizansō villa, he kept a pair of red-crested Japanese cranes, which he had imported from Matsumae. One day, one of the cranes was found dead in a nearby pond, with scythe wounds on its neck. Investigators could not find the perpetrator. A few days later, however, a man named Chōsaku, a servant to a nearby farming household, turned himself in for the crime, despite knowing it would probably get him executed. Mitsukuni had Chōsaku brought to him, and he summoned his retainers to observe the execution. He tapped Chōsaku four, five times on both shoulders with his sword. Then, suddenly, he turned to his retainers and called out: "Killing this man will not bring my crane back to life." He ordered Chōsaku released, and also ordered that the man be given rice—because Chōsaku, it turns out, had been driven to crime out of starvation.[67]

Mitsukuni's admirers cited this case as an example of his magnanimity and compassion. But Chōsaku's side of the story matters here, too. His desperation and starvation reflect some of the widespread suffering that Mitsukuni, no matter how "enlightened," failed to alleviate. During his reign, villagers endured high tax rates, and the effects of commercialization were exposing many farmers to greater economic uncertainty and increasing inequality within village communities. The domain reduced taxes and distributed food relief repeatedly during the 1680s, in response both to poor harvests and to growing poverty rates. The number of abandoned fields rose in many villages, a trend that reversed only after the end of Mitsukuni's reign and the adoption of a series of agricultural reforms in the 1690s.[68] Just a few years after his death, his successor was forced to implement a series of new taxes and other laws to raise more money and reduce expenditures, worsening conditions on the ground. Even samurai faced growing constraints: the domain's budgetary problems led to repeated austerity measures and the reduction of samurai stipends, forcing some families to borrow money and even food from Edo financiers.[69] For many of his subjects, Mitsukuni's reign was not a time to celebrate.

Mitsukuni died on the third day of the twelfth month of 1700. Poems and letters of mourning arrived from the imperial court in Kyoto, while a ditty in Edo noted the passing of the "two great treasures" of the realm: the shogunal gold mine on Sado Island, which had run dry, and Mito Kōmon, as Mitsukuni was popularly known.[70] In the nineteenth century, he became fodder for the affectionate stories, plays, and dramatizations that eventually led to the popular postwar television series *Mito Kōmon*.

Despite this posthumous celebration, Mitsukuni's legacy is a mixed one. On the one hand, he consolidated the administrative structures and institutions of Mito Domain and implemented a number of policies to promote its economic health. He oversaw a period of growth and prosperity in the castle town, and within Mito's Edo estates. He set a precedent for ambitious visions to improve infrastructure and engage in long-distance trade with Ezochi. On the other hand, many of these policies met with limited success. His agricultural policies sometimes had disastrous effects, ruining villages. He never effectively solved the fiscal problems caused by his domain's small tax base. His protection of merchants and artisans ultimately failed to prepare them for the commercialization of the Tokugawa economy. His plans for Ezochi came to naught. Benevolent rule could not transform fundamental structural problems in Mito's economy and society.

In a more positive light, Mitsukuni's scholarly and cultural achievements were undeniably significant. He recruited some of the best minds of his age to Mito, gathered an impressive array of historical and cultural documents, and raised the standards of historical scholarship in the *Dai Nihon shi*. His support for the arts and sciences led to a vibrant academic scene in Edo and Mito. Yet even here, his achievements contained contradictions. His belief in the centrality of the imperial line exposed a fundamental tension in the structure of the Tokugawa state, divided as it was between the nominal power of the emperor and the real power of the shogunate. Debates over how to interpret this paradox would cause huge rifts within Mito's academic and political elite in later years, rifts that would start to undermine the very basis of Tokugawa rule.

On balance, then, how should we evaluate Mitsukuni? How did this complex man compare to the standards of his time and place: Japan at the end of the seventeenth century, carefully limiting contact with the outside world, doubling down on a strict social order even as it started to fray? Put in this context, Mitsukuni was a leader ahead of his times, a visionary who believed Mito could inherit the Confucian moral values lost with the Qing conquest of China and set the standards for benevolent government for all of Japan. This vision, and the academic institutions and political reforms he created to put it into practice, reflect a ruler who developed a deep sense of ethics, who was open to the outside world, and who believed strongly in the possibility of reform and progress. His efforts often foundered on Mito's lack of economic and political resources, but the power and influence of his ambitious visions for reforming society stretched beyond his time in power, and beyond the borders of Mito.

At the same time, these achievements were quickly embellished and mythologized by later generations of Mito's leaders and scholars. Subsequent generations glorified his reign as Mito's Golden Age. Mito's later leaders looked up to Mitsukuni's moral compass, his scholarly commitments, and his devotion to pragmatic reform. At the same time, they often focused on those elements that aligned most closely with their own ideas and visions. Different people had different ideas about what Mitsukuni envisaged, and this led to academic disputes and political conflict, whether about the *Dai Nihon shi*, Japanese national identity, or samurai behavior in Mito. Today it can be difficult to tease apart the historical man from the many interpretations of his life and work that Mito's rulers and scholars produced, but this, too, is part of Mitsukuni's legacy: he successfully crafted his own reputation as an "enlightened ruler," setting the stage for the mythmaking that continues to this day.

Mitsukuni's death marked a turning point in Mito's history, from an age of growth and cultural flourishing to an era of stagnation and growing challenges. In the years to come, the domain's underlying political, economic, and social tensions caused more and more problems for the domain's leadership, and led to poverty, unrest, and demoralization for Mito's samurai and commoners alike. A deepening sense of domestic crisis—particularly when juxtaposed against an increasingly idealized Golden Age—drove later generations of Mito's scholars and leaders to pay greater attention to the practical challenges of governing. In this regard, Mitsukuni's accomplishments, as well as the problems he left behind, are crucial for understanding the roots of the reform movement that emerged a hundred years after Mitsukuni's rule—and for understanding the political factionalism that accompanied it, to terrible and violent effect. In addition to the effects of these economic, social, and political structures, the effort to turn Mitsukuni into a paragon of lordly virtue reverberated throughout Mito's history, inspiring his descendants and followers to justify their actions in his name, and appeal to his legacy as they pursued their own political projects. Mito's distinctive structural features and the legacy of Mitsukuni shaped the domain for the rest of its history, underpinning both the challenges of the eighteenth century and the dynamic changes in politics, society, and intellectual activity that ultimately redefined Mito as the center of a new ideology of radical reform in the nineteenth century.

NOTES

1. One *koku* is a measure of rice equal to approximately one hundred and eighty liters. It was the standard way to measure the size and status of domains during the Tokugawa period.

2. Takakura Taneaki, *Suifu chiri onkoroku*, in *Ibaraki ken shiryō: kinsei chishi hen*, ed. Ibaraki kenshi hensan kinsei daiichibu kai (Mito: Ibaraki-ken, 1968), 39; and *Kadokawa Nihon chimei daijiten*.

3. Population figures for warrior households are fiendishly difficult to estimate. The figures here derive from Mito shishi hensan iinkai, ed., *Mito shishi*, chū, vol. 1 (Mito: Mito shiyakusho, 1968), 44–52, 70–84, 162–96; chū, vol. 3 (Mito: Mito shiyakusho, 1976), 121–38. (Hereafter cited as *Mito shishi*.) The size of the retainer band did not fluctuate much over the course of the Edo period, despite Mito's commoner population shrinking. I have used the ratio of retainers in Edo and Mito in the 1830s to estimate a likely figure for 1700, recognizing that this is at best a rough estimate.

4. Yamakawa Kikue, *Women of the Mito Domain: Recollections of Samurai Family Life*, trans. Kate Wildman Nakai (Tokyo: University of Tokyo Press, 1992), 15–23, 101–4.

5. *Mito shishi*, chū, 1:291.

6. Takakura, *Suifu chiri onkoroku*, 79.

7. *Mito shishi*, chū, 1:462.

8. Takakura, *Suifu chiri onkoroku*, 104.

9. *Mito shishi*, chū, 2:403–8.

10. Takakura, *Suifu chiri onkoroku*, 179.

11. Takakura, *Suifu chiri onkoroku*, 176.

12. Takahashi Hirofumi, *Bakumatsu Mito-han to minshū undo: sonnō jōi undō to yonashi* (Tokyo: Seishi shuppan, 2005), 96–99.

13. Takakura, *Suifu chiri onkoroku*, 196–203.

14. Takakura, *Suifu chiri onkoroku*, 194.

15. Fabian Drixler has done extensive work on the demographic history of Mito and elsewhere in eastern Japan. See Drixler, *Mabiki: Infanticide and Population Growth in Eastern Japan, 1660–1950* (Berkeley: University of California Press, 2013), especially appendix 4, for population details.

16. For a brief discussion of Mito's permanent residence in Edo, see Seya Yoshihiko, *Ibaraki no shiwa* (Mito: Ibaraki shinbunsha, 2000), 188–92.

17. Hara Yūichi, "Mito-han Komagome-tei no kenkyū," *Tokyo Daigaku shi kiyō* 28 (March 2010): 41–63.

18. Seya, *Ibaraki no shiwa*, 188–92.

19. Seya, *Ibaraki no shiwa*, 188–92.

20. See, for example, Nagoya Tokimasa, *Mitogaku no kenkyū* (Kyoto: Shintōshi gakkai, 1975), Arakawa Kusuo, *Mito shigaku no gendaiteki igi* (Mito: Mito shigakkai, 1987), and Kajiyama Takao, *Gendai Mitogakuron hihan* (Tokyo: Kinseisha, 2007).

21. Yoshida Toshizumi, *Mito Mitsukuni no jidai: Mitogaku no genryū* (Tokyo: Azekura shobō, 2000).

22. Kurihara Shigeyuki, "Tokugawa Mitsukuni no seiji shisō," *Toritsu Daigaku hōgakkai zasshi* 18, nos. 1–2 (1978): 547–628; Bitō Masahide, "Tokugawa Mitsukuni no 'Dai Nihon shi,'" *Genroku jidai*, Nihon no rekishi 19 (Tokyo: Shōgakkan, 1975), 186–213.

23. Herschel Webb, "What is the Dai Nihon Shi?" *Journal of Asian Studies* 19 (1960): 135–49; Kate Wildman Nakai, "Tokugawa Confucian Historiography: The Hayashi, Early Mito School, and Arai Hakuseki," in *Confucianism in Tokugawa Culture*, ed. Peter Nosco (Princeteon, NJ: Princeton University Press, 1984), 62–91; Kate Wildman Nakai, "'The Age of the Gods' in Medieval and Early-Modern Historiography," in *Writing Histories in Japan: Texts and their Transformations from Ancient Times through the Meiji Era*, ed. James Baxter and Joshua Fogel (Kyoto: International Research Center for Japanese Studies, 2007) 11–39; Luke Roberts, "The Diverse Political Languages of Edo-Period Histories," in *Writing Histories in Japan*, 223–52; and John Brownlee, *Japanese Historians and the National Myths, 1600–1945* (Vancouver: University of British Columbia Press, 1997).

24. Koseki Yūichirō, *"Meikun" no kinsei* (Tokyo: Yoshikawa kōbunkan, 2011), 2–3.

25. Suzuki Eiichi, *Tokugawa Mitsukuni* (Tokyo: Yoshikawa kōbunkan, 2006), 1–34.

26. Suzuki, *Tokugawa Mitsukuni*, 38–41.

27. Suzuki, *Tokugawa Mitsukuni*, 48–52; Nakai, "Tokugawa Confucian Historiography," 72–74.

28. Kurihara, "Tokugawa Mitsukuni no seiji shisō," 548.

29. Tokugawa Mitsukuni et al., *Dai Nihon shi*, 134 vols. (Tokyo: 1851–1906). For brief overviews of the *Dai Nihon shi*, see Herschel Webb, "What Is the *Dai Nihon Shi*?" Kate Wildman Nakai, "Tokugawa Confucian Historiography," and Brownlee, *Japanese Historians*.

30. Suzuki Eiichi, *Mito-han gakumon, kyōiku shi no kenkyū* (Tokyo: Yoshikawa kōbunkan, 1987) 22–23.

31. Nakai, "Tokugawa Confucian Historiography," 64.

32. Nakai, "Tokugawa Confucian Historiography," 75.

33. Kurihara, "Tokugawa Mitsukuni no seiji shisō," 561.

34. Brownlee, *Japanese Historians*, 36.

35. Yoshida, *Mito Mitsukuni to sono jidai*, 132–52 and Nakai, "Tokugawa Confucian Historiography," 79–88.

36. Kurihara, "Tokugawa Mitsukuni no seiji shisō," 575–80 and Bitō Masahide, "Mitogaku no tokushitsu," in *Mitogaku*, ed. Imai Usaburō, Seya Yoshihiko, and Bitō Masahide, Nihon shisō taikei 53 (Tokyo: Iwanami shoten, 1973), 571–76.

37. This discussion is based on Kurihara, "Tokugawa Mitsukuni no seiji shisō," 575–77.

38. Nagoya Tokimasa, *Mitogaku no tassei to tenkai* (Mito: Mito shigakkai, 1995), 74–92.

39. See chapter 2 for a discussion of Fujita Yūkoku's appeal to Mitsukuni's legacy in his call to eliminate the moral essays from the *Dai Nihon shi*. For two modern examples by Mito scholars, see Nagoya, *Mitogaku no tassei to tenkai* and Arakawa, *Mitogaku no gendaiteki igi*.

40. Asaka Kaku [Tanpaku] and Imai Kōsai, *Shunsui sensei kōjitsu*, in Zhu Shun-shui ji, Shanghai junxueshe, 1926, 10–11. http://www.mgebooks.cn/detail.aspx?id =49391.

41. Suzuki, Tokugawa Mitsukuni, 116–17 and Xu Xingqing, "'Seizan inshi' 70-nen no saigetsu: Tokugawa Mitsukuni no gakumon, shisō keisei oyobi sono bunka isan," *Nihon shisō shi* 81 (2014): 8–25.

42. Rebekah Clements, "Speaking in Tongues? Daimyo, Zen Monks, and Spoken Chinese in Japan," 1661–1711," *Journal of Asian Studies* 76, no. 3 (August 2017): 603–26, and Julia Ching, "Chu Shun-Shui, 1600–1682: A Chinese Confucian Scholar in Tokugawa Japan," *Monumenta Nipponica* 30, no. 2 (Summer 1970): 177–91.

43. For details of Mito's academic development during Mitsukuni's time, see *Mito shishi*, chū, 1:655–806.

44. Bitō, "Tokugawa Mitsukuni no 'Dai Nihon shi,'" 198.

45. Mark Ravina's study of Uesugi Harunori in *Land and Lordship in Early Modern Japan* (Stanford, CA: Stanford University Press, 1999) stands out as an early English-language example; Koseki Yūichirō also focuses on Harunori in his discussion of the relationship between education, scholarship, and enlightened rulers in eighteenth-century Japan in *"Meikun" no kinsei*. For a more recent appraisal of benevolent rule, see Maren Ehlers's study of poor relief in Ōno Domain in *Give and Take: Poverty and the Status Order in Early Modern Japan* (Cambridge, MA: Harvard University Asia Center, 2018).

46. *Mito shishi*, chū, 1:374–402.

47. "Genroku gannen Mito-han kami senbai tasshi," [1688], No. 68 in *Ibaraki ken shiryō: kinsei shakai keizai hen*, ed. Ibaraki kenshi hensan kinseishi dai 2 bukai (Mito: Ibaraki-ken, 1988), 4:322–23.

48. Nogami Taira, *Mito-han nōson no kenkyū* (Tokyo: Fūtōsha, 1997), 39–42.

49. Nogami, *Mito-han nōson no kenkyū*, 189–92. See also *Mito shishi*, chū, 1:934–40.

50. See Ravina, *Land and Lordship* and Luke Roberts, *Mercantilism in a Japanese Domain* (Cambridge: Cambridge University Press, 1998).

51. Hokkaido gained this name in 1869, when the Meiji government formally laid claim to the region. Until then, the area north of Matsumae Domain—the vast majority of the island—was called Ezo or Ezochi by the Japanese, represented as Yeso, Yezo, or Yesso by foreigners. The indigenous Ainu name of the region is *Ainu moshir*. Sakhalin was called Karafuto when it was under Japanese rule; before that, it was often called Northern (or Outer) Ezochi. The Kuril Islands, several of which are contested between Japan and Russia today, are often known as the Chishima Islands in Japanese. For simplicity and familiarity, in this book I use Ezochi (before 1869) and Hokkaido (after 1869), Sakhalin, and the Kuril Islands.

52. Brett Walker, *The Conquest of Ainu Lands: Ecology and Culture in Japanese Expansion, 1590–1800* (Berkeley: University of California Press, 2001), 48–72.

53. Matsuura Akira, "The Trade in Dried Marine Products from Nagasaki to China during the Edo Period," in *Copper in the Early-Modern Sino-Japanese Trade*, ed. Keiko Nagase-Reimer (Leiden: Brill, 2016), 118–56.

54. This account is based on *Mito shishi*, chū, 1:639–54. See also Yoshizawa Gi-ichi, *Hoppō ryōdo tankenshi no shin kenkyū: sono Mitohan to no kakawari* (Tokyo:

Kinseisha, 2003), 30–35, for a discussion of the Kaifūmaru within the broader context of Mito's interest in Ezochi.

55. Kaifūmaru hokai kiji (n.d.), available at http://gazo.dl.itc.u-tokyo.ac.jp/kaishi-old/pages/4-1-28.html. Parts are reproduced in Kurita Hiroshi, *Kurisato sensei zatcho*, vol. 14 (Tokyo: Yoshikawa Hanshichi, 1901), 35–42. See also Mito shishi, chū, 1:648–52

56. Walker, *The Conquest of Ainu Lands*, 228.

57. See, for instance, J. Victor Koschmann, *The Mito Ideology* (Berkeley: University of California Press, 1987), 146.

58. Suzuki, *Tokugawa Mitsukuni*, 108.

59. Nagoya, *Mitogaku no kenkyū,* 178–90.

60. Nakai, "The Age of the Gods," 28.

61. Tokugawa Mitsukuni, "Seizankō zuihitsu," in *Nihon zuihitsu taisei, dai 2-ki,* ed. Nihon zuihitsu taisei henshūbu, vol. 14 (Tokyo: Yoshikawa kōbunkan, 1927), 373.

62. Tokugawa Mitsukuni, "Seizankō zuihitsu," 373–75.

63. *Mito shishi*, chū, 1:855–57.

64. This eyewitness description is from the diary of one of Mitsukuni's advisors, Inoue Gentō, translated into modern Japanese in Suzuki, *Tokugawa Mitsukuni*, 250–51.

65. Yoshida, *Mito Mitsukuni no jidai*, 73–124.

66. *Mito shishi*, chū, 1:940–46.

67. Suzuki, *Tokugawa Mitsukuni*, 275–77.

68. Yoshida, *Mito Mitsukuni no jidai*, 6–17.

69. *Mito shishi*, chū, 1:934–38.

70. Suzuki, *Tokugawa Mitsukuni*, 289.

Chapter Two

Eighteenth-Century Mito

Crisis, Reform, and the Birth of the Late Mito School

Foxes haunted Mito castle town in the eighteenth century. In Hosoya, on the banks of the Naka River, a spectral fox was known to wash *azuki* beans in the moonlight. If you relieved yourself on a particular haunted stone in Araki-chō, chances were high that a ghostly fox would jump out and punish you. Residents of Namimatsu-chō named *their* fox spirit Osaen after a nearby tea plantation; it was a frequent nuisance to locals. Even the castle had a resident ghost fox, called Chōgorō, who frequently bewitched passersby.[1]

The foxes haunting Mito's dark corners and lonely alleys symbolized a broader fall in fortunes of the castle town, and of the domain more widely, after the death of Tokugawa Mitsukuni in 1700. Economic crises caused social unrest among commoners and prevented fiscal reforms, leading to cuts to samurai stipends and rising debt levels for the domain. Divisions among Mito's retainer band were compounded by a series of weak daimyo who rarely or never visited Mito, preferring to stay on their luxurious Edo estates. Enthusiasm for the *Dai Nihon shi* project waned in parallel to the dwindling pool of fiscal resources for academic work, and the Shōkōkan's scholarly production stagnated. Fires, floods, and famine compounded these problems repeatedly throughout the eighteenth century. These challenges were demoralizing and drove Mito's people to protest with increasing frequency. Unrest, in turn, suggested to Mito's academic and political elite that the social order was fraying.

But somewhat paradoxically, out of this period of decline emerged a period of cultural and scholarly vibrancy. In the last third of the eighteenth century, a new cohort of academic and political leaders began to revitalize Mito's political, social, and scholarly fortunes. Key to this revitalization was the scholar Tachihara Suiken (1744–1816), who embraced many new intellectual developments that were reshaping traditional Neo-Confucian scholarship, particularly the work of Ogyū Sorai and Kokugaku[2] scholars. At the same time, Suiken was part of a "local turn" in Mito's academic world, a flourishing of regional scholarship that targeted practical topics and immediate challenges in and around Mito. Increasingly, Mito's academics worked on political, social, and economic problems alongside their more abstract historical and philosophical research.

Despite Suiken's crucial role in introducing a new approach to reformist governance and in reviving Mito's academic world, he has received almost no attention in Western scholarship on Mito.[3] Even Japanese scholars have given Suiken short shrift, with his students commanding much greater attention (and affection, in many cases) from intellectual historians and local scholars.[4] In part this is because Suiken was not a prolific writer: he produced almost no formal academic works, and his revisions to the *Dai Nihon shi* were criticized for their sloppiness. In particular, his plan to cut portions of the project was criticized from the outset as a violation of Mitsukuni's vision, and therefore a sort of heterodoxy, by Mito scholars.[5] Even today, Suiken is subject to this criticism, despite its clear roots in the factional disputes of his own time and the ahistorical assessment of Mitsukuni's vision as a timeless, unchanging "spirit" shaping Mito's scholarship.[6]

In both the political and academic realms, Suiken's dominant position in Mito during the 1780s and 1790s coincided with a turning point in the history of Mito and of Japan. In 1783, Suiken became advisor to the sixth Mito daimyo, Harumori. Over the next fifteen years the two men oversaw a robust program of domain reform, and played instrumental roles in the shogunate's Kansei Reforms, too. The program of domain reforms in Mito and across Japan signaled a new "proto-modern" set of ideas about domain administration, the economy, and social mores.[7] Although many of these ideas rested upon the traditional concept of benevolent rule, the target of reforms shifted away from the seventeenth-century focus on rulers' moral cultivation and cultural achievement toward the more concrete challenges of political economy. Meanwhile, new directions in the editing of the *Dai Nihon shi*, dominated by Suiken's student, Fujita Yūkoku, reflected a newfound emphasis on the cultural and political unity of Japan, centered on its uniquely long-lived imperial dynasty. This marked a transition from the abstract, universal moralizing role for historical research established during Mitsukuni's reign toward a more muscular program of defining national identity and using nationalism to organize society.

Alongside these shifts toward more modern ways of thinking about politics, social change, and Japanese history, the last decade of the eighteenth century was also marked by the spread of political factionalism in Mito. The relationship between Suiken and his student Yūkoku soured as the two men disagreed about the way forward for the *Dai Nihon shi*. Their disagreements drew in other academics, with Yūkoku inspiring a group of passionate, relatively ideological younger academics against Suiken's more moderate and pragmatic faction. This academic squabble spilt into the political realm, ultimately leading to Suiken's ouster from his positions of authority in 1803. Mito's scholarly revival at the end of the eighteenth century, therefore, also produced an increasingly bitter and acrimonious divide between radicals and moderates that complicated the broader reformist project tackling Mito's eighteenth-century crises.

MITO AFTER MITSUKUNI: STAGNATION AND UNREST IN THE EARLY EIGHTEENTH CENTURY

Mito's Golden Age reached its crest at the end of the seventeenth century, buoyed by the legacy of Mitsukuni's rule and the widespread economic and cultural boom across the Japanese archipelago. Mito castle town had blossomed into an academic and cultural center of thirty thousand people, with the *Dai Nihon shi* and related works earning respect in Edo and throughout Japan. Mitsukuni's successor, the third daimyo Tsunaeda (1656–1718; r. 1690–1718), continued to promote scholarship, and attempted to follow in Mitsukuni's footsteps by implementing various progressive reforms.

But Tsunaeda also inherited Mito's fiscal problems, notably the high costs associated with Mito's exalted status as a Tokugawa branch household, and particularly the costs of maintaining a full-time position in Edo. These expenditures outpaced Mito's comparatively small tax base, and high rates of inflation during the Genroku period (1688–1704) compounded the problem. In the same period, agricultural production in Mito Domain began to fall, with fields going fallow and tax revenues shrinking. The domain turned to loans from the shogunate and Kyoto-based financiers to fill budget holes, but these proved insufficient. In 1698, the domain began to request supplementary payments from samurai. In 1700, it requested payments from 153 wealthy commoners in order to pay for a special construction project at the Edo estate. Over the next few years, the domain would repeatedly order commoners to contribute to large, one-off expenses, often referred to as "money for the lord" (*goyōkin*).[8] These payments aggravated these commoner elites and, moreover, did not address the underlying mismatch between the domain's tax base and spending needs in Edo and Mito. Most pressingly for the domain government, shrinking budgets meant a reduction in stipend payments to Mito's samurai families, pushing many into poverty.

To tackle these structural problems, Tsunaeda recruited two masterless samurai (*rōnin*) from Kyoto: Yasuda Monzaemon and Matsunami Kanjūrō.

The unusual choice to seek aid from outside the domain hints at the increasing desperation of the domain administration, as well as the growing influence of Kyoto moneylenders who likely recommended these men to Mito's government.[9] Starting in 1704, Yasuda oversaw a program to issue paper money to help ease currency shortages, but this proved highly disruptive. The shogunate forced Mito to end the practice in 1707, but many commoners were not able to exchange their paper money for cash, causing more anger. Matsunami, hired in 1706, oversaw a much more comprehensive series of reforms, known collectively as the New Laws of the Hōei Era (1704–1707). These reforms encompassed fiscal reforms, such as budget cuts, tax increases, and new fees, as well as efforts to increase the amount of land under cultivation, in order to boost revenues. In addition, Matsunami sought to tap into Japan's commercial growth by promoting commercial agriculture, selling lumber, and easing restrictions on commerce in the castle town. Finally, he hoped to improve transport by digging a new canal to boost Mito's role in regional freight transport.[10]

Almost no one liked Matsunami's reforms. Farmers resented the need to divert labor to reclaim new fields and resisted the shift to commercial crops for fear of losing food supplies during lean years. Townspeople balked at the forced payments Matsunami demanded to fund his infrastructure projects, while his liberalizing economic policies angered the members of longstanding cartels and guilds. Low-ranking samurai resisted Matsunami's proposal to reduce government headcount. Military officials worried that improved roads and canals would make defense of the domain more difficult. Everyone complained about the hike in tax rates. The new canal sucked up vast amounts of labor, and the dangerous working conditions led to many deaths and injuries among the conscripted commoner construction force.

By the end of 1708, Mito's villagers had had enough. During the first month of 1709, a few dozen farmers from northern Mito crept into Edo. Each had been summoned by a secret document, circulated between villages across Mito Domain, with careful instructions for how to avoid detection on the highway. Once in the capital, these farmers found space in inns and lodges scattered across the Nihonbashi area, safe houses for petitioners whose owners feigned ignorance when Mito officials came searching. All those owners, that is, save one. A few of the Mito farmers decided that their particular inn did not meet their standards, so they took their metaphorical pitchforks and decamped to new lodgings in Asakusa. The innkeeper, angered by the loss of custom and the farmers' ingratitude, promptly reported them to Mito's officials, who tracked them down and hauled them in for questioning. The protestors seized the opportunity to hand over their list of demands, and Mito's officials, keen to avoid further unrest, agreed to cut some taxes and make a few small changes to domain administration. They sent the farmers away with strict instructions never to protest in such a way again.

The farmers respected this order for four days. They retreated to the outskirts of Edo, where three hundred of their compatriots from the southern part of the domain had gathered, preparing to stage their own protest. After discussing the domain's limited acknowledgment of the northerners' grievances, the two groups joined forces to renew their demands. They hatched a plan to accost Tsunaeda and his retinue during a procession to Edo Castle. Unfortunately, Tsunaeda's retinue changed their route at the last minute, forcing the several hundred farmers to run toward the main gate of the Mito estate, brandishing sticks, shouting "we are the honorable farmers of Mito, and are here to file a complaint!"[11] But they were unable to get into the estate, and they scattered back to their lodgings.

The next day, ringleaders opted for a new strategy. They sent three representatives to the estate of one of Mito's branch domains, who agreed to accompany them to the Mito estate. With this formal introduction, Mito's elders accepted the petitioners, and began to read the list of demands. They knew that more farmers were travelling to Edo from Mito—reports put the number at close to three thousand. Tsunaeda was scheduled to travel to a high-profile ceremony at Edo Castle in a few days. The embarrassment of massive protests by his subjects during such an event would be difficult to live down. The elders finally capitulated to the farmers' demands: they fired Matsunami and suspended his reforms. Taxation, labor duties, and other laws reverted to their pre-Hōei standards, with the exception of a few reforms that deregulated some commercial activities. This was a victory for Mito's farmers, but a blow to Mito's officials, who had pinned their hopes on these reforms as a way out of the fiscal hole left after Mitsukuni's rule. Instead, Mito fell deeper and deeper into debt. This led to cuts to samurai stipends, higher tax rates, and more "money for the lord."

Mito's leaders, however, refused to take responsibility for their failure to solve Mito's fiscal problems. Instead, they decided to pin the blame on Matsunami. They ordered him and his two sons tracked down and brought back to Mito, where they were thrown into prison in the sixth month of 1709. Matsunami was charged with carelessly revealing domain information to outsiders and otherwise failing to act with sufficient respect for the domain after his dismissal. Matsunami's sons died in prison a year later; Matsunami himself lived another six months before dying in his cell. Even after his death, Matsunami was not spared indignity: for generations, Mito's leaders continued to claim that he had brought "bad government" to Mito, ignoring the fact that he had been hired precisely to fix the problems Mitsukuni and Tsunaeda had been unable to solve.[12]

Echoing the 1709 uprising by Mito's farmers, the commoners of Mito castle town revolted against their worsening straits in 1726. In the tenth month, they submitted a mass petition to the domain demanding new efforts to protect their livelihoods from changing economic structures. They identified several key issues. First, the suburban villages bordering the castle town had turned into roaring centers of commerce. "Merchants of all stripes have set up shop in these villages, catching customers there and selling to them," they complained. Second, high taxes, fees, and labor requirements on urban households forced many artisans to leave the castle town. Third, rural wholesalers for rice, fish, and other products had begun trading directly with counterparts in Edo and Osaka, circumventing the castle town entirely. Finally, long-distance traders from northern Japan no longer bothered using Mito as a meeting point for trade with Edo and Osaka merchants; they instead traded directly with those merchants as larger and more robust trading networks stretched across Japan. The result of all these factors was a loss of economic vitality in the castle town, and with it a loss of population: the number of townspeople in Mito declined from 12,964 in 1700 to 10,991 in 1726.[13]

Natural disasters and weak government compounded the impact of rural commercialization and fiscal woes. In 1723, the Mito estate in Edo burned down and severe floods struck Mito, and then, in 1726, fire devastated the castle town. The 1730s and 1740s saw more floods and fires, not to mention a devastating outbreak of cholera. Mito's finances fell into worse straits, and the domain government grew increasingly divided between Edo, where the daimyo and his advisors lived, and Mito, where high-ranking retainers effectively controlled government. Throughout this period, domain was governed by a series of weak and short-lived daimyo, who rarely visited Mito itself. In 1749, the shogunate decided enough was enough and formally intervened in Mito's affairs, ordering a series of fiscal, administrative, and moral reforms. Externally imposed, these reform orders found few friends in Mito, and fizzled out by the mid-1750s, leaving only a deep sense of shame and embarrassment among the domain's samurai elite.

Even Mito's vaunted scholarship lost its luster in this gloomy era, although more slowly than social and economic conditions. Work on the *Dai Nihon shi* continued under Tsunaeda, who ordered the completion of the section of essays that assessed the events recorded in the main annals of the work. This section, called the *ronsan*, was directed by Mitsukuni's protégé, the scholar Asaka Tanpaku, who successfully oversaw the completion of the first draft of the annals and the *ronsan* for submission to the shogunate in 1720. Thereafter, however, work slowed considerably on the remaining portions of the *Dai Nihon shi*. The domain's fiscal problems led to a reduction in the Shōkōkan workforce, and the remaining scholars were middling historians, lacking the skills (and, it seems, the enthusiasm) to tackle the thorny process of revisions to the annals and *ronsan* essays.[14] Work had ground to a halt by the time of Tanpaku's death in 1737, and stagnated for the next five decades.

TACHIHARA SUIKEN'S
UPBRINGING AND EDUCATION

In the midst of this challenging era, Tachihara Suiken was born in Mito castle town on the eighth day of the sixth month of 1744. The Tachihara family had long roots in the Mito area, taking their name from a village in the southern part of Mito Domain. Suiken's grandfather, Tatsutomo, was promoted from commoner to samurai status in 1726. In 1727, Tatsutomo adopted a "bright and bookish" boy, and made him his heir. This was Suiken's father, Rankei. Rankei took over the household in 1743, upon Tatsutomo's death, and in 1744 was promoted to a mid-ranking samurai status with a small stipend. In 1757, he was promoted again, this time to the position of librarian at the Shōkōkan, a relatively prestigious job.[15] But he was never hired to work directly on the compilation of the *Dai Nihon shi* as the editors thought him an unremarkable scholar. Whatever Rankei's academic abilities may have been, education mattered a great deal to him and his wife, Ine, and they together devoted themselves to giving Suiken the best education they could. Their small stipend was not much to live on, but Rankei offered to copy whatever books Suiken wanted in order to encourage his love of reading. He urged Suiken to study the Chinese classics, as well as poetry and other subjects. Ine saved money on the family's clothing and meals to buy Suiken ink and paper. His parents made it possible for Suiken to devote himself to his studies.[16] Thanks to them, he became a precocious student. One of the directors of the Shōkōkan described Suiken as an "eagle hatched by a kite," a remarkable child produced by very ordinary parents.[17]

Suiken enjoyed a childhood education typical for samurai in mid-eighteenth-century Mito. His studies began with the Confucian classics, and particularly the interpretations by the Zhu Xi school of Neo-Confucianism that had found such favor with Mitsukuni. Mito's senior scholars prided themselves on their continued devotion to this school of thought, which emphasized the importance of individual moral development as the basis for ethical rule and behavior. This focus on morality underpinned the *Dai Nihon shi*, and was treated as orthodoxy throughout the Shōkōkan. Suiken absorbed these teachings from his father as well as from his father's teacher, the Shōkōkan co-director Nagoya Nankei, with whom he also studied poetry.

But Suiken soon encountered new ideas that challenged the orthodoxy of Zhu Xi Neo-Confucianism, ideas that would shape his intellectual outlook and

Figure 2.1.   Watanabe Kazan, Draft Portrait of Tachihara Suiken, 1818–1830
(Tahara City Museum)

inspire him to look beyond the narrow confines of the academic world. The earliest source of these new ideas was through Yatabe Tōgaku (1733–1789), a promising young scholar who taught in a *terakoya* school for children in the early 1750s. Only eleven years Suiken's senior, Tōgaku initially taught the Neo-Confucian curriculum familiar to the Shōkōkan, but in 1754 he was forced to leave Mito when his father conspired in a murder. While living in a nearby domain in 1757, he encountered a travelling scholar, Tanaka Kōnan, lecturing on the philosophy of Ogyū Sorai (1666–1728). Sorai had rejected the abstract, unchanging morality at the center of Zhu Xi-style Neo-Confucianism, and instead promoted the close reading of classical Confucian texts to understand the rites, laws, and customs that made government work. In other words, his was a political philosophy that advocated a pragmatic focus on effective governance, relying on empirical research in ancient texts to discover the rites and rituals that made for good rule. Building and maintaining good systems and institutions, rather than cultivating morality, was the most effective route to good government. The ruling elite could discover models of such systems by studying history—and also by looking at the successes and failures of their contemporaries. Tōgaku soon converted to Sorai's empirical approach to the Confucian classics, and upon his return to Mito a couple of years later he began to teach Suiken these new ideas. In 1760 Kōnan himself arrived in Mito, and Suiken eagerly attended his lectures. He soon fell in love with Sorai's pragmatic focus on political and social questions.

The senior scholars of the Shōkōkan, however, did not share Suiken's enthusiasm for Sorai, and they threw up obstacles to his academic career. They sought to eliminate Sorai's philosophy and methods from Mito's academies, and blocked Suiken's first job in the Mito Shōkōkan. Undeterred, Suiken moved to Edo in 1763, where he continued to study Sorai's work—and to clash with his superiors in Mito. They disapproved of his teaching Sorai in his private academy, whose students included future Mito luminaries such as Komiyama Fūken and Fujita Yūkoku. Finally, in 1775, Suiken snapped, and sent an aggressive defense of his intellectual interests to Mito's senior academics. "I love reading widely, and abhor narrow ways of thinking," Suiken began, before describing how his eclectic studies did not undermine the Neo-Confucian morality that his teachers held so dear. In fact, he argued, studying other ideas helps refine and strengthen more orthodox tenets. More pointedly, Suiken suggested that a cabal of jealous persons in the Shōkōkan leadership had ignored his efforts to defend his scholarly approach, despite his clear dedication to the goals of the institute. Perhaps, he wondered acidly, this was due to the rampant nepotism in the Shōkōkan's hiring practices, and the "rarity of staff members who exhibit any talent."[18] Unsurprisingly, Suiken's acerbic denunciation of the senior academics at the Shōkōkan did not go down well. We have no record that the directors even responded to Suiken's plea. It was only after the retirement and death of several senior directors that opposition to Suiken's eclectic approach to scholarship lessened.

Sorai was not the only new influence in Mito's academic circles, and Suiken was not the only Mito academic to take up new fields of study. The second half of the eighteenth century saw a boom in locally focused and practically orientated studies, including local history, agronomy, and social policy, which together diversified Mito's academic world. Suiken himself wrote a careful study of the rituals and celebrations that punctuated the annual calendar in Mito, one of his only written works.[19] His peer Takakura Taneaki (1749–1831) wrote a painstaking neighborhood-by-neighborhood history of Mito castle town, analyzing the decline of the city and relating anecdotes and legends that gave each area its character.[20] Other rural villagers wrote treatises on rural governance in the 1770s and 1780s.[21] And, as we shall see, Suiken trained a number of students in his eclectic, pragmatic, and locally focused approach to political, social, and academic challenges.

Figure 2.2.   Nagakubo Harutaka, Nagakubo Sekisui sensei zō
(Ibaraki Prefectural Library)

Nagakubo Sekisui (1717–1801) epitomized this trend toward scholarly diversity. Born to a farming family in the far north of Mito Domain, as a teenager he joined the "Seven Friends of Matsuoka," a group of doctors, priests, and farmers who spent their spare time discussing books and sharing poetry.[22] Sekisui moved to Mito to study classical Chinese poetry and astronomy with Nagoya Nankei, but, like Suiken, quickly sparred with Nankei over Ogyū Sorai's work. And also like Suiken, Sekisui travelled to Edo to study with several of Sorai's students. Through these studies, Sekisui developed a fascination about the world beyond Mito. In 1767, he travelled to Nagasaki, officially to collect a group of Mito castaways who had been repatriated from Annam. While there, he visited the Dejima compound of the Dutch, whose clothes, tools, and writings he meticulously observed and recorded in his diary. He also visited the Chinese district, where he eagerly purchased books and took note of the cultural habits of the Chinese residents. In 1774, after returning to Mito, he published the *Nihon yochi rotei zenzu*, one of the first maps of Japan to mark latitude and longitude and to emphasize the need for "accuracy in the representation of land." His attention to detail and scientific methods made this map one of the most popular in Japan until the late nineteenth century, and it was copied and adapted by mapmakers and artists around the country.[23] During his travels—perhaps in Nagasaki, but more likely during a visit to the shogunal libraries in Edo—Sekisui had also encountered a copy of the Jesuit missionary Matteo Ricci's 1602 map of the world. In the early 1780s,

Figure 2.3. Nagakubo Sekisui, Sankai yochi zenzu, 1785?
(Library of Congress, Geography and Map Division)

he made an accurate reproduction of this map, maintaining its proportions and carefully labeling the lines of latitude and longitude. He also offered a long explanation of the implications of these lines: the spherical shape of the earth, climatic differences relative to the equator, and even the concept of time zones.[24] Like his map of Japan, Sekisui's world map also became a bestseller.

Sekisui's upbringing in a farming household gave him firsthand experience of the sorts of practical issues that Sorai scholars cared about. He travelled throughout Mito Domain during the 1770s, observing the hardships facing villagers and proposing various agricultural reforms. Sekisui's sharp reports and academic reputation led to his promotion to samurai status and his appointment as tutor to the daimyo, Harumori, in the late 1770s, a position of considerable influence and power. In the years that followed, Mito's leaders frequently appointed academics from humble backgrounds to similar positions. Expertise in the practical problems of society became a path to political power in late eighteenth-century Mito. However, the rise of men from humble backgrounds to positions of power did not always sit well with the traditional establishment.

REDEFINING BENEVOLENT RULE
IN AN AGE OF SOCIAL CRISIS

Despite the slow pace of his academic career, Suiken's forthright attitude and political savvy won him friends in high places and opened the door to power and influence. The turning point in Suiken's career came in 1783, when Nagakubo Sekisui arranged for Suiken to become tutor to Harumori. Harumori, just a few years younger than Suiken, had become daimyo in 1766, at the age of sixteen. Determined to overcome the many crises facing Mito, he also aspired to become a "benevolent ruler," in part by following the example of Kumamoto Domain, which had successfully introduced a series of reforms in the 1760s.[25] In his role as advisor, Suiken was able to put his academic interests to practical use tackling Mito's many social and political problems. He and Harumori successfully developed a reform agenda that revived Mito's fortunes, and they weighed in on problems facing the shogunate, too. While they framed many of these reforms at both the domain and shogunal level in the language of traditional values, the content of their proposals reflected new, more comprehensive attempts to administer Mito through empirical study, a more sophisticated bureaucracy, and better training of officials. This new model of "protomodern" benevolent rule, part of a wider trend across Japan, explicitly sought to rebuild the domain's system of governance in response to the structural and political crises of the eighteenth century.

The natural disasters, economic sluggishness, and political paralysis that challenged Mito in the first half of the eighteenth century had only worsened since Harumori became daimyo. That very year, Mito castle town burnt down. In 1772, widespread crop failures and floods hit Mito. Starting in 1773, Harumori was forced to reduce his retainers' stipends by up to 10 percent. In 1774, disastrous harvests decimated tax revenues. In 1778, the shogunate once again intervened in Mito's political affairs, ordering another round of fiscal reconstruction—another humiliating experience for the domain. The castle town had lost much of its economic vitality by this point, underscoring Mito's economic woes: thirty sake brewers had operated there until the 1720s; by the 1780s, there were only four. Fifteen fishmongers had become three, all of whom were in dire straits and unsure whether their business could continue. There was no money for repairs to houses, and poor townspeople were living in bamboo or grass huts. Landowners could not find anyone to rent their buildings, even at zero rent. "It's hard to call this a town," lamented the town elders, noting that many shops had been replaced with vegetable patches. In all, the townspeople population had fallen from a recent peak of thirteen thousand to just five thousand, with one fifth of those residents actually working in other domains, and a further thirteen hundred or so out of work. Total commercial sales were one twentieth of their 1720s level.[26]

Takakura Taneaki, the local historian, blamed the castle town's decline on the ease of access to Edo, just three days away. Rural villagers and townspeople alike went to Edo "for even the smallest things," bypassing the wholesalers and merchants of Mito.[27] In addition, as the castle town grew during the seventeenth century, it had spilled over into the surrounding villages, blurring the boundaries between town and countryside. Enterprising townspeople often relocated to these peripheral areas, running their businesses from lands formally part of villages. This exempted them from the levies and taxes within the castle town but contributed to the town's loss of economic vitality in the eighteenth century—instead, the villages around Mito became increasingly wealthy.

Against this backdrop of population loss and commercial decline, however, Mito also saw the rise of an increasingly prosperous urban elite. Restaurateurs from Edo had set up shop in the Upper Town in the 1760s, and their establishments had quickly become entertainment sites, offering music and singing and even the ability to stay the night. Reading between the lines, these places offered more than food and music (and by the early Meiji period, the area's restaurants were well known as unofficial brothels).[28] By the 1780s, puppet theatre, kabuki, poetry, painting, calligraphy, engraving, swordsmithing, and sword decoration were all flourishing arts. Samurai and wealthy townspeople alike wore fancy clothes, attended plays and sumo matches, and adopted the newest fashions from Edo.[29] Sugar had become increasingly common across Japan, and excited locals thronged the new candymakers setting up shop in Mito.[30] Even outcastes seemed to be benefitting: Takakura complained that they had risen far above their station, with the women wearing fine fabrics and parading around the town.[31] The vibrant culture of Edo had arrived, spread by merchants, commercial publishers, and the constant back-and-forth of samurai between Mito and the domain's Edo estate.

This cultural vibrancy seems hard to reconcile with accounts of Mito's depopulation and poverty. It is perhaps easiest to explain it in terms of growing inequality: a prosperous elite, relatively secure in their comforts while the masses suffered. Harumori criticized this excessive material consumption as a mark of moral decline, which in turn had contributed to the disintegration of domain government. Demand for consumption and a desire for urban life had turned people away from farming, eroding tax revenue. Desperate for more revenue, the domain administration granted a growing number of wealthy commoners samurai privileges, such as the right to wear swords, in exchange for large payments. This eroded the status distinction between samurai and commoners. At the same time, there was a growing inequality of wealth between commoner elites and samurai, whose stipends had halved as the domain fell deeper into debt. This fraying of the status order emboldened commoners, who frequently protested against the domain and generally behaved with less deference to samurai.[32] Harumori issued harsh critiques against the moral failings of Mito's people, but unfortunately, after several decades of weak daimyo, Mito's high-ranking retainers had grown comfortable with the lack of strong oversight and reacted tepidly to Harumori's attempts at reform. Finally, fiscal constraints meant that Harumori was only able to travel to Mito once during his long reign, limiting his ability to oversee reforms personally.

Suiken and Harumori believed that the root cause of Mito's myriad problems lay in its severe loss of rural population, a sign of not only economic struggles but also moral decay and governmental weakness. Since 1730, Mito's village population had declined from a peak of three hundred and ten thousand people to just two hundred and thirty thousand people—a loss of 26 percent. The 1780s were particularly devastating: Mount Asama in Shinano Province erupted in 1783, covering much of eastern Japan in ash. Harvests failed that autumn, and famine quickly ensued. Mito saw relatively few deaths in this era, as Harumori's government relied heavily on granaries and other forms of relief, but repeated harvest failures destroyed many farming households. Farming families migrated en masse to Edo to seek employment, further undercutting the rural economy. But the most pernicious cause of depopulation, at least in the minds of reformist officials and scholars, was the prevalence of infanticide.

During the eighteenth century, infanticide was common practice in Mito. For many families, whether samurai or poor farmers, it was considered normal and indeed morally proper to control family size by limiting the number of children they raised. In times of economic hardship, it made sense to reduce the number of mouths to feed. In religious and ethical terms, most people did not consider birth to demarcate the beginning of independent life—after all, infants were still utterly reliant on their mothers. Children only became full human beings gradually, as they grew up. For these reasons, people in Mito, and in much of eastern Japan, had long relied on "thinning" (*mabiki*) to keep their families to a manageable size. Perhaps every third child born in Mito was "thinned" in the eighteenth century.[33] But Mito's officials saw this as a serious problem: Sekisui, for instance, raised the alarm about the prevalent practice of infanticide, and proposed a system of pregnancy surveillance and fines for parents who practiced infanticide as a way to shore up a declining rural population.[34]

Suiken shared Sekisui's concern about infanticide and other problems of rural administration with the group of young, reform-minded scholars who populated his private academy in Mito castle town. This was a diverse group: some came from samurai families with many generations of scholars, such as Komiyama Fūken. Others, like Kimura Kenji, were sons of farmers, using education as a way forward. Both Komiyama and Kimura wrote extensively on problems of rural administration and agronomy and believed that the practice of infanticide reflected poorly on the state of affairs in Mito. These ideas did not languish in Suiken's academy. He advocated for putting young, capable men into Mito's government, regardless of their family background. He found a sympathetic partner in Harumori, who appointed many of Suiken's students to important political and administrative roles.

Suiken's students devoted time and energy to surveys and proposals to stamp out the practice by strengthening the domain's administrative capacity. In 1789, Fūken showed Suiken a copy of a poster circulating around Mito that depicted a monstrous cat-faced woman, crushing her child under her foot (figure 2.4).[35] The poster was part of a rural campaign against infanticide in neighboring Tanagura Domain, and Suiken was reportedly thrilled to see evidence of a successful campaign.[36] In an essay submitted the following year, Kimura blamed widespread infanticide on excessive poverty among Mito's farmers. "Even commoners who are *not* impoverished still only eat miso once every couple of days, and some never eat meat or fish. They don't have a kerchief to wipe their noses after they sneeze, so they blow their noses with their fingers. They don't have cloths to wash their faces, and when they use the toilet, they don't use paper, but instead use leaves or straw." It was only natural, in Kimura's mind, that these impoverished commoners turned

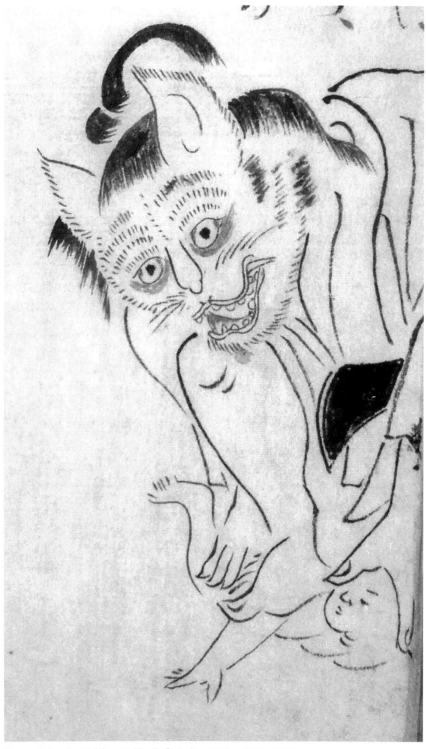

Figure 2.4. From Kimura Kenji, Sokuin goroku, 1791–1808
(Hokkaido University Northern Studies Collection)

to infanticide. Moreover, he blamed their miserable situation on the complete breakdown of governance in Mito.[37]

Harumori took Kimura's message to heart and introduced a comprehensive anti-infanticide program. He offered both carrots and sticks: on the carrot side, he rewarded families and villages that raised lots of children and publicized their virtuous fecundity. He also introduced a system of subsidies for childrearing. On the stick side, he issued severe bans on abortion and infanticide. He also introduced a system of pregnancy surveillance, under which village officials were responsible for reporting any pregnancies by women in their areas to the domain. Domain officials would regularly check in on these women to monitor their pregnancy.[38] Through the infanticide measures, Mito's rulers began to intervene more directly in village affairs, exerting greater control over a previously decentralized and semi-autonomous system.

These interventions worked, at least to a degree: the average number of children raised past infancy bottomed out at just under three children per woman in the late 1790s, and then began to grow again. By the middle of the nineteenth century, the rate had risen to nearly four children per woman.[39] Of course, plenty of women found ways around the new rules: records from this era contain a suspicious number of trips and falls by women in their eighth or ninth month of pregnancy, leading to statistically implausible numbers of "stillbirths" reported to the domain. Even into the twentieth century, there was evidence of infanticide on the fringes of the former Mito Domain.[40] Nevertheless, the efforts of activists like Kimura and leaders like Harumori to combat infanticide paid off. After nearly a century of failed reform efforts, the success of the campaign to reverse population loss signaled the beginning of a revival in Mito's government and society in the last decade of the eighteenth century. In the decades that followed, Mito's reformers would continue to use education, surveillance, and political intervention to increase their oversight over the commoner population, whether in matters of religion, military preparation, or political support.

Suiken and Harumori did not limit their sights to Mito's internal problems: they also turned their attention to political reform at the shogunal level. Harumori's base in Edo, the Mito Tokugawa family's exalted status, and the precedent set by Mitsukuni gave these men ample grounds to claim a role in shogunal politics. Moreover, they found an easy target in the person of Tanuma Okitsugu, whose twenty-year leadership of the shogunate began in 1767, just one year after Harumori became daimyo. Tanuma had promoted the spread of commerce and economic growth, largely to tackle the shogunate's own fiscal problems. In the minds of critics like Suiken and Harumori this had only given wealthy merchants greater power and undermined the position of samurai. Tanuma was to blame for the decline in moral standards and the corrosive spread of commercialism in rural areas. By the 1780s, they decided Tanuma had to go. In 1786, Harumori, along with the daimyo of the other Tokugawa branch domains of Kii and Owari, accused Tanuma of corruption, and forced him out of office. In his place, they installed Matsudaira Sadanobu, a traditionalist who had successfully improved the finances and government of his home domain, Shirakawa. Once appointed chief councilor, he embarked on the Kansei Reforms, a program to undo many of the developments of the Tanuma years. Keen to restore the traditional values of the shogunate, Sadanobu introduced moral reforms and a program of fiscal austerity.

Suiken played a central role in this political coup, which earned him both Harumori's trust and an influential position on the national stage. Nagakubo Sekisui told him that "your recommendation of [Sadanobu] is truly fortunate for the fate of our times."[41] It also gave Suiken the chance to weigh in on matters far beyond Mito's economic and political problems. In 1787, Sadanobu asked Suiken to list the greatest problems facing Japan. Suiken submitted three. He urged the shogunate to crack down on militant religious sects, reflecting the longstanding antipathy to wayward Buddhist temples in Mito. He argued that Korean embassies to Edo should end: they were simply too expensive, and did not produce any meaningful diplomatic benefit. Harumori formally submitted this proposal to the shogunate, which cancelled a planned diplomatic visit to celebrate the accession of the eleventh shogun Ienari that very year. And Suiken argued that the shogunate needed to deal with the arrival of Russian forces in the region of Ezochi, underscoring the new threat posed by the rise of Western imperialism as a global geopolitical force (see chapter 3). Here, too, the shogunate paid attention, although reluctantly. While Sadanobu believed that the high costs and logistical challenges of annexing Ezochi outweighed the benefits, by the late 1790s the shogunate decided to lay formal claim to the region to fend off the Russian threat.

In his dedication to reforms in Mito and in the shogunate, Harumori clearly emulated his ancestor Mitsukuni's efforts to become a benevolent ruler. And while Matsudaira Sadanobu has been remembered for the austere and deeply moralistic nature of his Kansei Reforms, the focus of the reforms within Mito reflected a deeply pragmatic orientation toward new social and economic problems, whether caused by infanticide, commercialization, or the ossification of government institutions in a divided domain. The growing prominence of specific, empirical research to inform policymaking also distinguished this era as a turning point in beliefs about governance. In this regard, Mito was not alone: these reforms were part of a wave of "protomodern" reforms that swept across Japan in the second half of the eighteenth century, as domains facing similar challenges as Mito experimented with new ideas.

But Mito's elite status among Japan's domains gave it a platform that allowed the domain's leaders to amplify their efforts within Mito and to influence the shogunate's reforms, as seen in Suiken's proposals to Sadanobu. Moreover, unlike stereotypes of Sadanobu's reforms, the reformist vision put forward by Suiken and Harumori was not simply a reactionary attempt to return to the past, even if it was cloaked in the language of traditional moralism. Rather, it reflected an awareness of new economic and geopolitical forces that required new ways of government at the domain and shogunal levels. Harumori and Suiken were by no means successful in every venture, and Sadanobu's Kansei Reforms fizzled out after a few years. But within Mito, their efforts set an important precedent: a willingness to comprehensively reimagine the workings of the domain and its society, and to take new and often radical steps to alter and reform those workings. Mito's reformers continued to use appeals to traditional moral values, like benevolent rule and the importance of proper social relations, but the *content* of their reform programs reflected a genuine desire to make their society stronger and more successful in the face of new challenges. Unsurprisingly, their attempts at reform almost immediately engendered debate and opposition, not only from the traditional establishment, but also among the diverse group of young scholars who formed Mito's revived and energized academic community under Suiken's leadership.

FUJITA YŪKOKU AND THE BIRTH
OF THE LATE MITO SCHOOL

Suiken's reformist interests extended to Mito's academic world, where he oversaw the beginning of a new phase in Mito's scholarly identity, often known as the Late Mito School. In 1786, Suiken became director of the Shōkōkan, finally displacing the conservative scholars that had resisted his Sorai-influenced scholarship and blocked his career. As the death or retirement of those scholars removed Suiken's strongest opponents, his close relationship to Harumori helped secure his promotion. As director, Suiken oversaw the recruitment of promising young students who injected life into the Shōkōkan with their intellectual skills. Suiken's choice of protégés reflected his reformist vision and his belief in the value of talent over heredity.

Perhaps the most able—and certainly the most controversial—of Suiken's protégés was Fujita Yūkoku, a precocious young man who emulated his teacher by seeking out new ideas, particularly the Kokugaku scholars of the eighteenth century. Yūkoku's work infused Mito's traditional scholarly emphasis on imperial history with a focus on Japan's unique, native traditions. His writings established the Late Mito School's distinctive blend of Kokugaku's ethnocentrism and exceptionalism, traditional Neo-Confucian moralism, and a pragmatic, reformist political philosophy attuned to the new domestic challenges and geopolitical threats of the late eighteenth century. It was through Yūkoku's work that Suiken's intellectual eclecticism and pragmatic orientation most powerfully shaped Mito's intellectual identity at the dawn of the nineteenth century.

Yūkoku was born in Mito castle town in 1774, the second son of a used-clothes merchant. This was a lucrative business—Mito was an important transshipment site for secondhand clothes from Edo to northern Japan—but a low-prestige one. Yūkoku's parents urged him to pursue education as a path to escaping this lowly status. Throughout his life Yūkoku expressed disdain for merchant activities, a common piety for Mito's samurai scholars that also suggests a deep desire to overcome his background. He excelled at school, mastering classical Chinese by his early teens. Suiken recognized his brilliance and arranged for his appointment to the Shōkōkan at the age of fifteen, then secured him promotions at the ages of eighteen and twenty-three. Yūkoku was granted a low samurai rank, too, which gave him a stipend and greater privileges within the academy. Suiken and Yūkoku's relationship was more like father and son than teacher and pupil.[42] Suiken's support gave Yūkoku breathtaking opportunities from a young age: in 1791, when Yūkoku was just eighteen, Matsudaira Sadanobu invited him to submit an essay on politics, and the result was a bold critique of the failures of the governing class: *Seimeiron* (*On the Rectification of Names*).

In *Seimeiron*, Yūkoku articulated a deeply ideological political ethics rooted in traditional values and the supremacy of the Japanese imperial tradition, reflecting a Sorai-like emphasis on *institutions* rather than individual moral behavior. Yūkoku argued that the proper relationship between lord and subject had grown obscured over time, hidden by the corrupting effects of commerce and the luxurious consumerism of urban life. If only "names and status distinctions were correct and rigid," he argued, distinguishing "the high from the low," then the realm could be governed justly.[43] On the one hand, Yūkoku's call to "rectify names" was an unremarkable call for reform, common to orthodox Confucianist arguments. But the real emphasis of his essay was on the system of status distinctions itself: the hierarchy of Japanese society, with the emperor at the top.[44] Morality flowed from this structure: so long as everyone knew their place and demonstrated loyalty to their superiors, the disorder that had caused economic, fiscal, and social problems could be fixed. This marked a key departure from the Neo-Confucian thinkers of the early Tokugawa period, both within Mito and elsewhere in Japan. Rather than assessing the moral behavior of individual emperors, shoguns, and lords, Yūkoku's vision of rectification emphasized loyalty to one's superior—ultimately the emperor—as the marker of morality and social order. Put simply, the early-Tokugawa ideal of "benevolent rule" as an individual moral trait was supplanted by the moral imperative of loyalty to one's superiors in the political hierarchy.

Yūkoku's emphasis on institutions led to another distinctive feature of his ideology: the uniqueness of Japan, whose imperial line, unlike those in China, had never been overthrown. In other words, the continued display of loyalty by successive shogunal clans had ensured the continued reign of the imperial dynasty, a marker of the validity of this moral system.[45] This distinctiveness made it easy for Yūkoku and his successors to argue that Japan, not China, was the morally superior nation, with the better claim to being a universal standard. *Seimeiron* established the youthful Yūkoku as a leading intellect in Mito, although Suiken chose not to submit the essay to the shogunate, fearful that it would invite criticism.

Scholars today often treat *Seimeiron* as the earliest and clearest expression of the principles of the Late Mito School, and the debates that have emerged reflect the difficulty of pinning down an eclectic philosophical school with a strong practical political orientation. First, there is vehement disagreement about the relative influence of different philosophical schools on Yūkoku and his successors. Bitō Masahide, J. Victor Koschmann, and H. D. Harootunian have argued in favor of the overwhelming influence of Ogyū Sorai, filtered through Suiken.[46] Yūkoku's focus on the political hierarchy underneath the emperor, and the means to preserve that system, reflects Sorai's institutional framework. Many local historians in Mito, who consider themselves heirs to Mito's historiographical traditions, reject this view, claiming that Yūkoku's emphasis on imperial loyalty and Japanese uniqueness reflect a different set of values: a deep reverence for Japan's imperial line, and the culture of loyalty that surrounded it. Kajiyama Takao, for instance, points out that Yūkoku criticized Sorai's failure to understand either the nature of Japan's political hierarchy or Japan's civilizational superiority.[47] In other words, while Yūkoku's *methods* may have reflected Sorai's empiricism, the most important factor is his *spiritual* devotion to exceptionalist ideas about Shintō and the emperor.

The question of philosophical influences leads directly into a second major debate: the degree to which the Late Mito School marked a departure from the scholarship of Mitsukuni and his contemporaries in the seventeenth century. Much of the debate centers on the question of national identity. On the one hand, Harootunian does not view Yūkoku as a "protonationalist," preferring to read the *Seimeiron* as a traditional expression of Japanese imperial

loyalty.[48] Mito scholar Nagoya Tokimasa argues Yūkoku was transmitting
Mito's spiritual tradition, which he defines as Mitsukuni's "true desire" to
emphasize loyalty to the emperor in the organization of the *Dai Nihon shi*.[49]
On the other hand, Bitō sees something new in Yūkoku's work: a deeper degree of devotion to the imperial line, a heightened emphasis on the continuity
of the imperial lineage—a view that was not common in the early Edo period,
when many scholars (including, perhaps, Mitsukuni himself) interpreted the
extinction of the Southern Court in 1392 as the end of an imperial dynasty.
Bitō also points out that the language of loyalty is itself a development of the
Late Mito School. While there had long been imperial loyalists throughout
Japan, Mito's scholars went to great lengths to promote imperial loyalism
as the bedrock of the entire Tokugawa political system, in part as a way to
legitimize their own heterodox teachings.[50] More recently but in a similar
vein, Mark McNally argues that Yūkoku's "exceptionalist tone" marked a
new recognition of Japanese distinctiveness and superiority.[51] In other words,
the emerging contours of the Late Mito School suggest a new sense of national identity: a coherent Japanese nation, defined by a political, ethical,
and religious system focused on reverence for an unbroken imperial line. By
resurrecting and amplifying an ancient discourse of imperial loyalty, Yūkoku
helped forge a new language of nationalism and Japanese uniqueness.

Zooming out from textual debates, the context of the *Seimeiron* and
Yūkoku's subsequent work lend credence to the argument that the Late
Mito School marked a departure from the scholarship of a century earlier.
Yūkoku's emphasis on Japanese exceptionalism reflected a new awareness of
geopolitical threats to Japan, particularly from Russia in Ezochi. Suiken and
Yūkoku's peers amassed a significant library about Ezochi, and later in life
Yūkoku would order his eldest son, Tōko, to defend Mito against British sailors, even if it meant death (see chapter 3). Yūkoku also reflected the strong
policy bent of Late Mito work: in the years that followed *Seimeiron*, Yūkoku
published essays on promoting agriculture, and wrote critical memorials to
Harumori regarding the domain's fiscal and economic problems. Yūkoku's
philosophical works were closely tied to his political and social critiques,
reflecting a new degree of integration between Mito's academic and political
worlds. This national perspective and integration of academic and political
work marked a shift in Mito's scholarly history.

The *Seimeiron* underscores the significance of the last decade of the eighteenth century as a transitional period, an era when new ideas about practical
political change and abstract national identity were taking form. Those ideas
would mature in the generation after Yūkoku, but the core principles of the
Late Mito School—loyalty to Japan's unique imperial lineage and the urgency
of addressing domestic problems to defend Japan against foreign threats, later

summed up by the slogan "revere the emperor, expel the barbarian"—can already be seen in Yūkoku's youthful *Seimeiron*. Given Yūkoku's age, it seems likely that the *Seimeiron* reflects many of Suiken's ideas, too. Suiken probably shared Yūkoku's intellectual positions regarding Japanese uniqueness, but he never developed this line of thought in a formal way.[52] But in one important respect, teacher and student were strikingly different. While Suiken's eclecticism led to a flexible pragmatism, Yūkoku turned his eclectic philosophical inspirations into a strident idealism. It was not long before their personalities clashed, over no less an issue than how, finally, to complete Mito's great scholarly project: the *Dai Nihon shi*, whose incomplete volumes weighed on the domain's scholars—and budget.

THE PROBLEM OF THE *DAI NIHON SHI* AND THE RISE OF FACTIONALISM

One of Suiken's first goals upon assuming the directorship of the Shōkōkan was to complete the *Dai Nihon shi*, which had been languishing since the death of Asaka Tanpaku fifty years earlier. This was not just for intellectual reasons: Harumori also placed enormous pressure on Suiken to complete the project, likely as a precursor to downsizing the Shōkōkan workforce to cut costs. Suiken decided the project should be done by 1800, the hundredth anniversary of Mitsukuni's death. With two sections of the text still outstanding, not to mention revisions to the first draft of the annals and essays submitted half a century earlier, this was a blatantly impossible task, and Suiken reluctantly proposed significant cuts to the project. However, Yūkoku adhered to a much stricter vision of the *Dai Nihon shi*, and he vehemently opposed Suiken's proposal, arguing that removing any portions of the text would undermine the ethical value of the project. The two men also disagreed on the content of the book: which sources to use, how to recount certain thorny historical episodes, and even whether the title was appropriate (Yūkoku argued that *Dai Nihon* ["Great Japan"] was not used by the court to refer to Japan, so submitting a book with that title to the emperor would be offensive).[53]

These debates grew uglier as time went on and, exacerbated by Yūkoku's increasingly abrasive personality, destroyed the relationship between Suiken and his student. Suiken made more and more errors as he hurried to finish drafts, irritating Yūkoku and other scholars. Meanwhile, Yūkoku's precociousness had made him arrogant. In 1793, Nagakubo Sekisui had to intervene to prevent him from submitting an aggressive memorial to Harumori, in which he criticized Harumori's failure to tackle rural depopulation and Mito's indebtedness. In 1797, Yūkoku wrote a public letter to his colleagues in the

Shōkōkan, implicitly criticizing Suiken on a number of philosophical and methodological points.[54] Shortly after this letter went public, a friend invited Yūkoku to a night out partying in the Yoshiwara brothel district of Edo—unbecoming behavior for a scholar and samurai from Mito, where moral reform was top of the agenda. Yūkoku was formally reprimanded and ordered to refrain from contact with Harumori for a short period of time. This angered Yūkoku, and he submitted a scathing memorial to Harumori that criticized the daimyo for his traditional views and his micromanagerial style. Harumori, furious at Yūkoku's blatant disregard for the order to refrain from contact, ordered Yūkoku back to Mito, and froze him out of scholarly work.[55] Suiken, embarrassed and offended, broke off contact with Yūkoku.

Yūkoku's fall from grace reflected the close interconnection between academic and political life in Mito under Harumori's reign, a feature that continued to grow. Academic debates became inseparable from the behavior of scholars outside the Shōkōkan. With Yūkoku's punishment, Suiken had regained control of the *Dai Nihon shi* project, but just two years later it was his turn to fall from favor, ostensibly for meddling in the domain's judicial system. Despite submitting a completed (albeit truncated) draft of the *Dai Nihon shi*, he was banned from the commemorative ceremony in which the text was presented to the spirit of Mitsukuni. After a lifetime working to achieve this goal, and a decade of desperately reducing the project's scope to get it done, this must have been a cruel disappointment. While Suiken fell from favor, Yūkoku found it once again. In 1799, his thoughtful proposal for tackling the problems of rural society earned him restoration to Harumori's good graces.[56] In 1803, he was appointed editor of the *Dai Nihon shi* in a sweeping personnel change that reversed Suiken's cuts to the project and removed Suiken from influence once and for all. In 1807, Yūkoku was appointed director of the Shōkōkan, cementing his influence over Mito's academic world.

In taking control of the *Dai Nihon shi*, Yūkoku was able to put his distinctive ideas about Japan's unique imperial polity into practice, and in so doing he cemented the shift in the Late Mito School toward an emphasis on Japanese exceptionalism. In concrete terms, this meant eliminating elements of the project that risked offending the court or undermining its moral supremacy. The project's title was an obvious point of contention, but perhaps more significant was his decision in 1809 to eliminate the *ronsan*, the series of essays that assessed the virtue of past emperors. The *ronsan* were a core component of the classical Chinese model of historiography that Mitsukuni sought to emulate, and Yūkoku's decision to remove them marked a decisive turn toward a distinctively Japanese model of history writing—one that did not critique the imperial dynasty but, rather, treated its unchanging nature with reverence.[57] Yūkoku and his defenders argued that the *ronsan* were not part of Mitsukuni's original vision, as they were composed by Asaka Tan-paku at the direction of Mitsukuni's heir, Tsunaeda. In their view, Yūkoku actually restored the "true vision" of Mitsukuni by eliminating the elements that did not emphasize and prioritize the distinctiveness of Japan's imperial tradition.[58] This is a rather ahistorical interpretation of events: it relies upon the transmission of an unchanging "spirit" or "intent" on the part of Mitsu-kuni and fails to account for the ways in which Mitsukuni's "spirit" could be interpreted and reinterpreted in different historical contexts. Moreover, Yūkoku's appeal to Mitsukuni's will seems to be a clear attempt to legitimize a competing vision for the *Dai Nihon shi*, in a situation where Suiken was still popular and had many loyal students, even after his ouster. In any event, Yūkoku successfully eliminated the *ronsan* and reinstated other components of the *Dai Nihon shi* that properly respected the imperial court and empha-sized the purported unbrokenness of its lineage. In this manner, he imbued the *Dai Nihon shi* with the values of imperial loyalty and Japanese uniqueness that today are regarded as the hallmarks of the Late Mito School.

Yūkoku's intellectual idealism and political ambitions came at a cost. They rent the Shōkōkan into two factions: purist reformers who studied under Yūkoku, and more pragmatic reformist scholars who remained loyal to Suiken. These moderates frequently gained the backing of a third group: the conserva-tive political establishment, who mostly wanted to prevent significant change. This establishment resented the ambitious but low-ranking samurai who came to dominate Mito's government. Ironically, given the intensity of the debates over the *Dai Nihon shi*, it was in the arena of politics, not philosophy, that the feuds between Mito's political factions worsened in the nineteenth century.

Suiken spent the rest of his life in quiet retirement. Freed from the obli-gations of domain work, he was able to cultivate friendships across Japan, and enjoyed writing poetry and entertaining at his home. He died in 1823, never having made amends with Yūkoku. Yūkoku died just three years later, a lonely, depressed, and alcoholic figure.[59] Although Harumori had supported a range of Yūkoku's proposals for administrative, agricultural, and academic reforms, his death in 1805 had dealt a blow to Yūkoku. With the death in 1816 of Harunori's son and successor, the seventh daimyo, Ha-rutoshi (b. 1773), Yūkoku had lost all backers in the upper echelons of the domain government. Yūkoku's abrasive manner had alienated his erstwhile friends and allies, and the domain's promotion of more moderate students of Suiken amplified Yūkoku's resentment and depression. Suiken's stu-dents continued to work in the Shōkōkan, and many became trusted advi-sors in the domain administration.

But it was Yūkoku's legacy that dominated Mito's scholarly world for the next sixty years. Yūkoku made two crucial contributions. First, he laid out a clear vision of the ideal society, one ordered by hierarchical status distinctions under a virtuous and divine emperor. This appealed to many samurai facing a loss of wealth and status and looking for a way to tackle the threats of societal disorder. Second, Yūkoku argued that the crises in society reflected a breakdown of that ideal order and required a new generation of leaders to restore society to its ideal form. He never resolved a key tension between these ideas: that returning to his idealized vision of the past might require the complete dismantling of the Tokugawa order. At the time of his death, this tension did not bother many Mito thinkers. Yūkoku did not want to overthrow the shogunate, or end the hierarchy of daimyo and vassals, samurai and commoners that spread an intricate and pervasive web of social control across the archipelago. Rather, Yūkoku believed that good lords could reassert this hierarchy, and thereby foster a harmonious, unified Japan, ready to face the looming threat of Western imperialism. He left it to his students, however, to explain just how that unity and strength could be attained.

At the dawn of the nineteenth century, a new generation of academic and political leaders had halted a long period of decline in Mito by introducing a series of practical reforms. Suiken and Harumori tackled domestic problems such as economic decline and infanticide by introducing new, more intense forms of government oversight into Mito's countryside, part of a raft of "protomodern" domain reforms taking place not only in Mito but across Japan. They played key roles in Matsudaira Sadanobu's rise to power and implementation of the shogunate's Kansei Reforms. Suiken and his reformist colleagues embraced new ideas, particularly those of Ogyū Sorai and Kokugaku scholars, and began tackling social, economic, and political problems. Although Suiken ultimately failed in his efforts to complete the *Dai Nihon shi*, he succeeded in bringing Mito's scholars firmly into the world of politics. For the remainder of Mito's existence, the marriage of scholarship and politics defined the domain, and gave birth to one of the most powerful political and ideological movements of the late Tokugawa period. But this all came at a cost: intense factionalism, triggered by Suiken's feud with his student Yūkoku, became a chronic and ugly characteristic of Mito's academic and political worlds for the remainder of the domain's existence.

NOTES

1. Takakura Taneaki [Issai], *Suifu chiri onkoroku*, in *Ibaraki-ken shiryō: kinsei chishi hen*, ed. Ibaraki kenshi hensan dai-ichibu iinkai (Mito: Ibaraki-ken, 1975), 149, 96, 98, 68.

2. *Kokugaku*, often called "nativism," refers to a strand of scholarship in Tokugawa Japan that challenged the dominant Neo-Confucianism of officialdom with a focus on

the distinctive literary and cultural traditions of Japan. Mark McNally offers a succinct overview and points out the risks of using nativism as a translation of Kokugaku in the introduction to *Like No Other: Exceptionalism and Nativism in Early Modern Japan* (Honolulu: University of Hawai'i Press, 2016), especially 1–6.

3. For instance, Klaus Kracht identifies no works on Suiken in his bibliography of Mito's intellectual history. H. D. Harootunian misidentifies him as Tachibana Suiken, and largely neglects him in his account of the rise of the Late Mito School. Harootunian, *Toward Restoration: The Growth of Political Consciousness in Tokugawa Japan* (Berkeley: University of California Press, 1970), 58–61.

4. The only biography of Suiken was published with the support of his descendant, hinting at the lack of enthusiasm for Suiken's work among later Mito scholars. Maeda Kōkyō, *Tachihara Suiken* (Mito: Tachihara Yoshishige, 1963). Yoshida Toshizumi, noting the curious lack of attention to Suiken, offers a brief biography in *Kansei-ki Mitogaku no kenkyū* (Tokyo: Yoshikawa kōbunkan, 2011), 8–39. Yoshida attributes this lack of attention to a more general lack of interest among Mito scholars in the historical origins (as opposed to ideological inspirations) of the Late Mito School.

5. Yoshida, *Kansei-ki Mitogaku no kenkyū*, 27–33

6. Bitō Masahide argued forcefully for the influence of Ogyū Sorai on Suiken as a key turning point in the reformulation of the *Dai Nihon shi* around more uniquely Japanese concepts; see "Mitogaku no tokushitsu," in *Mitogaku*, ed. Imai Usaburō, Seya Yoshihiko, and Bitō Masahide, Nihon shisō taikei 53 (Tokyo: Iwanami shoten, 1973), 564–66. Mito scholars, notably Nagoya Tokimasa and Kajiyama Takao, have reacted strongly, arguing that this view fails to account for the transmission of an unchanging emphasis on Japan's unique imperial lineage since Mitsukuni's time. They tend to ignore Suiken, however, in favor of Yūkoku. See Nagoya Tokimasa, *Mito Mitsukuni to sono yokō* (Mito: Mito shigakkai, 1985), especially chapter 5, and Kajiyama Takao, *Gendai Mitogakuron hihan* (Tokyo: Kinseisha, 2007), especially chapters 1 and 3.

7. The second half of the eighteenth century saw a series of "protomodern" reforms in many domains across Japan, whose leaders looked to one another for inspiration. Isoda Michinori, "Hansei kaikaku no denpa: Kumamoto-han Hōreki kaikaku to Mito-han Kansei kaikaku," *Nihon kenkyū* 40 (Nov 2009): 15. Other notable studies include Koseki Yūichirō, *"Meikun" no kindai: gakumon, chishiki to hansei kaikaku* (Tokyo: Yoshikawa kōbunkan, 2012), which focuses on Yonezawa Domain, and Mark Ravina, *Land and Lordship in Early Modern Japan* (Stanford: Stanford University Press, 1999), focusing on Yonezawa, Hirosaki, and Tokushima domains.

8. Terakado Morio, "Mito hanryō Hōei rokunen no zenpan ikki," in *Ibaraki hyakushō ikki*, ed. Ueda Toshio (Tokyo: Fūtōsha, 1974), 13–15.

9. This is Terakado's suggestion, based on work by Hayashi Motoi. Terakado, "Mito hanryō Hōei rokunen no zenpan ikki," 19.

10. *Mito shishi*, chū, 2:31–53.

11. Terakado, "Mito hanryō Hōei rokunen no zenpan ikki," 33.

12. *Mito shishi*, chū, 2:76–83. For a critical analysis of how Matsunami became a scapegoat for Mitsukuni's failures, see Ōishi Shinzaburō, "Matsunami Kanjūrō to Tokugawa Mitsukuni," in *Edo to chihō bunka*, ed. Ōishi Shinzaburō, vol. 1 (Tokyo: Bun'ichi sōgō shuppan, 1977), 85–106.

13. Details and quote from *Mito shishi*, chū, 2:157–66.

14. Suzuki Eiichi, *Mitohan gakumon kyōiku shi no kenkyū* (Tokyo: Yoshikawa kōbunkan, 1987), 32.

15. Maeda, *Tachihara Suiken*, 20.

16. Yoshida, *Kansei-ki Mitogaku*, 8–9.

17. Yoshida, *Kansei-ki Mitogaku*, 9.

18. Tachihara Suiken, "Suzuki sōsai ni atau," in *Mitogaku taikei*, ed. Takasu Yoshijirō, vol. 4, *Tachihara Suiken, Toyoda Tenkō shū* (Tokyo: Mitogaku taikei kankōkai, 1941), 203–7.

19. Tachihara Suiken, *Mito saijiki*, reprinted in Akiyama Fusako, ed., *Mito Saijiki: Mitohan no shomin shiryō shūsei* (Nagareyama: Ron shobō, 1983), 5–24.

20. Takakura, *Suifu chiri onkoroku*.

21. Suzuki, *Mito-han gakumon kyōiku shi no kenkyū*, 493.

22. Suzuki, *Mito-han gakumon kyōiku shi no kenkyū*, 493–97.

23. Marcia Yonemoto, *Mapping Early Modern Japan* (Berkeley: University of California Press, 2003), 37–39.

24. Gabor Lukacs, "Chikyū bankoku sankai yochi zenzu setsu: The First Japanese World Map with Latitudes and Longitudes and with an Extensive Japanese Explanatory Note," *The Cartographic Journal* 53, no. 2 (May 2016): 149–57.

25. Isoda, "Hansei kaikaku no denpa," 15–17.

26. "Tenmei 8-nen Mito shitamachi suibi shidai kakiage," in *Ibaraki ken shiryō: kinsei shakai keizai hen*, 4:284–89.

27. Takakura, *Suifu chiri onkoroku*, 180.

28. Takakura, *Suifu chiri onkoroku*, 121–23, and Ishibe Kanekichi to the editor, *Ibaraki shinpō* 124 (28 February 1878), reprinted in *Ibaraki ken shiryō: kindai shakai seiji hen*, vol. 1, 574.

29. *Mito shishi*, chū, 2:355–76.

30. Takakura, *Suifu chirhi onkoroku*, 121.

31. Takakura, *Suifu chiri onkoroku*, 151.

32. *Mito shishi*, chū, 2:286–316.

33. Fabian Drixler, *Mabiki: Infanticide and Population Growth in Eastern Japan, 1660–1950* (Berkeley: University of California Press, 2013), 1–22.

34. Fabian Drixler, *Mabiki*, 183, and Drixler, "The Discourse of the Louse: Regional Pride and Conflicting Cultures of Parenthood in mid-Tokugawa Japan," in *Kindheit in der Japanische geschichte*, eds. Michael Kinski, Elike Großmann, and Harald Salomon (Wiesbaden: Harrassowitz Verlag, 2016), 164–65.

35. Hand-drawn copy of a poster produced by Suzuki Busuke, contained in Kimura Kenji, *Sokuin goroku* (1791–1808), shikyo 32, Hokkaido University Library Northern Studies Collection, Sapporo, Japan. See Drixler, "The Discourse of the Louse," 159–90, for a discussion of this poster and its spread.

36. Letter from Kuno Junzō to Komiyama Masahide, in *Fūken nenroku*, vol. 1 [1807], 38; MS no. 826–27, National Diet Library Digital Library, dl.ndl.go.jp/info:ndljp/pid/2576962; also reprinted in Takahashi Bonsen, *Nihon jinkō kenkyū*, vol. 1 (Tokyo: San'yūsha, 1941), 504–7. Fabian Drixler addresses this episode in *Mabiki*, 143, suggesting that Suiken made a copy of the poster for himself, proclaiming it "a

model for the country at large"; my read of the letter is that it was not Suiken but the poster's author, Suzuki Busuke, who said this, upon learning that Suiken had seen the poster. (This reading is reinforced by a different record of this letter in Komiyama Masahide, *Fūken gūki*, vol. 5 [1809], 10; doc 826–24, National Diet Library Digital Library, dl.ndl.go.jp/info:ndljp/pid/2560380.) Either way, it is undeniable that Suiken saw the poster and must have thought highly of it, underscoring the significance of the network of academics and local activists in the Mito region.

37. Kimura Kenji, *Sokuminron*, in *Kinsei chihō keizai shiryō*, ed. Ono Takeo, vol. 1 (Tokyo: Yoshikawa kōbunkan, 1931), 2–19.

38. Drixler, "The Discourse of the Louse," and Drixler, *Mabiki*, 158–82.

39. Drixler, *Mabiki*, appendix 4.

40. Drixler, *Mabiki*, 232–43.

41. Quoted in Maeda, *Tachihara Suiken*, 575.

42. Maeda, *Tachihara Suiken*, 40.

43. Fujita Yūkoku, "On the Rectification of Names," quoted and discussed in J. Victor Koschmann, *The Mito Ideology: Discourse, Reform, and Insurrection in Late Tokugawa Japan, 1790–1864* (Berkeley: University of California Press, 1987), 43. Japanese original "Seimeiron," in Imai et al., *Mitogaku*, 9–14.

44. Bitō, "Mitogaku no tokushitsu," in Imai et al., *Mitogaku*, 571–76.

45. Mark McNally, *Like No Other: Exceptionalism and Nativism in Early Modern Japan* (Honolulu: University of Hawai'i Press, 2016), 174–75.

46. Bitō, "Mitogaku no tokushitsu"; Koschmann, *The Mito Ideology*, 43–48; Harootunian, *Toward Restoration*, 62–74.

47. Kajiyama, *Gendai Mitogakuron hihan*, 37.

48. Harootunian, *Toward Restoration*, 66–68.

49. For example, see Nagoya, *Mito Mitsukuni to sono yokō*, 3–18, and Kajiyama, *Gendai Mitogakuron hihan*, 40–62.

50. Bitō, "Mitogaku no tokushitsu," 561.

51. McNally, *Like No Other*, 175.

52. Kajiyama, *Fujita Yūkoku no monogatari*, 2:66–67.

53. For more on these debates, see Koschmann, *The Mito Ideology*, 34–43.

54. Yoshida, *Kansei-ki Mitogaku no kenkyū*, 292–98.

55. Seya Yoshihiko, "Kaidai," in Imai et al., *Mitogaku*, 479.

56. Fujita Yūkoku, "Kannō wakumon," in *Mitogaku taikei*, ed. Takasu Yoshijirō, vol. 3, *Fujita Yūkoku shū* (Tokyo: Mitogaku taikei kankōkai, 1941), 16–98. For a discussion, see Koschmann, *The Mito Ideology*, 82–94.

57. Suzuki, *Mito-han gakumon kyōiku shi no kenkyū*, 75–76.

58. See, for example, Kajiyama, *Gendai Mitogakuron hihan*, 223–38, and Kajiyama, *Fujita Yūkoku no monogatari*, 2:36.

59. Yoshida, *Kansei-ki Mitogaku no kenkyū*, 305.

Chapter Three

"Revere the Emperor, Expel the Barbarian"

Mito in the Age of Imperialism

The resurgence of Mito's academic and political world at the end of the eighteenth century coincided with the arrival of Russian traders, missionaries, and soldiers in the waters to Japan's north in the 1770s and 1780s. Russia was not the only Western empire making inroads into Northeast Asia, and over the next few decades, Japan's leaders watched anxiously as British, French, and American ships sailed past their islands with increasing frequency in pursuit of commercial wealth, trade routes, political conquests, and religious conversions. This global historical context shaped the development of Mito's reform movement for the remainder of the domain's history: Mito's scholars and political leaders framed their work through the lens of foreign crises. The ideas about national identity for which Mito became most famous, often summed up by the slogan "revere the emperor, expel the barbarian," were rooted in this context. The concepts of Japanese identity and, particularly, the unique significance of the imperial line, took on new significance when placed in the threatening geopolitical circumstances. The power of Mito's call to protect and strengthen Japan's national identity rested in part on the ability of the domain's scholars and leaders to persuade others of the urgency and severity of the imperialist threat.

In response to foreign imperialism, Mito's leaders also began advocating for the Tokugawa shogunate to adopt an aggressive expansionist policy of their own. Initially, Mito's leaders worried about Russia and its designs on Ezochi, as Japanese called Ainu territory stretching across present-day Hokkaido, Sakhalin, and the Kuril Archipelago. In their view, this northern region was Japan's weakest flank and required the most urgent attention. Mito's leaders were among the strongest advocates for colonization in Ezochi from the 1780s until the formal Tokugawa annexation of Ezochi in 1855 and then its incorporation into the imperial realm as Hokkaido in 1869. Although Mito did not play a heavy role in the post-1869 project of settler-colonialism in Hokkaido, the repeated proposals by Mito's leaders during the first half of the nineteenth century formed an important template for this modern conquest.

A number of leading Mito scholars and politicians shaped the discourse of national identity, military strengthening, and colonial expansion, and helped translate it into policy both within Mito and across Japan. Perhaps the most important figure in this story is Aizawa Seishisai (1782–1863). A brilliant scholar and powerful rhetorician, Seishisai refined and extended the ideas of the Late Mito School during the first half of the nineteenth century. He cemented Mito's reputation as the center of an emperor-centered philosophy of political loyalty and Japanese exceptionalism, often summed up by the slogan "revere the emperor, expel the barbarian." Ironically a keen student of the West, he argued in favor of building a state religion centered on the emperor as a way to unify the hearts and minds of Japan's people and strengthen the nation against foreign threats. His writings, most famously the *Shinron* (the *New Theses*), galvanized a generation of samurai across Japan to transform Japan into a modern state capable of fending off the growing threat of Western imperialism. Seishisai's students, most notably the ninth Mito daimyo, Tokugawa Nariaki, Nariaki's closest advisor, Fujita Tōko, and the military scholar Toyoda Tenkō, translated many of his ideas into policy during Mito's Tenpō Reforms and then, during the 1850s, into shogunal actions. They emphasized the importance of reforming Mito's samurai class, persuaded the shogunate to annex Ezochi and define a new northern border with Russia, and inspired a generation of activists in domains across Japan to pursue similar reforms, building a shared commitment to a unified, strengthened Japan.

By the middle of the nineteenth century, the geopolitical circumstances around Japan had changed—and Mito's "revere the emperor, expel the barbarian" philosophy changed, too. By the 1840s and 1850s, this ideology became more diverse, with some strands emphasizing national uniqueness, and others focusing more on the practical challenges of military defense. Mito ideas also spread far beyond the domain, and students of Mito's scholars began to interpret and reread those ideas in new directions. Some of Mito's scholars and leaders adapted their ideas to new circumstances, while other supporters, especially the younger, low-ranking samurai known as *shishi*, became increasingly radicalized in their support for the cause of keeping the foreigners out of Japan. Part of the potency of "revere the emperor, expel the barbarian" lay in the way it was redefined and reinterpreted throughout the mid-nineteenth century by these activists. Seishisai, for instance, grew to abhor the actions of the *shishi*, and he regretted the ways in which they used his ideas to destabilize the shogunate. His youthful anti-foreign beliefs grew more moderate over time, reflecting a pragmatic streak, but this shift in his beliefs was seen as a betrayal of principle by younger, more radical samurai in Mito and beyond. By the end of his life, Seishisai proved unable to control the ideas he had unleashed in *Shinron* and other writings. His life illustrates the power of Mito's ideas to mobilize and energize large numbers of people—but also the difficulty of controlling those ideas.

After the disastrous and devastating conclusion of Japanese militarism during World War II, scholars in Japan and the West seized on Mito's nineteenth-century scholars as key figures for understanding the rise of nationalism and ultranationalism in nineteenth- and early twentieth-century Japan. This work has focused primarily on Aizawa Seishisai and *Shinron*, which clearly articulated the amalgamation of Kokugaku and Confucian ideas in Late Mito thought and the resulting ideology of Japanese superiority and imperial loyalty.[1] Postwar liberal and leftist scholars saw in Seishisai's writings seeds of the extreme version of nationalism and emperor worship that led Japan into its disastrous imperial wars in the early twentieth century. They argued that his work represented a reactionary urge to return to a classical past, an anti-modern movement whose legacy held Japan back from fully embracing modern values in the twentieth century.[2] More recently, scholars have revisited Seishisai's writings, and the Late Mito School more generally, and have argued that his vision of state religion and Japanese exceptionalism was not a relic of a premodern, feudal age, but rather a distinctly new and modern development. The religious elements and national chauvinism that Seishisai and his Mito colleagues bequeathed to the nationalists of modern Japan were features common to nationalisms across the world.[3] Modern Japanese nationalism was modern in part *because of* its Kokugaku, Confucian, and even archaic elements, not despite them. Although scholars have begun to reassess Seishisai, they continue to focus on *Shinron* and Seishisai's ideological construction of national identity. Seishisai's position within the political landscape of Mito and Japan in the mid-nineteenth century has received little attention. This has led to an oversimplification of his life and ideas.[4] By situating Seishisai's life and career alongside that of other notable Mito scholars, and within both global and local historical contexts, the complex and overlapping nature of Mito's "revere the emperor, expel the barbarian" ideology becomes clear. The Mito anxieties about the foreign threat were informed by direct experience, both within Mito and in Ezochi, and translated directly to policy proposals that focused on the domain, the nation, and Ainu lands past Japan's northern frontier. The diverse interpretations of Mito's ideas ensured that they had far-reaching and profound implications for the shape of an independent, imperial modern Japan.

EZOCHI, RUSSIA, AND AIZAWA SEISHISAI

In 1792, a Russian diplomat named Adam Laxman arrived in eastern Ezochi seeking permission to trade with Japan. Laxman was not totally unex-
pected—reports of Russian explorers in and around Ezochi had reached the
shogunal authorities as early as 1771—but the formal overture marked the
first time in more than one hundred and sixty years that a foreign power had
arrived in Japan seeking a formal trade relationship.[5] Moreover, Laxman
came not to Nagasaki, the designated port for Western ships, but to a sparsely
populated region only nominally under Tokugawa control. The indigenous
Ainu population recognized Japanese authority, but only loosely, and many
Ainu groups resented Japanese power. These tensions had worsened over the
eighteenth century as commercial Japanese fishers and traders swarmed into
the region, exploiting Ainu labor and amassing enormous wealth and power.
Just three years before Laxman's arrival, the Ainu of eastern Ezochi had attacked Japanese merchants there, triggering a brief war that exposed the tenuous nature of Tokugawa authority and raised concerns about the possible role
of the Russians in turning the Ainu against the Japanese. Defense of Ezochi
was delegated to the small northern domain of Matsumae, but it was utterly
unprepared for the arrival of a Western imperial power in the region. In other
words, Ezochi in the 1780s encapsulated the distortions wrought by an increasingly commercial economy, coupled with unique ethnic and geopolitical
challenges. It was also very far away and very cold compared to mainland
Japan, adding to the shogunate's logistical headaches as they prepared to
defend the region against a feared Russian invasion.

   To Mito's political and academic leaders, Laxman's arrival signaled a
grave threat to Japan's territorial integrity. Ezochi had been a site of commercial interest for Mito's elite since the days of Mitsukuni, and Tachihara
Suiken was sufficiently concerned about the appearance of Russians in the
area to include it in his proposal for three priority reforms that he submitted to Matsudaira Sadanobu in 1787. Mito was not the only large domain
concerned about Ezochi: Sendai Domain, in particular, had a lively group of
scholars gathering information on the region, and Sadanobu felt that Nanbu
and Tsugaru Domains were the logical choice for bolstering defense in the
region. But the close ties between Mito's leaders and Sadanobu's administration, friendships with Sendai scholars, as well as the historical interests in
the region, gave Suiken and his students access to information that made the
problem of defending the north seem especially urgent.[6]

   After Laxman's arrival, Mito's officials planned an expedition to Ezochi
to gather more information. The daimyo Harumori asked Suiken to recom-
mend one of his students for the mission. Suiken nominated Kimura Kenji,

who had spent time in Sendai learning about events in Ezochi and come away desperate to focus on defensive questions. Kimura travelled to Ezochi on a reconnaissance mission in 1793, and after assessing the weakness of Japanese forces in southern Ezochi, he returned convinced that Mito needed to lead the way in defending Japan against Russian imperialism. Suiken secured him a spot on a shogunal mission to Ezochi just five years later. In the summer of 1798, Kimura landed on Etorofu, an island in the Kuril Archipelago. At the direction of the two shogunal officials leading his expedition, he inscribed a piece of wood claiming Etorofu as part of "Great Japan" (*Dai Nihon*), signing his name alongside the officials—as well as the names of the twelve Ainu men who guided them to Etorofu.[7] Kimura's wooden stake marked the first formal Japanese claim to territory in the Kurils, and highlights Mito's role in these early efforts to define and expand the modern borders of Japan—an emerging nation-state with imperialist ambitions of its own.[8] Kimura returned to Mito, where Harumori granted him samurai status for his activities and report; he spent the remainder of his life composing treatises on naval defense, although he never again travelled to Ezochi.[9] Meanwhile, Ezochi and the question of defense entranced another teenaged, aspiring Mito scholar Aizawa Seishisai.

Seishisai was born in the castle town of Mito in late spring 1782. His father, Kyōkei, was the first generation of his family to achieve samurai status: before that, the Aizawa family had served as bait-catchers for Mito's daimyo, procuring small birds to feed to the lord's falcons.[10] Kyōkei was by all accounts an able man: we do not know why he was raised to samurai status, but he was quickly promoted through the domain bureaucracy, ultimately heading Mito's rice warehouses in Osaka. Seishisai's mother, Noe, urged him to pursue his studies.[11] Both she and Kyōkei worked hard to give Seishisai an education: as he eulogized shortly after their deaths, they "borrowed money to buy me books, and found a tutor to educate me."[12] That tutor was Fujita Yūkoku, who lived in the same neighborhood as Seishisai. Yūkoku accepted Seishisai as a student in 1791, when Seishisai was ten. Yūkoku was only eighteen, but he was already renowned for his erudition and intellect and had just completed his famous essay, *Seimeiron*, making him a natural choice to teach the ambitious Seishisai. Perhaps, too, Yūkoku saw in Seishisai some kinship: both came from commoner families who had only recently worked their way into samurai status, largely due to their parents' devotion to their education.

Seishisai's education under Yūkoku included many of the principles that soon came to define the distinctive political philosophy of nineteenth-century Mito. Broadly speaking, these fell into four categories.[13] First, Yūkoku trained Seishisai in Ogyū Sorai's scholarly methods: reading original

Figure 3.1. Portrait of Aizawa Seishisai
(On loan to Ibaraki Prefectural Archives and Museum)

classical Confucian texts and paying attention to rites and rituals, rather than moral cultivation, as the essence of good governance. Second, he stressed the importance of the hierarchical social order and the virtue of loyalty. He emphasized that Japan had a distinct (and superior) social order by virtue of its unbroken and divine imperial line. For this reason, he told Seishisai, it was important to study Chinese history and philosophy, but not to treat China as a superior country. Third, Yūkoku taught Seishisai to combine his academic studies with careful attention to current affairs and pragmatic political problems. In particular, he emphasized Suiken's concerns with Russia and its purported designs in Ezochi, but he also drew Seishisai's attention to social problems and moral decline among Mito's commoners and samurai retainers. Finally, Yūkoku taught Seishisai about Mitsukuni's distinctive legacy: the importance of the *Dai Nihon shi* history project as a form of demonstrating imperial loyalty. Through his education under Yūkoku, Seishisai internalized the core values of Mito's academic revival; these values informed his research into the foreign threat and his subsequent proposals for how to address it.

In 1799, Seishisai got his first job as a researcher in the Shōkōkan, where he started working on the *Dai Nihon shi*. But for the most part he spent his time on a very different project: the gathering and analysis of information about the Russian Empire. Over the next fifteen years, Seishisai read everything he could get his hands on about Russia and the situation in the north: Chinese histories of Russia, accounts by Italian and Belgian missionaries in China, and travel reports by Japanese explorers in Ezochi. By the turn of the nineteenth century, Seishisai was probably one of the most informed people in Japan about Russia and the developments in Ezochi. The first result of this critical work, published in 1801, was *Chishima ibun*, in which Seishisai analyzed Russia's imperial expansion and mused upon its designs on Japan.

Chishima ibun marked a growing focus on Japan's place in the wider world and the articulation of a more muscular version of Japanese exceptionalism in Mito scholarship. Seishisai's research confirmed his concerns that Russia posed a great threat to an unprepared Japan, but it also led to a certain admiration for Russia, and particularly for Peter the Great (r. 1672–1725). In Seishisai's mind, Peter had "brought peace to his people, and prosperity to his country. . . . He planted grapes and other crops to feed his people; he built schools; he spread the law and religion; he trained soldiers and vanquished the nation's enemies. He took the . . . divisions of Russia of the past and turned them into a single, unified Russia."[14] Peter and Russia's other leaders had used Christianity to expand and consolidate their empire, turning it into a sort of "way" comparable to the imperial "way" of Japan. In contrast, Seishisai felt that Ezochi—and Japan more generally—had lost the purposeful structure of the imperial "way," the result of years of stagnation and decline. As a result, the region lacked a sense of unity, leaving it exposed to hungry, imperialist powers. He recognized that the moral virtuousness of a ruler was not enough to secure the realm against foreign threats; he argued that Japan needed to settle the "empty" Ainu lands of Ezochi with Japanese subjects, convert them to the imperial way, promote agriculture and social harmony, and establish firm borders around Japanese territory.

Through this analysis, Seishisai reflected the synthesis of universalist Confucian principles and native cultural and historical ideas that characterized the Late Mito School philosophy of Japanese exceptionalism, and demonstrated how these intellectual traditions could be put to use in the development of a new, more modern definition of the nation. At the core of this vision was the belief that Japan was a civilized center surrounded by "barbarian" adherents to Christianity and other heterodox belief systems. Seishisai relied on a classical Chinese concept of civilization, represented as the Middle Kingdom (*ka*), and barbarism (*i*), which became increasingly severe the farther one got from the civilized center. In line with Yūkoku's emphasis on Japanese superiority, Seishisai replaced China with Japan in this framework, arguing that the moral virtues of Japan's divine origins, its unbroken imperial lineage, and the values of loyalty and filial piety made Japan a superior country in a universal hierarchy of civilized and barbarian. Seishisai and the Mito scholars were not the first to identify Japan as the center of a civilized-barbarian hierarchy, but they defined the underlying principles of that view in a much more specific and *political* way, with reference to the new geopolitical landscape of Western imperialism.[15] Seishisai's ideas represented a shift to understanding Japan as a clearly defined national territory with a more modern conception of sovereignty and identity.[16] Also implicit in this assessment was an argument that Japan needed to become a different kind of country in order to survive in a world dominated by European empires. Japan's exceptional character might have been immanent to its divine origins and imperial lineage, but protecting and sustaining that character required a specific program of political action and social reform on the part of Japan's secular and military leaders.[17] In 1801, Seishisai did not yet have a clear program in mind, but he had already developed a strong belief in the necessity of such changes.

In the years that followed, Seishisai allied himself firmly with the Fujita faction in Mito's scholarly world and made a name for himself as one of Mito's most promising scholars, securing positions of increasing power in the domain. In 1803, Seishisai was transferred to the Shōkōkan's branch in Edo, where he quickly earned a reputation as "Teacher Sharp Tongue" (*suntetsu sensei*) for his biting critiques of domain officials.[18] Yūkoku had recently replaced Suiken as Shōkōkan director, reversing Suiken's cuts to the *Dai Nihon shi* and restarting the composition of the unfinished sections. Seishisai contributed to this work, but the next year tragedy struck when both his parents died within months of each other. Suiken entered a three-year mourning period and withdrew from formal work. In 1806, he returned to public life and quickly rejoined debates about the *Dai Nihon shi*, impressing his superiors with skillful arguments about the proper course to publishing the work. By 1807, his academic reputation had risen sufficiently to secure him appointment as tutor to the sons of Harutoshi (r. 1805–1816), the seventh daimyo of Mito. He became a close teacher and advisor to both Narinobu and Nariaki, who would become the eighth and ninth daimyo, respectively. In this role he taught the young lords-to-be the core principles of Mito's scholars. He served as Nariaki's teacher until 1820, when Nariaki turned twenty-one. During this period, Seishisai lived on Mito's Edo estates, and he enjoyed a period of good fortune. He married Kobayashi Moto in 1810, and welcomed his first child, a daughter, in 1813, with five more children over the next decade. He travelled to western Japan in 1819 to retrieve the remains of his father who had died in Osaka, along the way making pilgrimages to various sites sacred to the imperial household, reinforcing his academic and ethical commitments to the imperial line as the source of political legitimacy and Japanese exceptionalism. He then returned to Mito in 1820 where he opened a private academy. In 1823, he was appointed deputy director of the Shōkōkan, the second most powerful position in the academy. Seishisai was proving himself an able scholar and astute political actor.

As Seishisai's career progressed, he began to refine his call for urgent political reforms in the face of foreign threats. In 1806, Russian ships attacked Japanese trading posts on Sakhalin and the Kuril Islands, underscoring the ongoing risk they posed to Japan. This threat, as Seishisai argued to Harutoshi in 1807, required a total renovation of the ruling class and military organization. Moreover, if Mito's rulers could implement such a transformation, they would serve as role models for the entire country. Not only would this strengthen Japan against foreign imperialism; it would also be a glorious honor for Mito's ancestors.[19] Harutoshi took Seishisai's call seriously and began making preparations for naval defense and other reforms, but unfortunately, he died in 1816, and reforms lost steam. Nevertheless, Seishisai continued to stress the importance of reform to strengthen Mito and Japan against external threats. His deep and thorough research into Russian history and the events in Ezochi grounded abstract ideas of Japanese exceptionalism in a concrete set of concerns about the integrity and strength of the Japanese imperial realm. In his view, Mito's rulers could not ignore changing global circumstances. They had to reimagine their own political and social order to prepare for a new age.

THE ŌTSUHAMA INCIDENT
AND SEISHISAI'S *SHINRON*

After 1806, the Russian threat in Ezochi receded. But in Mito it seemed as though the threat of foreign invasion was growing. In 1807, villagers on Mito's coast sighted a foreign ship sailing offshore—the first such sighting since 1611. Over the next forty years, officials recorded 104 foreign ships passing Mito's coastline. Those ships were mostly whaling ships from Britain and the United States, attracted to the fertile waters of the Japan Grounds, a stretch of the Pacific Ocean between the Leeward Islands of Hawai'i, eastern Honshū, and the Ogasawara (Bonin) Islands. By the early nineteenth century, European and American whalers had chased their prey here, not least because whaling grounds closer to home—off New England or in the South Atlantic—had been depleted by Westerners' voracious appetite for oil and other cetacean products. Mito's officials responded to these sightings by dispatching hunting parties and fishermen, but no records remain of foreigners putting to shore in Mito, with one exception—the Ōtsuhama Incident of 1824. This episode brought the transformations wrought by Western commercial expansion and global imperialism straight to Mito's shores. It also validated the concerns of Seishisai and his fellow scholars, affirming the urgency of their call for domain reforms to tackle a crisis that threatened all of Japan.

On the twenty-eighth day of the fifth month of 1824, twelve English sailors put to shore at Ōtsuhama, the beach next to the fishing village of Ōtsu in the northern reaches of Mito Domain. They belonged to a fleet of four whaling ships anchored offshore and had come in search of fresh food and water. The sailors readily exchanged their guns for some chickens and let themselves be taken into custody.[20] Perhaps surprisingly, the residents of Ōtsu seemed unperturbed at the arrival of these foreigners. Some offered food, others tried to barter, while many were content to watch from a safe distance. Some carefully recorded the encounter (see figure 3.2). The villagers of Ōtsu still considered the foreigners barbarian—the Englishmen were filthy, not least because they never washed their hands—but they did not seek to repel the foreigners or avoid contact with them. And at least one of their number was able to communicate with the whalers in rudimentary English. This man, named Yūzaburō, was a bonito fisherman, and his story illustrates a world of foreign contact among Mito's villagers.

By the mid-1820s there was mounting evidence that Mito's bonito fishermen were interacting with these foreign vessels. Bonito clustered in the waters about one hundred and twenty nautical miles off the Mito shoreline, "a world that belonged to fishers alone," beyond the sight, knowledge, or control of land-based officials.[21] It was in this maritime space, in 1824, that

Figure 3.2. From Katō Shōra, "Bunsei 7 kōshin natsu ikoku tenmasen Ōtsuhama e jōriku narabini shokizu tō," c. 1824, Shōrakan bunko 43
(Ibaraki Prefectural Library)

Yūzaburō likely encountered the crew of the four English ships. Every summer, Mito fishermen travelled far out to sea in pursuit of the bonito. They did not shy away from the Western whalers, who were generally friendly. The bonito fishers traded clothes and food for trinkets, coins, and other goods, and at least one spent several days on an English ship, observing the harpooning and rendering of whales. The fishers brought these goods home, and they circulated throughout the villages of coastal Mito. The trade was apparently robust enough that local merchants sent goods on commission for the fishermen to trade. A local antiquarian scrupulously recorded some of the coins, pocketknives, rings, clothing, books, and even newspapers that were found throughout the area. He also recorded a rudimentary lexicon of English words that the fishers used to communicate, hinting at the richness of their encounters. Despite the peaceful nature of these encounters and exchanges, Ōtsuhama's villagers had no choice but to report the arrival of the Englishmen to the domain authorities. The officials and scholars in Mito castle town were much less sanguine about the arrival of the foreign ships. Within a few days, thousands of soldiers from Mito and its neighboring domains had descended upon Ōtsu and nearby villages. In addition to informing the shogunate, the domain decided to interrogate the Englishmen themselves, and dispatched two scholars, one of whom was Seishisai.

Seishisai jumped at the opportunity to apply his knowledge of foreign affairs to the crisis at hand, although his preconceptions shone through clearly in the course of his interrogation. He rushed to Ōtsuhama, where, over the course of three days, he interviewed John Gibson, captain of one of the ships, and other members of the crew. The first order of business was to work out where these sailors were coming from and what they were doing in Mito. The Englishmen could not read any Japanese text, whether Chinese characters or Japanese *kana*, and when Seishisai wrote "Russia" in Cyrillic, he also got blank stares. Finally, Gibson started writing the English alphabet, and reading the letters out loud. At this point Seishisai suspected that the men might be Dutch, but after Gibson started reciting "one, two, three . . ." instead of "een, twee, drie . . ." he realized that they were, in fact, English.[22] The difficulty of ascertaining what language the men spoke—and Seishisai's limited skills in Russian, Dutch, or English—did not bode well for the rest of the interrogation, but, surprisingly, he was able to garner a lot of information from the Englishmen. He pulled out a world map and had Gibson show where he had come from, the routes he had sailed, and other pieces of information. To explain why the Englishmen were there, Gibson blew out hard to imitate a whale's spout and used his hands to mimic a harpooner at work. The ships came from London and had been at sea for thirty-two months, he explained, drawing a moon and the number 32.[23]

Seishisai did not believe Gibson for a second. After watching the whale-imitating charade, he noted that "I resented Gibson for not revealing the truth of the matter, and, thinking about how to use my body language to press him further, I stared intensely at his face. He blushed and changed the topic by drawing another harpoon and other items, seemingly trying to speak vaguely."[24] Seishisai was convinced that Gibson and his men had arrived in Japan to scout out the land in preparation for a full-on invasion and were merely pretending to care about whales. Shogunal officials, including more competent interpreters, arrived in Ōtsu after a few days, and quickly resolved the situation by confirming the whalers' intent and sending them on their way with supplies and a stern warning never to return. Seishisai decried this as a foolish and naïve move that failed to take into account the Englishmen's wily natures. He argued that his conversation with Gibson had revealed how, "under the pretext of trade or whatever, [the English] approach and become friendly with peoples in all areas, secretly probing to see which countries are strong and which weak. If a nation's defenses are weak, they will seize it by force, but if there are no weaknesses to pounce on, they take it over by leading the people's minds astray with their wicked doctrine of Christianity."[25] For decades, Seishisai had built up an image of the West as a devious civilization, able to use the seemingly peaceful avenues of religion and trade to subvert the integrity of foreign nations and bring them under control.[26] His encounter with the Englishmen at Ōtsuhama confirmed these fears—or, perhaps, he found what he wanted to find in his interrogation of Gibson and his crew.

Other Mito scholars were even angrier at the shogunate's response. While Seishisai was using crude sign language to talk to the hungry English sailors, Fujita Yūkoku, back in Mito, summoned his eighteen-year-old son, Tōko, and gravely described the threat that the Englishmen represented to Japan's security and integrity. Tōko, enraged, threw himself to the front of the room, and swore to his father that he would slay the Englishmen, even if it meant suffering execution as punishment for his audacity. For the first time in his life, he resolved to die. Death was a price worth paying for proving his loyalty to the emperor by destroying the foreigners.[27] On his father's orders, Tōko rushed off to prepare for the journey to Ōtsu, gathering his swords and finding horses to take him north. Just as he was about to depart, however, the news arrived: shogunate officials had taken over from Seishisai, sending the Englishmen away with food and only a stern warning not to return. Tōko was devastated; he had missed his chance to prove his reverence for the emperor and his commitment to expelling the barbarians. He quickly came to resent the shogunate's weak and misguided reaction.

Despite the shogunate's restrained response, Seishisai saw in the Ōtsuhama Incident a golden opportunity to promote his arguments for reforming and strengthening Mito and Japan. He was doubly lucky when, in the second month of 1825, the shogunate introduced a more aggressive policy toward foreign vessels that put ashore on Japanese territory: the so-called "Don't Think Twice" edict. On the surface, the edict was simple: the shogunate ordered coastal officials to fire on foreign vessels that approached land. In practice, there were plenty of exceptions—Dutch, Korean, and Chinese ships were exempt, as were clearly disabled ships—and the edict also stressed that officials were to deter landings, not actually attack or pursue any ships unless they put to shore.[28] Nevertheless, the edict marked a change from existing policy and practice, under which—as seen in Ōtsu in 1824—officials usually offered food and water to any foreign ships and accepted any Japanese castaways attempting to return to Japan before politely asking the foreigners to sail away.

More significantly, the "Don't Think Twice" edict also cemented into policy the notion that isolation (*sakoku*) was the law of the land, giving a boost to Mito's proponents of a hardline "expel the barbarian" policy. Seishisai and fellow activists would, in later years, repeat over and over again that foreigners could not enter Japan because they had been banned since the beginning of the Tokugawa era. Tokugawa policymakers dealing with Western overtures for trade and diplomacy in these years also made this argument. But it was not true: it was the creation of harsher policies like the "Don't Think Twice" edict that led to such claims.[29] Nevertheless, by the time the shogunate repealed the edict in 1842, the idea that *sakoku* was the ancient law of the land went largely unchallenged in Japanese political and academic circles. The shogunate's shift to an isolationist policy in the aftermath of the Ōtsuhama Incident signaled to Seishisai that his vision for strengthening Japan against the Christian West had a growing political audience. To capitalize on this opportunity, he quickly wrote a manifesto for restructuring Japan: *Shinron* (*New Theses*), which he completed in 1825.

In *Shinron*, Seishisai identified the myriad problems facing Japan and outlined how to tackle them. Japan was facing a world situation unlike anything experienced before; the Western barbarians at Japan's shores were fundamentally different than previous waves of barbarians; and Japan's leaders therefore needed to overhaul Japan in order to address these unprecedented circumstances.[30] Seishisai synthesized his decades of research into foreign affairs to describe the power of Western nations, identifying above all the strength they derived from spiritual and religious unity, and the allegiance of their peoples to a single nation. Even more than military might, this spiritual strength was the gravest threat to Japan. In Seishisai's mind, "Christianity was the sole reason" for foreign rulers' success in uniting their "stupid commoners," despite the fact that it was "a truly evil and base religion."[31] To tackle this threat, Seishisai called for comprehensive reforms, from "reviving the samurai spirit" to introducing a peasant militia, creating coast guard forces and firearm factories, and strengthening the great domains around the country by reducing the expensive trips to and from Edo required by the shogunate.[32] The "Don't Think Twice" edict was a perfect focal point for national mobilization: "We must fire up our spirits, annihilate the impudent barbarians, and thereby demonstrate the greatness of our virtue to the entire world," Seishisai proclaimed.[33]

Expelling the barbarians was only part of the equation: Seishisai also argued for a spiritual mobilization to unify the people. In the remaining portions of *Shinron*, he described this spiritual unity, which he called "the national essence" (*kokutai*), and explained why it had disappeared from Japan and how it might be regained. At its core, *kokutai* rested upon the loyalty of subject to ruler, which in turn paralleled the filial relationship between child and parent. The originator of these values was the Sun Goddess Amaterasu, the ancestor of Japan's emperors. In addition to the ethical relationship between child and parent, subject and ruler, Amaterasu and her descendants valued military preparedness and the welfare of the people. Together, these values constituted

Japan's national essence.[34] In this way, *Shinron* became an expression of the core ideas of the Late Mito School: the blend of the universal ethical values of the Confucian tradition, such as loyalty, filial piety, and social hierarchy, and native Japanese ideas about religion and politics, particularly the divine origins and unbroken lineage of imperial rule.[35] Tying these universal values to the imperial household also allowed Seishisai to illustrate how the national essence might be strengthened in the face of new threats. In particular, he emphasized the importance of respect for Amaterasu and the imperial line ("revere the emperor," or *sonnō*), which could be expressed through the revival of imperial rites and rituals and their integration with political governance (*saisei itchi*).[36] In narrower religious terms, this meant keeping Christianity at bay, and replacing the corrupting influence of Buddhism and other foreign ideas with indigenous Shintō beliefs, reformulated as a form of state religion. This syncretic religious approach represented a radical break with the strict Confucian orthodoxy of the shogunate, as well as a savage attack on the long-standing prestige of Buddhist temples.

Finally, *Shinron* was no model of sober, academic prose, and Seishisai's manifesto targeted all levels of the Tokugawa social and political order. This was a biting, polemical tract, designed to galvanize Mito's rulers and the shogunate into action. Littered with references to loathsome barbarians, stupid commoners, and dimwitted scholars, *Shinron* savagely attacked everyone: meek officials, Buddhist priests, scholars of the West, believers in folk religion, ignorant peasants, lazy samurai, and corrupt aristocrats of times past. Seishisai's skill as a rhetorician matched his strong moral convictions and deep knowledge of social and political affairs. *Shinron* also implicitly challenged the shogunate by suggesting an end to key policies, such as the regular travel of daimyo to Edo and the separation of warriors from the land. This was not Seishisai's intent—he believed that the shogunate actually epitomized the ethic of loyalty in its subservience to the emperor—but *Shinron* came perilously close to undermining the structures of shogunal authority. Seishisai had crafted a powerful and dangerous call to arms. For these reasons, the daimyo of Mito, Narinobu, took one look at *Shinron* and flatly refused to pass it on to the shogunate. He also warned Seishisai to take his name off it even when circulating it privately.[37] *Shinron* would not be formally published for another thirty years.

The Ōtsuhama Incident persuaded Mito's elites that the risk of foreign contact was real. Sadly for Yūzaburō and his fellow fishermen, Mito's officials were not particularly pleased to discover the extent of this informal diplomacy in their domain. Officialdom put a moratorium on bonito fishing to prevent further contact, and, in early 1825, they arrested Yūzaburō after hearing rumors that he had continued to visit Western ships after the

Ōtsuhama Incident. He was taken to the castle town for questioning, and then imprisoned for three months. After his release, he returned to Ōtsu, but then he disappears from the documentary record. Seishisai and other officials were convinced that the Westerners would manipulate Japan's "stupid commoners" with Christianity, paving the way for an imperialist takeover. These views supported—and were supported by—a belief that Japan had always been "closed" to the outside world. But Yūzaburō's role in the Ōtsuhama Incident offers another perspective. In places like the bonito waters in the Japan Grounds, fishermen like Yūzaburō met Western whalers with an openness and curiosity that suggests many commoners were not quite so afraid of the foreign barbarians as Seishisai thought they ought to be.

In the years after completing *Shinron*, Seishisai became one of the most influential and high-ranking scholars in Mito, putting him in a privileged position to influence the domain's politics—and before long, he was able to capitalize on that position. In 1826, Fujita Yūkoku died, and Seishisai was appointed in his place as one of the directors of the Shōkōkan, securing his position at the top of Mito's academic world. In late 1829, the daimyo Narinobu died, prompting a fierce debate between conservatives and reformers over the succession. Seishisai joined other reformers in an illegal trip to Edo to urge the domain's senior officials to choose Narinobu's younger brother, Nariaki, as the next daimyo, arguing that it was better to keep the succession within the Mito bloodline rather than adopt an heir from outside the domain (see chapter 4). In more practical terms, Nariaki represented the best bet to enact the reforms that Seishisai and his reformist colleagues so desperately sought. After a decade studying with Seishisai, Nariaki had fully embraced Seishisai's view of the world.

Fujita Yūkoku's son, Tōko, joined Seishisai on the quest to put Nariaki in power. Under the influence of his father, Seishisai, and other reformist scholars, Tōko absorbed their anxiety about the foreign threat, which became a core part of his intellectual and political identity. After the disappointingly peaceful resolution of the Ōtsuhama Incident in 1824, Tōko had travelled to Edo, where he continued his studies with the domain's leading scholars, deepening his understanding of the values and beliefs of the Late Mito School. He read Seishisai's *Shinron* soon after it was completed, and lived with Yoshida Kōdō (Noriyo), Mito's resident Kokugaku enthusiast, thus absorbing both Seishisai's Confucian-inflected worldview as well as the more exceptionalist elements of Kokugaku thought.[38] During this period Kōdō was also serving as a tutor to Nariaki, and they appeared to have discussed Tōko—although the two did not meet while Tōko was in Edo.[39]

The reformers' extraordinary journey paid off: the shogunate approved Nariaki as Mito's ninth daimyo in the tenth month of 1829. Nariaki embarked

Figure 3.3. **Portrait of Tokugawa Nariaki, c. 1889**
(Ibaraki Prefectural Archives and Museum)

upon a robust program of reforms rooted in Seishisai's call to strengthen society in order to face the foreign threat. Seishisai and Tōko became central figures in Nariaki's reform administration (see chapter 4), advocating for domestic reforms as well as preparations for foreign threats. They developed a philosophy and policy of defensive reform that focused on improving the hearts and minds of Mito's people, encouraging respect for the imperial line, and defending the realm against Western imperial powers. In practical terms, this meant extending Japan's authority over its northern borders, and bolstering the military skills and martial spirit of Mito's people.

EZOCHI AND THE FOREIGN THREAT
DURING MITO'S TENPŌ REFORMS

For Seishisai, Tōko, and other reformers during Nariaki's administration, which lasted until his ouster in 1844, the question of repelling foreign threats went hand in hand with colonial ambitions in Ezochi. Alongside his work at the Shōkōkan and as an advisor to Nariaki, Seishisai continued to teach Mito's young samurai at his private academy in the center of the castle town. There, he trained a generation of Mito's youth to pay attention to the crises of the realm and seek radical interventions to address them. In the 1830s he published two essays that clarified the ideas of *Shinron* and framed them in simpler language that his samurai students and educated commoners could understand.[40] Even while *Shinron* remained unpublished, Seishisai's ideas spread through his students and writings. They found an enthusiastic following among a cohort of young samurai from low-ranking families, many of whom agreed with his view of the social and political problems they saw around them in Mito and looming across the seas. Tōko shared Seishisai's concern that it was only a matter of time before a foreign military threat appeared on Mito's shores, and he urged Nariaki to strengthen Mito's defenses. In one of his first memorials to Nariaki, submitted in the seventh month of 1830, Tōko pointed to attacks on Mito ships transporting rice, as well as the frequent sightings of foreign ships passing offshore, to underscore the urgency of this military threat. He proposed a two-pronged approach: a comprehensive set of military preparations, focused primarily on reviving the military spirit of Mito's samurai, and a program of shipbuilding to develop naval capacity.[41] This proposal was relatively vague, and largely reiterated the ideas of Tōko's father Yūkoku, but nevertheless it underscored the centrality of "expelling the barbarian" to the Mito reform agenda.

In 1837, prompted in part by the arrival of the American merchant ship *Morrison* to Uraga in the sixth month, Tōko revisited the question of defense. Building on Seishisai's ideas in *Shinron*, he proposed the resettlement of Mito's samurai in rural areas (*dochaku*). Resettling the samurai had multiple benefits: it would teach the samurai how to be self-sufficient and enable them to oversee the improvement of rural morals, in addition to boosting Mito's defenses, especially along its long, exposed Pacific coastline.[42] Nariaki created a high-level position for naval defense and assigned it to a prominent reformer.[43] He built new fortifications on the coastline, including gun emplacements. He also imported weapons and built a forge in the castle town to produce cannons.[44] And, despite Tōko's objections, non-samurai began to be mobilized as soldiers; in 1838, a number of Shintō priests and Shugendō adherents were incorporated into new militia units, as were one thousand hunters a few years later.[45]

Perhaps the most dramatic display of Nariaki's commitment to an aggressive defense policy was the reintroduction of massive hunting parties, which gave retainers the chance to practice their military skills—and demonstrated Nariaki's dedication to military preparedness. In 1840, the first party took place just south of Mito Castle, with "3,000 mounted soldiers and 20,000 foot soldiers" parading in front of a crowd of onlookers. Over the next two decades, Nariaki oversaw nine similar events.[46] Under his rule, Mito became one of the first domains to manufacture modern firearms and ammunition, many of which were based on Western models. Nariaki hired teachers from Nagasaki who had access to Dutch manuals and expertise. He also implemented Tōko's plan to resettle samurai along Mito's coast, where they would serve as a first line of defense against Western incursions.[47] These investments, together with military training, strengthened Mito's reputation as a bastion of military expertise in the face of foreign threats.

Meanwhile, Nariaki obsessed about Ezochi. He was convinced that the region—including the entire Kuril chain—was part of Japanese territory, and he resented the fact that effective Japanese control reached only as far as Etorofu, leaving the rest of the islands susceptible to Russian incursions. It would not be long before the Russians seized a foothold in Ezochi proper (today's Hokkaido), and from there they would be able to reach any port in mainland Japan.[48] To counter this threat, Nariaki developed an increasingly elaborate

Figure 3.4. Nariaki's Hunting Display, c. 1840
(Tokiwa Shrine, Mito)

proposal to colonize Ezochi, urging the shogunate to adopt a policy of agricultural migration and the establishment of full Japanese control over Ezochi, the Kuril Islands, and Sakhalin. Guarding Japan's "northern gate" was the "great worry of the Land of the Gods," he said, before implying that the shogunate risked its reputation by not taking aggressive defense measures.[49] Shogunal officials were more than a little insulted by Nariaki's insinuations, but they largely agreed with the need to develop a policy to colonize and administer Ezochi—after all, they had done just that between 1799 and 1821, when they tried and failed to annex the region.

But the shogunate was not willing to accept Nariaki's boldest proposal that he remove himself personally to Ezochi with a large portion of his family, along with the younger sons of samurai families and a large number of farmers and artisans. Together, they would build a new castle town in the center of Ezochi to serve as the headquarters of a large settler colony, turning the region into an agricultural breadbasket while also defending Japan.[50] Nariaki envisaged assimilating the Ainu, turning them into imperial subjects by teaching them Japanese and encouraging them to adopt Japanese customs. This, in his view, would ensure their loyalty to Japan and increase the legitimacy of Japanese claims to sovereignty over the region vis-à-vis the Russians. This proposal was fabulously expensive, and in the end offered Nariaki's enemies a chance to accuse him of grandiose ambition, but nevertheless it reflects the degree to which Mito's leaders treated Ezochi as a fundamental cornerstone of protecting and strengthening Japan against Western imperialism.

Mito's leaders undeniably took an aggressive position on defense policy. More moderate voices in Edo and around Japan proposed allowing trade with foreigners, a concession that might buy time for Japan to build up its strength. Nariaki rejected this argument as a sniveling admission of weakness, pointing instead to the example of the regent Hōjō Tokimune (1251–1284), who had executed Mongol emissaries in 1275 as a show of strength and defiance. But Nariaki was still pragmatic: he rejected proposals to build oceangoing ships and demonstrate Japan's military strength abroad, arguing that Japan's people "lacked passion and were weak of mind."[51] The core messages of Seishisai's *Shinron* echoed clearly: suspicions of the motives of traders alongside deep distrust of the ability of Japan's soldiers to stand up to the beguiling and duplicitous foreigners.

News from abroad soon amplified the urgency and intensity of Mito's message about defense, even as it directed attention away from the Russian threat in the north. On August 29, 1842, representatives of the Qing emperor signed a humiliating treaty with British envoys aboard a British warship anchored at Nanjing. The treaty, which concluded the Opium War and pried China open to foreign traders and missionaries, sent shockwaves around East Asia: the mighty Qing Empire had succumbed to a small, remote European nation. Over the next few years, the Qing signed similar treaties with the United States and Russia. No longer could Asia's rulers ignore the West. For Japan's leaders, news of Qing China's defeat made Seishisai's warnings about Western imperialism much more urgent. The shogunate repealed the "Don't Think Twice" policy that year: the enormous firepower Britain exhibited in China made it realize that it could not afford to provoke the Western powers by firing upon their ships.

THE MANY MEANINGS OF
"REVERE THE EMPEROR, EXPEL THE BARBARIAN"

Unfortunately for Nariaki, Tōko, and Seishisai, this growing sense of alarm did not prevent their enemies from forcing them out of power in 1844. All three men were imprisoned for several years, and their supporters in Mito were sidelined (see chapter 4). While in prison, however, Mito's scholars did not stop working on the foreign crisis, which was only growing worse. Over the next ten years, the work of Mito's leading scholars found new audiences across Japan. Seishisai's *Shinron* circulated rapidly, attracting students to Mito. At the same time, Tōko and Toyoda Tenkō, another young Mito scholar, began to modify Seishisai's ideas. Both retained Seishisai's hardline stance toward foreigners, but Tōko began to interpret the "revere the emperor" part of Mito's philosophy in more nationalistic terms, while Tenkō updated Seishisai's prescriptions to adapt to a rapidly changing geopolitical context. Paradoxically, "revere the emperor, expel the barbarian" began to lose some of its internal coherence, even as it grew more influential across Japan.

In 1844, the Dutch King Willem II wrote a letter to the shogunate urging Japan to open to Western trade and foreign relations, citing the inevitability of such an outcome after events in China. In 1845, a British ship landed in the Ryukyus, seeking trade, with a French vessel arriving there the following year. In 1846, the U.S. commander James Biddle sailed into Edo Bay seeking to sign a treaty similar to the Treaty of Nanjing. Shogunal officials rebuffed Biddle, but they knew they were working on borrowed time. On the thirteenth day of the tenth month of 1852, Seishisai noted that "rumors that the British warships in Guangdong (Canton) will head for Kanagawa next year have reached us here in Mito. I cannot understand why the shogunate is pretending otherwise."[52] The British did not arrive the following year, but the Americans did. On 1853/6/3 (July 8), Commodore Matthew C. Perry steamed into Edo Bay with four menacing warships belching smoke and a determination not to leave without a commitment to a treaty. Perry issued an ultimatum: he would return in a year to negotiate a treaty, or to bludgeon the shogunate into submission. He then sailed away. The threat of attack finally persuaded the shogunate that it could no longer avoid the matter.

Over the decade culminating in Perry's arrival, the sense of crisis across Japan about the country's lack of preparedness for the new world order grew more acute. In this context, Seishisai's analysis of the foreign threat in *Shinron* gained new relevance. Despite Narinobu's refusal to circulate the text in 1825, Seishisai's students and colleagues had created anonymous copies of *Shinron* that they circulated privately, through a growing network of students who shared Seishisai's concern with the state of the realm and his interpretation of Japan's divine and ethical national essence. Since then, samurai across Japan had started reading copies of *Shinron*, and Seishisai gained students from as far away as Kyūshū. The fact of Seishisai's authorship was somewhat of an open secret, and in 1848, one of Seishisai's students, Takahashi Taichirō, published a printed version of the text that included a postscript noting Seishisai as the author.[53] By the early 1850s, Seishisai's call to "expel the barbarians" had found a widespread following. A new wave of samurai from around Japan travelled to Mito to study with Seishisai and learn how best to confront the foreign threat. *Shinron* became the bible for these fervent young men, Seishisai their high priest.

Two figures in particular stand out for their devotion to Seishisai's teachings and for their role in laying the groundwork for the overthrow of the Tokugawa and the restoration of imperial rule in 1868. The first was was Maki Izumi, a Shintō priest from Kyushu, who read a copy of *Shinron* soon after it was written and travelled to Mito in 1844 to meet with Seishisai. They spent many hours discussing national affairs.[54] After Mito, Maki travelled to Kyoto, where he developed ties to several court families, and began to share Seishisai's "revere the emperor" ideas among courtiers hungry to restore political power to the throne. Maki spent ten years in prison after trying to reform his home domain, Kurume, with Mito's "dangerous" ideas, but after his release in 1861, he returned to Kyoto, where he joined radicals from Chōshū in pushing for the restoration of imperial rule.

The second figure to spread Seishisai's work in influential directions was Yoshida Shōin, a specialist in military education from the far western domain of Chōshū, and later an architect of Chōshū's rise as the center of the pro-imperial, anti-Tokugawa movement. The first time Yoshida encountered Seishisai's work was when he read a secret manuscript copy of *Shinron* in 1850 during a visit to Hirado Domain, whose daimyo was friendly with Tokugawa Nariaki. The next year in Edo, Yoshida studied with military scholar Sakuma Shōzan, who spoke highly of Seishisai's work on coastal defense. Through these connections, Yoshida's interest in Seishisai work, and particularly his call for military mobilization, increased. Finally, at the end of 1851, Shōin excitedly embarked on a trip to Mito, where he spent a month over the New Year. Seishisai hosted him several times, plying him with sake and conversation deep into the night. Yoshida left thrilled at the spirit of Mito's samurai and their devotion to fixing the problems facing Japan. He reread *Shinron* after Perry's arrival in 1853 and recognized its value as a practical text for galvanizing and mobilizing men to fight for their country.

Tōko, too, began to extend Seishisai's ideas in new directions. Time in prison meant time to write, and he composed several of his most important essays in 1844 and 1845, all of which addressed the Russian threat, the need for stronger defense policies, and dedication to the principles of imperial loyalty. His first composition, *Kaitenshishi*, is an annotated autobiographical poem that starts with the memorable line, "I resolved to die three times, and yet did not die," a sign of Tōko's moral convictions and passion.[55] The title refers to his desire to transform a decaying country, and the poem became widely admired among the *shishi*, or "men of high purpose"[56] and supporters of the "revere the emperor, expel the barbarian" cause throughout Japan. The source of the country's decay, as Tōko lays out in the first lines of the annotation, was the foreign threat, epitomized by the Ōtsuhama Incident—the first of Tōko's three moments of resolve. Later in the poem, Tōko recounts the dangers Russia posed to Ezochi, and bemoans the lack of urgency among samurai across Japan. He explicitly accused the shogunate of failing to pursue a colonization plan in Ezochi—a clear reference to Nariaki's unrealized proposal from 1839.[57] The poem concludes with a fiery statement of Japan's unique national essence (*kokutai*) and, particularly, a call to let Japan's martial spirit shine forth. This would strengthen the shogunate, force the barbarians to retreat, and bring order to the realm.[58]

In his second piece, a prose memoir of the Tenpō Reforms, titled *Hitachiobi*, Tōko defended the actions of his lord, Nariaki, and the goals of Mito's reform movement.[59] Here, too, he discussed the foreign threat and the necessity of taking a hardline stance against foreigners. After a long rehearsal of the history of Japan's foreign policy and developments abroad, exhibiting clear debts to Seishisai's research, Tōko discussed recent events within Mito. Nariaki was deeply concerned about "foreign ships roaming the seas, and sometimes even coming ashore, or offering goods to fishermen while on the water," and had prioritized coastal defense to drive these foreign vessels away.[60] Tōko again recounted Nariaki's Ezochi plans and reiterated the need to shore up Japan's northern flank by annexing the region.[61] Tōko's third piece, *Seiki no uta* (*Song of the Righteous Spirit*), was a long, Chinese-style poem about the core Mito ideas of reverence for the emperor and patriotism based on loyalty, honor, and military prowess, values that Tōko argued were unique to Japan. With references to Mount Fuji and the forty-seven rōnin, the poem centered Japanese geography and history, and tied it to an awesome imperial way. Tōko made a compelling case for the need for individuals to commit to the defense of Japan, inspiring *shishi* across Japan in the years that followed.[62] All of Tōko's texts, written in clear, passionate language, made the ideology of "revere the emperor, expel the barbarian" accessible and relevant to a wide audience of samurai and commoner activists across Japan.

Tōko's writings reflected many of the core ideas developed by Mito's scholars since the late eighteenth century, but he crafted a more potent form of "revere the emperor, expel the barbarian" that relied more heavily on notions of Japanese uniqueness than on the abstract Confucian ethics of Aizawa Seishisai. Where Seishisai had focused his energy on the ruling class, seeing ordinary people as merely "ignorant masses" who needed to be kept away from dangerous ideas like Christianity, Tōko believed that it was the connection between ordinary people and the imperial household that formed the basis of Japan's "national essence" (*kokutai*), its unique identity and spiritual strength. Seishisai believed that samurai needed to educate the masses in how to be loyal and dutiful to the emperor, but Tōko argued that it was the daily practice of worshipping Shintō deities that tied ordinary people to the imperial line—an innate, organic feature of individual Japanese lives.[63] Even when writing in Chinese poetic styles, Tōko emphasized "national particularism instead of universality."[64] With these writings, Tōko broke away from Seishisai's more abstract view of the samurai ethics of loyalty and duty as the moral basis of national strength. He became the leading proponent of a more radical view of Japanese uniqueness, one that was rooted in the distinctive history, myths, and customs of Japan rather than the expression of universal Confucian values. At the same time, Tōko made ordinary people matter: their beliefs, rituals, and actions could defend and preserve Japan's uniqueness. He saw education as a way to make all Japanese people aware of this fact. Self-awareness would lead to action, and action would strengthen Japan against its domestic crises and the foreign threat.[65]

While Tōko aimed to refine "revere the emperor, expel the barbarian" into a more nationalistic, distinctly Japanese ideology, Toyoda Tenkō focused more concretely on the steps needed in a post-Opium War East Asia. With Perry's arrival, he argued, Russia and England were no longer the real threat. Instead, Japan's policymakers had to deal with the United States. The United States had many similarities with England, including a hunger to get rich through trade and a willingness to use religion and force to swallow up other people's lands and colonize distant territories. But, unlike England, the United States was a young nation, ruled by eager, hungry, and ambitious men. In this sense, the Americans were more like the Mongols, keen to muscle themselves onto the world stage in pursuit of power and domination. This made them incredibly dangerous.[66] The only appropriate response, in Tenkō's view, was to reinstate the "Don't Think Twice" edict of 1825 and demonstrate Japan's overwhelming martial strength. This meant making coastal defense the top priority for every domain and the shogunate and mobilizing the people—not just samurai, but anyone with good proposals for coastal defense, even among "the lowest villagers and townspeople." All Japanese subjects needed to devote themselves to the protection of the realm.[67]

By the early 1850s, Mito's ideas had grown powerful as they circulated across Japan, especially after Perry's arrival confirmed the urgency of grappling with questions of national strength and foreign threats. However, they also grew more diversified: Seishisai's emphasis on rituals and state religion as an ethical system of political rule had given way to a more emotional appeal, in Tōko's case, to national identity and personal devotion. Meanwhile, Tenkō's focus on the logistics of coastal defense led him to a much greater willingness to mobilize large swathes of the Japanese population in the name of strengthening and protecting the nation. Alongside the increasingly diverse interpretations of "revere the emperor, expel the barbarian" emerging among Mito's scholars, their followers also began to interpret their ideas in new ways. Seishisai recognized that his ideas could be read in ways that went far beyond his intent, with the potential to destabilize the social order to which he remained firmly loyal. In 1852, for instance, he groused that various requests for copies of his work were all for pieces that "lamented the state of the world." He wished, instead, that his central idea—namely the importance of studying and understanding Japan's *kokutai*—had gained more traction among his followers than had his vitriolic disquisitions on the foreign threats and domestic crises facing the land.[68] Moreover, for men without particular loyalty to Mito or the Tokugawa family, the strident call for change emanating from Mito's scholars easily lent themselves to a deeper criticism of the shogunate. Their work hinted at the possibilities not to reform the Tokugawa system—but to replace it altogether.

TOWARD OPENING THE COUNTRY

Although Nariaki fell from power in 1844, he remained convinced that he had a role to play in shogunal politics, particularly with regards to defense and foreign affairs. In 1845 he began corresponding with Abe Masahiro about these issues, reiterating the importance of military reforms, such as defense spending and the colonization of Ezochi. He also underscored his conviction that, as the leader of a *gosanke* branch of the Tokugawa household, he was obligated to weigh in on matters of national policy. In the second month of 1846, Nariaki insisted that he be shown diplomatic letters from the Dutch to the shogunate and criticized Abe for failing to take a more aggressive stance against foreigners. In the face of this pestering, Abe had little inclination to support Nariaki, although he agreed in principle about the importance of coastal defense.[69]

The shogunate's decision in 1853 to accept Perry's demand for a treaty created an opening for Mito's leaders to seize national authority on the question of how to handle the barbarians. The shogun's leaders appointed Nariaki to the position of defense minister shortly after Perry's ultimatum, giving him a major platform to promote his reform agenda, although policy disagreements quickly derailed his efforts. Nariaki summoned Tōko to Edo early in the seventh month to advise him on defense and foreign policy. Before leaving for Edo, Tōko stopped at Yoshida Shrine, just south of Mito Castle, to offer a prayer "for the renewal of the true spirit of the realm."[70] His many years of activism had paid off; as Japan faced its greatest foreign crisis in two centuries, Tōko's message of spiritual mobilization against the foreign threat compelled the shogunate to place Mito men in government.

In the summer of 1853, Nariaki submitted to Abe Masahiro, the shogun's chief councilor, sweeping reform programs that focused on a two-pronged policy: prepare Japan for war, while simultaneously presenting a conciliatory face in treaty negotiations, relying on delays, obfuscation, and diplomacy to buy Japan time to build up its defenses.[71] This two-sided approach reflected the emerging consensus among Mito scholars, best encapsulated by Toyoda Tenkō, that the threat of war would inspire lackluster samurai to reform their ways and hone their martial skills. It also reflected their practical awareness of the limits of Japan's defensive capabilities. Nariaki urged the shogunate to issue a formal order for national unity, arguing that not only samurai but also townspeople and villagers needed to be mobilized as part of a general mobilization.[72] The shogunate issued a "great command" to that effect in the eleventh month. On 1854/1/14 (February 11), however, Perry returned with a determination to begin treaty negotiations, derailing Nariaki's desire to stretch out the diplomatic process. Nariaki tried to persuade the shogunate to put Perry off, but ultimately Perry's gunboat diplomacy and a strong faction in favor of conciliation overrode Nariaki's protests. The shogunate ultimately signed the Treaty of Peace and Amity with the United States on 1854/3/3 (March 31), creating two open ports at Shimoda and Hakodate. This treaty ushered in a new era of Japanese foreign relations, one in which the Western imperialist powers were impossible to ignore—but, at least provisionally, one in which they could be managed. Nariaki, angry, submitted his resignation as advisor shortly after the signing of the Kanagawa treaty. Although he had left his formal role,

Nariaki continued to advise Abe, and Tōko continued to work feverishly on the problems of diplomacy and defense throughout 1854. On 1855/8/14, Abe once again asked Nariaki to become a regular advisor to the shogunate on military affairs and coastal defense.

Negotiating actual treaties inevitably meant that Mito's anti-foreign ideologues had to temper their more idealistic calls for complete expulsion. Tōko and Seishisai both softened their hardline views somewhat, although both remained ambivalent about the wisdom of the shogunate's decision to sign treaties. Tōko came to accept the need to introduce Western military technology, for example—but he grew increasingly pessimistic about Japan's weakness as the shogunate signed "unequal treaties" with Russia and then Britain, so called for the various clauses that weakened Japanese sovereignty by granting those empires legal, military, and commercial rights on Japanese soil.[73] Writing to his family back in Mito in the summer, Tōko spoke proudly of his work on these matters, "the greatest issue facing the realm."[74] By the end of the year, though, the work was taking its toll: in the eleventh month of 1854, Tōko told his sister that "suddenly my hair has gone white, and it feels as though I have aged four or five years in the space of one."[75] Tragically, Tōko died in 1855 during the Ansei Earthquake—a devastating blow to Nariaki and Mito's reformist scholars.

In the aftermath of Perry's arrival, Seishisai, too, had criticized the shogunate for urging the country to remain calm and excoriated the regime for even considering trade with the Americans.[76] But Seishisai's position was more ambivalent than these angry words suggest, and he adopted a surprisingly pragmatic approach to foreign treaty negotiations. This was partly for political reasons: Seishisai, ever the Tokugawa loyalist, preferred to seek reform from within the shogunate than lob criticisms from the sidelines. In a deeper sense, Seishisai recognized that geopolitical realities had changed. If Russia had been the problem in *Shinron*, it really only affected Japan's northern edge. Now, with various Western powers arriving from all sides, bearing clear evidence of technological and military superiority, Seishisai recognized that "expel the barbarian" was no longer so simple. Not only were the barbarians themselves more sophisticated than they had been thirty years earlier, the domestic political scene had grown more complicated as various shogunal factions, myriad domains, a resurgent court, and a dispersed but influential group of radical young samurai all clamored for attention. With these circumstances in mind, Seishisai focused his energy on preventing the opening of Osaka to foreigners, rather than pushing for a complete ban on new foreign trading posts or diplomatic posts in Japan. Osaka's proximity to the imperial capital, Kyoto, made it too risky to allow foreigners there—not only because they might easily attack Kyoto, but because it would focus national attention on the shogunate's defensive capabilities in the area. This would only invite criticism, Seishisai argued, weakening the shogunate's authority.[77]

The treaty negotiations were also closely entwined with the problem of Ezochi, and it was here that Mito's reform proposals had their most enduring impact. Abe asked Nariaki for his opinion about Ezochi, which the shogunate had returned to Matsumae Domain's oversight in 1821. The Russians had moved quickly after Perry's first visit to assert their presence around Ezochi, and they began treaty negotiations of their own with the shogunate in 1854. These negotiations included debates about where, precisely, the border between the two countries should go, and Nariaki urged the shogunate to reannex Ezochi to lay claim to as much territory as possible. Despite the Russian threat, he was confident that "within ten years, Japan's sixty-odd provinces will become seventy-odd in number."[78] In 1855, the shogunate formally annexed the region, including most of Matsumae Domain, and established a magistrate at Hakodate, finally fulfilling the longstanding desire of Mito's leaders to assert Japanese control over the region. This coincided with the signing of a treaty with Russia that defined a new border, located between Urup and Etorofu in the Kuril Islands. The shogunate agreed to jointly administer Sakhalin (Karafuto) with the Russian Empire. Nariaki also pressed the shogunate to embark on settlement and urged Abe to relocate vagrants from the Kantō area to take up farming in Ezochi. After the 1855 Ansei Earthquake, he also proposed moving newly homeless Edoites there, too. Although he accepted that Mito would not play a major role in the settlement process, the domain did open a small trading post in western Ezochi—not quite the sweeping vision Nariaki laid out in 1839, but nevertheless an important step toward the wholesale colonization that followed two decades later.[79] Ezochi thus became part of the emerging Japanese nation-state, and unlike most other Japanese colonial acquisitions, it has remained part of the Japanese nation-state today, under the name Hokkaido.

The foreigners, meanwhile, wanted more than token diplomacy and a refueling stop, and, in 1856 the American consul, Townsend Harris, arrived in Japan to begin negotiations for a trade treaty that would allow for much greater contact between Japan and other nations. Nariaki was vehemently opposed, but the majority of the shogunate's chief councilors supported a treaty. Finally, in the sixth month of 1857, Abe died suddenly, ceding power to the pro-treaty Hotta Masayoshi. Nariaki, now isolated, resigned from his post that summer.[80] From the sidelines, Nariaki continued to fume about the progress of treaty negotiations. In 1857, the shogunate decided to accept American demands for a trade treaty, which established consulates in Edo and opened more ports to foreigners than under the diplomatic treaty of 1854. Nariaki urged the shogunate to reject the request, but he recognized that concessions would be necessary, so he made a bold suggestion: "there could be no greater expression of our friendship [with foreigners] than for the shogun to send me to America." Nariaki would lead three or four hundred men, the younger sons of farmers, samurai, and townspeople, and serve as "a middleman for the goods in which Americans want to trade."[81] In return, the Americans would agree to stay out of Japan, thus preserving the sanctity and security of the realm. Nariaki's astonishing proposal went nowhere and raised suspicions of his motives. It annoyed the shogunate's leaders, who became even more suspicious of Mito when they discovered a plot by Mito farmers to assassinate Harris. Relations between Mito and the shogunate worsened further.

Despite Nariaki's objection, Hotta announced his intention to sign a treaty with Harris on the last day of 1857. Nariaki was furious; Seishisai, inverting the famous slogan, sneered that the treaty was an example of "blaspheme the emperor, coddle the barbarian."[82] In early 1858, Hotta announced plans to seek the imperial court's approval for the treaty, in a bid to shore up support, but to Hotta's shock the court refused to back the shogunate—a serious blow to its authority. Furious, Hotta and his allies blamed Nariaki and Mito activists for stirring up the court's opposition. In the aftermath of the court debacle, Hotta resigned, and the shogunate councilors desperately looked for an able leader to restore the shogunate's strength. In the fifth month of 1858, they appointed Ii Naosuke, the daimyo of Hikone and a stalwart supporter of the shogunate's traditional power structures, as the young shogun's regent. Ii was firmly opposed to Nariaki's "expel the barbarian" philosophy, and unlike Abe or Hotta he was not interested in compromise and conciliation. Ii had little interest in expanding participation in the shogunate to other lords, and he was staunchly in favor of signing treaties with the West. Ii immediately consolidated power by pushing out pro-Nariaki, anti-treaty forces in government and signing the Harris treaty without waiting for further approval from the court. Nariaki, upon hearing the news, made an uninvited visit to Edo Castle to demand, at the very least, submission of the treaty to the court for approval. Ii refused to do so, and—enraged by Nariaki's lack of respect—punished him and his allies in a dramatic purge. Nariaki was confined once again to house arrest, and many of his allies and supporters also faced punishment (see chapter 5).

Nariaki's ouster signaled the end of the resistance to foreign trade treaties within the highest echelons of the shogunate. But it did not mean the end of the road for Mito's strong anti-foreign ideas. Instead, those energies dispersed across Mito and across Japan. Perry's arrival amplified the voices of more radical supporters of "revere the emperor, expel the barbarian" policies. These radicals agitated for harsher measures against the foreigners and began to cultivate allies in the imperial court and in Chōshū, the site of growing anti-Tokugawa sentiment. This loose coalition of anti-foreign political activists, many of whom were low-ranking samurai with little formal political power, were the seeds of the *shishi* who would shape the politics of the next fifteen years with radical reform movements, coup attempts, and anti-foreign terrorism. In the spring of 1860, a group of these radicals sought revenge for Ii's purge of Nariaki and other Mito men by assassinating Ii at Sakurada Gate (see chapter 6). Just a few months later, on 1860/8/15, Nariaki died in Mito, leaving the domain without a strong leader to rein in the actions of its most radical samurai. As a result, some of the earlier proponents of Mito's ideas began to question them, backing away from the more extreme positions of the diehard *shishi*. Ironically, the most prominent example was none other than Aizawa Seishisai.

Even though Seishisai despised the Harris treaty, he was even more worried about the disobedience and unrest among Mito's *shishi* following Nariaki's ouster and death. In 1862, Seishisai published a short essay, "A Plan for Tasks at Hand," in which he justified his support for opening the country.[83] He recanted the philosophy of "expel the barbarians" and the Tokugawa's "closed country" policy. Rather than a timeless law of the land, he argued, it was a historical artifact that had been put in place during the 1630s to cope with rebellions by Christian samurai. Two centuries later, it was no longer fit for purpose. In an age when Western imperialist powers were working in concert to muscle their way into Asia, he warned, "if we do not enter into friendly relations with foreign countries, we will make them all our enemies." This view came from a clear-eyed assessment of Japan's weaknesses: its outdated weapons, its weakened samurai class, and its inability to afford any possible indemnities should it lose a war with a Western power. Instead, he praised the shogunate's pursuit of policies to enrich the country and strengthen the army (*fukoku kyōhei*). Many of these policies reflected Seishisai's proposals from *Shinron*, such as the relaxation of *sankin kōtai*, which took place in the summer of 1862. These policies, supported by Nariaki's son (and Seishisai's former student), Tokugawa Yoshinobu, would buy Japan time to improve its military strength.[84]

Seishisai's political views had grown more moderate, but his writing contained the acerbic barbs familiar to readers of *Shinron*. This time, however, they were directed at many of those very readers. He criticized the thoughtlessness of the "hot-blooded young men" advocating armed expulsion of the foreigners, arguing that they failed to consider the possibility of losing. He also attacked their selfishness: "one cannot say of a man that he behaves like a loyal subject if he acts as though the country were private property that he can toss lightly away." He dismissed the "hotheads" as arrogant, deluded extremists, manipulating the emperor and putting the entire country at risk as they steadfastly refused to acknowledge changing political and geopolitical circumstances. By the early 1860s, political instability had become a greater threat, in Seishisai's mind, than the principles of "expel the barbarian." Mito's *shishi* scorned Seishisai's essay, calling it the writings of a senile old fool. Bands of men continued to engage in political violence against foreigners and shogunal officials, undermining shogunal authority. A year later, in the summer of 1863, Seishisai died in Mito, with no end in sight to the political turmoil within the domain or the domestic and foreign crises engulfing the shogunate.

Seishisai hoped to inspire a grand restoration of the Tokugawa social order with *Shinron* and his teachings. To the end of his life, he was unwilling to recognize the central paradox in his ideas: that radical reform might mean the collapse of the very system he hoped to preserve. His criticisms of the "hot-blooded young men" in "A Plan for Tasks at Hand" reflect his continuing faith in an ethical and political order centered on hierarchy and loyalty, represented by the Tokugawa shogunate's loyalty to the imperial court. Yet by the 1860s, this was an increasingly futile argument. It was becoming increasingly clear that loyalty to the emperor might better be served without the shogunate and the elaborate, fractured geography it ruled. By the time of Seishisai's death it was also becoming clear that "expel the barbarian" was no longer a viable political option. The foreigners were in Japan to stay, and experienced observers both within and outside the shogunate recognized this fact. "Revere the emperor, expel the barbarian" had lost its political coherence. But it had not yet lost its rhetorical power, and for the remainder of the decade it would inspire radicals in Mito and across Japan to commit acts of violence against foreigners and those Japanese who supported, however reluctantly, the extension of foreign relations.

Since at least the 1780s, Mito's reformist scholars had paid special attention to the threat foreign imperialists posed to Japan. The most urgent of these threats was Russia, and the question of how to protect northern Japan preoccupied Mito's scholars and leaders until 1824, when the Ōtsuhama Incident revealed that Britain, too, posed a threat. News of the Opium War reinforced that concern, while the increasing frequency of ships bearing envoys, missionaries, and traders from the United States and France showed that the imperialist threat was not isolated to Japan's northern flank. Nevertheless, Mito's leaders continued to emphasize the need to shore up the north and advocated for an imperialist project of their own: the seizure and colonization of Ezochi, land of the Ainu, to prevent it falling into Russian hands. By the mid-1850s, this advocacy had worked: the shogunate annexed Ezochi and agreed to new national borders with Russia, establishing the shape of modern

Japan. Meanwhile, the imperialist threat induced Mito's scholars to develop the powerful version of national identity, centered on the superior nature of a divine, unbroken imperial line, for which the domain is most famous. This ideology spread quickly around Japan and inspired people, particularly the low-ranked, radical *shishi*, to begin forging a new nation-state out of the fractured Tokugawa polity. Mito's leaders, alarmed, ultimately rejected this development, but they were unable to stop it.

Mito's "revere the emperor, expel the barbarian" ideology is easily associated with a virulent xenophobia. After all, the language used by scholars such as Aizawa Seishisai is scathing and polemical, rooted in a philosophical system based upon a hierarchy of civilizations and written in response to a clear and growing threat—one that had already wreaked havoc on neighboring China. But despite his reputation as a xenophobic ideologue, Seishisai's career and later political views suggest a more complicated picture of a scholar whose strong beliefs in Japanese exceptionalism and classical history sat alongside a keen perceptiveness about a changing domestic and international system. Comparing his work to the ethnocentric focus of Tōko's essays, or the technical sophistication of Toyoda Tenkō's proposals for military reform, shows how Mito's scholars deployed a number of rhetorical strategies to pursue a shared goal of strengthening their society. Put differently, the xenophobia and archaic radicalism of "revere the emperor, expel the barbarian" was just one part of this philosophy. Mito's scholars were also deeply realistic about the possibilities of political change, even if they were naïve about the extent to which their rhetorical saber-rattling could undermine their own efforts to forge greater unity under the Tokugawa shogunate.

The last years of Seishisai's life epitomized the complex and ultimately contradictory nature of Mito's "revere the emperor, expel the barbarian" ideology. Seishisai maintained his distrust of foreign empires and his belief in Japanese superiority throughout his life, but he also recognized the importance of using the necessary political means to protect a weak Japan. He was willing to absorb ideas from abroad, whether Peter the Great's approach to government in Russia or, in later years, the technology on offer from the Dutch or the Americans. In large part based on these foreign examples, he developed a more modern conception of the Japanese state, one that relied upon a state religion and imperial mythology to forge political unity and ethical principles. His belief in Japanese superiority rested upon his commitment to the social and political hierarchy of Tokugawa Japan, and the ideals of loyalty and obedience that underpinned it. Loyalty to the throne, explained and reinforced through a system of rites and rituals, lay at the core of his vision of a resurgent and unified Japan, able to function in the modern world of global empires. As a result, the erosion of this belief system by the middle of the nineteenth century by radical samurai willing to overturn the system in the name of protecting Japan struck him as a graver threat than the black ships steaming into Edo Bay. He criticized his most ardent followers for failing to recognize this fact, and for failing to uphold these ideals in their shortsighted and bloodthirsty actions. But he also failed to entertain other models of imperial loyalty that did away with the mediating function of the Tokugawa shogunate. In the end, he never resolved the tension between loyalty to the Tokugawa family and loyalty to the imperial court. Perhaps luckily, he did not live to see how much worse Mito's factional disputes and bloodletting would become, as factions fought over precisely that tension.

NOTES

1. Bob Tadashi Wakabayashi, *Anti-Foreignism and Western Learning in Early-Modern Japan: The "New Theses" of 1825* (Cambridge, MA: Council on East Asian Studies, Harvard University, 1986) and J. Victor Koschmann, *The Mito Ideology* (Berkeley: University of California Press, 1987).

2. Perhaps most famous is Maruyama Masao, who argued that Seishisai's version of nationalism was anti-modern because he feared the stupidity of ordinary people instead of trying to mobilize them in the defense of the nation. *Studies in Tokugawa Intellectual History*, trans. Mikiso Hane (Princeton, NJ: Princeton University Press, 1974), 356. H. D. Harootunian, in *Toward Restoration* (Berkeley: University of California Press, 1970), similarly argues that the Mito scholars were not protonationalists but, rather, seeking a return to a classical age, on the basis of their vision of an idealized ancient Japan.

3. Kiri Paramore, "Political Modernity and Secularization: Thoughts from the Japanese Eighteenth and Nineteenth Centuries," *Journal of Religious History* 36, no. 1 (March 2012): 19–30, and Mark McNally, *Like No Other: Exceptionalism and Nativism in Early Modern Japan* (Honolulu: University of Hawai'i Press, 2016).

4. Until very recently, Seishisai's Japanese biographers universally ignored the later part of his life, leaving out his role in the factional disputes that wrecked Mito in the 1850s and 1860s. See, for example, Seya Yoshihiko, *Aizawa Seishisai*, (Tokyo: Bunkyō shoin, 1942) and Nishimura Fuminori, *Aizawa Hakumin* (Tokyo: Shōkasha, 1936). Ami Takao is the first to treat Seishisai's later life fully in Ami, *Aizawa Seishisai no shōgai* (Mito: Kinseisha, 2016). Other treatments of the Late Mito School, notably those by Harootunian and Koschmann, tend to focus on the ideological function of the texts and reform programs in Mito, rather than the dynamics between political actors.

5. Sapporo-shi kyōiku iinkai, ed., *Shin Sapporo shishi*, vol. 1 (Sapporo: Sapporo-shi, 1986), 416.

6. *Mito shishi*, chū, 3:926.

7. Yoshizawa Giichi, *Hoppō ryōdo tankenshi no shin kenkyū: sono Mito-han to no kakawari* (Tokyo: Kinseisha, 2003), 37–38.

8. Etorofu had long been home to the Ainu and a trading post for Japanese and then Russians since the seventeenth century. In the 1854 treaty signed between Japan and Russia, Etorofu marked the northern border of Japan in the Kurils. In 1875, Japan gained the entirety of the Kuril chain. Russia seized the Kurils after World War II, and most residents—whether of Ainu or Japanese descent—moved to Hokkaido. Japan disputes Russian sovereignty of Etorofu to this day.

9. Yoshizawa, *Hoppō ryōdo tankenshi*, 6–7.

10. The Aizawa family trace their roots to the Heian-era courtier Fujiwara no Korechika. They first arrived in the Mito area during the sixteenth century, serving the Satake family before the arrival of the Mito Tokugawa. Personal correspondence with Aizawa Takuya, April 2021.

11. Ami Takao, *Aizawa Seishisai no shōgai*, 13–16.

12. Seya, *Aizawa Seishisai*, 17–18.

13. This overview is based on an essay Seishisai wrote in 1850 describing his training under Yūkoku: Aizawa Seishisai, "Kyūmon ihan," in *Nihongaku sōsho*, ed. Nagasaka Kaneo (Tokyo: Yūzankaku, 1939), 8:38–90.

14. Aizawa Seishisai, *Chishima ibun*, quoted in Kurihara Shigeyuki, "*Chishima ibun* kō," *Nihon rekishi* 469 (June 1987): 55.

15. In English, Ronald Toby first articulated the development of a Japan-centered "civilized-barbarian" hierarchy, pinpointing Tokugawa diplomatic practices and the consequences of the collapse of the Ming Dynasty in 1644 as key turning points. Toby, *State and Diplomacy in Tokugawa Japan* (Princeton, NJ: Princeton University Press, 1984).

16. Kurihara, "*Chishima ibun* kō," 52–57.

17. Kiri Paramore discusses how Seishisai emphasized social and political integration, rather than simple technological superiority, as the source of Western strength. In this regard, religious and political unity could be used to build a modern state—it was not simply a throwback to classical times. He developed this idea most fully in *Kikōben*, which he wrote in 1828. See Paramore, "Political Modernity and Secularization," esp. 26–28.

18. Seya, *Aizawa Seishisai*, 27.

19. Seishisai's memorial is discussed in Ami, *Aizawa Seishisai no shōgai*, 54–55.

20. David Howell has beautifully retold the Ōtsuhama Incident with a focus on Yūzaburō. This section draws on his essay "Foreign Encounters and Informal Diplomacy in Early Modern Japan," *Journal of Japanese Studies* 40, no. 2 (Summer 2014): 295–327. ·

21. Howell, "Foreign Encounters," 318.

22. Kurihara Shigeyuki, "*Shinron* izen no Aizawa Seishisai: chūkai *An'i mondō*," *Tokyo toritsu daigaku hōgakkai zasshi* 30, no. 1 (1989): 187–93. See also Ernest Clement's translation of a version of this account in "Mito Samurai and British Sailors in 1824," *Transactions of the Asiatic Society of Japan*, Fourth Series, Vol. 33, Part 1 (1905): 86–131, and Wakabayashi, *Anti-Foreignism and Western Learning in Early-Modern Japan*, 58–99 for a lengthier discussion of Seishisai's views on Christianity, the West, and Western imperialism.

23. Kurihara, *"Shinron* izen no Aizawa Seishisai," 194.

24. Kurihara, *"Shinron* izen no Aizawa Seishisai," 194.

25. Aizawa, *An'i mondō*, quoted and translated in Wakabayashi, *Anti-Foreignism and Western Learning in Early-Modern Japan*, 90.

26. Wakabayashi, *Anti-Foreignism and Western Learning in Early-Modern Japan*, 68–76.

27. Fujita Tōko, "Kaitenshishi," in *Fujita Tōko zenshū*, ed. Takasu Yoshijirō (Tokyo: Shōkasha, 1935), 1:7–13.

28. Howell, "Foreign Encounters," 312–13.

29. For a discussion of how increased encounters with foreign powers led to this xenophobic policy, see Wakabayashi, *Anti-Foreignism and Western Learning*, 58–99.

30. Wakabayashi, *Anti-Foreignism and Western Learning*, 108.

31. Aizawa, *Shinron*, in Wakabayashi, *Anti-Foreignism and Western Learning,* 200.

32. Aizawa, *Shinron*, 214–44.

33. Aizawa, *Shinron*, 243.

34. Koschmann, *The Mito Ideology*, 64–67.

35. This description of the synthesis of Confucian and Kokugaku ideas is somewhat oversimplified, largely because synthesizing different traditions inevitably meant rejecting parts of each. Mark McNally briefly discusses Seishisai's complicated views of Confucian and Kokugaku ideas in *Like No Other*, 183–87. Kajiyama Takao, focusing on Mito's most prominent Kokugaku scholar, Yoshida Kōdō (Noriyo), notes the varying degrees of receptiveness to Kokugaku among Mito's nineteenth-century scholars. Seishisai was notably critical of Kokugaku, particularly for its failure to acknowledge the universal ethical principles (the Confucian "way," or *dō*), and he argued frequently with Kōdō. Fujita Tōko lay somewhere in the middle of the spectrum. Kajiyama, *Mito no kokugaku: Yoshida Kōdō wo chūshin toshite* (Mito: Mito shigakkai, 1995), 261–85. Despite this, given the imperial focus of Mito's scholarly traditions, and the content of Mito scholars' foreign-policy work in the nineteenth century, I agree with Wakabayashi that the discourse of Japanese exceptionalism in the Late Mito School rested upon the work of Kokugaku scholars in the eighteenth century, even if Seishisai and other Mito scholars were forthright in their criticism of much of that work. Wakabayashi, *Anti-Foreignism and Western Learning in Early-Modern Japan*, 35–40.

36. Aizawa, *Shinron*, 263–64.

37. *Mito shishi*, chū, 3:931.

38. Suzuki Eiichi, *Fujita Tōko* (Tokyo: Yoshikawa kōbunkan, 1998), 30–36.

39. Suzuki, *Fujita Tōko*, 35.

40. "Tekiihen" in 1833 and "Sōen wagen" in 1834. An annotated modern Japanese translation of "Tekiihen" is found in Tsukamoto Katsuyoshi, trans., *Shinron, Tekiihen* (Tokyo: Iwanami Bunko, 1942). There are no critical editions of "Sōen wagen," although a printed version of the text has been reproduced in *Nihon kyōiku bunko*, shūkyō hen (Tokyo: Dōbunkan, 1911), 372–417 and in *Nihon kokusui zensho*, vol. 10 (Tokyo: Nihon kokusui zensho kankōkai, 1915–1918).

41. Fujita Tōko, "Jōi ni tsuite," in Takasu, *Fujita Tōko zenshū*, 6:20–44.

42. Fujita Tōko, "Bushi dochaku no gi," in Takasu, *Fujita Tōko zenshū*, 6: 258–97. Koschmann suggests that defensive concerns were secondary but given the consistent focus on the foreign threat by Mito's scholars throughout this period, the investment in personnel and defensive outposts, and the growing knowledge of Western designs on China, it seems likely that Tōko and his peers were sincere in their concerns. Koschmann, *The Mito Ideology*, 103.

43. *Mito shishi*, chū, 3:216.

44. *Mito shishi*, chū, 3:229–33.

45. *Mito shishi*, chū, 3:240.

46. Nagai Hiroshi, *Tokugawa Nariaki: Fukakujitsu na jidai ni ikite* (Tokyo: Yamakawa shuppansha, 2019), 71.

47. *Mito shishi*, chū, 3:214–44.

48. Fujita Tōko, *Hitachiobi*, in Takasu, *Fujita Tōko zenshū*, 1:424.

49. Tokugawa Nariaki, "Suifu-kō kensaku," in *Mitogaku taikei*, 5:238.

50. Tokugawa Nariaki, "Hoppō mirai kō," in *Mitogaku taikei*, 5:273–308.

51. Fujita Tōko, *Hitachiobi*, 420–21.

52. Aizawa Seishisai to Terakado Masajirō, 1852/10/13, in *Aizawa Seishisai shokan shū*, ed. Osaka daigaku Aizawa Seishisai shokan kenkyūkai (Kyoto: Shibunkaku, 2016), 32.

53. Seya Yoshihiko, "Kaidai," in Imai et al., *Mitogaku*, 427–28.

54. *Mito shishi*, chū, 3:976–79.

55. Fujita Tōko, *Kaitenshishi*, 3–247.

56. Thomas Huber, "Men of High Purpose and the Politics of Direct Action, 1862–64," in *Conflict in Modern Japanese History: The Neglected Tradition*, ed. Tetsuo Najita and Victor Koschmann (Princeton: Princeton University Press, 1982), 107–27.

57. Fujita Tōko, *Kaitenshishi*, 209.

58. Fujita Tōko, *Kaitenshishi*, 246.

59. Fujita Tōko, *Hitachiobi*, 249–478. For a brief discussion, see Fritz Opitz, "Die Lehensreformen des Tokugawa Nariaki nach dem 'Hitachi-Obi' des Fujita Tōko (Ein Beitrag zur Lehensgeschichte der Tokugawa-Zeit)," PhD Diss., Ludwig-Maximilians-Universität zu München, 1965.

60. Fujita Tōko, *Hitachiobi*, 415.

61. Fujita Tōko, *Hitachiobi*, 424–25.

62. For a translation and discussion of this poem, and its impact on *shishi*, see Matthew Fraleigh, "Songs of the Righteous Spirit: The 'Men of High Purpose' and Their Chinese Poetry in Modern Japan," *Harvard Journal of Asiatic Studies* 69, no. 1 (June 2009): 109–71.

63. Yoshida Toshizumi, *Mitogaku to Meiji ishin* (Tokyo: Yoshikawa kōbunkan, 2003), 215–18.

64. Fraleigh, "Songs of the Righteous Spirit," 156.

65. Suzuki, *Fujita Tōko*, 208. For a more general discussion of how the Mito scholars' work functioned as ideology, mobilizing commoners as political actors, see Koschmann, *The Mito Ideology*, 130–51.

66. Toyoda Tenkō, "Bōkai shinsaku," in Imai et al., *Mitogaku*, 344.

67. Toyoda, "Bōkai shinsaku," 348.

68. Aizawa Seishisai to Terakado Masajirō, 1852/10/4, *Aizawa Seishisai shokan shū*, 31; see also Nara Katsuji's remarks on Seishisai's letters in his appendix to that volume, in which he elaborates on Seishisai's thoroughgoing focus on status and loyalty, even at the expense of promoting nationalism.

69. Conrad Totman, "Political Reconciliation in the Tokugawa Bakufu: Abe Masahiro and Tokugawa Nariaki, 1844–1852," in *Personality in Japanese History*, eds. Albert Craig and Donald Shiveley (Berkeley: University of California Press, 1970), 180–208.

70. Quoted in Suzuki, *Fujita Tōko*, 233.

71. Nariaki's proposals are printed in *Dai Nihon komonjo: bakumatsu gaikoku kankei monjo* (Tokyo: Tokyo teikoku daigaku bunka daigaku shiryō hensangakari, 1910–2003), 1:509–22 and 2:4–14. W. G. Beasley has translated part of the proposal into English in *Select Documents on Japanese Foreign Policy* (London: Oxford University Press, 1960), 102–7.

72. *Mito-han shiryō* (Tokyo: Yoshikawa kōbunkan, 1917), jō, 2:52.

73. Suzuki, *Fujita Tōko*, 249.

74. Quoted in Suzuki, *Fujita Tōko*, 234.

75. Quoted in Suzuki, *Fujita Tōko*, 246.

76. Seishisai to Terakado, 1854/3/14, in *Aizawa Seishisai shokan shū*, 37.

77. Isaka Kiyonobu, *Aizawa Seishisai no bannen to Mito-han* (Tokyo: Perikansha, 2017), 58.

78. *Mito-han shiryō*, jō, 8:407.

79. *Mito shishi*, chū, 4:782–87.

80. *Mito shishi*, chū, 4:497–501.

81. Tokugawa Nariaki to Rōjū, December 30, 1857, in Beasley, *Select Documents on Japanese Foreign Policy*, 168–69.

82. Seishisai to Terakado, 1858/5/24, in *Aizawa Seishisai shokan shū*, 74.

83. Quotes from Aizawa Seishisai, "A Plan for Tasks at Hand," trans. Donald Keene, *Monumenta Nipponica* 62, no. 1 (Spring 2007): 75–86.

84. This essay's publication coincided with the Bunkyū Reforms, which were forced upon the shogunate by a coalition of great lords, led by Satsuma's Shimazu Hisamitsu and the court. As part of these reforms, Nariaki's son, Tokugawa Yoshinobu, became regent, one of the most powerful positions in the shogunate (see chapter 5). Seishisai was one of Yoshinobu's teachers, and he may have written this essay as a public show of support for Yoshinobu's new position and the shogunate's official stance in favor of opening relations with the West.

Chapter Four

The Politics of Mito's Tenpō Reforms

Between 1829, when Tokugawa Nariaki became Mito's ninth daimyo, and 1844, when he was ordered into retirement by the shogunate, an extraordinary group of reformers held power in the domain. Together they implemented a sweeping, radical program to confront the social, political, and moral ills that had plagued Mito for more than a century, such as the collapse of the domain's tax base, the dissipation of martial values and military preparedness, and the corruption of the domain leadership—all factors that Tachihara Suiken, Aizawa Seishisai, and other reformers had identified for years. Moreover, Mito's reforms attracted attention from around Japan and inspired the shogunate's own version of the Tenpō Reforms. During Mito's reform movement, and in the decades that followed, likeminded observers from around Japan extolled it as an example of how to strengthen Japan. Military reform, samurai education, an emphasis on talent over heredity, commoner mobilization, new economic policies, religious controls, and more muscular, charismatic forms of leadership all distinguished Mito's Tenpō Reforms, and illustrate the radical nature of their challenge to traditional society. Mito's reformers sought to oust the traditional establishment, reform the political order, and rebuild their society.

This radical project was couched, however, in the language of tradition. In this regard, Mito's Tenpō Reforms resembled reform movements throughout Tokugawa history: reformers expressed a desire to return to an idealized past, one that predated whatever social, economic, or moral decline was plaguing the present. Scholars of the Tenpō Reforms have tended to focus on this traditional language: H. D. Harootunian credits Mito's nineteenth-century scholars with "restating the traditional assumptions" of Tokugawa society, for example, while J. Victor Koschmann, in his seminal study of Mito, argues that the reformers "repossessed" the seventeenth-century ideology that underpinned the Tokugawa order.[1] Koschmann in particular notes that this was a contradictory and tension-riddled effort, because the Mito reformers also recognized that they had to actively intervene in quite dramatic ways to restore these traditional practices and social structures. The stereotype of the Tenpō Reforms, more broadly, is that they were a failure, a futile attempt to revive a traditional past.[2] More recently, however, historians have begun to revisit this view and have started recognizing in the series of domain-level reform movements—including Mito's—a broad transformation to more modern concepts of government: centralized, with modern military technology and organization, and centered around the calculating operation of political power, rather than the exercise of morality.[3] By looking at domain-level reforms across Japan from the end of the eighteenth century and through the nineteenth century, it becomes clear that a broad set of changes helped establish and legitimize new forms of politics that intimately shaped the structure of post-Tokugawa Japan. Mito was no exception, and indeed the domain's outsized status and reputation ensured that its reform movement attracted attention from across Japan.

Koschmann also focused on how the texts and actions of Mito's reformers functioned as ideology, that is, as mechanisms for mobilizing Mito's samurai and rural elite to become political actors in the middle of the nineteenth century. In this chapter, I do not dispute this function: it is certainly true that Mito's reformers successfully mobilized a large swath of Mito's rural elites to support their agenda. However, they were equally effective in mobilizing a backlash, initially among members of the traditional samurai establishment, and later among ordinary people throughout Mito. The reform coalition itself also suffered, with moderate and radical camps diverging over a number of policies. This political factionalism and the violent conflict it engendered are equally important consequences of Mito's reformist agenda.

Finally, both Harootunian and Koschmann argue that the Mito reformers were particularly interested in the domain as the "microcosm" (to use Koschmann's term) of the proper social order.[4] That is, they envisioned the domain as the proper site for articulating the relationship between social reform and demonstrations of loyalty to the imperial realm. But it did not take long for Mito's reformers to set their sights on the shogunate, which embarked upon its own version of the Tenpō Reforms in the early 1840s. Although political backlash in the mid-1840s cut reforms short, in both Mito and in the shogunate, they were revived in the 1850s. By that point, observers around Japan had begun to introduce similar measures in their own domains. Mito's reform agenda was not limited to the domain's borders.

The central figures in the reform movement were Nariaki and his most trusted advisor, Fujita Tōko (1806–1855). Nariaki has often been described (and dismissed) as a radical xenophobe, a close-minded reactionary whose bellicose attitude undermined the delicate diplomatic efforts of the shogunate and established a streak of anti-foreignism that lingered well past the 1860s. Diplomatic historians and scholars of Tokugawa politics have focused on his hot temper and strident anti-foreign statements, primarily within the context of the diplomatic negotiations of the 1850s.[5] Meanwhile, despite his central role in Mito's political reform movement and intellectual tradition, Fujita Tōko has received little sustained attention in the West in recent years. Meiji-era foreign observers of Japan commented on his significance in inspiring Japanese nationalism and the overthrow of the Tokugawa order, but in the aftermath of World War II, Tōko, like Seishisai and other Mito scholars, was treated as a source of ultranationalism and militarism.[6] Unlike Seishisai, however, whose works have undergone reassessment in recent years, Tōko remains a more elusive figure.[7] In general, scholars have focused their analysis primarily on Tōko's intellectual contributions, and most attention has gone to the *Kōdōkanki* and its commentary. In terms of his role in Mito's reform movement, scholars have emphasized the ideological nature of Tōko's reformism, while downplaying the political elements of that project.[8] In Japanese, Suzuki Eiichi offers a more complex analysis of Tōko's place within Mito's political landscape, illustrating how his personality and upbringing shaped his political activities and enabled him to influence people and events across Japan. This chapter builds on Suzuki's approach to demonstrate how Tōko's political identity and changing ideological positions worked together to produce Mito's reform movement. Finally, figures in the moderate camp of reformers barely feature at all in Western scholarship on Mito's reforms. Here, the scholar and devoted rural reformer Komiyama Fūken (1764–1840) stands in for the moderates, serving as a counterpoint to Tōko's radicalism. His copious journals are a crucial source to read alongside the writings of Tōko and Nariaki in order to gain a fuller picture of the reality of the Tenpō Reforms for the people who lived through them.

Mito's Tenpō Reforms reflected the ideological goals of their authors. They also were the product of intense political battles: Nariaki and his reformist officials against the traditional establishment, radical reformers against their moderate counterparts, and the administration against an often reluctant commoner population. These battles intersected with circumstance, most notably the devastating famine years of the mid-1830s, to produce a complicated and increasingly fractious political and social landscape within Mito. Nevertheless, by the 1840s, Mito's reformers had succeeded in implementing a number of changes to their domain's political, social, and economic structure, attracting interest and attention from elsewhere in Japan. Despite the fall from power of the reformist administration in 1844, Mito's reforms continued to influence supporters elsewhere in Japan. Nariaki's return to power in the 1850s rested in no small part on the reputation he and his fellow reformers had achieved as a result of their efforts to transform Mito during the Tenpō years.

THE RISE OF THE REFORM FACTION

Tokugawa Nariaki was never meant to become lord of his domain. Born in 1800 as the third son of the seventh daimyo, Harutoshi (1773–1816, r. 1805–1816), he spent most of his childhood in Mito's Edo estate at Koishikawa, watching his eldest brother, Narinobu (1797–1829, r. 1816–1829), prepare to succeed their father as lord of Mito. By the time Narinobu became daimyo in 1816, Nariaki's other brothers and sisters had been sent off as adoptive heirs or daughters-in-law to other powerful daimyo across Japan or court nobles in Kyoto. In later years, this family network formed an important basis for Nariaki's political alliances. But as a child, Nariaki had little reason to expect needing such alliances; he stayed in Edo, a spare heir should Narinobu die young or fail to produce a child. As brother of the daimyo, he had the best tutors, including Aizawa Seishisai and Yoshida Kōdō (Noriyo), who together gave him a rigorous training in Confucian ethical and political classics as well as Kokugaku works on Japan's history and mythology. Seishisai later boasted of his student's precociousness: at the age of four, Nariaki asked his father to have two samurai retainers take over from his wet-nurses. That same year, he began reading the Confucian canon; he moved onto Japanese poetry composition at age five. Nariaki had an astute understanding of ethics, and he quickly and perceptively grasped the state of the world. From age nine, his attention turned to martial arts, including shooting, spearwork, riding, and weaponry—all skills that he mastered, inspiring Mito's retainers to improve their own efforts. Finally, at the age of nineteen he began learning the music and dances associated with the imperial court and Shintō rituals, studies that he continued throughout his life.[9] Seishisai's description is no doubt embellished, but it gives some sense of Nariaki's training.

    Nariaki's reformist education led him to develop sharp criticisms of Mito's various social and political problems. He was obsessed with wasteful spending by the domain government, which had indebted Mito while also failing to alleviate widespread poverty among Mito's subjects. A classic example was a ceremony designed to display the domain's benevolence and charity. The domain spent three hundred *ryō* to capture various animals, which they then brought to Koishikawa and, in a choreographed display of mercy, released in the garden in front of an audience of prominent priests. Rather than spend the money on this pointless exercise, Nariaki grumbled, the domain should simply give poor subjects the cash.[10] Nariaki also fumed from the sidelines as his brother responded placidly to the 1824 Ōtsuhama Incident. Seishisai, Fujita Tōko, and other reformers were frustrated by Narinobu's lack of urgency about the foreign crisis, which symbolized a general lack of enthusiasm for the reforms they deemed essential to solving Mito's social and economic woes and facing the foreign threat. Nariaki, close to the reformers, may have advocated privately for these causes: his brother granted him the literary title "Sleeping Dragon" (*senryūkaku*), hinting at his strong convictions and political beliefs.[11] But with no formal political position in the domain, Nariaki had little standing to push for reforms.

Fujita Tōko also grew up in the heady milieu of Mito's reformers, and, like Nariaki, developed a sharp willingness to confront the entrenched interests of the traditional establishment. He was born in the Uwabaikō neighborhood, just to the west of Mito Castle, in the third month of 1806. His father, Yūkoku, was then head of the Shōkōkan research institute and a close advisor to the seventh daimyo, Harutoshi. Yūkoku's rise to the upper echelons of the domain gave Tōko a privileged place in Mito, but from the perspective of the traditional elite he was one of an upstart group of ambitious, lower-ranked samurai, like Seishisai and many other reformers. This difference in status and rank became an important element in Tōko's political activism

Figure 4.1. Portrait of Fujita Tōko
(Ibaraki Prefectural Archives and Museum)

and accentuated the ideological differences within Mito's samurai class. His reformism was not simply ideological: it was also highly political, aimed at replacing the traditional establishment with a new cohort of younger, less exalted samurai, chosen on the basis of their merit rather than heredity.

Tōko's education focused on the classical Confucian ethics and Japanese history that formed the core of the Late Mito School curriculum. Yūkoku's strong commitment to the ethical and historical principles of loyalty and obedience stuck with the impressionable young Tōko. In 1826, Yūkoku died, leaving Tōko to run the Fujita household. He began working at the Shōkōkan and took over Yūkoku's academy in 1827, and in 1829, he was appointed to a directorship at the Shōkōkan, marking his arrival into the upper echelon of Mito's academic world. Like his father, Tōko was uncompromising and forthright in his opinions, and had little compunction about offending powerful people, including his new bosses. Shortly after arriving at the Shōkōkan, he submitted a scathing memorandum that outlined "five evils" in the institute, including the promotion of corrupt and immoral men and the general lack of rigor in the curriculum.[12] He argued that scholars had forgotten the importance of putting their academic work to practical use, and that the best men—in particular Seishisai—were not given the most important roles. Tōko's memorandum did not eliminate the ills of the Shōkōkan—in fact, it amplified a rift between the senior members of the institute in Edo and the reformist faction led by Tōko in Mito. Nevertheless, it highlighted Tōko's newfound position of influence in Mito, and his willingness to single out the traditional establishment as the target of his reformist energies.

Alongside his challenge to the Shōkōkan leadership, Tōko focused his energy in the summer of 1829 on Mito's intensifying succession crisis. The eighth daimyo, Narinobu, was a sickly man with no children, and Mito officialdom had been worrying about his succession for several years. Narinobu's condition had taken a turn for the worse in 1828, and various factions in Mito were scheming to pick a successor. The traditional establishment negotiated with the shogunate for Narinobu to adopt one of the shogun's sons as an heir, as this might bring much-needed fiscal aid from the shogunate. Tōko and the reformist faction threw their energies into supporting Nariaki, whom they recognized as a standard bearer for their cause. The two sides continued to jockey for influence into 1829. As Narinobu grew sicker, "both Mito and Edo fell into great turmoil: there hadn't been such a disturbance in the domain since its founding."[13] The reformists decided to make a last, desperate stand, and a group of leading scholars—including Seishisai and Tōko—left Mito without permission to petition officials in Edo to persuade Narinobu to choose Nariaki as his heir. Travelling without a permit was a serious offense, and Tōko later claimed that he was prepared to die for the second time in his life if it would put Nariaki in power.[14] Tōko knew that the reformists in Mito needed to show the conservative elite in Edo that they were strong in numbers and in conviction. On the fourth day of the tenth month, three days after they arrived in Edo, Narinobu died, threatening to make matters even more contentious. Conveniently, however, Narinobu's advisors quickly discovered his will, which stated his intention to adopt Nariaki as his heir. Four days later the shogunate confirmed Nariaki's succession as daimyo, paving the way for a reformist agenda that transformed Mito.[15]

The fight over Nariaki's succession heightened the tensions between establishment and reformist factions among Mito's samurai, tensions that would persist throughout his reign. Nariaki immediately punished several establishment figures for their opposition to his succession. But this faction included most of Mito's highest-ranking retainers, who could not easily be removed from power. To soothe the establishment retainers' outrage at the reformers' illegal trip, Nariaki punished thirty members of the reformist faction, although these punishments were short and perfunctory. To avoid the uncertainty and chaos surrounding his succession—and to ensure control over his legacy—Nariaki quickly wrote a will laying out the procedure for determining his heir. He insisted that the bloodline of Mito's first lord, Yorifusa, drive the search for an heir should anything befall him before he produced a son of his own.[16] These efforts helped calm tempers on all sides in Mito and Edo, at least for a little while.[17] Nevertheless, Nariaki had no intention of governing as a moderate, and he quickly turned to an unabashedly reformist agenda.

MITO'S TENPŌ REFORMS:
PERSONNEL, LEADERSHIP, AND FACTIONALISM

For the next fifteen years, Tōko served as "Nariaki's brain," the guiding force for a comprehensive reform agenda that aimed to revitalize Mito and prepare it for the new age of global imperialism.[18] Mito's reforms, often called the Tenpō Reforms after the Tenpō era (1830–1844), sought to sweep away the accumulated social and political ills of the previous century through comprehensive reforms of the domain's political, social, and economic order. Scholars have focused on four major areas of reform, as laid out by Tōko several years into Nariaki's reign: reforming the tax code via a land survey; restoring samurai morals via a new education system and school; reviving military defenses, particularly along the coast; and returning samurai from their urban homes in Edo and Mito to the countryside.[19] Scholars have focused on these four areas to show how the ideas of the Late Mito School played out in the realm of politics. As Victor Koschmann argued, these efforts were "aspects of a formal, structural rectification designed to approximate the contours of an archetypical order. . . . They represented the authority of Shinto myth and the persuasiveness of neo-Confucian arguments for the possibility of spontaneous resonance between human minds and the Mind of Heaven-and-Earth."[20] All of these projects served ideological purposes, insofar as they represented the philosophical values of the Late Mito School and aimed to motivate new forms of action among Mito's people.

This emphasis on ideology, however, oversimplifies the story of the Tenpō Reforms by focusing just on these four categories. These categories do not account for the wider reformist project to overturn the hold of the traditional establishment, and, in time, Tōko's efforts to outwit the moderate faction of reformists. These political projects, alongside the urgency of defending Mito's long coastline from foreign ships, were just as important to Mito's reformers as the more abstract project of transforming the hearts and minds of Mito's people. As a result, Mito's Tenpō Reforms were messy and contradictory. They required political compromises that were vital to their implementation, but also led to worsening disagreements and factionalism.

On 1829/10/18, the day after his confirmation as daimyo, Nariaki wrote to his senior retainers with instructions to make "love of the people" as the highest priority of domain governance. He pinpointed the years immediately after Mitsukuni's death as the start of a downward slide in good government and singled out excessive taxation as a symbol of the government's failure to be benevolent rulers.[21] Although these tax reforms took some time to implement, Nariaki also demonstrated his commitment to good government by hiring reformist officials to oversee civil government. Shortly after New Year's Day, 1830, he issued a broad edict to villagers laying out the steps of moral and economic reform necessary, in his view, to improve their livelihoods and wellbeing.[22] Meanwhile, Nariaki announced a parallel set of edicts to Mito's samurai. First, he said, the true way of the samurai was the study of literary and martial arts, and all his retainers should pursue these studies with vigor. Second, no matter their rank or position, any retainer with an opinion or proposal should submit a memorandum to express their views.[23] These simple proclamations encapsulated Nariaki's approach to government. The importance of education as a way to strengthen the samurai, both morally and militarily, lay at the heart of his ideology. And Nariaki's willingness to hear all manner of opinions illustrates his forthright, direct, and pragmatic approach.

Nariaki confirmed his interest in hearing the best ideas, no matter the rank of their source, by promoting able men to his administration. Most notably, this meant promoting a number of the low-ranking samurai who had supported his succession. This group, numbering about sixty or so, were predominantly lower ranked, and removed from the traditional corridors of power in the domain administration. Most prominent in this group were the more radically inclined students of Fujita Yūkoku, such as Tōko and Seishisai, but there were also a number of more moderate reformers, identifying with the Tachihara Suiken faction.[24] Nariaki appointed young reformers to various posts in his government, most notably the rural district administrators (*kōribugyō*), and also as advisors and policymakers in both Edo and Mito. He also solicited a number of direct memorials from low-ranked retainers, bypassing the traditional political hierarchy. These memorials allowed reformists from both radical and moderate camps to propose changes to Mito's government and make the case for their particular reform visions. In this way, even without holding down posts in the upper ranks of the government, the young reformers were able to influence Nariaki's reform agenda.

Seishisai was among those who submitted memorials. Seishisai's assessment of Mito's reform priorities hewed closely to the issues he had raised in the *New Theses*, including the restoration of samurai vigor, the importance of moral leadership, and the need to strengthen civil government.[25] In the years that followed, he urged Nariaki to implement educational reforms that would cultivate the literary and military skills of Mito's samurai, which he argued were indispensable to the restoration of samurai government.[26] He also advocated religious reforms that gave Shintō greater weight in politics, at the expense of powerful Buddhist sects. In addition to soliciting policy proposals from Seishisai, Nariaki briefly appointed Seishisai as a rural administrator, where he was supposed to put his reform ideas into practice. This did not go well—Seishisai found it difficult to challenge entrenched interests, and he lacked managerial skills—and he returned to academic work after just a year. But he continued to support Nariaki's reform program and wrote extensively on ways to implement the spiritual, military, and economic changes necessary to strengthen Mito.

Tōko's early proposals illustrate how he sought to use reforms to seize political power within Mito from the traditional establishment. First and foremost was the importance of putting capable administrators with reformist goals into power. His first proposal to Nariaki emphasized the importance of placing "righteous men" (*seigi no jinbutsu*) in power. He identified the traditional establishment as a major obstacle to any reforms and, therefore, the first target for Nariaki's incoming administration. Not only were many of Mito's elites self-interested and corrupt, decades of conservative rule had "completely destroyed morals and discipline, impoverished samurai and commoner alike, depleted the domain's finances, and diminished the domain."[27] The first step in tackling these problems, Tōko argued, was to break the elite stranglehold on government, particularly by kicking out the half-dozen or so "evil men" who represented the worst of the pernicious conservatism at the top of Mito domain. In their stead, Tōko argued, Nariaki should promote men of talent, regardless of their status or rank, in order to carry out the "great work" of reform. Tōko even suggested two reformists as ideal choices: Kawase Shichirōemon and Seishisai. Seishisai needed no introduction, of course, as his reputation for a sharp intellect and smart policy proposals was well established. Kawase, on the other hand, was not a good scholar, but he was extremely good at putting ideas into practice. He grasped problems quickly and was an effective decision-maker. The two men complemented each other, in Tōko's view, by combining the power of academic analysis with effective administrative and political leadership.[28] Tōko's vision of leadership was already becoming clear: in contrast to the emphasis on moral leadership and ethical cultivation during the early years of Mito Domain, he advocated a more muscular approach to politics, one that was uncompromising in its goals and methods. He aimed to sweep away the traditional establishment, and with it the many woes affecting Mito and its people, in order to establish a spiritually, militarily, and economically strengthened domain that would serve as a model for Japan.

Perhaps unsurprisingly, he volunteered himself as an example of a righteous leader, and in the spring of 1830, he took up a post as district administrator for the Hatta region, about twenty-five kilometers north of the castle town. Mito's reformists strongly believed in the importance of the rural economy, and since the time of Tachihara Suiken's pro-natal policies had advocated increased surveillance and supervision of village life. Tōko travelled around his district, interrogating headmen to determine their character and urging them to crack down on luxury and decadence in their villages.[29] He also built a series of granaries to help control food prices and encouraged village headmen to promote agriculture. While these methods were hardly revolutionary or unique to Mito, they were framed as part of the longstanding efforts in Mito to overturn a century of population decline and reinvigorate rural life.[30] In this regard, the Tenpō efforts marked a continuation of reform policies introduced under Suiken.

Tōko quickly discovered, however, that direct oversight of rural areas meant being away from the center of political power in the castle town. In Hatta, the office for the district intendant was a simple building with a thatched roof, containing a kitchen and two six-mat tatami rooms, perhaps three hundred square feet in all—quarters just about suitable for a young bachelor on temporary assignment. Tōko was immediately overworked: "doing even the smallest tasks, the equivalent of chopping up a chicken, feels like butchering a whole cow," he complained to a friend six months into his post.[31] Such a workload left little time to develop reform policies for the domain. Tōko soon proposed a consolidation of the district administrators and a relocation of their offices to the castle town. In the late fall of 1830, Nariaki agreed to Tōko's proposal as part of a sweeping overhaul of Mito officialdom that put many reformists into power. Tōko was appointed as administrator for the larger Ōta district, which made up more than a quarter of Mito's territory and included 126 villages. The district office was located in the castle town, and Tōko returned there in the second month of 1831. Tōko felt much happier about this move back from the countryside: "gazing at the buildings and garden, it felt like meeting an old friend."[32] Shortly after returning to the castle town, Tōko married Sato, the daughter of one of his fellow district administrators. He settled into his new job, which involved managing a large staff and attending frequent meetings at the castle. The comfort of home no doubt supported his professional ambitions.

Once again close to the domain government and his fellow reformers, Tōko continued to agitate for the promotion of reformist officials. Perhaps unsurprisingly, Nariaki faced significant resistance from the traditional establishment. The establishment tried to prevent the appointment of reformers, or to reassign them to less influential posts. In response, Tōko and his reformist colleagues hardened their resolve against the establishment, suggesting that opposition to the elites was inevitable in the name of reform. He sent angry letters to Nariaki about personnel changes with which he disagreed, including a failure to promote Seishisai. Tōko persuaded the other district intendants to join him in petitioning Nariaki to appoint more reformists to various positions. Nariaki, however, responded with a stern warning for the intendants to focus on district administration, not meddle in personnel appointments elsewhere in the domain government. Nariaki's admonition infuriated Tōko. Claiming illness, he stopped going to work in the second month of 1832. Nariaki tried to placate him, urging him to focus his energy on the job he had been assigned. Rather than mollify the pouting Tōko, this just made him even angrier.

Perhaps most corrosively, the pro- and anti-reform factions grew increasingly vitriolic in their descriptions of one another. Tōko began referring to the reformists as "righteous," in contrast to the "degenerate" establishment. In turn the establishment began to refer to the reformists as *tengu*, a kind of mountain demon, perhaps to disparage their upstart ways and tendency toward arrogance.[33] These epithets, moreover, quickly turned from labels affixed to policies and principles into smears of personalities and characters. The political debates around Nariaki's succession had quickly become personal, revealing deep animosity between the reform administration and the traditional establishment. In the fourth month of 1832, Tōko submitted an angry memorandum to Nariaki, outlining the problems affecting Mito's government. The biggest problem remained the endemic opposition to reforms among senior officials. He excoriated their decadence, lack of self-control, and unwillingness to correct "outdated beliefs." Only by changing the system of government appointments to a more meritocratic system, ending the factional disputes among scholars, and focusing on moral improvement could Nariaki "bring good government to Mito, and thereby strengthen Japan."[34] Nariaki did not change his mind based on Tōko's memorandum; instead, he decided it was time to get Tōko out of Mito for a while. He promoted him to a job in Mito's headquarters in Edo, where Tōko moved in the summer of 1832.

In Edo, Tōko became one of Nariaki's closest aides, and in that role, he continued to target the traditional establishment. He helped draft Nariaki's edicts to his retainers, emphasizing the importance of moral behavior and open communication from low-ranking samurai directly to Nariaki. He developed plans to tackle Mito's fiscal woes by eliminating supplemental payments to Mito's highest-ranked retainer, and more generally targeting the expensive lifestyles of elite retainers.[35] In 1834, he set his sights on the powerful Buddhist temples that, despite two centuries of efforts to limit Buddhism in Mito, remained influential. He proposed relocating a number of samurai to the area around the Mito Tokugawa mausoleum in Ōta, which would enable the domain to take control of this sacred site away from local temples. This relocation was also designed to reduce the number of samurai in need of high stipends for expensive urban life.[36] Finally, he continued to urge Nariaki to promote his fellow reformers.[37]

Alongside the fight against the traditional elite, Tōko tackled a more delicate problem: the latent factionalism within the reformist coalition. The roots of this factionalism dated back to the academic dispute between Tachihara Suiken and Fujita Yūkoku (see chapter 2). Tōko criticized this dispute, arguing that it eroded the quality of academic work in the Shōkōkan.[38] After his father's death, Tōko had made amends with the Tachihara family, and he spoke highly of men from both factions who had joined together to push for Nariaki's appointment as daimyo in 1829.[39] In practice, however, it proved difficult to avoid disputes within this coalition as academic disagreements spilt over into policy debates. The first two years of Nariaki's regime witnessed the fraying of the reformist coalition, as more moderate figures began to ally with the traditional establishment against some of the reformers' more radical and fast-paced changes.[40]

The most prominent member of the moderate group of reformers was Komiyama Fūken, whose incrementalist and bottom-up approach to change often sat at odds with Tōko's top-down approach. Fūken, the son of a low-ranking samurai retainer and the daughter of a farming family, charted a familiar course for Mito's best and brightest, excelling in school before becoming a pupil of Tachihara Suiken in the Shōkōkan. He was close to both

Figure 4.2. Portrait of Komiyama Fūken
(Ibaraki Prefectural Archives and Museum)

Suiken and to Fujita Yūkoku, but he soon decided to put his academic skills to practical use, and he left the Shōkōkan to become a district administrator in 1799. He remained in that position for twenty-one years, and by all accounts was a devoted official. He believed firmly that the cure for Mito's rural ills lay in improving the morals and livelihoods of the domain's rural residents through education and reform. He was an ardent anti-infanticide campaigner, distributing posters and other manifestos to local villagers and sharing them with his teacher, Suiken. He even went so far as to make picture books for illiterate or semi-literate farmers, exhorting them to avoid gambling, try new cultivation methods, and stop practicing infanticide.[41] Through this experience in the field, Fūken developed a pragmatic, down-to-earth approach to reform.

Fūken joined Tōko and other radicals to put Nariaki in power in 1829, but once in Nariaki's administration, Fūken's incremental approach began to diverge from Tōko's centralizing impulses. This played out during the debate over reforming the district administrator system, when Fūken argued in favor of keeping administrators close to villagers in order to cultivate the support of wealthy farmers and other rural elites. Tackling rural depopulation, declining tax revenue, and the commercialization of village life would be more effective if done at a smaller, more local scale. It also meant working from the bottom up, in incremental steps, seeking compromise and support in order to prevent anger and unrest.[42]

This tension between moderates and radicals played out throughout the 1830s and into the 1840s. Nariaki, hearing of the dispute among the district administrators, feared that they would cause his entire reform agenda to falter. He singled out the "Fujita faction" for its dogmatism and bade them exercise self-restraint.[43] But these tensions were not, at least yet, irreconcilable. Many of the ideological programs associated with Tōko and the radicals, such as military preparations, education reform, and rural administration, reflected the influence of moderate reformers. In other cases, such as efforts to address economic issues within the castle town, attempts to reach a compromise delayed or undermined the reform agenda. The complex interplay between moderate and radical proposals hints at the changing political dynamics within Mito Domain, and Tōko's efforts to seize more power for the young, low-ranking reformist movement.

Meanwhile, Nariaki did not just want to effectively administrate a reform agenda; he also sought to define himself as a "benevolent ruler," and thereby inspire his retainers to regain their morale and energy as the ruling class. Although he openly appealed to the ideals of the early Tokugawa era, holding up Mitsukuni's reign as a prelapsarian Golden Age of enlightened leadership, in practice, Nariaki's style of governance reflected an emerging idea that "enlightened rule" meant the effective deployment of political power, rather than the moral cultivation of the leader.[44] He drew legitimacy from the familiar concepts of samurai statecraft, but he pushed the boundaries of those concepts by intervening more forcefully in the lives of his subjects, both commoners and retainers, whether through strict behavioural restrictions, new forms of welfare and taxation, or new institutions for education and military training. These efforts reshaped Mito's political landscape by opening up political participation to a wider group of samurai, but they also destabilized the traditional political order. Reform could be a perilous business.

By the middle of 1832, Nariaki had grown frustrated with the slow pace of change due to factional squabbling and establishment obstruction, and he decided to make his first formal trip to Mito to take personal charge of the reform movement. Because of Mito's fiscal straits, domain officials had to raise money from merchants and wealthy farmers to pay for the trip, and Nariaki insisted upon a stripped-down itinerary to cut costs and demonstrate the importance of austerity. He also hoped to model the ideal samurai lifestyle: simple clothes and food, a lack of pretense, and earnest devotion to one's duties. It would be much easier to persuade officials in Mito of the importance of these efforts in person, as well as to gain a clearer understanding of the matters facing his realm. Nariaki arrived in Mito on 1833/3/5 and spent his first month in Mito inspiring his retainer band to take up the cause of reform.

Late in the third month, Nariaki issued the *Kokushihen* (*Declaration of Intent*), a manifesto that neatly summed up many of the dominant threads of Mito thought, including the sacred origins of Japan's imperial line, the need to defend the nation by strengthening the shogunate, and a commitment to Confucian ideals of loyalty, filial piety, and social hierarchy. Nariaki explained that samurai needed to learn these values in order to fulfill their role as rulers. In order to do so, they had to devote themselves equally to both academic learning and martial training. Nariaki went on to express his disappointment that Mito's samurai had failed to take their education seriously. Instead, they passed off others' ideas as their own, without thinking deeply about them. Rather than engage in honest and direct conversations with their friends and colleagues, they used false flattery and insincere praise to paper over problems. Dilettantes collected helmets or swords or longbows but did not maintain a full set of armor or weapons to go into battle. Members of various martial arts guilds competed with one another but failed to develop well-rounded skills. For generations, samurai had observed the domain's prohibition on sumptuous clothes and excessive partying largely in the breach. Many were drinking too much and then getting into loud and embarrassing fights. Rather than use their stipends to put their children in school, higher-ranking samurai spent them on brothel visits and theatre performances.[45] Nariaki ended his manifesto on a sorrowful note, complaining that, despite a brief burst of enthusiasm after his succession, few of his retainers were now sending him proposals for new reforms. Nevertheless, he hoped that they would take to heart his vision: that only through strong bonds of seniority and friendship, forged through honesty and loyalty, could the domain's samurai emerge as a worthy governing class. To develop those bonds, they needed to study the moral values that underpinned them.

Response to the *Kokushihen* was cautiously optimistic about its potential to inspire Mito's samurai to take their jobs more seriously. Komiyama Fūken hoped that it would energize lazy officials, but he warned that the problem was not one of theory but, rather, one of practice. Fundamentally, it was not that young samurai did not understand the principle of studying both literary and martial arts; rather, it was that they lacked stamina, dedication, and care.[46] This view, coming from the by-then elderly Fūken, may have been unusually disgruntled, but a general sense that Mito's young samurai lacked rigorous training led Nariaki to begin discussions about building a new domain academy. Nariaki also introduced a number of programs to boost samurai skills and consolidated the many martial arts guilds in Mito to get rid of more esoteric, impractical skills in favor of more sensible ones, such as shooting, archery, and horseback riding.[47] Finally, Nariaki tried to improve his retainers' attitudes toward their role as a ruling class. In the *Kokushihen*, he urged his retainers to respect the hard work of farmers that made it possible for them to eat rice every day. In this vein, he created tiny dolls of farmers, which he distributed to the women and children in his household. These farmer dolls were supposed to remind them of the sacrifices that supported their livelihoods.[48]

Nariaki's energetic efforts during his first visit to Mito earned him praise from reformers, but they ruffled more than a few feathers among the traditional elite. That elite, largely based in Edo, had many friends in the shogunate, including the *rōjū* Mizuno Tadaakira. On 1833/12/28, Mito's senior retainers received a formal warning from the shogunate about the "poor spirits among Mito's people," a signal that Nariaki's reforms were causing discontent. Fūken blamed the radical faction of reformers for turning every issue into a fight about principle, an unfortunate spillover from the theoretical debates of the academic classroom.[49] The radicals did not even mention the warning, perhaps a reflection of their embarrassment.[50] Although Mizuno died just two months later, leaving the shogunate in the hands of men friendlier to Mito, the warning emboldened the traditional elite and slowed the pace of Nariaki's reforms. Nariaki returned to Edo in the spring of 1834.

THE TENPŌ FAMINE AND
REFORMS IN TOWN AND COUNTRY

In the *Kokushihen*, Nariaki focused on the spirit and morals of his samurai retainers. But samurai made up only part of Mito's population, and urgent concerns about the state of Mito's commoner population were quick to rise to his attention after his arrival in Mito in 1833. In fact, the first matter of business to come before him on the very same day he arrived was a concern from Fūken, who was serving as the town magistrate. Fūken argued to Nariaki that disagreements between the town magistrates and the rural intendants (including Tōko) were preventing the efficient resolution of problems. In concrete terms, this included the question of how to oversee and manage day laborers, who tended to live in nearby villages but come into the castle town for work.[51] More generally, the castle town was struggling with high poverty and dissolute morals. This was not a new complaint: Tachihara Suiken had also worried about the growing inequality between poor townspeople and a wealthy merchant elite, and stern rejoinders against luxury, gambling, and other forms of frivolity had been staple features on the town noticeboard since the eighteenth century. The accumulated dislocations of an increasingly commercial, archipelago-wide economy were a major source of Mito's ills, and these changes needed new governmental structures to address them. Fūken, ever the pragmatist, suggested a regular meeting of the various magistrates to discuss issues that spanned their geographic or institutional remits, although it is unclear whether this in fact ever happened.[52] Nevertheless, this issue encapsulated the thorny challenges facing Nariaki: factional disputes plaguing his young administration, long-standing economic and social issues, and the sheer logistical complexity of running a reform government.

The castle town and its woes proved particularly challenging for the reform administration. The town had been struggling for decades, losing population while dealing with corrupt local officials, rising inequality between wealthy merchants and poorer commoners, economic competition from suburban and rural merchants and manufacturers, and rising poverty rates. By 1833, the commoner population had shrunk to seven thousand people, roughly two-thirds the size at its peak a century earlier. Central Mito was a patchwork of empty houses and abandoned properties, some of which had been turned over to vegetable gardens.[53] During the 1830s, a new, consolidated town government was put in place, with the goal of making administration simpler and more transparent. Alongside administrative reforms, the domain also cracked down on the culture of consumption and entertainment that was a feature of urban life, particularly among wealthy merchants. A series of edicts in the 1830s banned luxury of all kinds and imposed strict rules on everything from clothing to housebuilding.[54] Domain officials reminded everyone that restaurants were only for the use of travellers and, even then, no semblance of entertainment should take place within them. Under no circumstances should Mito's residents be going out to eat![55]

Mito's urban elite did not take kindly to these efforts to improve their lives, and they lobbied against measures that threatened to undermine their livelihoods. In response, the domain banned merchants from other domains from trading in Mito, and they reformed financial regulations to make it easier for merchants and artisans to finance their businesses. They offered relief for poor townspeople, and tried to control prices, particularly for rice. These efforts largely failed: powerful merchants from Edo and elsewhere easily avoided the regulations put in place in Mito, and many wealthy castle-town merchants simply started trading from nearby villages. These policies were also fundamentally at odds with the simultaneous efforts to promote agriculture by cracking down on urban life, adding to chaos and confusion in the castle town during this period.[56]

The reformers met with greater success in the countryside, but only after considerable debate. Tōko's goals ranged widely and built upon a legacy of rural reform proposals among Mito's reformers, dating back to the late eighteenth century. They included the selection of more talented local officials, regulations to reduce consumption and luxury, and a series of economic interventions designed to improve agricultural productivity. Tōko strongly disapproved of the commercialization of the rural economy and sought to stamp out cash crops and other forms of commerce. Here, however, he faced resistance from Komiyama Fūken, who argued that cracking down on cash farming would dispirit entrepreneurial farmers and further depress the rural economy. Fūken was able to persuade Nariaki on this point: when Tōko proposed closing down rural sake brewers to focus rice production on food supply, Fūken argued that such a closure would mean the loss of a large source of demand for Mito's rice, flooding the market and pushing down prices, adding hardships to farmers.[57] Fūken also raised a familiar issue that, in his view, had been a moral stain and economic impediment for years: the practice of infanticide. Although efforts since the late eighteenth century had helped slow the practice, Fūken urged Nariaki to devote moral and monetary energy to supporting families with children. Not only would this stamp out one of Mito's distinctive "evil customs," it would help revive Mito's economy by creating more workers.[58] Although infanticide had been a regular topic for Mito's nineteenth-century reformers, it became more urgent in the summer of 1833 as terrible weather and poor harvests signaled the onset of a serious famine.

Heavy storms devastated northeastern Japan in the summer of 1833, causing flooding and severe crop failures. Word of peasant uprisings in response to rising prices reached Mito by late 1833. That fall, half of the townspeople in the Lower Town requested food assistance. Harvests improved the next two years, but 1836 saw another round of bad weather and bad harvests. The domain's tax revenues fell to a quarter of their normal amount, a sign of the devastation in rural areas. In the winter of 1837, two thousand townspeople requested food assistance. In 1838, another crop failure led to one of the worst years of famine across eastern Japan.[59] The domain officially reported zero famine deaths, although Komiyama Fūken privately noted that many such deaths were attributed to illness, rather than famine, in order to prevent public unrest.[60] In reality, starving commoners, including many refugees from further north, died in villages and the castle town. A series of fires in towns around the domain led to suspicions of arson by angry refugees.[61]

The onset of famine required urgent measures from Nariaki's administration, but it also provided an opportunity to demonstrate "benevolent rule"—and persuade recalcitrant elites to accept reforms. During the summer of 1833, with reports of harvest failure reaching Mito from domains to the north, Nariaki ordered a ban on sake brewing to preserve rice supplies.[62] After a bad storm late in the eighth month, he toured the domain to inspect damage, and issued bans on cash crop cultivation as well as plans for tax relief and emergency grain storage.[63] In addition to the domain's existing emergency granaries, Tōko introduced a supplementary granary system to smooth prices and mitigate the worst of the rice shortages. To encourage mutual support, the domain dangled the promise of a status promotion to reward wealthy villagers who helped others. Distributing rice to starving peasants was as good a demonstration of benevolent government as anything, and helped garner support for the reform administration in later years.[64] Nariaki established a fund for childrearing support for poor townsmen, and instructed the town magistrates to gather local midwives for a moral lesson in the evils of infanticide.[65] Moreover, the belt-tightening necessary to get Mito through lean years offered a good opportunity to persuade Mito's traditional establishment to accept cost-cutting measures, such as sumptuary restrictions and cuts to the number of servants in each household.[66] The challenges of famine years distracted from some of Nariaki's grander ambitions, such as building his new academy, but in the end, Mito weathered these years better than it had the great famines of the eighteenth century. The domain's success earned praise from elsewhere in Japan. One Edo broadsheet ranked various domains on the success of their famine policies; Mito got top marks.[67] Good harvests returned in 1839, and Mito slowly recovered.

Nariaki's program to love Mito's people was not purely altruistic: it also reflected his anxiety about potential popular unrest. Even before his first visit to Mito, there were signs that Nariaki's reforms might cause discontent among commoners. Early efforts at rural reforms met with fierce resistance from local villagers, who distrusted the new officials.[68] As Nariaki prepared his first visit, Fūken warned him that his plans to cancel the traditional gift of sake to the town elders risked angering the entire population of townspeople, a threat significant enough to worry the town magistrate's office about their ability to keep matters under control.[69] By the end of that visit, soaring rice prices had produced unrest in Ōtsu, in far northern Mito, and Fūken urged Nariaki to act quickly to prevent any uprisings by angry villagers targeting rice merchants. During the worst years of the Tenpō Famine, refugees from northern Japan flowed into Mito, raising tensions and leading the domain to order all outsiders expelled from the domain.[70] Nariaki also kept nervous tabs on large rural uprisings in Kai Province in 1836, for instance, which were just one of "a wave of unprecedented popular protest" across Japan in response to economic problems and famine.[71] In 1837, a disgruntled samurai named Ōshio Heihachirō led an uprising in Osaka, burning much of the city to the ground. Nariaki could not take for granted the support (or at least the acquiescence) of his own subjects.

In the end, though, it was precisely Nariaki's actions to stave off famine and prevent similar unrest from spreading to Mito that helped consolidate support for his reform agenda and prevented popular unrest. In addition to ordering Fujita Tōko to implement various rural reforms and relief measures Nariaki dispatched personal emissaries to other domains to ask for rice aid, limiting food shortages.[72] He also cultivated local elites and priests to prevent localized discontent from growing into larger movements and introduced greater surveillance of villages. This carrot-and-stick approach to local politics worked. The relative success of famine relief policies helped persuade villagers of the value of Nariaki's reform agenda, and Mito saw no major uprisings during this period.

The reformers' efforts to demonstrate good governance during times of famine no doubt helped the domain weather the famines of the 1830s, but they came at a serious political cost. To cope with plummeting tax revenue, the domain administration halved the stipends of Mito's samurai—and then halved them again. Government offices had their budgets slashed. In normal times samurai may have put up with these cuts as a form of collective sacrifice, but Tōko's reform efforts included additional reductions to samurai income, compounding the cuts and creating an obvious source of resentment. In 1837, at the height of the famine, he proposed ending the practice of paying samurai a stipend, instead returning to a direct fief system whereby their income was calculated from specific land holdings. This would help keep the domain's budget in balance and give samurai—many of whom spent much of their lives in Edo—a greater sense of connection to the domain.[73] However, in years of poor harvests, this meant serious losses for samurai, as the Tenpō crises made clear. In response to strong resistance from his retainers, Nariaki quietly tabled Tōko's proposal.[74]

REFORMING THE SHOGUNATE

Despite the ongoing hardships caused by famine and the resistance of many samurai to new policies, Nariaki, Tōko, and their reform-minded peers continued to pursue their agenda. From the late 1830s into the early 1840s, they introduced major new reform programs, increased their attacks on Mito's conservative establishment, and created new bodies of political support. Although moderates shaped the course of many of these reforms, eventually Tōko and more radical reformers consolidated power within the reform administration. The reformers succeeded in implementing a number of their ideological goals, mobilizing pro-reform samurai, and nurturing political subjectivity among a rural elite that was gradually incorporated into the domain's political and educational institutions. The reformers also looked beyond Mito and began to push for reforms at the level of the shogunate, complementing their calls for military reform and the colonization of Ezochi (see chapter 3). These actions also marked the next phase in a political project to strengthen Nariaki's role and the position of the reformist coalition—although their actions also heightened discontent among the traditional establishment, sowing the seeds of a major backlash against the Nariaki regime

The reformers agonized about losing momentum for their agenda as the Tenpō Famine dragged on. Early in 1836, Tōko and Nariaki hatched a plan to call the bluff of reluctant retainers. Nariaki locked himself into his rooms and refused to attend New Year's ceremonies. He told his officials that he was considering resigning because of their failure to support his reform agenda. This was a thinly veiled threat: if he resigned, high-ranking aides would suffer severe punishment for having failed to support their lord.[75] The gamble worked. Nariaki's finance officials agreed to a wide-ranging plan to cut costs: ten years of austerity budgeting, a reduction in support for families and servants of samurai on official business, a decrease in the size of the women's quarters of the daimyo's household, and an end to the permanent stationing of Mito's samurai in Edo. These measures met with loud protests, and ultimately, they failed to fix Mito's fiscal problems, but they nevertheless dealt a serious blow to the traditional establishment and marked a victory for Tōko and his reformist allies.

Emboldened, in 1837 Nariaki and Tōko revived and extended their reform agenda, outlining the four major proposals that have featured so prominently in studies of Mito's Tenpō Reforms: a comprehensive land survey; the resettlement of samurai in rural areas; the establishment of a domain school; and the end of the permanent residence of Mito's daimyo in Edo. Tōko's signature achievement was the land survey, which began in 1840. His goal was to create an accurate assessment of Mito's agricultural productivity and thereby rebalance the domain's budgets. He also aimed to tackle the problem of inequality in the domain by identifying and taxing more productive fields at a higher rate. These fields had largely fallen into the hands of wealthy landlords, whose concentrated assets gave them power and influence over the poor tenant farmers who were an increasingly large percentage of the rural population. Tōko, like other radicals, believed that a top-down rectification of the land system was the essential first step to solving these problems.

Unsurprisingly, moderates like Komiyama Fūken disagreed with Tōko's approach, arguing that it made more sense to judiciously lower excessive taxes to encourage work, and to introduce childrearing subsidies, moral education, and infanticide regulations.[76] Fūken opposed Tōko's land survey, warning that it might trigger uncontrollable uprisings and presciently arguing that it would fail to address the real problem of reduced tax revenue while allowing wealthier farmers to consolidate their control over good land. In the end, Tōko recognized the futility of imposing the survey by fiat. In order to head off almost certain opposition, domain officials decided early on to gain the support of local elites—the landlords, wealthy farmers, and other local notables who dominated Mito's villages. Negotiations with these elites led to compromises on who would supervise the surveys, how to categorize the productivity of the land, and even the length of the measuring rods used, but the domain secured the grudging support of villagers.[77]

The short-term results of the survey were disheartening, but they did produce a silver lining in the form of a new political alliance in support of reform. The amount of cultivated land in Mito was nearly a quarter less than official estimates. From the domain's perspective, this fact was mitigated by the fact that much of the land was more productive than previously thought, meaning there was no significant change to tax revenues. But for farmers, the survey was mostly bad news. Rich farmers whose holdings had grown over time were now slapped with greatly increased tax bills after years of paying tax on much lower assessments. Poor farmers generally saw only minuscule decreases in their tax burdens. "The rich peasants are bitter, the poor peasants are not particularly happy, and the overall resources of the domain have been reduced," Tōko reflected glumly. Nevertheless, he still considered the survey an important first step toward reestablishing balance and good governance in Mito.[78] Moreover, the survey had a long-term effect that proved to be politically valuable for Tōko. Although wealthy farmers did see sudden tax increases, the survey confirmed their rights to the high-quality lands they had amassed over the years. Astute local elites recognized this potential, and they also extracted samurai titles and other privileges in exchange for supporting the survey process. These local notables, scattered across the Mito countryside, began to form a powerful alliance with the reformist wing of the domain government.[79]

In the castle town, the most significant component of the 1837 reform program was the construction of a new school: the Kōdōkan. Through the Kōdōkan, Nariaki sought to train his retainer band to be better leaders by applying the ideals of the Late Mito School. In practical terms, this meant following the example of Tokugawa Ieyasu, who "quelled the troublesome and put them on a righteous path," and "revered the emperor and expelled the barbarian. He did so through both martial and academic skill."[80] In other words, Mito's samurai should learn how to prevent (or suppress) unrest, develop a firm appreciation for the virtues of imperial loyalty, and fiercely protect Japan from foreign threats. The Kōdōkan grounds, located next to Mito Castle, contained buildings for teaching as well as shrines to both Confucius and Shintō deities, reflecting the Late Mito School's emphasis on the "unity of Confucian and Shintō thought" (*shinju itchi*). Large training grounds for archery and other martial arts emphasized the principle that "academic and martial arts cannot be separated" (*bunbu wakarezu*). The Kōdōkan also embodied the belief that education went hand in hand with governance, and many high-ranking domain officials had jobs at the school. Aizawa Seishisai served as headmaster, overseeing a reformist curriculum that taught the unity of filial duty and loyalty (*chūkō futatsu to nashi*), and the principle that "one should not discriminate between the value of academic study and practical work" (*gakumon jigyō sono kō koto ni subekarazu*).[81] All retainers were required to send their sons to the Kōdōkan, and close to 90 percent of them did so, a sign of Nariaki's success in consolidating power. The school was less successful at persuading its students to study both academic and military arts with equal enthusiasm: the young men of Mito had a decided preference for martial arts.[82] Nevertheless, the school was considered a promising start, and several branch schools opened in rural towns to serve commoners seeking a similar education.[83]

Nariaki's vision for the Kōdōkan included a counterpart at the edge of town: the sprawling gardens of the Kairakuen, designed to complement the rigors of the Kōdōkan with a space for students to rest after exerting themselves in study or military training. The complex included groves of cherry and plum trees, as well as a wooded area and bamboo groves. A pavilion for poetry reading and parties perched on the edge of the bluff, overlooking Lake Senba to the south. There were also testing grounds for tea and mulberry bushes, hinting at the pragmatic streak that ran throughout the Tenpō reforms. Unusually for a Tokugawa-era lord, Nariaki also opened these gardens to Mito's commoners, arguably making the Kairakuen Japan's first public park. Nariaki worked hard to demonstrate his commitment to his subjects' welfare and recognizing their role as fundamental members of the domain. He reshaped the castle town in pursuit of his political agenda, inscribing his values and vision onto the urban landscape.

The renewed reform agenda polarized Mito's samurai class. In 1839, more than seventy members of Mito's traditional establishment had signed an unprecedented petition urging Nariaki to retract some of his reforms and delay a trip to the domain. Others bristled at Nariaki's austerity measures and at the promotion of men like Tōko to high positions. Nevertheless, in 1840 Nariaki promoted a number of reformists to positions historically reserved for the traditional establishment. Tōko was appointed chamberlain (*sobayōnin*), a dizzying elevation for a man whose grandfather had peddled secondhand clothes. Several of his colleagues were promoted to Nariaki's council of elders, ruffling more than a few feathers among Mito's high-ranking families.[84] In the meantime, the moderate voices in the reform coalition were in retreat. Komiyama Fūken's reservations about Tōko's land reforms disappointed Nariaki, who began to ignore him; Fūken died in 1840, taking with him a key voice of moderation. Other members of the Tachihara faction, disillusioned by Tōko's radical approach, began to sympathize with the traditional establishment. Even as Tōko and the radical reformers grew more confident in their project, they were eliciting deeper and deeper resentment from the traditional elite.

Despite losing the goodwill of many members of the traditional establishment, Nariaki gained new supporters. The establishment of the Kōdōkan, alongside military reforms such as the mass hunting parties, inspired younger samurai, particularly those with radical sympathies. Nariaki's promotion of "revere the emperor, expel the barbarian" and other tenets of Mito scholarship gained him admirers in Mito's academic world. He also started to gain supporters among Mito's commoners. The most important of these were wealthy farmers, who supported the land survey and other agricultural reform efforts and, because they had access to education, were well acquainted with the work of Mito's reformist scholars.[85] These local elites became an important constituency of the rural schools around Mito, where they formed a block of "revere the emperor, expel the barbarian" adherents. Nariaki also supported religious reforms that promoted Shintō education and religion. These actions endeared him to Shintō priests around Mito, as well as to scholars of Kokugaku interested in studies of Japan's indigenous history and religious traditions.[86] Together, these groups formed a coalition of political support for Nariaki and his reform agenda and marked a shift in the balance of power within Mito'toward a younger, restless, and ambitious group of reform-minded samurai and commoners.

However, as part of his religious reforms Nariaki also ordered Tōko to reduce the influence of Buddhist temples, seen as a corrupting foreign presence. Although Mito had long kept its temples on a short leash, they were nevertheless powerful and well connected, especially to the shogunate in Edo. Influential priests and their allies began to sound the alarm in Mito and Edo about Tōko's aggressive attacks on their property and prestige. To make matters worse, Tōko continued to take a hard line against any hint of anti-reform backlash. When Nariaki promoted Yūki Toraju, the son of a powerful, establishment family, to a high-ranking role in his administration in 1843, Tōko threatened to resign. Nariaki tried to placate him with a raise, which Tōko frostily rejected as a thinly disguised bribe. Tōko stopped going to work, again claiming illness, and asked to be released from his positions. Incensed, Nariaki refused, and admonished Tōko: "Toraju comes from an exalted and high-ranking family that has served as senior retainers for generations, whereas you, Tōko, are only the second generation since your family was lifted out of townsman status." Clearly there were limits to Nariaki's willingness to rely on "men of talent" at the expense of hereditary elites—at the very least, he could not ignore altogether the traditional power and authority of Mito's high-ranking retainers.[87] While publicly these establishment retainers dared not challenge Nariaki and his allies, privately many of them resented the power and prestige granted to Tōko, as well as his uncompromising attitude.

While pursuing reforms and currying support within Mito, Nariaki and Tōko also began intervening in the politics of the shogunate. In 1838, upon the accession of the twelfth shogun, Ieyoshi, Nariaki had submitted to the shogunate a highly critical (and unsolicited) memorandum that outlined a series of problems, such as corruption, loose morals, foreign affairs, fiscal issues, and commercial extravagance, and offered his unvarnished opinion that Mito's example ought to inspire the shogun to adopt reforms. He emphasized the importance of selecting able men to serve as councilors and urged those leaders to gather advice directly from low-ranked samurai in order to get an accurate picture of affairs, and to avoid the scheming of high-ranking officials and the women's quarters.[88] He exhorted the shogunate's leadership to seize control of political decisions in order to tackle the "domestic ills and foreign threats" that endangered Tokugawa society.

Nariaki used both intrigue and persuasion to induce the shogunate to take up his call for reforms. Nariaki recommended several reformist officials to serve as chief councilors, and quickly secured the promotion of Sanada Yukitsura, the reformist daimyo of Matsushiro Domain, to the position of chief councilor. Nariaki justified his interference in the shogunate's personnel decisions by claiming that, as the daimyo of one of the three *gosanke* households, he had a special interest in the fate of the shogunate.[89] He also cultivated the support of Mizuno Tadakuni, a long-serving chief councilor, who had indicated some receptiveness to reform. Nariaki felt that Mizuno, a womanizer and gourmand, was entirely unsuited to being a leader, but Mizuno became chief councilor in 1839 and then, after the death of the retired shogun Ienari in 1841, he purged the shogunate and embarked on a reform program that lasted until his ouster in 1843. During this period, which coincided with the most intense period of reform within Mito, Nariaki wrote to him repeatedly with ideas for reforms, and grew to appreciate his leadership.[90] Although there is little evidence that the shogunate explicitly adopted Nariaki's ideas, Mizuno introduced a number of reforms that aligned with Mito's, including measures to boost rural population, rural administrative reforms, and religious consolidation.[91] Nariaki's proposals were also gathered and published for a general audience, suggesting a wide appetite for his ideas not just in Mito, but also across Japan.[92]

Unfortunately, Mizuno faced his own set of complex political factions, making his position a fragile one. Many of the shogunate's reforms were disruptive and unpopular, causing anger to spread. Despite a certain degree of support from Mizuno, the political environment for Nariaki in Edo and Mito remained fragile. On the one hand, his outspoken personality won him admirers, and his powerful position as the leader of a Tokugawa branch family gave him a platform to push for national reforms. But his aggressive approach and his attack on traditional power centers, whether in his own retainer band or at the level of national politics, made him many enemies, who were eagerly waiting for the opportunity to pounce.

The conditions were set for the fall of Mito's reform administration: a coalition of disgruntled opponents, tense relations with the shogunal authorities, and a number of disruptive reforms that could easily be used as evidence of unseemly ambition. The final blow came in 1843, when a rival factional of shogunal officials led by Abe Masahiro ousted Mizuno from power, paving the way for Mito's anti-reform factions to reassert themselves. It did not take long for them to take their revenge on Nariaki. In the fifth month of 1844, Nariaki was summoned to Edo, where he was greeted by a terse order from the shogunate to resign as daimyo of Mito. It was not unusual for the shogunate to order such punishments for lesser-ranked lords, but to do so to the leader of a powerful Tokugawa branch family had only rare precedent. He was ordered to hand over the position of daimyo to his eldest son, Yoshiatsu, then only twelve years old. The formal reasons for his dismissal were a litany of the negative effects of his reform efforts, revealing the anti-reform forces behind the shogun's decision: too many guns manufactured, too many military drills, the creation of military academies, overambitious religious reforms, a failure to cut spending, and arrogant plans for Ezochi (see chapter 3).[93] Nariaki offered a robust defense of these efforts, but it did not matter. The anti-reform officials did not intend to litigate the dismissal. Nariaki, forced into retirement and sentenced to house arrest in Edo, was left to fume at his loss of power. And with Nariaki went the entire reform administration. Tōko, Seishisai, and other officials were placed in house arrest or confinement, and the traditional establishment took power again.

THE LEGACIES OF THE TENPŌ REFORMS

For many years, scholars assumed that the Tenpō Reforms were a failure, both within Mito and in the shogunate.[94] And it is true that the backlash against them in 1844 halted or reversed many of the specific reform efforts. Nevertheless, the legacy of this work lived on in several important ways. First, their ideas found a strong following in other parts of Japan, inspiring a number of efforts to replicate or build upon Mito's reforms. Second, Mito's reformers—including Nariaki—found themselves back in power by the early 1850s, allowing them to restart many of their Tenpō-era efforts. And ultimately—as we will see in the next chapter—the Tenpō experience inspired Nariaki to push hard for the shogunate's Ansei Reforms in the mid-1850s. Within Mito, however, the revival of reforms during the 1850s also led to worsening factionalism and the collapse of effective domain government.

Mito's Tenpō Reforms had attracted outside attention almost from the very beginning. During the Tenpō period, several samurai from Kyushu domains visited Mito, keen to learn about Mito's reform project.[95] They returned home and tried to implement similar changes in their home domains. They were not always welcomed: in many places, conservative factions pushed back vigorously, as in Mito. But they largely succeeded in raising awareness of Mito's reform movement across the archipelago.[96] Perhaps the most notable was Murakami Kazuhiro from Kurume, who wrote an extensive account of his travels to Mito in 1843. This trip was part of an excursion to several northeastern domains to gather information about their administrative reforms, and reflected a growing interest in new forms of governance across Japan. In particular, Murakami pointed to the willingness of Mito's reformers to tackle underlying systemic issues, such as tax policy, military training, and hiring practices, rather than just the moral cultivation of the ruling class. He took away an important lesson: namely, the importance of revising policies and institutions to reflect new circumstances.[97] Moreover, Murakami and his lord, the tenth Kurume daimyo, Arima Yoritō, placed Mito's efforts within a longer sweep of domainal reform across Japan, including Kumamoto's Hōreki Reforms in the 1750s, Yonezawa's Meiwa-An'ei Reforms of the 1770s, and Mito's Tenpō Reforms. While often couched in traditionalist language, these reforms also contained important shifts toward more modern forms of governance and administration.[98] Seen from afar, Mito's reformism was part of a set of ideas for how to reform the Tokugawa political system in order to address the new crises of the nineteenth century. Institutional and systemic reforms were only part of this process, however, and as we shall see in the following chapter, new styles of leadership were also part of this story.

For Mito's reformers, the second half of the 1840s were a frustrating period of powerlessness and reversals. Although the shogunate relaxed their punishments relatively quickly, power in the domain remained in the hands of the anti-reform establishment. This remained a difficult period for Tōko, who was beset by hemorrhoids and other ailments contracted in Koishikawa. Tōko was finally set free in the second intercalary month of 1852, although with the conservatives still in power he did not return directly to politics. Instead he expanded his private academy, taking on thirty students, including several girls, by the following year. Tōko's classes included recitation and debate, primarily on the *Analects*.[99] In the senior classes, Tōko often hosted lecturers from other academies throughout Mito. He conducted debates about moral character and the state of politics, recreating a space for reformist politics within Mito even though he was shut out of formal government roles.

In Nariaki's case, meanwhile, his skillful mobilization of popular support quickly led to a robust exoneration movement. In the seventh month of 1844, a group of farmers travelled to Edo to protest Nariaki's innocence to influential daimyo of other domains. Former members of his reformist administration asked the shogunate for a pardon, with the most radical defying orders to stay in Mito and travelling to Edo, where they delivered petitions to the shogunal councilors. Groups of Shintō priests lobbied for Nariaki's exoneration. These actions alarmed Nariaki, who begged the domain administration to prevent such hotheaded acts, lest the shogunate punish Mito even more severely. For Nariaki, the fight for reform was less important than preserving the integrity of Mito. After taking the unimaginable step of forcing Nariaki out, who knew what the shogunate might do to the domain or his family next? Despite his concerns, his supporters in Mito continued to organize on his behalf, and in the tenth month of 1844, thousands of farmers from across Mito gathered together to demand his release. Other groups of villagers made plans to travel en masse to Edo to make their case. Rumors swirled that pro-reform samurai had forced the farmers to attend, and that may have been true for some villagers, but the size of the group, and their fervent demands, hints at the genuine support for Nariaki among villagers across Mito Domain.[100]

The agitation by Mito's commoners worried Abe Masahiro, who feared greater unrest in Mito. He released Nariaki late in the eleventh month, two hundred days after his arrest. Many of the pro-Nariaki farmers and samurai were punished for travelling to Edo, but this mostly served to mark them as true loyalists. These devoted reformers wasted little time in criticizing their moderate peers who had stood by, waiting to see how events ended up. But they directed their greatest anger at Mito's conservative establishment. The movement to free Nariaki had exposed and deepened the domain's ideological fault lines, which divided the reform wing into radical and moderate camps and set both those camps against an anti-reform establishment.

Although Abe had released Nariaki from confinement, he did not intend to allow him to interfere directly in Mito's fragile politics. The domain remained under the nominal control of the young Yoshiatsu, with actual power resting with a regency dominated by Mito's traditional, conservative establishment. These conservatives, stung by the actions of Nariaki's supporters and fearful of Nariaki's own actions, punished many reformers and even sent spies into Nariaki's household. Nariaki invented a secret code to write letters to his supporters, in which he decried the "evil men" in Mito's government, over and over again.[101] His supporters petitioned everyone they could: the leaders of Mito's branch households, other Tokugawa branch families, high-ranking shogunal officials, and the daimyo of other, unrelated domains. Yet none were willing to support Nariaki against the shogunate, no matter how sympathetic they were to his cause. Months turned into a year, and still Nariaki could not take part in politics.

In the summer of 1846, two foreign requests for trade persuaded Abe to reconsider his harsh stance against the Mito reformers. The first came from the French in the Ryukyus, and Abe tried to deal with it by instructing Satsuma Domain to handle the matter. This only served to enrage Nariaki, who accused Abe of weakness. The second incident was harder to deflect: the American Commander James Biddle sailed into Edo Bay, terrifying the city's residents and embarrassing the clearly unprepared shogunate. Abe realized that he could scarcely afford criticism, not least from Nariaki, who was widely respected for his views on defense. Abe decided to extend an olive branch to Nariaki, gradually relaxing the punishments on Mito reformists and engaging in energetic defensive preparations over the rest of the year. Between 1847 and 1852, Abe worked hard to improve relations between Mito and the shogunate by restoring Nariaki's reputation and intervening in Mito's government to limit the power of Mito's traditional establishment. In 1848, Abe directly criticized the establishment government in Mito, and reduced some of the punishments on Nariaki's supporters. In mid-1849, he permitted Nariaki to participate in domain politics again. In 1851, he quietly suggested that Mito's government punish the remaining establishment leaders, restoring the power of the reformist faction. Finally, in late 1852, Nariaki and Yoshiatsu were summoned to Edo Castle, marking a full reconciliation between the shogunate and Mito, and Nariaki's return to power as a retired daimyo.[102]

During the mid-1850s, the revival of reformist power meant the revival of many of the Tenpō Reforms in Mito: promotion based on merit, the expansion of the Kōdōkan, new military reforms and defensive preparations, the construction of naval ships, renewed attention to rural revitalization and controlling the commercial economy, and continued attempts to promote Shintō at the expense of Buddhist temples.[103] Although Tōko's focus was on foreign affairs, he was closely involved in these domain efforts, especially a project to mobilize farmers as soldiers for coastal defense.[104] Tōko's work demonstrated the continued salience of the Tenpō-era reform agenda into the 1850s. Nariaki, too, paid attention to domain reforms, particularly after 1855, when he resigned his position as a shogunal advisor. One notable accomplishment was the completion of the Kōdōkan campus in 1857, allowing the school to move out of its temporary quarters. Alongside the Kōdōkan, the domain opened a number of regional schools for relocated samurai and commoners.[105] He moved forward with ambitious changes, including the recruitment of commoners to a new military force (the first domain, along with Tosa, to do so), and the construction of a reverberatory furnace for weapons manu-facturing.[106] In comparison to the Tenpō era, this later period saw a greater emphasis on military reforms—unsurprising given the onslaught of gunboat diplomacy since Perry's arrival in 1853. Unfortunately, these reforms added considerably to domain spending and wrecked attempts to restore fiscal sol-vency. The domain tried to solve both these problems by offering commoners samurai status in exchange for a fee, but they found few eligible candidates.[107] Despite these shortcomings, the Tenpō reform vision continued to reshape Mito well into the 1850s.

But Nariaki's return to power did not soothe the antipathy between re-formists and the traditional establishment—if anything it served to further enrage the anti-reform forces. Nariaki cracked down on the conservative establishment, placing many of them under house arrest and removing others from office, generating resentment. Rumors swirled about a plot to drive a wedge between Nariaki and his son, the daimyo Yoshiatsu. More pragmati-cally, conservatives argued that Nariaki's rule was excluding a large number of Mito's retainers, making it unfair and one-sided. Amid this contentious period, on 1855/10/2 Tōko died during the Ansei Edo Earthquake. Nariaki was distraught, and the loss of Tōko threatened to undermine the reform-ist agenda within Mito. Around this time, Nariaki grew more paranoid. He started punishing establishment officials for fomenting factionalism and fail-ing to support his reforms. In spring of 1856, he executed one of the leaders of the conservative establishment, ostensibly for bribery and graft, but driven in part by rumors that he was plotting Nariaki's assassination. Nariaki undeni-ably proved his strength, but it was a rash move. Over the next few months, a series of arrests and punishments for other establishment samurai further exacerbated tensions between Mito's reformist and conservative factions.[108] The ugliness of this political factionalism quickly swallowed up the progress of reforms within Mito and left a much deeper scar on Mito society.

The reform movement that swept through Mito from the 1830s to the 1850s built on the work of earlier scholars, such as Tachihara Suiken and Fujita Yūkoku, as well as reformers in domains across Japan. The reformers sought to overhaul first Mito and then Japan in order to confront longstand-ing domestic problems and newfound foreign ones. Under the forceful and charismatic leadership of Tokugawa Nariaki and overseen by a group of in-fluential scholars, the reforms were part of a broader trend toward reinventing the structures and philosophy of rule in late Tokugawa Japan. No longer was moral cultivation and ethical leadership sufficient for benevolent rule; rather, reformers like Tōko and Nariaki sought to inspire their subjects to participate in politics. They placed ambitious and capable young men into power and formed groups of supporters among commoners and priests.

As Victor Koschmann and others have persuasively argued, this high-lights the power of Mito's ideas and reform activities as forms of ideology, qualifying individuals to act. But Mito's reforms also reflect the messy process of politics: the constant negotiation between rival reform factions, the challenge of matching ideals to on-the-ground reality, and the pervasive and chronic resistance to reforms by powerful and high-ranking establishment figures. Political ambitiousness also meant that Mito's reformers looked beyond Mito to reform Japan: far from treating the domain purely as a "microcosm" of their idealized country, they recognized and leveraged the power of the shogunate to further their own agendas, and insisted that their expertise and Mito's exalted status gave them the right to influence shogunal politics.[109] This, too, was a crucial legacy of the Mito reform movement, as it inspired other daimyo across Japan to begin seeking a greater say in national politics. In the aftermath of Commodore Matthew Perry's arrival in 1853, Nariaki was able to capitalize on Mito's reform experience and his own reputation as a foreign policy expert to lead a number of these great lords in a project to reshape the shogunate, putting Mito's reform values into practice on the national stage.

NOTES

1. H. D. Harootunian, *Toward Restoration: The Growth of Political Consciousness in Tokugawa Japan* (Berkeley: University of California Press, 1970), 48; J. Victor Koschmann, *The Mito Ideology: Discourse, Reform, and Insurrection in Late Tokugawa Japan, 1790–1864* (Berkeley: University of California Press, 1987), 27.

2. See, for example, Harold Bolitho, "The Tenpō Crisis," in *Cambridge History of Japan*, vol. 5, *The Nineteenth Century*, ed. Marius Jansen (Cambridge: Cambridge University Press, 1988), 116–67.

3. Isoda Michinori,"Mito-han tenpō kaikaku no dōjidaitekina hyōka to eikyō: shin shiryō 'Mito kenbunroku ron' no bunseki," *Ibaraki kenshi kenkyū* 95 (March 2011): 31–50; see also Mark Ravina, "Kindaika kindaisei to meikun no saikentō," *Rekishi hyōron* 717 (January 2010): 37–50 and Koseki Yūichirō, *"Meikun" no kinsei* (Tokyo: Yoshikawa kōbunkan, 2011).

4. Harootunian, *Toward Restoration*, 91–94; Koschmann, *The Mito Ideology*, 125.

5. For example, Conrad Totman, "Political Reconciliation in the Tokugawa Bakufu: Abe Masahiro and Tokugawa Nariaki, 1844–1852," in *Personality in Japanese History*, eds. Albert Craig and Donald Shively (Berkeley: University of California Press, 1970), 183; William G. Beasley, *Select Documents on Japanese Foreign Policy* (London: Oxford University Press, 1960), 11–15; Mark Ravina, *To Stand with the Nations of the World* (Oxford: Oxford University Press, 2017), 86.

6. Richard Chang, for instance, says Tōko's ideas "well represent bakumatsu xenophobia." Chang, "Fujita Tōko's Image of the West," *Journal of Asian History* 2,

no. 2 (1968): 130–40. See also Chang, *From Prejudice to Tolerance: A Study of the Japanese Image of the West, 1826–1864* (Tokyo: Sophia University, 1970).

7. Klaus Kracht provides a brief account of his life, based largely on Tōko's autobiography, in his study of Tōko's most famous work, the commentary on the *Kōdōkanki*. Klaus Kracht, *Das Kōdōkanki-jutsugi des Fujita Tōko (1806–1855): Ein Beitrag zum politischen Denken der Späten Mito-Schule* (Wiesbaden: Otto Harrassowitz, 1975).

8. This is due to the focus on intellectual history among scholars of Mito, including Koschmann in *The Mito Ideology* and Mark McNally in *Like No Other: Exceptionalism and Nativism in Early Modern Japan* (Honolulu: University of Hawai'i Press, 2016).

9. Aizawa Seishisai, *Rekkō gyōjitsu* (Tokyo: Tokugawa Akitake, 1874 [1861]).

10. Seya Yoshihiko, *Mito no Nariaki* (Mito: Ibaraki shinbunsha, 2000), 41–42.

11. Nagai Hiroshi, *Tokugawa Nariaki: fukakujitsu na jidai ni ikite* (Tokyo: Yamakawa shuppansha, 2019), 32.

12. For a discussion of these ills, see Suzuki Eiichi, *Fujita Tōko* (Tokyo: Yoshikawa kōbunkan, 1998), 45–46.

13. Ishikawa Seishū, *Mito kinen*, in *Ibaraki ken shiryō: kinsei seiji hen*, ed. Ibaraki kenshi hensan kinsei kinseishi dai 1 bukai (Mito: Ibaraki-ken, 1970), 1:648.

14. Fujita Tōko, *Kaitenshishi*, in *Fujita Tōko zenshū*, ed. Takasu Yoshijirō (Tokyo: Shōkasha, 1935), 1:14–38.

15. The role of Narinobu's will in determining Nariaki's succession sounds suspiciously convenient to some historians, given the highly fraught circumstances. The will itself has been lost, making it impossible to investigate its authenticity. *Mito shishi,* chū, vol. 3 (Mito: Mito shiyakusho, 1976), 19–20.

16. *Mito-han shiryō*, bekki (Tokyo: Yoshikawa kōbunkan, 1917), 1:35.

17. For details of the tensions and Nariaki's attempt to mollify both sides, see *Mito shishi*, chū, 3:21–25.

18. The phrase is from Suzuki, *Fujita Tōko*, 81.

19. These four topics were laid out in a memorial issued by Nariaki, but likely composed by Tōko, in 1837. See *Mito shishi*, chū, 3:60. They reflect longstanding priorities among Mito's scholars, including Aizawa Seishisai, who discussed many of these issues in *Shinron*.

20. Koschmann, *The Mito Ideology*, 84.

21. *Mito han shiryō*, bekki 1:312; see also Seya, *Mito no Nariaki*, 59–62.

22. "Fukusei jōken," 1829/1, *Ibaraki ken shiryō: kinsei seiji hen,* 1:170.

23. Nagai, *Tokugawa Nariaki*, 39.

24. *Mito shishi*, chū, 3:27–32.

25. Ami Takao, *Aizawa Seishisai no shōgai* (Tokyo: Kinseisha, 2016), 101–2.

26. Seya Yoshihiko, *Aizawa Seishisai* (Tokyo: Bunkyō shoin, 1942), 142–43.

27. Fujita Tōko, "Seigi no jinbutsu wo suisen suru ni tsuite," in Takasu, *Fujita Tōko zenshū*, 6:13.

28. Fujita Tōko, "Seiji no jinbutsu wo suisen suru ni tsuite," 16.

29. Suzuki, *Fujita Tōko*, 67–68.

30. See, for example, Nariaki's letter to district intendants on 1830/11/10, *Mito-han shiryō*, bekki 1:362.

31. Quoted in Suzuki, *Fujita Tōko*, 64.

32. Fujita, "Kaitenshishi," 122.

33. *Mito shishi*, chū, 3:47.

34. Fujita Tōko, "Hanhei sankajō (Jinshin fūji)," in Takasu, *Fujita Tōko zenshū*, 6:198–99.

35. *Mito shishi*, chū, 3:41–43.

36. Fujita Tōko, "Nishiyama tonden ni kansuru kengi," in Takasu, *Fujita Tōko zenshū* 6:45–74.

37. Suzuki, *Fujita Tōko*, 83–85.

38. Fujita, "Hanhei sankajō," 160.

39. Fujita, "Hitachiobi," in Takasu, *Fujita Tōko zenshū*, 1:265–78.

40. *Mito shishi*, chū, 3:45.

41. Nakata Shōichi, *Mito-han to ryōmin* (Tokyo: Kinseisha, 2008), 201–7.

42. Koschmann, *The Mito Ideology*, 84, 100.

43. Suzuki, *Fujita Tōko*, 62–63.

44. Isoda, "Mito-han Tenpō kaikaku," 40–41.

45. Tokugawa Nariaki, "Kokushihen," in *Mitogaku*, ed. Imai Usaburō, Seya Yoshihiko, and Bitō Masahide, Nihon shisō taikei 53 (Tokyo: Iwanami shoten, 1973), 210–27.

46. Komiyama, "Tenpō shūhanki," in *Ibaraki ken shiryō: bakumatsu hen*, ed. Ibaraki kenshi hensan bakumatsu ishinshi bukai, vol. 1 (Mito: Ibaraki-ken, 1971), 297.

47. *Mito shishi*, chū, 3:121–62, 245–84.

48. Nagai, *Tokugawa Nariaki*, 77.

49. Komiyama, "Tenpō shūhanki," 322.

50. *Mito shishi*, chū, 3:52–54.

51. Komiyama, "Tenpō shūhanki," 291.

52. Komiyama, "Tenpō shūhanki," 276.

53. "Tenpō 4-nen Mito jōka han'ei shihō kakiage," [1837], No. 60, in *Ibaraki ken shiryō: kinsei shakai keizai hen*, ed. Ibaraki kenshi hensan kinseishi dai 2 bukai (Mito: Ibaraki-ken, 1988), 4:289.

54. "Tenpō 1-nen Shōgatsu fukusei jōken" [1830/1831], in *Ibaraki-ken shiryō, kinsei seiji hen*, 1:170.

55. "Fukusei oyobi ryōriten nado torishirabe no ken" [1833/9/21], in *Ibaraki-ken shiryō, kinsei seiji hen* 1:187.

56. *Mito shishi*, chū, 3:366, 405–8.

57. Komuro Masamichi, *Sōmō no keizai shisō* (Tokyo: Ochanomizu shobō, 1999), 211–22.

58. Komiyama, "Tenpō shūhanki," 289.

59. *Mito shishi*, chū, 3:691–752.

60. Yoshida Toshizumi, *Mitogaku to Meiji ishin* (Tokyo: Yoshikawa kōbunkan, 2003), 95–96 and *Mito shishi*, chū, 3:729.

61. Komiyama Fūken, "Fūken sensei hiroku," in *Ibaraki ken shiryō: bakumatsu hen*, 1:422–23.

62. "Kyōsaku ni tsuki zōshu kinshi no ken," 1833/8/10, in *Ibaraki ken shiryō: kinsei seiji hen*, 1:184.

63. These edicts are reproduced in *Ibaraki ken shiryō: kinsei seiji hen*, vol. 1, 182–87.
64. Inui Hiromi, *Mito-han Tenpō kaikaku to gōnō* (Tokyo: Seibundō, 2006), 17.
65. Komiyama, "Tenpō shūhanki," 310.
66. Komiyama, "Tenpō shūhanki," 313.
67. *Mito shishi*, chū, 3:738
68. *Mito shishi*, chū, 3:598–608. For a longer discussion of popular unrest, see Takahashi Hirobumi, *Bakumatsu Mito-han to minshū undo* (Tokyo: Seishi shuppan, 2007), 127–29. Some Mito scholars criticize Takahashi as too pessimistic toward Nariaki's efforts, citing the lack of (official) famine deaths as evidence of Nariaki's relative success, but his work is an important contribution in the vein of "history from below," analyzing village protests and the experience of outcastes in Mito Domain.
69. Komiyama, "Tenpō shūhanki," 266.
70. For a detailed discussion of rural tensions during the Tenpō famine, see *Mito shishi*, chū, 3:691–762.
71. Bolitho, "The Tenpō Crisis," 121.
72. Fujita Tōko, "Teishi nichiroku," in Takasu, *Fujita Tōko zenshū*, 4:317.
73. Fujita Tōko, "Jōge fuyū no gi," in Takasu, *Fujita Tōko zenshū*, 6:209–39.
74. *Mito shishi*, chū, 3:138.
75. Suzuki, *Fujita Tōko*, 112–14.
76. Suzuki Fusako, "Mito-han Tenpō kaikaku no ichi kōsatsu: Komiyama Fūken to hansei kaikaku," *Ochanomizu shigaku* 15 (1972): 64–83.
77. Inui, *Mito-han Tenpō kaikaku to gōnō*, 23.
78. Fujita Tōko, "Hitachiobi," 469, transl. Koschmann, *The Mito Ideology*, 99.
79. Takahashi, *Bakumatsu Mito-han to minshū undo*, 78–79.
80. Tokugawa Nariaki, "Kōdōkanki," in Imai et al., *Mitogaku*, 230.
81. Fujita Tōko, "Kōdōkanki jutsugi," in Imai et al., *Mitogaku*, 259–338, and Tokugawa Nariaki, "Kōdōkan gakusoku," in *Mitogaku taikei*, ed. Takasu Yoshijirō (Tokyo: Mitogaku taikei kankōkai, 1941), 5:183.
82. Suzuki Eiichi, *Mito-han gakumon kyōiku shi no kenkyū* (Tokyo: Yoshikawa kōbunkan, 1987), 289–311.
83. *Mito shishi*, chū, 3:199–204
84. *Mito shishi*, chū, 3:70–71.
85. For a discussion of the effects of these reforms in mobilizing a new class of supporters, see Koschmann, *The Mito Ideology*, 130–51. Koschmann draws on Inui Hiromi's work on the Suda household, a wealthy farming family in southern Mito Domain, which has been republished in Inui, *Mito-han Tenpō kaikaku to gōnō*.
86. Koschmann, *The Mito Ideology*, 146–47.
87. Quoted in Suzuki, *Fujita Tōko*, 172–75.
88. Tokugawa Nariaki, "Suifu-kō kensaku," in Takasu, *Mitogaku taikei*, 5:194–97.
89. Nagai Hiroshi, *Tokugawa Nariaki*, 114.
90. *Mito han shiryō*, bekki, 1:136–46, 187–89.
91. On Nariaki's influence on Mizuno, see Inui, *Mito-han Tenpō kaikaku to gōnō*, 60–63. For an overview of the shogunate's reforms, see Bolitho, "The Tenpō Crisis," 139–58.

92. Seya, *Mito no Nariaki*, 123–27 and Tokugawa, "Suifu-kō kensaku," in Takasu, *Mitogaku taikei*, 5:191–272.

93. *Mito shishi*, chū, vol. 4 (Mito: Mito shiyakusho, 1982), 10–11.

94. Matthew Lamberti, in his biography of Nariaki, describes the Tenpō Reforms as a failure, as does Harold Bolitho in his survey of the Tenpō Reforms. Lamberti, *A Political Study of Tokugawa Nariaki of Mito*, PhD Diss., Columbia University, 1968, 7 and Bolitho, "The Tenpō Crisis," especially 158–64.

95. For accounts by several of these officials, see Kuno Katsuya, *Tahanshi no mita Mito* (Tokyo: Kinseisha, 1990).

96. Bitō Masahide, "Mitogaku no tokushitsu," in Imai et al., *Mitogaku*, 556–57.

97. Isoda, "Mito-han Tenpō kaikaku," 31–50.

98. Isoda, "Mito-han Tenpō kaikaku," 47–48. See Koseki, *"Meikun" no kinsei*, particularly the introduction, for a discussion of the historiographical trend toward recognizing late-Mito reform movements as part of a modernizing trend. See also the special issue of *Rekishi hyōron* 717 (January 2010).

99. Suzuki, *Fujita Tōko*, 230.

100. *Mito shishi*, chū, 4:86–92 and Nagai, *Tokugawa Nariaki*, 127.

101. Seya, *Mito no Nariaki*, 161.

102. Totman, "Political Reconciliation in the Tokugawa Bakufu," 180–208.

103. *Mito shishi*, chū, 4:504–5.

104. *Mito shishi*, chū, 4:633.

105. *Mito shishi*, chū, 4:671–98.

106. Nagai, *Tokugawa Nariaki*, 150–51.

107. *Mito shishi*, chū, 4:636–37.

108. *Mito shishi*, chū, 4:550–64.

109. Koschmann, *The Mito Ideology*, 125–29.

Chapter Five

Nariaki, Yoshinobu, and the Birth of Modern Japan

For the last fifteen years of the Tokugawa period, two of the most important and influential politicians in Japan were from Mito: Tokugawa Nariaki and his seventh son, Yoshinobu. Nariaki served as defense minister and shogunal advisor in the crucial years after Commodore Matthew Perry's arrival in Japan in the summer of 1853, working closely with the shogunate's council of elders to develop their response to the demands for foreign treaties. Although he ultimately failed to prevent the signing of commercial treaties with the foreign powers, he nevertheless thrilled samurai and commoners alike in his strident call for repelling the foreign threat. Meanwhile, he joined an alliance of influential lords of major domains in calling for greater participation in national government. Nariaki's charismatic leadership emboldened this group of "great lords" to shape shogunal policy, most visibly by advocating for Nariaki's son, Yoshinobu, to become heir to the thirteenth shogun, Iesada, in 1858. As Nariaki failed on the question of foreign trade, this group also failed in the shogunal succession crisis, and they and their domains suffered during the Ansei Purge of 1858–1859. Nevertheless, the work of the great lords, and their attachment to Nariaki and Mito's teachings, became the foundation of a renewed attempt in the 1860s to create a more open and participatory form of national government in the shogunate. By 1863, Yoshinobu had become the leading figure in this effort once again. For the next five years, he sought to balance his loyalties to the imperial court with his duties to the Tokugawa family. When, as shogun, he reached the limits of that approach, he decided that his greater loyalty lay with to the court and his country—no surprise for a man who had been steeped in the language of imperial loyalty since his childhood in Mito. In late 1867, Yoshinobu surrendered the Tokugawa mandate to rule, setting off the tumultuous political transition known as the Meiji Restoration.

Nariaki's divisive personality produced sharp critics, starting with his contemporaries, and his paranoid bellicosity has made him somewhat of a villain
in standard accounts of late Tokugawa history.[1] But Nariaki's reputation as a
"xenophobe and an iconoclast" does not fully account for his efforts to build
coalitions among the great lords or his struggles to control the more extreme
elements within Mito.[2] Recent work has revisited Nariaki's political role in
the shogunate, as well as the popular support for Nariaki that emerged after
his fall from power.[3] But few scholars have taken Nariaki as the focus of their
work, even in Japanese; only two modern biographies exist.[4] In Yoshinobu's
case, the demands of realism that shogunal politics imposed upon Yoshinobu
forced him to make compromises, often with brutal consequences for his erstwhile supporters among Mito's radicals. He developed a calculating approach
to power, willing to exploit differences within and between the court, various
domains, and the shogunate itself. Perhaps as a result, he was never fully accepted by any of these groups and has therefore remained a somewhat elusive
figure in the political histories of the Meiji Restoration.[5] Certainly being declared an enemy of the court in the aftermath of the Battle of Toba-Fushimi
did not help, and he presided over the collapse of a social and political system
that was no longer fit for purpose in an age of aggressive imperialism. For
much of the Meiji period he remained out of the public eye, refraining from
any effort to rehabilitate his image. It was only with the oral history work
conducted by Shibusawa Eiichi around the turn of the twentieth century that
Yoshinobu began to tell his version of events, which—fifty years after the
fact—are problematic, to say the least, as a reliable account of the 1860s.[6]
And despite being the only Mito Tokugawa member to become shogun, he
has received remarkably little attention among Mito's historians compared to
Mito's most famous scholars, daimyo, and radical samurai.[7]

     The role of Nariaki and Yoshinobu during the 1850s and 1860s reveals
the importance of Mito's ideas and people at the highest levels of national
politics until the very end of the Tokugawa period. Nariaki and Yoshinobu
rose to power on the strength of their family's status, on the reputation of
Mito's reform movement, and through careful politicking. Nariaki relied on
an extensive network of family and friends to navigate the treacherous ter-
rain of shogunal politics in the last thirty years of the Tokugawa period, and
he successfully positioned Yoshinobu to succeed him as the Mito figure with
the greatest national prominence. Both men skillfully responded to many of
the political upheavals that characterized this tumultuous era: the arrival of
foreign ships, and the subsequent decision to accede to demands for diplomacy and trade; pressure from below in the form of radicals, in Mito and
around Japan, who adhered to the same ideals that Nariaki and Yoshinobu
professed; and the resurgence of the imperial court as a political actor, which

exposed the limits and contradictions in the Tokugawa system of power and legitimacy. In this context, "revere the emperor, expel the barbarian" and other aspects of Mito's teachings inevitably lost some of the idealism that was so inspiring to the radical *shishi* who engaged in campaigns of terror around Japan in the decade after Perry's arrival. Nariaki and Yoshinobu often struggled, for example, to appease their most radical supporters while still capitalizing upon their support. And ultimately it became impossible to ignore the logical inconsistency between loyalty to the throne and loyalty to the shogunate. This philosophical challenge, coming on top of the deep structural problems in Tokugawa society, ultimately proved too much for the shogunate. As politicians in an increasingly national arena, Nariaki and Yoshinobu helped reshape Japan into a stronger, more unified, and more centralized nation-state—even though that came at the expense of their family's 260-year hold on power.

MITO'S FAMILY, FRIENDS, AND SUPPORTERS

Mito's outsized political influence in the late Tokugawa period depended not only upon the domain's high rank within the Tokugawa family and the reputation of its reform movement. It also rested upon an elaborate and far-reaching personal network that connected the Mito Tokugawa family to the shogunate, the court, and important daimyo families across Japan via marriage, adoption, and friendship. These personal relationships reinforced the efforts by Tokugawa Nariaki and his seventh son, the fifteenth shogun, Tokugawa Yoshinobu, to reimagine the political structure of Japan by including a greater number of powerful lords and paying greater attention to the wishes of the imperial court. By the 1850s, when Nariaki returned to power and joined the shogunate, a powerful group of influential lords had begun to stake out a new vision of national political participation and authority.

Tokugawa Nariaki's ten wives exemplified the political value of personal relationships. His primary wife, Yoshiko (1804–1893), was the ninth daughter of Prince Arisugawa Orihito (1755–1820), and the first member of a royal family to marry into the Mito household. She brought with her a gift that symbolized her imperial roots: a cutting from a cherry tree cultivated in the imperial palace since the ninth century. For the rest of his life, Nariaki relied upon Yoshiko as a trusted advisor and demonstrated his reverence for the imperial line through New Year's ceremonies in her honor.[8] Yoshiko's elder sister was the principal wife of the twelfth shogun Ieyoshi (1793–1853), and she maintained close ties with her relatives in Kyoto. Nariaki's other wives came from slightly less exalted backgrounds, but they also reinforced Nariaki's ties to important families within Mito and around Japan. His second wife was the daughter of the senior Mito house elder. Next was the daughter of a retainer to the daimyo of Itoigawa Domain. Another four were the daughters of courtier families in Kyoto, underscoring Mito's dedication to the imperial court. Two were the daughters of *hatamoto* retainers of the shogun. Finally, Nariaki was also married to the granddaughter of Tachihara Suiken—a reminder that, despite the disputes between the Tachihara and Fujita factions within Mito's reformist coalition, those factional divides were not insurmountable.[9]

Nariaki's thirty-seven children also provided an avenue for spreading Mito's influence across Japan. Although nearly half of them died very young, Nariaki was determined to put the others to good use. He remembered all too clearly the disputes over his own succession as daimyo, and he intended to en-sure a clear line of succession to his offspring. Yoshiko gave birth to his first son, Tsuruchiyomaro (later known as Yoshiatsu), in 1832, and Nariaki began preparing him to become daimyo almost immediately. But he also paid spe-cial attention to his seventh son, Shichirōmaro, who was born on 1837/9/29.[10] Nariaki recognized in the young Shichirōmaro a future leader and wanted to keep him within the family until he was a teenager to nurture his character and skills. He also worried about the health of Tsuruchiyomaro and wanted to prepare Shichirōmaro to serve as daimyo if necessary.[11] Shichirōmaro never became daimyo, but he did go on to be an influential leader: the fifteenth and final Tokugawa shogun, Yoshinobu. Nariaki's attitude toward and treatment of Shichirōmaro, therefore, is worth exploring to understand the influence of Nariaki and Mito's ideas on the highest levels of the Tokugawa shogunate during the last years of its existence.

Nariaki believed strongly that his sons should be educated in Mito, rather than on the Mito estates in Edo, in order to instill discipline and a respect for Mito values. This was a difficult task in Edo, where the diversions and distractions of the vibrant city could derail a young man. Growing up in Mito at the height of his father's reform administration, Shichirōmaro absorbed Mito's scholarship and political ideology. Nariaki carefully supervised Shichirōmaro's upbringing, insisting that he follow the model imposed on all of Nariaki's retainers: equal training in the civil and martial arts, with special attention to the principles of loyalty and Japan's unique imperial history. Shichirōmaro studied Chinese and Japanese classics with Aizawa Seishisai and other leading scholars at the Kōdōkan. But he much preferred training in archery and horseback riding, roaming for miles at a time across Mito Domain. Nariaki finally had to punish the young Shichirōmaro to get him to devote equal attention to both parts of his education.[12] He attended Nariaki's large hunting parties, learning about the importance of modernizing and strengthening the samurai in the face of the foreign threat. Through his

Figure 5.1.   Portrait of Tokugawa Yoshinobu
(Ibaraki Prefectural Archives and Museum)

formal education in Mito's pro-imperial ideology at the Kōdōkan, he developed a deep respect for the imperial household—reinforced by his blood ties
to the imperial court through his mother Yoshiko. Nariaki later told him that
his duty was to support the shogunate—but should shogunate and court come
to war, then he was not to draw his bow against the imperial court, even if it
meant disobeying the shogun.[13]

Nariaki's family ties even played a role in his fall from power in 1844. In a
defense of his actions, he claimed that the shogunate had grown suspicious of
his desire to invite Yoshiko to Mito with him in order to pay their respects to
the Mito Tokugawa family graves just north of the castle town. In Nariaki's
view, this request, coupled with his unusually lengthy, four-year stay in Mito,
and his request to lead the colonization of Ezochi, had led some in the shogunate to suspect him of forging an independent power base. He denied this
intention, of course, and noted that the shogunate had approved his lengthy
return to Mito. (They had also denied Yoshiko's request to travel, and their
eldest son, Yoshiatsu, would have remained in Edo.) Nevertheless, shogunal
officials were wary of letting Nariaki build up a family power base in Mito.[14]

After Nariaki's ouster in 1844, he and his supporters turned to his family networks in search of a path back to power. After fruitless appeals to
shogunal officials, in the spring of 1846 a glimmer of hope appeared in the
form of a doctor's serving girl. The girl, whose name we sadly do not know,
was the daughter of Nakamura Heizaburō, a low-ranked samurai who had
hired out his daughter to work for Saka Gen'eki, a doctor in the women's
quarters of the shogun's castle, to support his family. Saka was sympathetic
to Nariaki's cause, and through the Nakamuras he warned Nariaki's supporters that their aggressive petitions for his exoneration were only annoying the
shogun. He recommended a more delicate approach: persuading the powerful women in the shogun's household to adopt their cause. At this point, the
Mito Tokugawa family practice of intermarrying with the shogunate and
other elites proved its use. Nariaki and his family members were connected
to several women in the shogun's household. Nariaki and his supporters
started sending gifts and messages in hopes of persuading them to put in a
good word with the shogun. Unfortunately, Nariaki's hopes foundered upon
the internal politics of the women's quarters. For instance, rivalry between
two of the most senior women, Anegakōji and Mihoyama, made for delicate
negotiations. Ultimately, Nariaki's overtures ended with only vague promises
to discuss his circumstances with the shogun. Nariaki's supporters, dejected,
gave up on the shogun's household.[15]

Despite this disappointing outcome in the women's quarters, Mito's ties
to the shogun himself proved useful as Abe Masahiro carefully drew Nariaki back into the shogunate's political fold. Ieyoshi doted on Shichirōmaro,

who was his nephew (his wife was Yoshiko's sister). In 1847, Abe arranged for Ieyoshi to appoint the young boy the head of the Hitotsubashi household. The Hitotsubashi was one of the "Three Lords" (*gosankyō*) branch houses of the Tokugawa household. These branches, slightly lower in rank than the "Three Houses" (*gosanke*) of Mito, Owari, and Kii, were often given priority when selecting heirs for a shogun who had no child of his own. Appointing one of Nariaki's sons as head of the Hitotsubashi household was a significant gesture and gave Nariaki a major avenue of political influence within shogunal politics. Along with the appointment, Ieyoshi gave Shichirōmaro a new name: Yoshinobu. The ten-year-old Shichirōmaro-turned-Yoshinobu left the Mito household and took on his new role. After arranging for Yoshinobu's adoption into the Hitotsubashi family, Abe arranged in 1848 for Nariaki's eldest son Yoshiatsu to marry the Princess Ito, who had been adopted by Ieyoshi. The next year, Ieyoshi made a personal visit to the Mito Estate at Koishikawa, further improving ties and creating a path for Nariaki's rehabilitation.

Nariaki recognized that adoption and marriage could ensure goodwill and informal alliances with the court, the shogunate, and other important domains around Japan, and he wasted little time in securing those relationships. Several of Yoshinobu's siblings also took up new homes, creating a family network across Japan that spread and reinforced Mito's values and political power. Yoshinori, Nariaki's fifth son, became the daimyo of Tottori Domain in 1850. Naoyoshi, Nariaki's eighth son, became daimyo of Kawagoe Domain in 1854; Mochimasa, Nariaki's ninth son, was adopted by the daimyo of Oshi Domain in 1849, although he was disowned ten years later during the Ansei Purge; he later became daimyo of Okayama Domain, in 1863. Five more brothers became daimyo for smaller domains across Japan, while Akitake, Nariaki's eighteenth son, became the last daimyo of Mito after Yoshiatsu's death in 1868. Nariaki's daughters, too, played an important role in Nariaki's family politicking, marrying into large and influential *tozama* domains. His eldest daughter, Sakahime, was betrothed to Date Munenari, the daimyo of Uwajima Domain, although she died soon after in 1839. His sixth daughter, Matsuhime, married Nanbu Toshihisa, daimyo of Morioka Domain between 1849 and 1868. Yayohime, Nariaki's ninth daughter, married Date Yoshikuni, the daimyo of Sendai, in 1852, while Sadako, Nariaki's eleventh daughter, eventually married into the Arisugawa royal line, underscoring the ties between that court family and the Mito Tokugawa.[16] These connections illustrate the degree of support and friendship for Nariaki among prominent daimyo families and in Kyoto.

Despite his new family and title, Yoshinobu continued to enjoy a close relationship with his father. Nariaki wrote often and at length and visited

Yoshinobu frequently in the following years. He urged Yoshinobu to continue his studies of both civil and martial arts, and repeatedly laid out his diagnosis of the ills of 1850s Japan: the weakness of samurai spirit, the threat posed by the West, and the loss of morals. He tried to inculcate in Yoshinobu the importance of serving his country. In addition to repeated visits and letters, Nariaki also sent copies of his own writings about leadership and reform.[17] Yoshinobu watched his father build political alliances through family ties and friendships as part of a concerted effort to implement national reforms to strengthen Japan against the foreign threat.

Nariaki's circle of friends and allies extended beyond the families into which he married his children. He grew close to a group of prominent daimyo—most famously Shimazu Nariakira of Satsuma, Yamauchi Yōdō of Tosa, Matsudaira Shungaku of Fukui, and Date Munenari.[18] These men were daimyo of large domains, far from Edo, and, like Mito's rulers, historically excluded from formal roles in the shogunal government. They were a particularly capable group of men: highly educated and politically astute, with good advisors and relatively stable domains. As domestic and foreign crises grew more severe in the middle of the nineteenth century, they recognized the need for more transformative change. They found a call to arms in the writings and teachings of Mito's scholars and in Nariaki's leadership. These leaders sought him out for his expertise on foreign affairs during the 1840s and into the 1850s, exchanging letters about military preparation, the threat foreign powers posed to Ryukyu, and pointers on *rangaku* scholarship. They emulated Mito at home, too, strengthening their military forces and shoring up their domain economies. They developed a strong appreciation for the potential of the imperial court to unify Japan and open up space for able leaders to take more prominent roles in governing the nation.

Nariaki also had supporters among a diverse group of samurai and courtiers across Japan, many of whom had studied the writings of Aizawa Seishisai and Fujita Tōko, the rhetoric of "revere the emperor, expel the barbarian." In some cases, these men shared Mito's ideas with their lords, supporting their domain's efforts at reforms. In other cases, Mito's ideas found homes among more radical, minority factions. This was the case in Chōshū, for example, as well as at the imperial court. As we have seen, people around Japan flocked to Mito and studied with the domain's leading scholars, taking those messages home with them. The strident call to defend the nation and overhaul a decaying society resonated especially with young, lower-ranked samurai, priests, and educated commoners. In domains across Japan, adherents to these ideas promoted their own version of reforms.

Samurai from Satsuma domain, in the far southwest of Japan, were particularly attracted to Mito's teachings. Arimura Shunsai, a young samurai stationed at Satsuma's Edo estate, sought out Fujita Tōko and became a devoted follower. He extolled Tōko to his peers, including Ōkubo Toshimichi and Saigō Takamori, two reform-minded young samurai who would go on to be leading figures in the Meiji government. Ōkubo never managed to meet Tōko, but Saigō, especially impressed by Tōko's work and character, secured a meeting in the spring of 1854, when they discussed the importance of restoring imperial rule and the need to form a coalition of samurai cutting across domain lines. Saigō took this message to heart, urging his home domain to lead the charge to restore the emperor to power. He visited Tōko several times while in Edo, attending Tōko's lessons and writing letters home that extolled the ideas of Mito.[19] He described listening to Tōko as "bathing in spring water: all unrest and confusion disappear and my heart and mind become quiet and pure."[20] Saigō was "at a loss for words" at Tōko's death in 1855, calling it "a great tragedy for the realm."[21] Saigō also introduced Tōko's ideas to friends from other domains, such as Hashimoto Sanai, an influential advisor from Fukui.[22] In later years, Saigō told friends that of his elders, he respected Tōko most of all, and of his peers, he endorsed Sanai. Through these connections, Tōko's vision for imperial restoration found a home in the domains that would go on to lead the political revolution of the late 1860s.

On the other hand, some of Tōko's followers gradually backed away from his uncompromising stance and the radicalism that he inspired. Yokoi Shōnan, for instance, a colleague of Hashimoto Sanai in Fukui, initially agreed with Tōko's views, but became more critical as he watched Mito tear itself apart with factionalism. Yokoi enthusiastically supported Tōko's call to strengthen Japan and reform Japanese politics and society, but he condemned the fanaticism of Tōko's more radical followers. He quickly recognized the futility of trying to reverse the opening of the country and praised the more pragmatic position of Aizawa Seishisai and his followers, who were advocating a practical foreign policy based on opening Japan. Despite these criticisms of Tōko's followers, Shōnan mourned Tōko, saying, "there are few men like Tōko anywhere in Japan."[23]

Other students of Mito's scholars pushed their ideas in more radical directions. Yoshida Shōin had already started to lose faith in Aizawa Seishisai's argument that the Tokugawa shoguns were exemplars of imperial loyalty, realizing instead that individual samurai might be able to express such loyalty directly to the emperor, rather than via the shogunate.[24] He established a small school in 1857 where he taught Mito's values to a generation of Chōshū samurai, including men who would go on to become leading figures in the Meiji Restoration and the post-Restoration government, such as Kusaka Genzui, Takasugi Shinsaku, Katsura Shōgorō, and Itō Hirobumi. Yoshida was unfettered by Mito's kinship to the Tokugawa family, however, and this made him more willing than Seishisai to challenge Tokugawa rule. He advocated for grassroots uprisings by loyal samurai and villagers—a position adopted during his stay in Mito—and took a more belligerent position on the question of how to deal with the Westerners. His student Takasugi Shinsaku established the Kiheitai, Japan's first modern regiment, clearly inspired by some of Mito's teachings: he wrote "loyal to the bone" (*chūgi kotsuzui wo uzumu*), a phrase from Fujita Tōko's work *Kaitenshishi* (see chapter 4), on the Kiheitai's banner, underscoring Mito's central role in turning Chōshū into a base of "revere the emperor, expel the barbarian" activism in the last years of the Tokugawa era.[25]

Like Shōin, the Kurume priest Maki Izumi ultimately went further than the Mito scholars in advocating for the restoration of direct imperial rule, abandoning Seishisai's belief in the moral value of the shogunate as a model of Confucian loyalty, and he called for military uprisings against the shogunate. He committed suicide in 1864 after a failed coup attempt in Kyoto. Although his uprising had failed, he had succeeded in planting Seishisai's ideas of imperial restoration deep within the imperial court.[26] The court had long held respect for Mito, dating to at least the time of the second daimyo, Mitsukuni, because of the emphasis on imperial supremacy in the *Dai Nihon shi* and other writings. For a faction of more radical courtiers, such as Sanjō Sanetomi, Seishisai's writings offered a manifesto for more direct political change, including the restoration of direct imperial rule.

For all of these men, Mito's ideas were an inspiration, even if in time they interpreted those ideas in new ways and drifted away from the loyalty to the Tokugawa system that mattered so much to Aizawa Seishisai, Fujita Tōko, and Tokugawa Nariaki. They also played an important role in spreading these ideas among their friends and peers and helped make Nariaki a popular figure among anti-foreign *shishi* and daimyo across Japan. Their enthusiasm for "revere the emperor, expel the barbarian" formed an important source of support for the efforts of Mito's leaders to rebuild the Tokugawa shogunate in stronger, more inclusive ways during the 1850s.

THE ANSEI REFORMS AND THE
SHOGUNAL SUCCESSION CRISIS, 1853–1858

Nariaki's popularity among the great lords, and the strength of his reputation as a leader and foreign policy expert, was made evident in 1853, when Shungaku and Nariakira both urged Abe Masahiro to appoint him as naval advisor to the shogunate shortly after Perry's arrival.[27] Abe Masahiro's decision to seek input from daimyo signaled his willingness to expand decision-making power beyond the traditional inner circle of shogunal leadership. Nariaki and the other great lords seized the opportunity to advocate vociferously for reform and a hard line against the Americans. For the next two years, Abe oversaw a reform program, named after the Ansei era (1854–1860), that sought to consolidate national power, strengthen Japan against foreign threats, and revitalize the shogunate's finances. Nariaki played a crucial role in these projects, which drew heavily on Mito's Tenpō-era efforts. In the summer of 1855, Abe asked Nariaki to review a thirty-seven-point plan for shogunal reforms, which included a number of items straight out of the Mito playbook: a number of cost-cutting measures; a school for "civil and literary arts" in Edo; putting a halt to farmers giving up agriculture; a number of military investments; and plans to colonize Ezochi. Nariaki endorsed many of these ideas, but also warned Abe that he needed to prioritize carefully. He urged Abe to find talented men to take charge of individual reforms, rather than rely on the slow machinery of the shogunate. He was particularly passionate about Abe's proposal for new schools, emphasizing the importance of sending the sons and heirs of high-ranking samurai to learn how to become good rulers. He stressed the urgency of "enrich the country, strengthen the military" (*fukoku kyōhei*), a slogan that was dominating shogunal discourse at this time—and would go on to be a key pillar of the young Meiji regime after 1868. He warned that both sides of this equation were important: without a strong military, economic growth would just leave Japan exposed to foreign conquest, while a lack of resources would hamper military preparations.[28]

Nariaki's views on the colonization of Ezochi, and particularly the role of Matsumae Domain, speak to his belief in the importance of strengthening national government. Matsumae had strenuously resisted shogunal attempts to take more control in Ezochi at the turn of the nineteenth century, and they did so again in 1854 and 1855. They relied on income from Ezochi's commercial fishing industry and had no desire to cede the monopoly on access to Ezochi, even though they lacked the ability to defend the region. Nariaki urged Abe to seize their entire domain via attainder, stressing that they cared more about preserving their fishing rights than they did the protection of the realm.[29] Given Nariaki's efforts to secure control of Ezochi for Mito in the 1830s, it is easy to read this as self-interested—but by the 1850s, he no longer expected Mito to lead the colonization program. His interests had shifted to support the centralization of authority under the shogunate.

Nariaki's work as a shogunal advisor enhanced his reputation among anxious Japanese subjects and likeminded leaders. His strident calls for military preparation thrilled Edo's anxious residents, who circulated broadsheets portraying him as a great general. After years of grousing about Nariaki's zealous push for austerity and moral reform, Edo's samurai and common folk now embraced him as the answer to their prayers in a time when war seemed imminent. His plan to warn Japanese people to prepare for war seemed to be working.[30] His reputation as a fearless defender of the realm spread beyond Edo, too. At the same time, Nariaki's appointment as advisor marked a loosening of the traditional structure of political power in the shogunate. The historical exclusion of the *gosanke* houses from political office had ended, and this signaled that other excluded voices might now have a greater say in political decisions. This precedent was compounded by Abe Masahiro's political style, which relied heavily on cooperation and consultation with powerful lords. While this helped him weather the immediate crises of the early 1850s, it also emboldened those lords to seek greater influence in national government.[31] In the end, though, Nariaki's efforts in the shogunate were more limited than he had hoped, as he faced considerable backlash from the traditional powerholders. It also unlikely that, despite his calls for promoting able men, that he truly wanted all daimyo to participate in government.[32] Nevertheless, his participation in shogunal government between 1853 and 1855, and the reforms that he proposed, helped loosen the structures of Tokugawa power and opened up new visions of unity government.

After 1855, Nariaki's position in Edo grew more tenuous as debates over policy and fights over power divided the shogunate. The shogunate was a large, unwieldy, and slow-moving entity, and its leadership—despite Abe's prodding—did not take kindly to Nariaki's impatient demands for change. Abe, in a bid to soothe the anti-Nariaki camp, appointed one of their leaders, Hotta Masayoshi, to the governing council of elders, a move that backfired by creating division even within the government. Abe himself was forced to resign his position as chief councilor in the fall of 1855, ceding the role to Hotta (although he stayed on as a councilor). The next year, Townsend Harris arrived to begin negotiations for a trade treaty. Hotta supported the treaty, enraging Nariaki (see chapter 3). Young supporters of Nariaki watched this unfold and, frustrated, took to the streets in increasingly radical protest, further antagonizing the anti-Nariaki side. In 1857, Abe died, and Nariaki lost his closest ally in the shogunate; he resigned soon after. With his departure, the great lords seeking a more consensus-driven approach to national government lost an influential voice in government.

Perhaps more importantly, however, for the fortunes of the reformist lords was the political instability caused by the death by heatstroke of the shogun Ieyoshi on 1853/6/22, just after Perry's departure. Ieyoshi could hardly have died at a more inopportune time. His government was frantically trying to address its most significant foreign policy crisis in more than two hundred years. To make matters worse, Ieyoshi's son, the thirteenth shogun, Iesada, was a sickly man. His first two wives had died childless, and he had no children by his third. He cared little for politics, leaving the fraught negotiations over foreign treaties in the hands of his councilors. From the start of his reign, the question of who would succeed him preoccupied shogunal officials and other influential lords. With the foreign threat at Japan's door, the country needed a capable leader—and the shogunate needed a shogun who could preserve its authority in a time of crisis.

The reformist lords immediately began lobbying for Tokugawa Yoshinobu to become Iesada's successor. Yoshinobu had already developed a reputation as a smart and capable young man, and he firmly argued against the opening of negotiations with Perry, demonstrating his ideological commitment to Nariaki's hardline stance on foreign affairs.[33] The lords argued that Yoshinobu was older and more experienced than the alternative, the daimyo of Kii Domain, Tokugawa Yoshitomi. The great lords recognized Yoshinobu's aptitude and potential to be a strong leader and saw him as their best shot at achieving their goals of national unification and a bigger role for themselves in government. More practically, perhaps, they expected that the young Yoshinobu would rely on the advice and support of Nariaki and his allies, giving the great lords unprecedented influence over shogunal politics and allowing them to pursue their national reform agenda.

Abe tried to suppress this movement, but after his death in 1857, the great lords began openly promoting Yoshinobu. They met with each other to discuss the need for reform, pretending to be "studying together" to avoid shogunal anger.[34] However, the families that traditionally dominated the shogun's government opposed the appointment of Yoshinobu for reasons of history and politics. Kii was one of two traditional producers of shogunal heirs, making Yoshitomi the logical choice. His backers also feared that Yoshinobu's candidacy would give the reformist lords too much influence. The establishment mobilized quickly and aggressively against Yoshinobu's candidacy to prevent any erosion of its power. In 1858, shortly before Iesada passed away, Yoshitomi was named his successor, soon becoming the thirteenth shogun Iemochi. Nariaki and other backers of Yoshinobu made an unannounced visit to Edo Castle in a last-minute bid to stop the announcement, but they succeeded only in antagonizing Ii Naosuke, the new chief councilor.

The resolution of the succession dispute coincided with the crisis around the signing of the U.S.-Japan trade treaty. Hotta Masayoshi's failure to secure court backing for his treaty negotiations, and subsequent resignation, had led to the appointment of Ii Naosuke as regent to the young Iesada in the fifth month of 1858. Uninterested in compromise and determined to reassert the shogunate's traditional prerogatives, Ii unilaterally approved the Harris Treaty, infuriating Nariaki and his supporters among the great lords. Nariaki, Matsudaira Shungaku, and other lords condemned Ii's actions. Although Yoshinobu refrained from commenting on the shogunal succession question, he demanded an audience with Ii to condemn his failure to consult the court on the treaty.[35] Ii reacted swiftly and coldly: he quelled opposition by sentencing Nariaki to house arrest and then targeted many of his supporters in the so-called Ansei Purge.[36] Yoshinobu was banned from Edo Castle on 1858/7/5, a punishment soon converted into forced retirement and house arrest. The reformist lords had been swept from power, and Yoshinobu was confined to his home.

The Ansei Purge marked a resurgence of shogunal power and a setback for the reformist lords. Nariaki's ouster from power triggered a robust exoneration movement in Mito that quickly turned violent, and he begged his followers to stay calm lest the shogunate take even more drastic measures against the domain. His words, however, were not enough. On the third day of the third month of 1860, a group of seventeen samurai from Mito and one from Satsuma gathered in the rain outside the Sakurada Gate of Edo Castle, where they waited for a procession of Hikone samurai accompanying Ii to the castle. The Hikone men were in raincoats, with their swords sheathed. A gunshot rang out, and the Mito men descended upon Ii's palanquin. Ii was killed immediately, along with a number of his guards. The attackers cut off Ii's head and ran off with it. Five of them died in the fighting. Eight more committed suicide when they realized their injuries would prevent them from escaping.

Nariaki, who received the first reports of the attack the next day, was shocked and appalled. "No matter how bad Ii might have been, he was appointed by the shogun for good reasons," he wrote to Yoshiatsu. Attacking Ii was tantamount to attacking the shogunate. "The realm will fall to anti-Tokugawa daimyo, or it will fall to the foreigners," Nariaki warned, urging him to repair relations with Hikone immediately.[37] Nariaki was no doubt distancing himself as far as possible from the attackers to avoid further punishment for himself or his domain. But his stance also reflected a deeper contradiction in his philosophy of leadership. Throughout his career, Nariaki sought to demonstrate a new form of "benevolent rule," a more muscular and charismatic approach to leadership that grappled with the political, social, and diplomatic threats facing Japan by mobilizing new groups of people and educating them in a new set of ideals. By taking this vision to the national stage, Nariaki sought to preserve and strengthen the shogunate. Criticism and reform was a means to strengthen and preserve the hegemony of Tokugawa rule, even if its structure ought to change. Yet, his bellicose language, his forthright critiques, and his policy of urging the country to prepare for war (while secretly adopting a more conciliatory approach to foreign diplomacy) all combined to radicalize many younger, lower-ranking samurai who had earnestly studied Mito ideas and pledged to uphold the Mito slogan of "revere the emperor, expel the barbarian." Once those ideas took hold, Nariaki

Figure 5.2. Hasuda Ichigorō, Sakuradamon-gai no hen zu, 1860
(Ibaraki Prefectural Library)

had no hope of reining them in again. Although he condemned the Sakurada Gate attackers and pronounced himself horrified, Nariaki could not avoid all responsibility for fanning the flames of violence against the shogunate, fatally undermining its authority.

Nariaki died just a few months after the assassination of Ii, during a moon-watching party in Mito on 8/15, likely of a heart attack. He was buried in the family cemetery at Zuiryūzan, north of Mito castle town. After his death, the domain turned inward, preoccupied by the political struggles between radical, moderate, and establishment factions. Within just a few years, this factionalism had spiraled into civil war. The shogunate no longer trusted Mito, and crackdowns made life difficult for reformists, pushing them to the fringes where they plotted violent attacks on foreign embassies and shogunal officials. Meanwhile, at the national level, the coalition of daimyo that had formed around Nariaki continued to pursue his vision of political reform and military strengthening. But as the foreign threat intensified, other daimyo and the court began to lose faith in the shogunate, eroding its legitimacy and weakening its control over Japan.

MITO'S RADICALS AND YOSHINOBU'S ASCENT

After Nariaki's death, Mito domain lost its prominent place on the stage of national politics. But his death did not mean the loss of the vision of the reformist lords, or the loss of Mito's ideals. Instead, the focus of the reform project shifted to Yoshinobu, who shared many of his father's ideals and had witnessed at close quarters the complex and shifting political factions in Edo and across Japan. With his father's death, Yoshinobu became a symbol for Mito's radical younger samurai, too, as well as their supporters elsewhere in Japan. He became the new figurehead for supporters of "revere the emperor, expel the barbarian," a slogan whose motivational strength had been dramatically proven at Sakurada Gate. The combination of his political skill and symbolic position as a son of Mito made him a crucial figure in the realignment of Japanese politics that unfolded in the aftermath of Ii Naosuke's assassination.

The years around 1860 were marked by the growing influence of radical *shishi* and their allies at the expense of the shogunate. After Nariaki's death in the eighth month, the shogunate felt that the radical threat had receded sufficiently, and they loosened Yoshinobu's punishment. However, when the shogunate failed to prevent the British ambassador Rutherford Alcock from travelling near the emperor's city of Kyoto on an overland trip from Nagasaki to Edo, a group of samurai, priests, and merchants snuck out of Mito and attacked the British legation at Tōzenji on 1861/5/28. Although they failed to kill Alcock, the attack prompted another set of reprisals against the radicals and their sympathizers within Mito.[38] In the aftermath of the Tōzenji attack, the shogunate was forced to accept British demands for greater security, including the stationing of British troops at Shinagawa, close to Edo's southern entrance. This enraged the Mito radicals and their supporters, who saw this as an unacceptable foreign intrusion into the shogun's seat of power. Other shogunal decisions, such as allowing the British to survey Japanese waters and moving forward with plans to open Hyōgo as a treaty port, were also deeply unpopular. This anger culminated in yet another attack by Mito's radicals. On 1862/1/15, a group of them tried to assassinate the shogunate's chief councilor, Andō Nobumasa, as he entered Edo Castle's Sakashita Gate. The attackers had made a secret agreement with radicals from Chōshū, and in their manifesto they accused Andō of accommodating the barbarians and thereby disgracing Japan.[39] Andō escaped death but was seriously injured, hobbling the shogunal leadership even further.

Political leaders around Japan observed the loss of shogunal strength at the hands of Mito radicals during the Sakurada, Tōzenji, and Sakashita attacks, and started seeking ways to gain power at the shogunate's expense. Most significant among these observers were Chōshū and Satsuma, although the two domains pursued very different approaches to gain power. On the one hand, Chōshū adopted a hardline anti-foreign policy and began working with radical courtiers, most famously Sanjō Sanetomi, to demand that the shogunate break its treaties with the Western powers. On the other hand, Satsuma's leadership (now dominated by Shimazu Hisamitsu after Nariakira's death in 1858) sought to revive the coalition of great lords that had lost power during the Ansei Purge, aiming to get the shogunate and the court to work together in a unity government. Hisamitsu argued to the court that Matsudaira Shungaku and Yoshinobu should oversee this project.[40] Scheming in Kyoto by Chōshū and Satsuma, as well as radical courtiers, led to the dispatch of an imperial envoy to Edo to demand the expulsion of the foreigners, a host of reforms, and the appointment of Shungaku and Yoshinobu as senior officials. After arriving in Edo on 1862/6/7, the envoy received a group of Mito radicals, who urged him to push for Yoshinobu's appointment as "vice shogun," and to insist that the shogun travel to Kyoto to confirm plans to expel the barbarian.[41] At this moment, at least, the interests of Mito's radicals aligned with the interests of the great lords.

The shogunate reeled at the court envoy's demands, which tacitly condoned the Mito violence that had struck at the heart of the shogunate over the past two years and gave Yoshinobu and the great lords an enormous opening to seize power. Shogunal officials were deeply skeptical of Yoshinobu, whom they viewed as an ally of the Mito radicals. They had even considered removing him from the Hitotsubashi household and returning him to Mito as Yoshiatsu's adopted son, with instructions to pacify the domain—a clear effort to get him out of Edo and the national limelight.[42] When that failed, they had released Yoshinobu and Shungaku from their punishments in 1862/4 in an attempt to head off the demands from the great lords.[43] Yet, facing clear imperial instructions, the shogunate had no choice but to accept the court's demands. On 7/6, Shungaku was appointed chief councilor, and Yoshinobu guardian to the young shogun. Yoshinobu now stood near the top of the shogunate, and the court and the great lords drew closer to their goal of sharing power in national government.

Yoshinobu's political interests were not entirely aligned with those of the other lords due to his loyalty to continued Tokugawa hegemony. Almost immediately, he began to side *against* Shungaku, who wanted to open up the shogunate to participation from all domains, not just the traditional vassals of the Tokugawa household. Shungaku also wanted to grant clemency to opponents of the Ii and Andō regimes. Yoshinobu opposed both these moves, throwing his weight behind the shogunal establishment in Edo—perhaps because he worried about Tokugawa authority eroding too quickly, or perhaps because of a shrewd political calculus to earn the backing of Edo's officials.[44] Matters came to a head in the ninth month when the imperial court sent Sanjō Sanetomi to extract a promise from the shogunate to annul the existing foreign trade treaties and to send the shogun himself to Kyoto to meet with the court. Yoshinobu, siding with the shogunal establishment (and perhaps recognizing the futility of reopening the treaty question with the foreign powers) argued that annulling the existing treaties was impossible, but Shungaku decided to adopt the court's anti-treaty position. Yoshinobu found himself trapped. He grudgingly changed his position, but then on 10/21 he submitted his resignation. Yoshinobu sulked for five days or so before being persuaded to return to his post, but just three weeks later he resigned again.[45] Finally, after the shogun agreed to travel to Kyoto to discuss the anti-treaty question directly with the court, shogunal officials persuaded Yoshinobu to travel to Kyoto early in the new year of 1863 ostensibly to prepare for the shogun's visit but also hoping that the court's fond view of Yoshinobu and his Mito roots would lead to reconciliation between court and shogunate.

The political machinations that led to Yoshinobu's appointment as shogunal guardian illustrate the complex set of cleavages and alliances that structured Tokugawa politics in the 1860s. Three broad divides were at play. First, the shogunate's traditional establishment was pitted against the great lords, who had placed their hopes in Yoshinobu for a greater political role in national politics. Some of these lords, especially Satsuma, were willing to use the court to pressure the shogunal establishment to accept greater participation. Second, a divide was developing between the shogunate and an emerging alliance between Chōshū and radical courtiers, bolstered by sympathetic radicals from Mito and across Japan. Radicals, both in Mito and across Japan, saw Yoshinobu as the heir to Nariaki's strident anti-foreign and pro-imperial vision of a reformed Japan. In the early 1860s, neither Chōshū nor the court was in a position to overthrow the Tokugawa, but they saw in Yoshinobu a potential ally in their quest for a greater role in determining Japan's fate. Third, the great lords had little interest in entertaining radicalism, which was threatening to undermine their power within their domains. They shared this view with the shogunal establishment, who were desperate to quell radical unrest. The great lords grew increasingly suspicious of agitation by Chōshū, and worried about the pro-Chōshū radical faction growing within the court. They feared that hotheaded action would trigger war with the West and domestic disorder, sending Japan down China's humiliating path after the Opium War.[46] In the years to come, Yoshinobu would try to manipulate these alliances and exploit these divisions in order to strengthen his own hold on power and pursue his vision of a stronger, more unified Japan.

RESTORING SHOGUNAL AUTHORITY

After arriving in Kyoto on 1863/1/5, Yoshinobu's primary goal was to shore up the shogunate's authority vis-à-vis the court and to establish a model of cooperation between the court, the shogunate, and the great lords. Immediately, however, he ran into the intersecting political divisions and alliances that had shaped his rise to power. First, the shogunate's officials in Edo resented the court's demands for a shogunal trip to Kyoto and were keen to reassert Tokugawa supremacy. But the court was under the sway of the radical faction, in alliance with Chōshū, that was keen to limit the shogunate's power. The court insisted that the shogunate close the treaty ports, a stern repudiation of Ii Naosuke's unilateral decision to sign the Harris Treaty in 1858. Yoshinobu sympathized with this criticism of the shogunate's earlier actions, but he also believed that the shogunate need confirmation of its authority to rule on behalf of the court in order to maintain legitimacy and effectively mobilize the country against the foreign threat. If he could extract such a confirmation, he could sideline Chōshū and reduce the radicals' influence at court. But it was only by promising to revise the treaties that the shogunate could reconcile with the court, a policy that the shogunal establishment deeply opposed. Yoshinobu, however, calculated that it was more important to restore shogunal authority in the eyes of the court; the issue of the ports could be hammered out in detail later, as could tensions with Edo.

In a meeting with Emperor Kōmei on 1863/3/5, Yoshinobu extracted a formal confirmation of the Tokugawa family's position as shogun, responsible for protecting Japan against foreign threats, in exchange for agreeing to close the treaty ports within a matter of weeks. But this statement was soon followed by a second imperial notice outlining the importance of shogunal allegiance to the court, a not-so-subtle assertion of imperial authority.[47] Over the previous year, Yoshinobu had demonstrated his pragmatic streak, using the treaty issue as a tool to curry favor first with the Edo establishment, then—after changing his view—with the court. But siding with the court had not secured full recognition for Tokugawa authority, revealing the ongoing power of the anti-Tokugawa faction at court.

Meanwhile, the great lords were growing angry at the continued agitation of radicals. The most frustrating from Yoshinobu's perspective were a group of men from Mito, who had arrived in Kyoto in two waves, and quickly became embroiled in the city's radical politics. Ironically, the first, smaller group accompanied Yoshinobu, who had few retainers of his own in the Hitotsubashi household, and whose sympathies lay (at least in part) with Mito's reformers. Two months after Yoshinobu, a second group of around one thousand men travelled to Kyoto with Yoshiatsu, who had been assigned to the shogun's entourage. Initially, Yoshiatsu was due to remain in Edo, but the court asked specifically that Mito men travel with the shogun, no doubt reflecting the respect for Mito's imperial loyalism and, perhaps, the partisan interests of the radical faction at court.[48] Many of these Mito men were radicals, including, most notably, Fujita Tōko's son Koshirō. Soon after their arrival in Kyoto, many of them met up with radicals from other domains, strengthening their commitment to "expelling the barbarian," a goal that seemed within reach as the shogun made his visit to the emperor.[49] Before long, however, tensions started running high, and Date Munenari warned that the radicals risked causing serious unrest in the city, or—worse—falling under the spell of Chōshū.[50] The great lords' coalition was fraying: Shungaku resigned from government, stymied by both shogunal officials and pressure from radicals, while Shimazu Hisamitsu denounced Yoshinobu and Shungaku for accepting the unworkable radical policy of "expelling the barbarians."

Thus, while on the surface Yoshinobu had reasserted the shogunate's prerogative in foreign affairs, in doing so he had lost the support of the great lords and committed the shogunate to an impossible task: Britain and the other foreign powers had made it clear they would resist with military force any attempt to close ports. Nevertheless, he believed that accepting the court's demand was the only way to ensure the survival of the shogunate.[51] Yoshinobu returned to Edo on 4/23 to oversee the negotiations to close the ports, but he made little progress: Edo officials resisted the plan and the British refused to entertain the possibility. Yoshinobu tried to resign, pointing to his isolation within the shogunate as a symbol of his ineffectiveness, although the shogun personally intervened to persuade him to stay on.[52] Meanwhile, seeing the shogunate dragging its heels, Chōshū decided to carry out the emperor's wishes unilaterally, and began firing on foreign ships passing through the Straits of Shimonoseki, enraging the foreign powers. In an effort to control Chōshū, the shogunate announced on 8/12 it would close one treaty port, Yokohama, but even this continued to meet foreign resistance—while angering die-hard anti-foreign radicals who refused to countenance any modification of the emperor's will.

And then, on 8/18, a stroke of luck befell Yoshinobu and the shogunate, creating a window of opportunity for Yoshinobu to renew his efforts at bringing together court, shogunate, and the great lords. A group of radicals in Kyoto, including men from Chōshū and the Kurume priest (and Aizawa Seishisai student) Maki Izumi, attempted a coup in Kyoto, setting fire to large swaths of the city and enraging the Emperor Kōmei. Seizing the opportunity, Shimazu Hisamitsu ousted the radical faction at court and their Chōshū allies. Yoshinobu, keen to seize the opportunity, dispatched an embassy to Europe to renegotiate the treaties, signaling his commitment to carrying out the imperial will. Late in the eleventh month of 1863, he arrived in Kyoto to take part in a renewed effort by the great lords to establish a unity government and suppress radical influence at court.[53] He took control of the wayward Mito men, restoring Mito's reputation in the eyes of the other great lords.

Early in the New Year of 1864, the shogun arrived once again in Kyoto, ostensibly to further Yoshinobu's project of reconciling court and shogunate. But the shogun received a surprising letter from the emperor outlining a new policy compromise: the court would cease advocating for total expulsion of the foreigners; in return, the shogun was to cooperate with the great lords to affect a national unity government. This marked a subtle but important shift in court policy and undermined Yoshinobu's firm commitment that the shogunate would expel the foreigners. By asking the shogun directly to pursue a unity government, the court challenged Tokugawa primacy, which was one of Yoshinobu's core principles in his delicate effort to balance the interests of the shogunate with those of the great lords. The imperial letter tilted the playing field too far in the great lords' favor. On 1864/2/15, Yoshinobu learned that Hisamitsu had secretly intervened with the court to draft the letter. At a meeting of the great lords at court the next day, Yoshinobu snapped. After perhaps one drink too many, he launched into a furious tirade, condemning Hisamitsu's plan as an effort to undermine the shogunate as it tried to fulfill imperial wishes by closing Yokohama.[54] Yoshinobu believed in "revering the emperor," but he also refused to abandon loyalty to the shogunate. When push came to shove, Yoshinobu was unwilling to entertain a ruling coalition of court and daimyo that did not account for Tokugawa primacy. Shocked by the outburst, Hisamitsu abandoned the effort to craft a unity government. The other great lords also left Kyoto. The dream of a coalition government had collapsed after just a few months. Three days later, the shogun reiterated his promise that his government would close Yokohama.[55]

Abandoning efforts to work with the great lords, Yoshinobu swiftly consolidated Tokugawa power in Kyoto. On 1864/3/26, he was appointed supreme commander for imperial defense, effectively making him the most powerful shogunal official in Kyoto. Importantly, this was an appointment by the court, not the shogun, signaling his loyalty to the imperial throne and his desire to forge ties between the two centers of power.[56] He turned the imperial guard into a modernized military force, using Western drills, uniforms, and firearms, and also started building battalions of peasant soldiers—a clear legacy of Nariaki's military reform efforts.[57] He relieved a number of daimyo of their various Kyoto guard duties, replacing them with men from Aizu, Kuwana, and his own Hitotsubashi household, all close supporters of the shogunate. The lords of these three domains were all related by blood, the great-grandsons of Mito's sixth daimyo Harumori—another result of Mito's influential family politics. On 4/20, the emperor confirmed the Tokugawa shogun's ruling authority, in exchange for a promise to close the ports and punish Chōshū for its role in the previous summer's violence in Kyoto.

Yoshinobu had successfully restored some of the shogunate's authority vis-à-vis the court and had ensured Tokugawa primacy vis-à-vis the great lords. But this came at a cost to his political reputation vis-à-vis the shogunal establishment. Yoshinobu's consolidation of power in Kyoto meant he was far from Edo and the shogunal establishment. Edo officials resented Yoshinobu for his pro-expulsion views, which they saw as unworkable. They also grew angry at Yoshinobu's seeming indifference to the scourge of radicalism. Yoshinobu's support for expulsion signaled a broader sympathy with the aims of radicals, and this, in the view of many shogunal officials, encouraged violence against the shogunate. Nowhere was this clearer than in his natal domain, Mito, where the Tengutō Rebellion erupted in the spring of 1864, quickly leading to full-on civil war (see chapter 6). The Tengutō repeatedly stated their desire to assist the shogunate in the expulsion of the foreigners, and their actions grew bolder as Yoshinobu doubled down on the expulsion plan. The spread of violence and warfare in Mito and across the northern Kantō put pressure on the shogunate—but it also increased the volatility and unpredictability of domestic and foreign politics, complicating Yoshinobu's efforts to balance the interests of the court, the shogunate, the various great lords, and his own ideological commitments.

The shockwaves from Mito's civil war soon reached Kyoto, where they intersected with the ongoing political challenge of Chōshū. Since the crackdown on the domain on 1863/8/18, the great lords, the court, and the shogunate all agreed that the domain needed to be punished for fomenting rebellion. But they could not agree on a solution and the breakdown of the unity government in the spring of 1864 delayed matters further. Yoshinobu, sympathetic to Chōshū's anti-foreign goals, wanted to take a more conciliatory approach, relying on persuasion to bring the domain back into the fold. Satsuma and Aizu, however, disagreed vehemently, pointing to the continued agitation of Chōshū radicals within Kyoto and their efforts to regain a foothold within the court. Matters came to a head on 1864/6/5, when Aizu men killed a group of Chōshū radicals at the Ikedaya inn in Kyoto. Yoshinobu, worried that a vengeful Chōshū would send troops to the restive capital, finally adopted a more aggressive position, demanding the court order Chōshū's troops to stand down. This regained Yoshinobu the trust of Satsuma and bolstered his alliance with Aizu. On 7/18, he persuaded the shogunate to ask the court to order an attack on the Chōshū radicals, triggering a fierce two-day battle. Fires broke out and quickly spread across the city, burning nearly thirty thousand houses to the ground.[58]

Emperor Kōmei was furious and ordered the shogunate to punish Chōshū for its radicals' behavior. Shogunal officials, however, had little appetite for a military expedition and were angry that Yoshinobu had secured the court order. They were preoccupied with the Mito rebels and a diplomatic spat with the British. Reluctantly, the shogunate ordered various daimyo to send troops to Chōshū, but ultimately the shogunate and Chōshū negotiated an uneasy truce. Chōshū punished its radical leaders, and the shogunate's forces called off their mission, without either side firing a shot. Meanwhile, exasperated Edo officials announced the end of efforts to close the ports. This was part of a concerted effort to shut out Yoshinobu from power. This effort reached such a level that Satsuma proposed to a despondent Yoshinobu late in the eleventh month to abandon the shogunate altogether and try once again to build a new form of government centered on the court.[59]

Satsuma's proposal was a step too far for Yoshinobu, and instead mobilized him to repair his relationships with Edo officials while shoring up support in Kyoto. He refused to leave the capital to oversee the expedition against Chōshū, recognizing the fragility of his base in the city. But he also recognized that he needed to assuage shogunal concerns about his radical sympathies. The most obvious target was the rump band of the Tengutō making their way to Kyoto to appeal to Yoshinobu (see chapter 6). Late in the eleventh month, Yoshinobu raised a force of ten thousand men to defeat this ragtag army. With their hopes for Yoshinobu's support dashed, the Mito men surrendered at Tsuruga on 12/16. Yoshinobu refused even to meet the Tengutō men, judging the political risk too high. And while he did not plan to have them executed, he ultimately acquiesced to the demands of other shogunal officials. Of the roughly eight hundred men who surrendered, 352 were executed like common criminals during the second month of 1865.

This brutal episode ruined Yoshinobu's legitimacy in the eyes of many radical adherents of Mito's "revere the emperor, expel the barbarian" ideology. But it also marked a significant blow against the radical cause across Japan, and at least temporarily gave the shogunate breathing room to strengthen its military forces. In personal terms, Yoshinobu's cold-bloodedness toward his Mito compatriots has been interpreted as a Machiavellian move. The shogunate had grown wary of Yoshinobu's base of power in Kyoto, and his intervening to protect the Mito rebels would have raised their suspicion further. Supporting the shogunate's hardline stance enabled him to maintain his role as a key intermediary with the imperial court.[60] In later years, however, Yoshinobu offered a different reason for his actions. He argued that the rebels had committed an unforgivable offense by exacerbating the factionalism in Mito and rebelling against their daimyo and the shogunate.[61] He feared that the naïve radicalism of the rebels would only tear apart the country at a time of extraordinary weakness in the face of the foreign threat. In any case, Yoshinobu's harsh stance against the Tengutō marked a turning point. Over the next three years, he became a more forceful political actor, willing to challenge opponents aggressively as he took on greater responsibilities. His anti-foreign views, however, also began to soften as he dealt with diplomatic realities and the military threat posed by foreign powers. By the time he became shogun in 1866, he had embraced the need to open the country in order to preserve its integrity, fully rejecting the cause of the Tengutō radicals.

HYŌGO, CHŌSHŪ, AND THE LAST SHOGUN

In 1865, however, Yoshinobu continued to support the court's demands to close the ports, even as the foreign threat grew increasingly severe over the course of the year. Not only had the foreign powers refused to accept the closure of Yokohama, they had also demanded a massive indemnity from the shogunate for Chōshū's attacks on foreign vessels in 1863. The weight of these demands strained the relationship between the shogunate and the court, who continued to feel that the shogunate was far too accommodating. In the spring of 1865, the young shogun Iemochi travelled to Kyoto to try to improve the situation. Unfortunately, Harry Parkes, the new British ambassador, was keen to squeeze the shogunate wherever possible to extract more concessions, insisting on the opening of Hyōgo (Kobe) as a new port for foreign trade. Given Hyōgo's proximity to Kyoto, Parkes knew that this was unacceptable to court hardliners, but he sent ships to Hyōgo anyway to expose the shogunate's weakness and drive a wedge between Edo and the court.[62] On 1865/9/26, anxious shogunal officials proposed accepting Parkes's demand to open Hyōgo to prevent war. Yoshinobu furiously insisted that they seek imperial consent. The shogunal officials ignored him and decided to press ahead with opening Hyōgo. In response, the court punished members of the shogun's council, a blatant intervention into the shogunate's internal disciplinary structure. The shogun and his councilors decided enough was enough. Resentful of the court's unhelpful and bellicose interference, they submitted the shogun's resignation. This effectively left the court to deal directly with the foreigners anchored off Hyōgo, causing chaos in Kyoto.[63]

Yoshinobu, the logical successor to Iemochi, had no interest in taking responsibility for this mess. Instead, he turned the chaos to his advantage. In a series of hurried meetings early in the tenth month, he persuaded Iemochi to stay in his role in exchange for forcing the court to approve the foreign treaties (although not, in the end, to open Hyōgo), essentially conceding its demands for foreign expulsion. This compromise satisfied Parkes and the other foreigners, at least for the time being, and also mended ties between the shogunate and Yoshinobu, allowing him to become a pivotal figure once again in Kyoto.

Unfortunately for Yoshinobu and the shogunate, the tentative resolution of the foreign treaties issue meant only that the simmering issue of Chōshū came once again to the fore. The truce of late 1864 had done little to stem Chōshū's defiance of the shogunate, and the domain continued to train Western-style military troops and purchase weapons. Meanwhile Yoshinobu's disinterest in Satsuma's proposal for a new attempt at unity government pushed Satsuma closer to Chōshū's antagonistic stance toward the shogunate. To make matters worse, the imperial court had softened its stance toward Chōshū and its own radical courtiers. To stanch Chōshū's ascendancy, Yoshinobu advocated for a display of force against the rebellious domain—the only way, in his view, to assert the shogunate's power. He urged the court to approve a second punitive expedition but was overruled repeatedly in favor of more conciliatory approaches. By the spring of 1866, however, Chōshū's brazen intransigence could no longer be ignored, and the court and shogunate swung behind Yoshinobu's plan.

The Second Chōshū Expedition, also known as the Summer War of 1866, proved to be a disaster.[64] The shogunate's troops were disorganized and poorly trained. They suffered humiliating losses at the hands of Chōshū's modernized troops. The shogunate was unable to persuade many domains to send troops to help with the war effort. The most notable absence was

Satsuma, which had fully reversed its anti-Chōshū stance of 1864. The shogunate's prestige and reputation took hit after hit as Chōshū's superior firepower sent shogunal troops fleeing. The young, radical leaders of Chōshū's modernized troops were strong devotees of Mito's "revere the emperor, expel the barbarian" ideology. They went to battle with banners emblazoned with quotes from Fujita Tōko's poetry. How ironic, then, that one of their targets was Nariaki's son, Yoshinobu.

And then, on 7/20, Iemochi died.

Yoshinobu was still the obvious successor, with unmatched lineage, rank, and experience. He had the trust of key court figures, including that of Emperor Kōmei. He led one of the most modern military forces in the country in the form of the imperial guard. But Yoshinobu was not stupid, and he had no desire to take on full responsibility for an embattled institution. Instead, he agreed to succeed Iemochi as head of the Tokugawa family, but not to take the title of shogun. Much later in life, he explained that he was already thinking about ending the shogunate and restoring direct imperial rule.[65] But given his tendency to make cautious, strategic decisions, his choice could more simply have reflected a desire to wait and see how the political winds shifted. Yoshinobu also agreed to continue the war effort against Chōshū, and he started modernizing the shogunate's troops along Western lines, insisting that soldiers use firearms, for instance, rather than bows and arrows. For the first time in more than two hundred years, the head of the Tokugawa household prepared to lead his troops into battle. On 8/11, however, news of a major Chōshū victory reached Yoshinobu. Realizing the futility of fighting against a superior foe, he changed plans and persuaded the emperor to seek an armistice, using Iemochi's death as a pretext to save face.

And so ended the Summer War, a humiliating episode for the shogunate that underlined the woeful lack of military preparedness and its weakening grasp on political authority. In the war's aftermath, Yoshinobu faced the daunting task of restoring the shogunate's tattered authority. In addition to its humiliation at the hands of Chōshū, a spate of popular uprisings across Japan broke out, challenging local government and further eroding the shogunate's popular legitimacy. Officials in Edo treated Yoshinobu and the court with suspicion. The great daimyo had given up the dream of a unity government. And foreigners insistently pressed their case to open Hyōgo.

Yoshinobu realized that only a fundamental transformation of the shogunate could enable Tokugawa power to continue and protect Japan from foreign attacks. On 1866/9/2, he announced an innocuous sounding set of reforms that masked a determination to radically overhaul the Japanese state.[66] He consolidated control over the shogunate by replacing key advisors and putting supporters into key positions in the Tokugawa branch families.

Yoshinobu mended ties with the various vassal daimyo who had been so suspicious of his efforts to work with the great lords. He reorganized the military further, introducing modern weapons from France and making military obligations less burdensome on small domains. He established permanent diplomatic missions to London and Paris, and, at the invitation of Napoleon III, sent his younger brother to represent him at the 1867 Paris Exposition.[67] On 12/5, Yoshinobu accepted the title of shogun, becoming the fifteenth ruler of the Tokugawa dynasty. Unfortunately, just three weeks later the Emperor Kōmei suddenly died, costing Yoshinobu one of his strongest backers in the imperial court. The end of 1866 was thus bittersweet for Yoshinobu.

Over the next few months, Yoshinobu carefully negotiated between the court, Chōshū, the great lords, and the foreigners. He secured the court's acceptance of the opening of Hyōgo in exchange for leniency toward Chōshū at a conference of the great lords, outmaneuvering their efforts to challenge Tokugawa primacy in national affairs and arguing that building "national wealth and strength" required adopting foreign technologies, an argument his father had made a decade earlier.[68] He hosted a banquet for foreign representatives to underscore his regime's control of diplomatic affairs. He wooed the court with money and marriage offers and demonstrated his commitment to imperial authority by moving into the shogun's Kyoto palace, Nijō Castle, on 1867/9/21. This move also countered the influence of the great lords in Kyoto and forced the court to relax its anti-foreign stance further. By the autumn of 1867, Yoshinobu had established the framework of a modern, bureaucratic, centralized state. He had put in place one of the most capable group of shogunal leaders in decades. He had hired Leon Roches, the French representative in Japan, to offer advice and guidance on military and political reforms. He had reasserted the shogunate's prerogatives and had secured the support of the imperial court.

In some ways, Yoshinobu's actions reflected the principles and values of his home domain Mito: revering the imperial court while strengthening Japan against the foreign threat. In other ways, though, Yoshinobu's reforms went far beyond what Mito's men of just a decade before could have imagined. They marked a complete transition toward a modern government and military, with a cabinet, ministries and salaries determined by role, rather than status. Decision-making was centralized, but the shogunate consulted frequently with the great lords. The shogunate was now committed to foreign diplomacy and trade. In other words, under Yoshinobu the Tokugawa shogunate ceased to be a defender of the old order. Instead, it started to build a new, modern Japan, part and parcel of an interconnected, imperialist world.[69]

This reassertion of Tokugawa authority came at a cost. With hopes of coalition government gone, the great lords had retreated to their regions. Angry at their loss of influence at court, and resentful of continued Tokugawa dominance, they plotted military action to topple Yoshinobu's government. Satsuma and Chōshū started independent foreign relations, a development particularly welcome to the British, who resented the shogunate's reliance on French aid.[70] Ordinary Japanese protested across Japan, driven in large part by the severe economic dislocations caused by the expansion of foreign trade. Prices soared, inequality worsened, and the high costs of Yoshinobu's reform efforts led to higher taxes. On 1867/9/26, Yoshinobu announced an even more comprehensive round of reforms, this time focused on raising revenue and fixing the shogunate's budget. These reforms underscored the shogunate's plan to replace Japan's patchwork polity of domains and retainer territories with a centralized state—but one run by the Tokugawa. This move confirmed for many domains that Yoshinobu was not simply trying to preserve the status quo, with its loose confederation of vassals enjoying considerable autonomy, but rather seeking to seize much more power as the leader of the central state.

Discontent mounted over Yoshinobu's ambitions and, just one week after he announced these latest reforms, the shogunate received a proposal from Tosa, urging Yoshinobu to return his ruling prerogatives to the imperial court, paving the way for a coalition government of daimyo and court nobles, all under the authority of the emperor. Within days, Yoshinobu accepted the proposal: he agreed to restore power to the emperor. On 10/12, he announced his intentions to his officials. On 10/13, he told representatives of the daimyo. On 10/14, he returned the Tokugawa ruling mandate to the emperor (*taisei hōkan*), and the court formally promulgated the return of power the next day. Although he did not surrender his title as shogun, after less than a year in the position, Yoshinobu ended 260 years of Tokugawa hegemony.

Why did Yoshinobu abandon his position so readily? It turns out that Tosa's proposal was not a surprise—in fact, Yoshinobu himself may have quietly asked Tosa to submit it. Certainly Yoshinobu was ambivalent about holding national power; his reluctance to accept the title of shogun in 1866 may have reflected this. But, more fundamentally, he recognized that the shogunate was irredeemably weakened in the aftermath of the Summer War and was unable to defend Japan unilaterally. He saw all around him signs of chronic unrest: attacks by violent radical samurai, popular unrest over economic dislocations and the treaty issues, and the continued machinations of the great lords. Worrying reports that both Satsuma and Chōshū were mustering troops to march on Kyoto had reached the corridors of Nijō Castle. Yoshinobu accepted that the only way to strengthen Japan and defend it against the imperialist powers was to sacrifice the shogunate and unite the country behind the court.[71]

It is too simplistic to say that Yoshinobu's childhood education in Mito predestined him to give up the shogunate. After all, he had spent much of the previous four years manipulating the court in order to preserve Tokugawa primacy, and he knew too much about the factionalism there as well as its fundamental lack of governing experience to treat it as a hallowed entity. But his upbringing did teach him the value of the imperial line as a source of national unity, and he remained committed to defending Japan. He firmly agreed with Aizawa Seishisai's view that a divided Japan was at great risk of falling victim to foreign takeover. By 1867, it had become clear that the shogunate could not unify Japan: there was simply too much resistance to Tokugawa authority, and too much division within the shogunate. Only a new political system, centered on the emperor, could unite the disparate interests of Japan's lords. In place of the shogunate, Yoshinobu hoped that his latest reforms would serve as the foundation for a unity government of the great lords serving in council to the court. As the head of the Tokugawa family— possessor of the greatest amount of territory of any daimyo—he no doubt expected to remain one of those lords.

THE COLLAPSE OF THE TOKUGAWA SHOGUNATE

Events moved quickly—and not according to Yoshinobu's plan. The court, severely unprepared to govern, hemmed and hawed about taking on responsibility for things like foreign diplomacy, while domains loyal to the shogunate, particularly Aizu and Kuwana, angrily resisted creating a power-sharing government with the Tokugawa's historical enemies in Chōshū or Satsuma. Daimyo of all stripes refused to come to Kyoto to join a governing council, pretending to be sick or otherwise busy to avoid getting trapped in the brewing storm. On 12/9, Satsuma and Chōshū seized control of the court in a coup, announcing plans to form a new government without the participation of Yoshinobu or other shogunal officials. Once in control of the court, hardliners clamored for Yoshinobu's resignation as head of the Tokugawa household and the surrender of all Tokugawa territories. The court was reluctant: Yoshinobu's reputation had soared since returning authority to the emperor. And Yoshinobu was furious, seeing in this act a self-interested power grab. Yoshinobu angrily left Kyoto for the Tokugawa stronghold of Osaka on 12/12 in order to regroup. On 12/22, Yoshinobu agreed to surrender his title, but refused to surrender his lands, denouncing Satsuma. On 12/24, supporters of the shogunate in Edo attacked Satsuma's estates, inflaming tensions and pushing Aizu and Kuwana to seek war.

A week later, Yoshinobu dispatched his armies to Kyoto, where they met Satsuma and Chōshū forces at the Battle of Toba-Fushimi, on the outskirts of the imperial capital. Between 1/3 and 1/6, the shogunal armies suffered defeat after defeat. Satsuma and Chōshū had thoroughly modernized their forces and were hungry for victory. Yoshinobu had developed a modernized infantry, but they lacked strong leadership. The troops belonging to Aizu and other vassal domains were hopelessly outdated. But above all, the shogunal forces lacked the drive and passion of their enemies. Many of Yoshinobu's lieutenants saw the writing on the wall for the shogunate. Yoshinobu had little appetite for battle and particularly wanted to avoid fighting in Kyoto. He claimed later he had no choice but to respond to an attack by Satsuma troops.[72]

On 1/6, Yoshinobu boarded a ship from Osaka to Edo in a hasty and undignified retreat. With Satsuma and Chōshū marching on Osaka, bearing the imperial banner, he knew that staying put would mark him as an enemy. By leaving for Edo, he hoped to signal his submission to the court. Nevertheless, the next day the court issued an order to defeat Yoshinobu, labeling him an enemy of the court for occupying Osaka and failing to send the belligerent leaders of Aizu and Kuwana home from Kyoto in late 1867.[73] Yoshinobu arrived in Edo 1/12, and—for the first time since becoming shogun—entered Edo Castle. By 1/16, he had decided that he would not fight to preserve Tokugawa preeminence. From then on, he oversaw a "program of capitulation," reducing the size of his government, opening up channels to the court to hand over power, and, on 2/12, entering voluntary confinement at Ueno to signal his subordination to the imperial forces.[74] Yoshinobu ordered Edo Castle be left undefended. On 4/4, the imperial armies, led by Satsuma and Chōshū forces, entered Edo Castle with no resistance. For all intents and purposes, the Tokugawa shogunate no longer ruled Japan.

Tokugawa Nariaki and his son Yoshinobu had taken the ideas and policies of Mito's reformers to the national stage, where they sought to transform Japan's system of government into a more modern, centralized institution that could repel the foreign threat and unite Japan's people under the imperial court. These men were among the most influential politicians of their day, and they spread a language of political reform that inspired people across Japan to begin reimagining their country as a modern nation-state.

Nariaki remained as divisive after death as he was during his life. To his opponents, Nariaki was selfish, arrogant, stubborn, and vindictive—and many blamed him for Mito's worsening factionalism and descent into civil war. His supporters admired his convictions and his willingness to take bold action to save Japan. They pointed to his consistent desire to strengthen and support the shogunate, and criticized the corrupt and timid members of the establishment in both Mito and the shogunate for undermining his efforts. These equally passionate responses reflect Nariaki's charisma and forcefulness, and the radicalism of his vision of how to unify Japan and preserve its independence. In the long term, Japan achieved this vision. But at the time of his death, Nariaki left behind a domain—and a country—collapsing into chaos.

Assessments of Yoshinobu are also rather mixed. In many respects he was a brilliant politician, clear-eyed about the challenges facing the shogunate and Japan. But he also lacked a human touch and failed to rouse popular sympathy. His decision to retreat rather than fight in the early days of the Boshin War is puzzling.[75] His leadership meant making compromises and tradeoffs for both principled and self-interested reasons. At the same time, however, his story also illustrates how Mito's ideals were the basis for the most far-reaching attempt to reinvent the Tokugawa order to prepare it to lead a nation into the modern world. Yoshinobu achieved a platform for disseminating Mito's reformist ideals unmatched by any of his predecessors. Yoshinobu, drawing on Mito's reform legacy, helped push Japan toward its modern form.

Both Nariaki and Yoshinobu helped promote a new vision of political power in mid-nineteenth-century Japan, one centered on a renewed imperial court, one that drew on able and talented leaders, and one that was strong enough and flexible enough to cope with the myriad domestic and especially foreign threats that were overwhelming the traditional order. In the end, Mito's leaders were unable to maintain control of the process of political modernization that unfolded in the 1860s: neither Nariaki nor Yoshinobu could escape the imperative of family loyalty, even as they fought against the structures of Tokugawa rule. This tension ultimately proved unworkable, and as this fact became clearer to more and more people around Japan, the shogunate's base of power eroded faster than Yoshinobu could reform its institutions. But other reformists, including many friends and supporters of Mito, had also taken up the cause of political transformation. They, too, believed in the Mito cause of revering the imperial court, and without the encumberances of family loyalty, were able to sweep away Tokugawa rule. That process, however, was also driven by self-interest, political angling, and—especially in Mito—cycles of vengeance and violence. In the end, Mito's most prominent leaders were unable to prevent their home domain from being torn apart by the ideological and political pressures they sought to apply to Japan at large.

NOTES

1. Seya Yoshihiko discusses Nariaki's divisive legacy and the concomitant lack of attention to him in the first part of *Mito no Nariaki* (Mito: Ibaraki shinbunsha, 2000).

2. Mark Ravina, *To Stand with the Nations of the World* (Oxford: Oxford University Press, 2017), 86.

3. See, for instance, Shinozaki Yūta, "Ka'ei-ki ni okeru Tokugawa Nariaki 'san'yo' no jittai to eikyō," *Meiji ishin shi kenkyū* 15 (March 2018): 1–21 and Monma

Takeshi, "Tokugawa Nariaki no meiyo kaifuku o meguru dōkō," *Kinsei kindai ikōki no rekishi ishiki, shisō, yuisho*, ed. Kindai Ibaraki chiikishi kenkyūkai (Tokyo: Iwata shoin, 2017), 21–51.

4. Seya, *Mito no Nariaki*; Nagai Hiroshi, *Tokugawa Nariaki: fukakujitsuna jidai ni ikite* (Tokyo: Yamakawa shuppansha, 2019). In English, the only full-length study of Nariaki is Matthew Lamberti's unpublished 1968 Columbia PhD dissertation, *A Political Study of Tokugawa Nariaki of Mito, 1800–1860*.

5. Iechika Ryōki, *Tokugawa Yoshinobu* (Tokyo: Yoshikawa kōbunkan, 2014), 5. There are numerous studies of Yoshinobu's career as shogun; alongside Iechika, the best is Matsuura Rei, *Tokugawa Yoshinobu* (Tokyo: Chūō Kōronsha, 1975). In English, Conrad Totman, *The Collapse of the Tokugawa Bakufu, 1862–1868* (Honolulu: University of Hawai'i Press, 1980) offers the most detail, although primarily within the context of shogunal politics.

6. Shibusawa Eiichi, ed., *Sekimukai hikki: Tokugawa Yoshinobu kō kaisōdan* (Tokyo: Heibonsha, 1966). Conrad Totman makes this critique of Yoshinobu's memoirs, and of Shibusawa's subsequent scholarship based on those memoirs, in *The Collapse of the Tokugawa Bakufu, 1862–1868*, 564.

7. One exception is Nagoya Tokimasa, *Mitogaku no tassei to tenkai* (Mito: Mito shigakkai, 1992), 49–73, although here the focus is primarily on how Yoshinobu "realized" the imperial loyalism of his ancestor Mitsukuni and father Nariaki.

8. Nagai, *Tokugawa Nariaki*, 185–87.

9. Nagai, *Tokugawa Nariaki*, 201.

10. In contrast to his reform agenda, Nariaki was not particularly inventive when it came to naming his twenty-two sons. After Tsuruchiyomaro, their names reflected the order of their birth: Ji- (2) rōmaro, Sabu- (3) rōmaro, Shi- (4) rōmaro, and so on.

11. Shibusawa, *Tokugawa Yoshinobu kō den*, vol. 1 (Tokyo: Ryūmonsha, 1918), 12.

12. Shibusawa, *Tokugawa Yoshinobu kō den*, 11–12, and Matsuura Rei, *Tokugawa Yoshinobu* (Tokyo: Chūō kōronsha, 1975), 8.

13. Shibusawa Eiichi, ed., *Sekimukai hikki*, 4.

14. *Mito shishi*, ed. Mito shishi hensan iinkai, chū, vol. 4 (Mito: Mito shiyakusho, 1982), 14–15. (Hereafter Mito shishi)

15. For a fuller discussion, see *Mito shishi*, 4:133–45.

16. There is a convenient chart of all Nariaki's children in Nagai, *Tokugawa Nariaki*, 198–200.

17. Ōniwa Kunihiko, *Chichi yori Yoshinobu-dono e: Mito Nariaki Hitotsubashi Yoshinobu ate shokanshū* (Tokyo: Shūeisha, 1997).

18. Mark Ravina discusses this group of reform-minded lords in *To Stand with the Nations of the World*, 83–106.

19. Tadano Masahiro, *Fujita Tōko no shōgai* (Tokyo: Kinseisha, 1997), 124–30.

20. Quoted in Mark Ravina, *The Last Samurai: The Life and Battles of Saigō Takamori* (Hoboken, NJ: John Wiley & Sons, 2004), 61.

21. Quoted in Tadano, *Fujita Tōko no shōgai*, 129.

22. Mitani Hiroshi, *Ishin shi saikō* (Tokyo: NHK Books, 2017), 137–40.

23. Yoshida Toshizumi, *Mitogaku to Meiji ishin* (Tokyo: Yoshikawa Kōbunkan, 2003), 202–14.

24. Kirihara Kenshin, "*Shinron* juyō no ichikeitai: Yoshida Shōin o chūshin ni," *Kokumin kokka keisei ki no chiiki shakai: kindai Ibaraki chiiki shi no shosō* (Tokyo: Iwata shoin, 2004), 73–76.

25. Nakata Shōichi, *Yoshida Shōin to Mito* (Tokyo: Kinseisha, 2015), and Yoshida, *Mitogaku to Meiji ishin,* 188–201.

26. H. D. Harootunian, *Toward Restoration the Growth of Political Consciousness in Tokugawa Japan* (Berkeley: University of California Press, 1970), 34–35, 281–314.

27. Mitani, *Ishin-shi saikō*, 133.

28. *Mito-han shiryō*, jō (Tokyo: Yoshikawa kōbunkan, 1917), 8:403–6.

29. *Mito-han shiryō*, jō, 11:569.

30. Seya, *Mito no Nariaki*, 166–67.

31. Ravina, *To Stand with the Nations of the World*, 86.

32. Shinozaki, "Ka'ei-ki ni okeru Tokugawa Nariaki 'san'yo' no jittai to eikyō," 18.

33. Iechika, *Tokugawa Yoshinobu*, 13.

34. Mitani, *Ishin shi saikō*, 136.

35. Iechika, *Tokugawa Yoshinobu*, 33.

36. For a fuller account, see William Beasley, *The Meiji Restoration* (Stanford, CA: Stanford University Press, 1972), 117–39.

37. *Mito-han shiryō*, jō, 33:958.

38. *Mito-han shiryō*, ge, 3:105–9.

39. *Mito-han shiryō*, ge, 4:154.

40. Iechika, *Tokugawa Yoshinobu*, 40–41.

41. *Mito shishi*, chū, vol. 5 (Mito: Mito shiyakusho, 1990), 68.

42. *Mito-han shiryō*, ge, 5:177.

43. Iechika, *Tokugawa Yoshinobu*, 42.

44. Totman, *Collapse of the Tokugawa Bakufu*, 12.

45. Totman, *Collapse of the Tokugawa Bakufu*, 37–39.

46. Mitani, *Ishin-shi saikō*, 197.

47. Totman, *The Collapse of the Tokugawa Bakufu*, 58.

48. *Mito-han shiryō*, ge, 6:258.

49. *Mito shishi*, chū, 5:75.

50. *Mito shishi*, chū, 5:104.

51. Iechika, *Tokugawa Yoshinobu*, 54.

52. Iechika, *Tokugawa Yoshinobu*, 59–60.

53. Totman, *Collapse of the Tokugawa Bakufu,* 91.

54. Beasley, *Select Documents in Japanese Foreign Policy*, 73–74.

55. Iechika, *Tokugawa Yoshinobu*, 70–71.

56. Iechika, *Tokugawa Yoshinobu*, 75.

57. Totman, *The Collapse of the Tokugawa Bakufu*, 166.

58. Totman, *The Collapse of the Tokugawa Bakufu*, 126.

59. Iechika, *Tokugawa Yoshinobu*, 91–92.

60. *Mito shishi*, chū, 5:466–70.

61. Shibusawa Eiichi, *Sekimukai hikki*, 85.

62. Beasley, *Select Documents,* 80–81, 291–92.

63. Totman, *The Collapse of the Tokugawa Bakufu*, 160–61.

64. The Summer War is Conrad Totman's term. Totman, *The Collapse of the Tokugawa Bakufu*, 227.

65. Shibusawa, *Tokugawa Yoshinobu kō den*, 3:259.

66. Totman, *The Collapse of the Tokugawa Bakufu*, 277.

67. Iechika, *Tokugawa Yoshinobu*, 163–73, and *Mito shishi*, chū, 5:551–53.

68. For details of the Hyōgo debate and Yoshinobu's arguments to the court in favor of opening, see Beasley, *Selected Documents,* 77–91, 306–20; quote in Shōgun Keiki to Imperial Court, April 9, 1867, 308.

69. Iechika, *Tokugawa Yoshinobu*, 139–40; see also Ravina, *To Stand with the Nations of the World*, 106.

70. Ravina, *To Stand with the Nations of the World*, 106–10.

71. Iechika, *Tokugawa Yoshinobu*, 177–80, 207–14. Until recently, historians have argued that Yoshinobu expected to maintain Tokugawa primacy in a different form after surrendering the ruling mandate, but Iechika argues that this was unlikely. Yoshinobu worked hard to persuade the court to accept the return of the mandate, and he genuinely recognized the Tokugawa shogunate's inability to act unilaterally to protect Japan.

72. Totman, *The Collapse of the Tokugawa Bakufu*, 433–36, and Iechika, *Tokugawa Yoshinobu*, 237.

73. Iechika, *Tokugawa Yoshinobu*, 224.

74. Totman, *The Collapse of the Tokugawa Bakufu*, 441.

75. Iechika discusses this unsettled assessment in *Tokugawa Yoshinobu*, 5–8.

Chapter Six

The Violent Restoration

Civil War and the End of Mito Domain

On 1858/8/3, the Mito domain government issued a warning to local officials: "As reports on the chaotic developments in Edo continue to arrive, our people's spirits will undoubtedly be inflamed."[1] The "chaotic developments" in question were the spate of punishments leveled by the shogunal regent Ii Naosuke against Tokugawa Nariaki, Tokugawa Yoshinobu, and their reformist supporters among the great lords, in retaliation for their unscheduled visit to Edo castle to protest Ii's signing of the Harris Treaty. These punishments were the beginning of the Ansei Purge, which marked a brief resurgence of the traditional powerholders in the shogunate and struck a blow against both the reform faction of great lords and radical anti-foreign samurai in Mito and across Japan.

Mito's officials were right to be concerned about the spirits of Mito's people. In the years after Nariaki's second ouster, angry protest and violent conflict became commonplace across Mito, and Mito's radical wing took that violence to Edo and beyond as they fought for the expulsion of foreigners and, increasingly, against the shogunate itself. This violence led to outright civil war within Mito by mid-1864, pitting radicals—low-ranking and rural samurai, wealthy farmers, and priests—against an alliance of moderate reformers and the traditional establishment. Warfare and the cycles of vengeance that followed killed thousands of men, ruining many a family on both sides of the ideological divide. The ideological battle of Mito's civil war intersected with a different set of conflicts, rooted in the structural changes in Mito's society and economy. The Tenpō Reforms had helped many of Mito's villages recover from their long eighteenth-century decline, but at the cost of increasing inequality within village society. While many richer villagers eagerly joined the radical "revere the emperor, expel the barbarian" movement, poorer villagers became the victims of extortion and forced labor demands by the battling political factions, heightening their resentment of their richer, collaborator village peers.

In the last fifteen years of Mito Domain, these conflicts and divisions reached tragic and devastating levels. The extreme factionalism, social unrest, and civil war also undermined what had been Mito's most urgent lesson for the rest of Japan: the need to forge a united nation in the face of domestic trouble and foreign threats. In the aftermath of Tokugawa Nariaki's death in 1860, Mito's leaders failed to unite their domain. Mito's radicals' outright defiance of the shogunate undermined their claim to be supporting the Tokugawa in the quest to unite Japan. The factionalism that had been building for decades became insurmountable, and the result was that Mito ceased to play a major role on the national stage after the mid-1860s. Moreover, the cycles of vengeance and retribution that developed after Mito's civil war ensured that the scars of factionalism lived with Mito's people for many, many years. They destroyed Mito's samurai class and tore the lives of ordinary people apart. At a national scale, the civil war that accompanied the 1868 Meiji Restoration was relatively inconsequential and bloodless, warranting barely a sentence or two in histories of Japan's modern revolution.[2] For the people of Mito, however, the birth of modern Japan was bloody, violent, and devastating, the conclusion to years of growing acrimony over the politics of reform.

THE ANSEI PURGE AND
MOUNTING UNREST, 1858–1860

Events in Edo during the summer of 1858 caused a wave of unrest in Mito that undermined the fragile balance of power between radical reformers, their moderate counterparts, and conservative samurai from the traditional establishment. Tokugawa Nariaki and his supporters were already bitter over the shogunate's decision on 6/1 to select Yoshitomi, the young Kii heir, to succeed the shogun Iesada. Ii Naosuke's decision to unilaterally sign the Treaty of Amity and Commerce with the United States on 1858/6/19 (July 29) further enraged Nariaki, his son Yoshinobu, and their supporters, who protested by confronting Ii at Edo Castle. Ii doled out a wave of punishments in return, sentencing Nariaki to house arrest. Yoshiatsu, too, was ordered to refrain from attending Edo Castle. News of Nariaki's punishment reached Mito immediately, and the reformist coalition of activist samurai, rural elites, and radical scholars made plans to travel to Edo to protest. In response, Ii interfered directly in Mito's domain government, ordering harsh crackdowns on Nariaki's most fervent supporters in the domain. Ii also set guards at the gates of Mito's estates in Edo, an insulting gesture that made Nariaki's supporters in Mito even angrier. Although the domain government remained in the hands of reformers, their power was under attack.

Meanwhile, Ii's unilateral action on the Harris Treaty, followed soon by treaties with four other Western powers, prompted a backlash from Kyoto, where a furious Emperor Kōmei decided to make the shogunate pay for its disregard of the imperial will. On 1858/8/8, the court issued the so-called secret edict, which criticized the signing of the Harris treaty and called on all of Japan's daimyo—not just the traditional powerholders in the shogunate—to meet to discuss how to solve domestic unrest by unifying the court and shogunate, and how to avoid the disgrace of foreign conquest.[3] Not only had the court issued a shockingly political statement, it had also sent a copy directly Mito, in blatant disregard of the normal channels of communication through the shogunate. The court also included an addendum addressed only to Mito that instructed the domain—and its "retired lord," meaning Nariaki—to enforce the instructions to the shogunate by circulating them to domains around Japan. This was a clear challenge to the shogunate's authority and reflected the work of Mito's leaders over the previous years to cultivate strong ties to the court.

The secret edict swiftly complicated an already fragile political situation for Mito's government. Mito's radicals joyously welcomed the secret edict, which they took as a sign that their criticism of Ii Naosuke and the Harris Treaty was on the right path. Moderate reformers, best represented by Aizawa Seishisai, reacted in horror. He feared that it would lead to terrible punishment for the domain by an angry shogunate. He also believed that it would trigger an irreversible divide between the court and shogunate, undermining the entire social hierarchy that he believed lay at the core of Japan's national essence. Seishisai criticized the radical faction within Mito—so many of whom had passed through his classroom—as a reckless and cavalier gang, willing to destroy the domain and abandon the ethical principle of loyalty to one's lord. He implored the domain to return the edict to the imperial court.[4] The daimyo Yoshiatsu and his advisors, trying to have it both ways, hesitantly committed to returning the edict. Ii, unsurprisingly, was furious, and added more pressure to the domain by forcing a number of reformist officials into retirement toward the end of the eighth month of 1858 and increasing the surveillance of Mito's estates in Edo.

In response to both Yoshiatsu's ambivalent position on the secret edict and Ii's aggressive stance toward Mito, radical samurai, villagers, and priests began streaming toward Edo. Officials managed to halt this group at Kogane, the third post station from Edo on the main Mito-Edo highway. There, several hundred men dug in their heels and issued calls for Nariaki's release and the shogunate's acceptance of the secret edict. Domain officials urged the radicals to disperse, but simultaneously pointed to the group as a warning to the shogunate of the depths of popular dissatisfaction with Ii's actions. Yoshiatsu successfully negotiated an end to shogunal intervention in Mito's affairs and then persuaded the Kogane men to return home by the end of 1858/9.[5]

Despite this détente, Ii was determined to secure a retraction of the secret edict, and he dispatched officials to Kyoto to resolve the crisis. There they heard rumors that Mito radicals had induced the court to issue the edict, and in the ninth month, Ii began a purge of Mito's radicals and their supporters in Kyoto. Facing intense pressure, radical Mito *shishi* sought support from Fukui, Tottori, Chōshū, and Tosa—all places friendly to Mito, or with a group of sympathetic radicals who had studied Mito's ideas. Unfortunately for Mito's radicals, however, none of these domains' governments were willing to offer public support in the face of Ii's crackdown. Nevertheless, upon hearing of these efforts Ii extended his purge of Mito's radicals to Edo beginning in the tenth month of 1858. He dispatched his deputy Manabe Akikatsu to Kyoto to persuade the court to retract the secret edict. He arrested several high-ranking Mito officials on conspiracy charges in the spring of 1859, and summoned others to Edo for questioning.

These actions enraged Mito's radicals. The domain administration repeatedly implored the radicals not to take rash actions, particularly in advance of Manabe's return to Edo in the third month of 1859. They warned about spies from the shogunate and ordered local officials to keep track of any radicals seen praying fervently at local shrines. They desperately tried to stop radicals from travelling towards Edo.[6] Meanwhile, Ii's crackdown continued, and more Mito radicals were imprisoned. Officials begged Ii to release Nariaki and Yoshiatsu from their punishments in order to ease tensions, but to no avail. By the sixth month of 1859, thousands of samurai, wealthy farmers, and Shintō priests gathered once again at Kogane Post Station, where they set up roadblocks to prevent officials from carrying the edict out of the domain. Domain officials were paralyzed. Radical voices supported the actions as a necessary stand against Ii's attacks on Mito, and as a sign of support for overturning the foreign treaties and expelling the foreigners. Moderates agonized that the actions would only invite harsher crackdowns: Aizawa Seishisai, for instance, was "at a loss for words" at the mayhem unfolding on Mito's highways.[7] Nariaki, too, was trapped: he recognized the futility and danger of the radicals' actions but was not willing to betray his supporters.[8]

The moderates' fears proved well founded. On 1859/8/23, the shogunate captured someone who claimed to be plotting on Nariaki's behalf and used this as a pretext to increase the punishments on Nariaki and Yoshiatsu. Nariaki was forced to leave Edo and enter house arrest in Mito. A number of Mito's radicals, including some high-ranking officials, were executed or sentenced to long prison terms. Ii ordered the bakufu junior councilor Andō Nobumasa to oversee Mito's government, effectively handing control to the traditional establishment. By the middle of the ninth month, Nariaki finally decided that the behavior of the radicals posed too great a risk to Mito, and privately urged radicals in Edo to return home.[9] These actions finally persuaded the radicals to abandon their stand at Kogane, and they dispersed by 1859/10/6. In exchange, the shogunate relaxed the punishments on Yoshiatsu and Mito's house elders—but they continued to arrest and imprison Mito's radicals, with a goal of removing them from Mito's Edo estates. Ii also continued to purge Mito's sympathizers, executing Hashimoto Sanai and Yoshida Shōin during the tenth month. The shogunate had dealt a severe blow to Mito's radicals and their supporters.

Other Mito commoners protested in less visible ways. Kurosawa Toki was a poet and teacher from the village of Suzugoya, about twenty kilometers northwest of Mito castle town. Through her literary networks and family she had absorbed the "revere the emperor, expel the barbarian" ideology flourishing in Mito's academies, and was well informed about Mito politics. She was a dedicated supporter of Nariaki, and she watched from Suzugoya as he fell victim to Ii Naosuke's purge. In the eighth month of 1858, a bright, white comet appeared over Suzugoya—a portent of ill times. Kurosawa interpreted the comet as a call to action, and in 1859, she embarked on a bold journey to Kyoto to submit an entreaty directly to the emperor, condemning Ii and seeking Nariaki's exoneration. Along the way, she composed in her head a long poem laying out her case, and once in Kyoto she asked Saida Koresada, a Kokugaku scholar, to submit it on her behalf to Emperor Kōmei. She then left Kyoto for nearby Osaka, where she was captured by shogunate police. For the next few months she was interrogated, mostly by officials trying to find the men who had put her up to this audacious task: after all, how could a women, acting alone, make her way to Kyoto? They did not believe her when she told them that she had no accomplices, and they threw her into prison. Kurosawa fell ill, but still the interrogators sought answers about her networks, refusing to believe her argument that she was acting solely in response to the comet of 1858 and out of her heartfelt dedication to Nariaki. On 1859/10/27, she was sentenced to banishment, but she soon returned quietly to Suzugoya.[10] Kurosawa's dedication to Nariaki hints at the depth of loyalty that he had gained among ordinary people across Mito domain.

Despite Ii's crackdown and the efforts of Nariaki and other Mito leaders to control radicals within the domain, anger and frustration continued to boil beneath the surface, and before long it erupted again. On 12/15, Yoshiatsu was summoned to Edo Castle, where Ii and Andō told him that they had secured

Figure 6.1.   Portrait of Kurosawa Toki
(Ibaraki Prefectural Archives and Museum)

from the court a revocation of the secret edict. They demanded that Yoshi-atsu hand over the document within three days or be deemed in violation of the imperial will. The edict itself, unfortunately, was in Mito—Nariaki had spirited it away from Edo earlier that fall—and Yoshiatsu immediately dis-patched an emissary to Mito to seek advice. Over the next few days, Nariaki and high-ranking officials in Mito debated what to do. With radicals largely in prison or absent, moderates carried the day, and proposed (as a compro-mise) returning the document directly to the court, thus satisfying the court's demand without surrendering directly to Ii and the shogunate. Unfortunately, this outcome satisfied no one: the shogunate refused to accept it, and a group of radicals in Mito, once they got wind of the leaders' proposal, promptly blockaded the Edo highway at Nagaoka, the first post station from Mito on the highway to Edo.

Unlike the earlier blockades at Kogane, the Nagaoka blockade was a clear and direct challenge to the domain administration. Only about sixty-five people or so participated, and—unsurprisingly, given the punishments meted out to radical samurai—they were predominantly priests, Shugendō worship-pers, and rural elites. But they were firmly opposed to returning the secret edict, arguing that the shogunate had forced the court to issue the retraction and therefore violated the true imperial will. To make matters worse, the domain leadership was starkly divided on the question of the secret edict. Nariaki wanted to delay as long as possible, preferably by getting a confirmation directly from the court; Yoshiatsu and officials in the Edo estates wanted to surrender the document immediately to the shogunate; and Seishisai wanted to return the edict to the court. Amid these debates, a skirmish broke out in the castle town between a few of the Nagaoka men and domain troops, raising fears that the band would launch a full-throated attack. One official committed *seppuku* in the castle grounds as the leadership dithered, raising tensions further. Finally, at Seishisai's urging, the domain dispatched troops to Nagaoka. The blockaders crept away before the troops arrived, ending the stalemate.[11]

While the Nagaoka blockade was preoccupying the attention of officials in Mito and Edo, another group of Mito radicals decided that the only way to overcome shogunal obstructionism was to assassinate Ii. With their actions limited by the crackdown in Mito, many of Mito's radicals had left for western Japan, where they sought out friends in the western domains that were the shogunate's historical enemies, most famously Satsuma and Chōshū. There, the young activists found willing allies in their quest to overthrow Ii and reject the treaties, all in the name of "revering the emperor, expelling the barbarians"—a sign of how widespread and influential Mito's teachings had become by the late 1850s. After failing to secure backing from Satsuma's leaders late in 1860/1, they decided to act alone, and they developed plans to attack Ii in Edo. Several of the Nagaoka blockaders joined the plotters in Edo after the dissolution of the blockade late in 1860/2. Domain officials reported the absconders to the shogunate, who put out arrest warrants, but they were too slow. On 3/3, sixteen Mito men, joined by one man from Satsuma, carried out their attack as Ii entered Edo Castle's Sakurada Gate. They killed Ii immediately.

News of Ii's assassination thrilled Mito's radicals, but it further embroiled Mito in political turmoil. The perpetrators defended their actions by claiming Ii had violated the imperial will, both through his unilateral signing of the foreign treaties and by machinating against the court's secret edict. They did not, however, argue in favor of overthrowing the shogunate altogether; rather, they claimed to set the shogunate back on its rightful path.[12] Nevertheless, the attack dealt a serious blow to Tokugawa legitimacy, weakening the shogunate vis-à-vis the great lords and the court. It also eroded the authority of Mito as one of the three Tokugawa branch houses. To many observers, Mito's samurai had allied with Satsuma, the Tokugawa's historical enemies, and turned against their household—hardly a model of loyalty and honor. With Nariaki's death just a few months later, in the eighth month of 1860, Mito lost its most charismatic leader, further reducing its preeminence on the national stage.

TAKEDA KŌUNSAI AND THE
POLITICS OF CONTAINMENT, 1860–1863

The Sakurada Gate attack demonstrated to the shogunate—now headed by Andō Nobumasa and Kuze Hirochika—the limits of Ii's harsh approach to the treaty issue, the court, and radical activists. They changed course and adopted a more conciliatory approach, including efforts to forge stronger ties between court and shogunate (see chapter 5) and a more lenient attitude toward Mito. They did, however, continue to insist on the surrender of the secret edict and the suppression of radical activism. To oversee this project, Yoshiatsu asked the shogunate to release a number of officials with radical sympathies from their punishments so that they could serve in government once again. This, he hoped, would help rebuild trust between the radical activists and their government, a necessary first step to bringing order back to Mito. Takeda Kōunsai (1804–1865) was among these officials, and his efforts at building peace—followed shortly by the failure of those efforts—exemplify Mito's tortuous politics during the early 1860s.

Kōunsai came from a long line of Mito retainers, and he was close to Mito's reformist scholars, joining Aizawa Seishisai and Fujita Tōko on their expedition to Edo in 1829 to lobby for Nariaki's accession as daimyo. Kōunsai was a firm believer in the ideas of the Mito scholars but, as he told

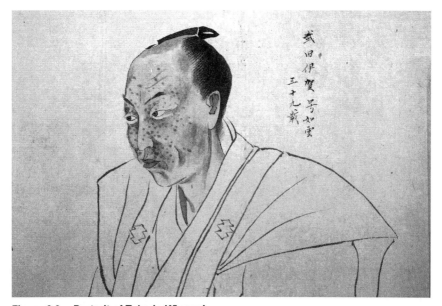

Figure 6.2. Portrait of Takeda Kōunsai
(Ibaraki Prefectural Archives and Museum)

his children, "you don't need to become a scholar" to put these values into action. The core of being a samurai was the willingness to die at any time in the defense of righteousness.[13] After Nariaki's succession as daimyo, Kōunsai quickly moved up the ranks of the reform administration, becoming a house elder, the highest rank of Mito's officialdom, in 1839. His elite position was a marked contrast to Tōko and other reformers who had much lower ranks. In a political system that prioritized hierarchy and family background, Nariaki and his reformist supporters relied heavily on men like Kōunsai, whose elite lineage made it much easier to justify his promotion to positions of power.

As house elder, Kōunsai dealt not only with issues in the domain but also with national politics. He urged Nariaki to reject foreign demands to open ports to trade, and he worked closely with officials in the shogunate and at the imperial court to promote the anti-foreign cause. He worried that foreigners were learning Japanese more quickly than Japanese officials were learning English, putting Japan at a disadvantage in negotiations—so he asked Nariaki to sponsor English teaching in Mito. A strong proponent of "expelling the barbarians," he welcomed the imperial edict of 1858 that ordered Mito to uphold that policy—and criticized Nariaki's son, the daimyo Yoshiatsu, for failing to take the shogunate to task for its weak approach.[14] Until his ouster during the Ansei Purge, Kōunsai was the most powerful member of Mito's radical faction in the domain government.

Kōunsai's high rank and radical sympathies made him a good candidate for extending an olive branch from the domain government to low-ranking, radical activists. In the aftermath of the breakup of the Nagaoka blockade and then the attack on Ii, some Mito men tried to flee to Satsuma Domain, although they were quickly arrested. Another group decamped to one of Mito's domain schools in the village of Tamazukuri, where they holed up and began plotting their next steps. These schools were originally created in the late 1850s to teach the reform ideas of Nariaki and the Mito scholars to commoners across the domain. The primary audience was local elites, such as village heads, Shintō priests, and rural samurai, with a large number of ordinary farmers joining these elites in military training, sometimes drilling daily out of their fervent commitment to "the Japanese spirit."[15] The radicals were not necessarily welcome in communities like Tamazukuri. To support themselves, they extorted and bullied local villagers for food and money, spreading resentment and fear among Mito's commoners and eliciting harsh crackdowns from the domain government. Kōunsai urged Yoshiatsu to adopt a more conciliatory approach, arguing that the crackdowns were inflaming the situation. He also warned that the root cause of the tension was a lack of balance and fairness in the domain's government: he blamed conservative figures for constantly undermining the reformist government and blatantly disregarding the ideas and dedication of the radical camp. Mito's establishment, he warned, was putting their private interests over the interests of the domain and, by extension, the grand cause of national salvation.[16] After securing Yoshiatsu's agreement, Kōunsai persuaded the leader of the Tamazukuri holdouts to surrender in the second month of 1861.

But this approach backfired: establishment elites protested this lenient treatment and demanded harsher crackdowns on radicals. The domain government acquiesced, issuing an order to local officials on 2/22 that they should kill ány radicals who resisted arrest.[17] In the fourth month, they announced another crackdown on radicals who had not surrendered with the Tamazukuri group. Just a few weeks later, however, on 1861/5/28, the attack by a small group of Mito radicals on the British legation at Tōzenji led to another round of reprisals against reformist leaders. The shogunate intervened in Mito's government, forcing Kōunsai into house arrest and restoring members of the traditional establishment to positions of power.[18] Unfortunately, these actions inflamed tensions yet again among Mito's radicals. Early in the New Year of 1862, a small group of Mito radicals snuck out of the domain to Edo, where they attempted to assassinate Andō Nobumasa as he entered Edo Castle's Sakashita Gate. Although they failed to kill him, they succeeded in further undermining the shogunate's authority and creating opportunities for Satsuma, Chōshū, the court, and other groups opposed to the shogunate's policies to gain power. Within Mito, the Sakashita attack inspired the radicals to continue agitating against the foreign treaties, and they found a receptive audience at the court. The shogunate, desperate to halt the rapid loss of its authority, punished officials associated with the Ii and Andō regimes, and released many of the victims of the Ansei Purge. On 1862/8/5, Yoshiatsu received instructions to once again participate in national political debates; shortly thereafter, a shogunal emissary paid respects at Nariaki's grave. Yoshiatsu ordered the release of radical officials in Mito, including Kōunsai; by the eleventh month, he had been restored to his official position as house elder.[19]

For the next year or so, Kōunsai and the radicals once again dominated Mito politics. Soon after regaining his position as house elder, he travelled to Kyoto at the request of the imperial court and spent the next few months attending policy meetings related to foreign affairs. He built close ties to high-ranking court officials and even received a personal gift of chopsticks from the emperor after dining with him. As a strong advocate of closing the ports, as well as a high-ranking representative of a Tokugawa household, he found himself in an influential position to pressure the shogunate to accept the court's demands for a harsher foreign policy. On 1863/3/5, Yoshinobu had accepted these demands on behalf of the shogunate and agreed to close the ports (see chapter 5). Kōunsai returned to Edo in the fourth month of that year to oversee the closing of Yokohama, and then went back to Mito two months later to oversee defensive preparations along the coast.

RURAL LIFE IN MITO, 1858–1863

The bewildering and rapid vicissitudes that swept Mito's political landscape between 1858 and mid-1863 took place alongside changes in the structures of life for Mito's commoners, particularly in rural Mito. Some of these changes in the rural economy had been unfolding for decades, since at least the Tenpō Reforms, while others reflected the more immediate pressures caused by the expansion of foreign trade in the late 1850s and the consequences of political turmoil within Mito. Rural unrest became a distinctive feature of Mito's countryside in this period, and it intersected in complicated ways with the ideological and political changes taking place among Mito's samurai and educated commoner elite.

Four interlinked trends defined Mito's villages in the middle of the nineteenth century. First, they began to prosper again, after nearly a century and a half of decline and stagnation. In part this was due to the effects of the domain's Tenpō Reforms of the 1830s and 1840s. Despite the fall of the reform government with Nariaki's ouster in 1844, major initiatives, such as the land survey and tax reforms, continued under the subsequent establishment regime, and then again after Nariaki's return to power in the 1850s. Over time, the domain was less effective at implementing these reforms, but they nevertheless helped stabilize local villages.[20] New land surveys focused on land reclamation, and although the destruction of many records makes it difficult to get a full picture of the domain, evidence suggests that village populations and agricultural productivity stabilized in this period.[21] Second, the initial enthusiasm among reformers such as Fujita Tōko for restricting commercial agriculture gave way relatively quickly to the more moderate view in favor of cash crops and export products. This included commercial food crops, such as soybeans, sesame, and *konnyaku*, as well as other cash crops, notably lacquer trees and safflower (*benihana*) for oil production.[22] This helped accelerate the trends toward commercial agriculture that had long been underway, especially in southern Mito.

Third, the extension of commercial agriculture caused new rifts in village society. In earlier periods of rural stress, poor farmers had often abandoned villages, fleeing to the castle town or Edo to eke out a living. They left behind villages dominated by wealthier, less precarious farmers. In the 1850s, however, there is evidence that class stratification had increased, with a new pool of poorer tenant farmers occupying a larger and larger percentage of village populations.[23] In other words, increasingly capitalist social relations were developing between landowners and tenant farmers producing cash crops for export and trade. Finally, as commercialization increased, many villages ceased to be self-sufficient and came to depend on markets that stretched to Edo and around the Kantō. By the early 1860s, this included the foreign trade passing through Yokohama. Foreign trade was highly disruptive to existing markets, with many Edo-based suppliers to Mito redirecting their goods to the lucrative Yokohama market. In 1860, the shogunate reminted its currency to address the problem caused by Japan's comparatively undervalued gold. This caused huge price increases for certain goods in Mito, such as tea, copper, and rice, and led to cash shortages. These economic dislocations strained commoners and samurai alike and complicated the domain's perennial efforts to solve its fiscal woes.

As a result of these changes, social tensions rose in this period across Mito, independently of the political cleavages between the radical, moderate, and conservative factions in Mito's government and among its educated elites. In the villages of southern Mito, where commercialization had spread the most, crime rates rose during the 1850s and early 1860s, causing disputes and anxiety about village stability.[24] Elsewhere, villagers argued over how to share the proceeds from increasingly commercial ventures. In 1862, a group of villagers from Koibuchi, a few kilometers southwest of the castle town, marched to the district administrator's office in the castle town to protest the village headman's failure to maintain infrastructure, failure to distribute revenues from lumber sales, and general failure to behave properly. In contrast to earlier moments of rural unrest, they were not demanding tax relief or aid for impoverished residents; rather, their complaints illustrate newfound dissatisfaction with the social hierarchy within the domain.[25]

The accelerated spread of a commercial rural economy was not directly tied to the political battles between radicals and conservatives, but the social tensions within Mito's villages did intersect with those ideological cleavages. Many rural elites became "mobilized" by the ideological work of the Mito scholars, through the land reforms, the promotion of some to rural samurai status, and the rural schools.[26] These elites supported the radicals in Mito's government, and many took time off from agricultural work to attend the rural schools, protest the punishment of Nariaki in 1858 and 1859, or accompany samurai travelling to Edo or Kyoto during the early 1860s. The domain government worried that village life was disrupted by the travels of these commoner supporters of the radical cause, a sign that these new forms of political activism were disrupting the structures of village life.[27] As political tensions between radicals and their opponents in Mito's government worsened in late 1863 and into 1864, they began to converge with these latent social tensions, pushing the domain toward civil war.

MITO'S CIVIL WAR, 1863–1865

The situation in Mito began to deteriorate in the last months of 1863 as national political crises once again inspired Mito's radicals to take up arms. Between the Sakashita Gate attack in early 1862 and the summer of 1863, the radical "expel the barbarian" faction seemed to have the upper hand in Kyoto, with backing from Chōshū, court nobles, and Mito's radical activists. But in the summer of 1863, Chōshū fell from power after overplaying its hand. Radicals were chased out of the imperial guard and other institutions, buying the shogunate time to negotiate a more moderate solution to the foreign crisis. In the aftermath of the crackdown on Chōshū in Kyoto in the eighth month of 1863, radicals across Japan once again turned to Mito Domain. Radical samurai and activists from around Japan sought help from Mito allies, most famously the Chōshū samurai Kido Takayoshi and the radical courtier Sanjō Sanetomi.[28] Some travelled to Mito, where they joined bands of Mito's radicals in the domain schools scattered across Mito's regional towns. By the end of the year, similar radical groups had sprouted up around the northern Kantō. The shogunate warned villagers of roving bands of "masterless samurai, claiming to be from Mito, who extort money or force farmers to join their bands, all in the name of 'expelling the barbarian.'"[29] With domain leadership in disarray, in Mito and elsewhere, many villagers armed themselves and chased down these marauding bands in vigilante posses.[30] The Kantō, heartland of the Tokugawa shogunate, was collapsing into anarchy.

In the aftermath of Chōshū's ouster from Kyoto, Yoshinobu and the shogunate quickly tried to capitalize on the imperial court's change of heart. Yoshinobu expressed his desire to carry out the court's order to expel the barbarians, dispatching an embassy to Europe to renegotiate the treaties (see chapter 5). These actions, however, raised alarm bells within Mito. Local officials warned that the shogunate's commitment to close the ports had excited radicals across Mito. Without concrete steps to achieve this, however, they feared that those radicals would prove uncontrollable.[31] Unfortunately, the shogunate could not countenance such blatant disregard for their authority by marauding gangs of radicalized samurai, farmers, and priests, acting outside the structures of domains or shogunal authority. No matter how much some officials, whether in the shogunate or in individual domains, sympathized with the goal of expelling the barbarians, they could not reconcile that sympathy with the clear challenge to the Tokugawa political system that the radical bands posed.

The shogunate, having regained some power in the aftermath of Chōshū's ouster from Kyoto, turned its attention back to the Kanto in late 1863, determined to stamp out this lawlessness. With the shogun himself ordered to stay in Kyoto by the court, Mito was given the responsibility for reinstating order in the Kanto. Yoshiatsu, stationed in Edo to oversee this operation, ordered Kōunsai to quell the unrest at its source: Mito's rural schools. Kōunsai must have felt a sense of déjà vu: four years after negotiating with the Tamazukuri holdouts, he faced another band of radicals in Mito's schools. As he had with the Tamazukuri band, he sympathized with the radicals' cause, but disagreed with their tactics. He urged the leader of the radicals, Fujita Tōko's son Koshirō, to wait a little longer before raising an army to physically expel the barbarians from Japan's shores. But Koshirō rejected Kōunsai's pleas and accused him of betraying the Mito cause. Kōunsai set up a military camp in southern Mito, while continuing to send envoys and negotiators to Koshirō to persuade him not to raise an army.

Unfortunately for Kōunsai and Edo officials' efforts to quell the unrest in Mito and across the northern Kantō, however, Yoshinobu's reassertion of his commitment to close the ports as part of his consolidation of power vis-à-vis the other great lords on 1864/2/15 excited Mito's radicals. Koshirō argued— not unreasonably—that his intentions were in line with Yoshinobu's policy. Kōunsai and other domain leaders sent a constant stream of envoys to dissuade Koshirō, arguing that raising an illegal army, even one that supported the shogunate's policies, would force the shogunate to destroy Mito Domain. Undaunted, Koshirō decided the time was right to lead an army to expel the barbarians from Yokohama and Japan. In 1864/3, Koshirō raised an army at Mount Tsukuba, just south of Mito, to lead a vanguard action to expel the foreigners. This band, popularly known as the Tengutō, attracted the support of not only radical samurai but also many of the rural elites and Shintō priests that had backed Nariaki's reform movement. The Tengutō travelled to the Tokugawa shrines at Nikkō and other nearby areas, with some bands resorting to extortion, arson, and even murder to secure supplies from local villages.[32] On the way to Nikkō, they issued a call to arms to radicals across Japan: "Serving the court above and assisting the shogun below, we intend to spread the authority of the divine land over the nations of the world."[33]

The Tengutō's claims to be "assisting" the shogunate did not convince either the domain government or the shogunate. Then, on the night of 1864/5/14, two placards appeared on walls in Mito castle town. The first, signed by "the righteous band," decried the establishment government as an "evil gang," and threatened them with "divine retribution." The second contained an even more dangerous statement: its author accused the shogunate of failing to uphold the imperial will and called on Mito's samurai to rise up and overthrow the Tokugawa shogunate.[34] On 5/30, the Tengutō decided to return to Mount Tsukuba to regroup. On the way, they set fire to the town of Tochigi after its intendant refused to give them money, and they threatened to burn down the castle town of Yūki. Local rulers demanded action from the shogunate, while the rebel band grew in size as sympathetic priests, villagers, and rural samurai joined.[35]

The Tengutō actions divided Mito's retainers. Radicals such as Kōunsai urged Yoshiatsu to announce his support for the insurgents' cause of expelling the barbarians as the only way to bring them under control. The traditional establishment, led by Ichikawa Hiromi, were apoplectic that Koshirō and his band were running amok across the Kantō, disregarding the orders of Mito's elders and besmirching the reputation of the domain. And moderate reformers, such as Aizawa Seishisai's followers, also believed that the risk posed to Mito's stability by the Tengutō actions outweighed any righteousness in their cause. The establishment and the moderates put aside their differences and agreed to work together against the radicals, forming a coalition known as the "Student Faction," after the many members who were studying at the Kōdōkan. After the placards condemning the shogunate appeared in the fifth month, members of this group travelled to Edo to demand that Yoshiatsu crush the rebels and expel radical sympathizers from Mito's government. Yoshiatsu, facing pressure from shogunal officials in Edo, had no choice but to expel reformists and put Ichikawa in charge of the domain government. Yoshiatsu sent Kōunsai back to Mito and ordered him into house arrest.[36] Ichikawa quickly gathered an army of several thousand to take on the Tengutō rebels. In the sixth month, the shogunate ordered the domains of the region to quash the rebellion and dispatched a shogunal army to join Mito's establishment forces.

The crackdown on reformers shattered the Student Faction's fragile alliance, however, as moderates recoiled at Ichikawa's seizure of power. They reunited with radical reformers against Ichikawa and the conservative establishment, and a group of reformers left Mito in mid-June to take their case to Yoshiatsu. Kōunsai, in confinement in Mito, watched as events spiraled out of control, and on 6/22 he agreed to join the reformers heading south for Edo, even though it meant violating his punishment. They got as far as Kogane, the post station just outside of Edo, where forces from Tsuchiura Domain, acting on the shogunate's orders, stopped them from travelling further. Yoshiatsu sent an envoy to the reformers at Kogane, begging him to send half of their men home and submit their opinions in writing. Kōunsai replied, arguing that the seizure of Mito's government by the conservative establishment was a direct violation of Nariaki's wishes and therefore had to be dealt with immediately—above and beyond the debates about closing the ports. Kōunsai stayed at Kogane for the next month, trading letters with Yoshiatsu about the dangers of Ichikawa's regime.

War between Ichikawa's troops and the Tengutō rebels broke out early in the seventh month. On 7/7, the shogunal armies attacked Koshirō's forces at Takasai, just west of Mount Tsukuba. After an initial victory by shogunal troops, the rebels counterattacked under cover of darkness and routed the pacification army. Ichikawa's men retreated to the castle town, where they imprisoned and killed family members of the Tengutō. This prompted the Tengutō to attack the castle town, but they failed to oust the conservatives, who consolidated power, disregarding instructions from Edo, where reformers still had power. The Edo-based reformers protested immediately to Yoshiatsu, demanding that he punish Ichikawa's unilateral seizure of power in the domain. Yoshiatsu was desperate to restore order in Mito but could not go in person to broker an end to the conflict, as he was in charge of Edo while the shogunate attempted to negotiate with Chōshū (see chapter 5). Yoshiatsu designated as his personal representative Matsudaira Yorinori, the daimyo of the Mito branch domain of Shishido, and ordered him to restore order to Mito.[37]

Yorinori was a poor choice for this effort. He had long been a supporter of Nariaki and Mito's reformers, and his sympathies lay with the anti-establishment factions in Mito, even if he agreed that the radicals were behaving inexcusably.[38] He privately believed that the Mito Tokugawa family was obliged to carry out Nariaki's will and expel the barbarians.[39] As he travelled to Mito, several partisan groups keen to oust Ichikawa and support the Tengutō rebels joined Yorinori. His force ballooned in size with thousands of samurai and commoners, many of whom were supporters of the Tengutō, or at the very least opponents of Ichikawa: Kōunsai, for instance, joined Yorinori as he passed through Kogane. Ichikawa, upon hearing of these developments, decided to treat Yorinori's army as allies of the Tengutō band. He refused to surrender the castle town, and even demanded that the shogunate send another army to quell Yorinori's force. Yorinori's men attacked Ichikawa's forces on the edge of the castle town on 1864/8/10. A week later, he formally joined Koshirō's troops and seized Nakaminato and started laying plans to retake the castle town. The pacification army had become part of the rebel force.

The situation in Mito rapidly disintegrated. The Tengutō forces relied on extortion and theft from local villages to supply their men, and, in some cases, they killed merchants whom they considered to have benefitted from foreign trade. With the domain government effectively not functioning, villagers began to band together to resist the Tengutō men. The village of Koibuchi, where social tensions were already high, joined with dozens of nearby villages and put up a force of more than two thousand men to fend off the Tengutō attacks. This force eventually joined the battles against the Tengutō men.[40] Poorer villagers also began targeting village elites, many of whom supported the Tengutō or had even joined their forces. The number of smashings and attacks on the homes of rural samurai, local officials, rich farmers, merchants, and priests soared during the summer of 1864.[41] On 8/15, a band of one hundred Tengutō men demanded rice from Gohei, the hereditary leader of Mito's outcastes. He refused, leading them to burn down twenty houses. Gohei in turn raised an army of five hundred men and joined the Koibuchi forces against the Tengutō. Of course, the Tengutō were not the only ones to demand money and labor from Mito's commoners. Ichikawa's men also ordered villagers to provide cash, especially around Nakaminato and Mount Tsukuba.[42] Even in the castle town—ostensibly controlled by Ichikawa's men—discontent rose, with townspeople protesting high rice prices on 8/7.[43] Mito's commoners suffered at the hands of both factions in the civil war, and their discontent continued to grow as fighting intensified.

Shogunal officials, furious that Yorinori had not only failed to resolve the conflict in Mito but indeed had worsened the situation, ordered a second pacification army to chase down the first one. This army arrived in Mito on 8/24, and fierce fighting raged between the Tengutō and Yorinori's forces, on the one hand, and the alliance between the shogunate's army and Ichikawa's men, on the other. Over the next month, hundreds of men died, and large swathes of the domain were destroyed.[44] On 9/16, Yorinori finally agreed to surrender, along with his men. On 9/26, he was sentenced to death for failing to carry out his orders to pacify Mito; he committed *seppuku* that night.

Koshirō and Kōunsai, however, escaped with a thousand or so holdouts from Nakaminato after another month of fighting against the shogunal pacification army. After a ragged march from the coast, they regrouped in the mountains north of Mito, appointed Kōunsai their leader, and decided to march to Kyoto, where they hoped to appeal to Yoshinobu and explain that their aims in raising an army were to carry out the "revere the emperor, expel the barbarian" cause. They set off through the steep mountains of central Japan, maintaining a low profile: Kōunsai was focused on reaching Kyoto above all else. He ordered his men not to pillage or harass villages they passed through, painfully aware of the Mito men's poor reputation in the villages of northern Kantō. In order to secure the acquiescence of other daimyo whose domains he needed to cross, he promised to avoid their castle towns. For two weeks, the Tengutō men stuck to back roads and avoided trouble. Ichikawa was distracted with restoring order in Mito, and the shogunal forces had yet to regroup in Edo. Kōunsai, with his relatively small force, seemed like a minor threat.

It did not take long, though, for reports of Kōunsai's march to reach Edo. No one knew exactly where Kōunsai was headed, and the shogunate feared that it might be Edo or even Yokohama for a direct attack on the treaty port. The shogunate quickly issued orders to domains across central Japan to capture or destroy Kōunsai's army. Kōunsai's men encountered their first armed resistance on 11/16 in Shimonita, on the northwestern edge of the Kantō Plain. The skirmish was short-lived, and the Tengutō men escaped with few casualties. They pressed on into the mountains of central Japan, moving swiftly. They were challenged again at Wada Pass, where they again repelled their opponents. They continued through the mountains, persuading Iida Domain to let them pass freely, before descending into the lowlands around Nagoya, where the Owari branch of the Tokugawa household also let them pass, under heavy guard.

Shogunal officials continued to demand that the Tengutō men be stopped, and as the group neared Kyoto, fears of unrest in the imperial capital induced the court to weigh in. On 11/29, Tokugawa Yoshinobu received the court's permission to lead an army toward Nagoya in order to prevent the Mito men from reaching Kyoto. Kōunsai's hopes of appealing to Yoshinobu's sympathies were dashed. With no hope of beating the shogunate's military forces in battle, Kōunsai left the main highway to Kyoto and led his men into the mountains north of Nagoya in hopes of breaking through to the Sea of Japan and approaching Kyoto from the north. They crossed into Echizen Province on 12/5, where snow was already deep. By this point, the group had developed a fearsome reputation, and local communities waited in terror for the Tengutō men to pass their way.[45] They negotiated safe passage through Ōno Domain and doggedly pushed onward to the coast, in heavy snow. On 12/11, they arrived in Shinbo, where the forces of Kaga Domain awaited them.

Kōunsai, trapped, asked to negotiate with the Kaga forces, who accepted the request and also agreed to forward a petition to Yoshinobu. In it Kōunsai argued that the imperial desire to expel the barbarians had fallen by the wayside, ignored and derailed by the shogunate and other forces. Mito had been taken over by the evil Ichikawa, disgracing the legacy of Nariaki. He and his men had no choice but to act to uphold the imperial will and the honor of Mito Domain. For a few tense days, negotiations continued between Kōunsai, Yoshinobu, and other shogunal and domain leaders. Kōunsai did not want to fight, and Kaga Domain wanted to arrange a peaceful surrender, but Yoshinobu and other shogunal leaders wanted a punitive attack to destroy the Mito radical movement and serve as a warning to other radicals elsewhere in Japan. Yoshinobu's arguments carried the day, and the date for an attack was set for 12/17. Kaga desperately urged Kōunsai to surrender before then, in hopes of preventing bloodshed. Kōunsai submitted his surrender notice to Kaga's forces on 12/16, and his force of 823 men were taken into custody.

Events moved swiftly and brutally after Kōunsai's surrender. Yoshinobu was satisfied by the capture of Kōunsai's men by Kaga, but the leader of the shogunate's second pacification army in Mito demanded harsher punishments, in line with the execution of Yorinori and his rebels in Mito earlier that year. On 1865/1/20 Yoshinobu acquiesced. The Mito men were transferred to herring storehouses: reeking, cramped, and windowless buildings with no comforts. They continued to plead their case, insisting on their commitment to the shogunate's formal policy of expelling the barbarians and the importance of preserving Nariaki's honor in Mito. But the shogunate could not countenance such a blatant rebellion against its authority; there was to be no leniency for Kōunsai and the Mito radicals. Kōunsai was sentenced to death and executed on 2/4, along with two of his sons who had joined his expedition, as well as Koshirō and other leaders of the Mito group. By 2/23, 352 Mito men had been executed in Tsuruga. Another 130 men were exiled, while several hundred farmers who had been conscripted into the small army were sent back to Mito. The Tengutō men, committed to the Mito ideal of "revere the emperor, expel the barbarian," had met their grisly and tragic end.

THE CONSERVATIVE REGIME, 1864–1868

After Yorinori's surrender and execution at the end of the ninth month of 1864 and the flight of Koshirō, Kōunsai, and the rump band of Tengutō men a month later, Ichikawa reasserted establishment control over Mito. He soon exacted revenge on the supporters and families of Mito's radicals. The wives and children of Tengutō men, including those of Takeda Kōunsai, were captured and thrown into prison. Many died there, either at the hands of the executioner or by starvation and illness.[46] More than three dozen Mito samurai who had led the fighting against Ichikawa's troops were executed in 1865/3, decimating the ranks of Mito's younger generation of samurai.[47] Others were jailed, their stipends and properties taken away: "several hundred families were removed from the domain roster . . . everywhere one saw masterless, tumbledown samurai mansions."[48] The moderate camp of reformers tried to persuade Ichikawa to be lenient toward the Tengutō men, but they had little sway within the government. Ichikawa began personnel reforms in early 1865 that consolidated his power, pushing the moderates away and rewarding other establishment figures with stipend increases and promotions. He started to reverse and unwind the reform agenda and banned the teachings of Mito's reformist scholars at the Kōdōkan.[49]

Central to Ichikawa's project to reassert control was his effort to disarm Mito's commoners and restore the traditional status order by stripping commoners of the privileges they had acquired during the course of the Tenpō Reforms and Mito's civil war. In 1865/1, the domain imposed strict rules on who could carry swords and who could bear surnames, and restricted gun ownership to hunters. Rural schools were dismantled, commoners were banned from training in martial or military arts, and village militias were outlawed.[50] A few months later, the domain followed this edict with an offer of amnesty to any villager who had participated in the violence of the previous summer, in exchange for a commitment to agricultural work and community peace.[51] In the eighth month, the domain admonished villagers for "forgetting their place," urging them to return to the traditional morals and customs of the status order.[52] Ichikawa was determined to reintroduce conservative values and return Mito to an older social model.

Ichikawa's efforts to reassert establishment control met with anger and discontent from all quarters and, before long, word of his harsh tactics reached Kyoto and Edo. Moderate Mito samurai based in Kyoto, repelled by Ichikawa's actions, approached the daimyo of Okayama and Tottori—both brothers of the late Nariaki—to ask for their support in a plan to get the imperial court to intercede in Mito; the court eventually instructed the shogunate to consult with them before making any decisions regarding Mito. Ichikawa, alarmed, tried to build ties with the shogunate to shore up his position. However, on 1865/10/24 and 10/25, Ichikawa's administration executed dozens of his opponents without warning, seizing them in the middle of the night. Ichikawa had heard that the shogun Iemochi might resign in favor of Yoshinobu, whom he considered an ally of the radicals (see chapter 5); he feared that Yoshinobu might intervene on the behalf of Mito's radicals. Unfortunately for Ichikawa, the executions backfired: shogunal officials were outraged that he had taken such a drastic step, and ordered that Mito's government seek approval from the shogunate prior to taking similar actions in the future. This directive marked the subjugation of Mito to outside authority, and a growing loss of trust in Ichikawa's regime among shogunal and court officials.[53]

Conditions on the ground in Mito also contributed to the febrile atmosphere in the domain. Many commoners and rural samurai were unhappy at Ichikawa's efforts to strip their newfound power and status. Compounding matters, rice prices soared throughout 1865. In 1866/2, two rural samurai and a local priest petitioned the domain government to redistribute some of the assets seized from Tengutō men to the "noble commoners" who had fought on Ichikawa's side against the radicals. They also urged the government not to abolish local militias but, instead, to form a much larger force, some twenty thousand strong—a figure that would have represented a sixth of the male population of Mito Domain.[54] This did not come to pass, but it reflects some of the anger at Ichikawa's actions, as well as the newfound political identity that had emerged through the civil war. In 1866/3, the outcaste leader Gohei, who had joined Ichikawa's forces after the Tengutō burned down his village, refused to return to the leatherwork that was traditionally relegated to outcastes, another sign of reluctance to Ichikawa's conservative backlash.[55] In 1866/4, a large *uchikowashi* protest broke out in Nakaminato, pitting the parishioners of a local shrine against merchants who had received domain permission to cut trees on shrine land. The uprising quickly spread in size, and before long rumours that Mito was on the verge of yet another round of outright warfare had reached worried observers in Edo, Kyoto, and beyond. In response, Ichikawa took even harsher steps, throwing a number of moderate reformers into prison in an attempt to maintain his grip on power.[56]

By the summer of 1866, neither the court nor the shogunate could ignore the situation in Mito. The court summoned Mito's senior house elder and asked whether they should order Ichikawa and his administration to commit suicide as a way to heal the rifts within the domain. Deciding this was likely to make things worse, not better, the court instead asked the shogunate to establish a dedicated "Office of Mito Reform" to oversee a more moderate approach to rehabilitating the domain's government. This backfired, too: Ichikawa and his men resisted shogunal attempts to interfere and maintained their hold on power into the fall of 1867, when Yoshinobu's return of the Tokugawa ruling mandate set off a series of events that plunged Mito once again into war.[57]

MITO'S RESTORATION

Yoshinobu's decision to return power to the imperial court in the tenth month of 1867 caused consternation among Mito's samurai. Ichikawa insisted that the domain, as a Tokugawa branch family, support the shogunate without reservation. The court, favoring Mito's radicals, disapproved of Ichikawa, and urged Yoshinobu and Yoshiatsu to remove him from power. Yoshinobu, however, was distracted by events in Kyoto, and had no appetite to intervene in Mito. As the divide between court and shogunate grew in the weeks after Yoshinobu's decision, culminating in the seizure of the throne by Satsuma and Chōshū in the coup of 12/9, the loyalties of pro-imperial Mito radicals diverged. Many chose to join Satsuma and Chōshū, while others demanded reforms in Mito to bring the domain in line with the wishes of the new imperial government. After Yoshinobu retreated from the Battle of Toba-Fushimi, some Mito men returned with him to Edo, while others agreed to serve the new imperial government. Some of the Mito men still in Kyoto sought permission to return to Mito to oust the Ichikawa regime. They secured a court order to do so on 1/19 and left for Edo, where they retook Mito's estates from the conservative establishment. They then marched onward to Mito, arriving in the middle of the third month. Fearing the vengeance of these radicals, Ichikawa chose to flee Mito, joining the Tokugawa loyalist forces in the north. He and his men fought with Aizu and other northern domains against the imperial armies until Aizu's surrender in the ninth month of 1868.

Ichikawa's flight suddenly lifted years of suppression of the reformist factions and unleashed a wave of violence and chaos. Radicals quickly seized power and threw establishment figures into jail or house arrest in an outpouring of pent-up resentment. As tensions worsened, on 4/5 Yoshiatsu died after a serious illness, leaving the domain government without a clear leader.[58] Just ten days later, Yoshinobu returned to Mito at the order of the court. But once there, he avoided politics completely. Instead, he confined himself to the Kōdōkan classroom where, as a young boy, he had first studied Mito's "revere the emperor" ideas. Yoshinobu's presence calmed matters slightly, but only for a little while. No doubt his cold disregard for Mito's Tengutō rebels left him with few friends among his erstwhile supporters. Meanwhile, Takeda Kanejirō, the grandson of the Tengutō leader Takeda Kōunsai, sought vengeance for his grandfather's execution. He secured an imperial order to uphold Nariaki's legacy and oust the "traitors" in Mito's conservative establishment. He arrived in Edo on 4/28, where he embarked on an assassination campaign against many members of the conservative faction on Mito's Edo estates. A few weeks later, he set his sights on Mito, leaving Edo on 5/22. Once there, Kanejirō and his followers embarked on a brutal and bloody campaign of "divine retribution," murdering dozens of establishment samurai and their families, leaving their bodies in the streets or hanging from bridges.[59] People fled the castle town. Finally, on 6/11, a group of five hundred samurai and scholars marched on the castle, demanding that the new government stop Kanejirō's rampage. The government summoned Kanejirō; he refused to come. The government, furious, discussed sending soldiers to kill Kanejirō, but he had amassed a stockpile of weapons in his home and had a large group of supporters. Another devastating battle within the castle town seemed imminent.[60]

News of the showdown reached Yoshinobu in the Kōdōkan and he finally decided to intervene. He dispatched a mediator to the castle, who negotiated punishments for both sides—but also the promotion of Kanejirō to councilor, to mollify his supporters. The settlement averted another outbreak of civil war, but tensions remained high. Yoshinobu left Mito shortly thereafter, relocating to the Tokugawa homeland in Sunpu (Shizuoka). There, he entered a life of seclusion for the next thirty years, staying out of the public eye. Even as people elsewhere in Japan began to turn to the task of building a new, modern nation, the people of Mito could not escape the factionalism and civil war of the 1860s.[61] Yoshinobu's intervention could not solve the deep rifts that had destroyed Mito.

After Yoshinobu left in the summer of 1868, tensions rose again. The domain reissued strong prohibitions against murder and robbery and demanded that samurai families rein in the bad behavior of their sons and brothers.[62] In 1868/9, Ichikawa returned to Mito and attacked the castle before holing up in the Kōdōkan for several days. In the ensuing battles at the school, dozens of men on both sides died. Ichikawa broke free on 10/2 and fled south, where he skirmished with government troops, losing more men. Ichikawa escaped again but was tracked down and captured a few months later. In the early spring of 1869, in front of hundreds of spectators on a field on the outskirts of Mito, he was put to death by crucifixion as punishment for his attack on the domain government.[63] Ichikawa's execution marked the end of warfare in Mito. But it did not mark the end of factionalism, and Mito lived with the scars of these battles for a long time.

Tokugawa Akitake, the eighteenth son of Nariaki, became the last daimyo of Mito on 1868/11/5. He inherited a domain in tatters. Mito's retainer band had shrunk from thirty-five hundred samurai in 1840 to fewer than nine hundred men. Retribution and punishment of Ichikawa's supporters continued into the summer of 1869, with some three hundred men executed between late 1868 and mid-1869. Morale had evaporated, the domain's economy lay in ruins, and Akitake faced instructions to reorganize and standardize administration as part of the imperial regime's centralizing efforts. As part of the nation-wide abolishment of the domains, he formally returned his family's title to Mito Domain to the imperial court on 1869/3, but stayed on as the governor. As he faced these daunting circumstances, Akitake warned the imperial government of the difficulties they faced in governing Mito: "This is a remote, stubborn country. Especially over the past five years, destruction has been severe, and the people's hearts are still unsettled. There are many who will not understand the need to reform the habits of the last two hundred years, and they may well rise up . . . [It may be necessary] to use sword and shield to pacify the region."[64]

Mito Domain ceased to exist on 1871/7/14, and in short order the central government merged the main territory of the domain with surrounding areas to form Ibaraki Prefecture. Akitake resigned from his position as governor. Mito became the prefectural capital, but the dissolution of the domain was yet another blow to the city's pride. The central government dispatched governors from elsewhere in Japan to assert control, bringing in soldiers to keep the peace. In 1872, a mysterious fire broke out, destroying the castle, which hosted the temporary prefectural offices. It was widely attributed to resentment against the new government and its military forces.[65] For several years after the Meiji

Restoration, Mito took on the character of an occupied town, and Ibaraki gained the reputation of a "hard-to-govern" prefecture.[66]

For Mito, neither the Restoration of 1868 nor even the abolition of the domain in 1871 marked an end to the domain's troubles. It would take many years for the wounds caused by the violence and chaos of the late 1850s and 1860s to heal, and, in some ways, Mito never recovered the stature it had enjoyed as the beacon of "revere the emperor, expel the barbarian" philosophy, the model for modernizing reforms and the source of national leadership in the middle of the nineteenth century. Rather, for Mito's people the transition from Tokugawa to Meiji was bloodstained and divisive. Whether among the warring factions of Mito's elite, or in the villages divided by social change and ideological awakening, the birth of modern Mito was a traumatic experience.

The violence and chaos of the last years of Mito also go a long way to explaining why Mito disappeared from the main narrative of the Meiji Restoration. Although the ideas generated by its scholars continued to influence activists and politicians at all levels and in all places, the factionalism within the domain pushed both radicals and reactionaries to extreme positions. After the death of Nariaki, there was no strong leader to hold these divergent views together. Mito ceased to represent anything but division—a poor model for a country whose aspiring leaders, no matter their disputes and differences, largely shared a hunger to unify Japan and establish it as a modern nation.

NOTES

1. "Yūshisha chin'yu no ken," in *Ibaraki ken shiryō: kinsei seiji hen*, ed. Ibaraki kenshi hensan kinseishi dai 1 bukai (Mito: Ibaraki-ken, 1970–), 1:228.

2. Andrew Gordon, for example, devotes only one paragraph to the civil war in his classic textbook, *A Modern History of Japan: From Tokugawa Times to the Present* (Oxford: Oxford University Press, 2014), 59. For a more recent appraisal of the significance of the Boshin civil war as a transformative moment in Japan's military and political history, see Hōya Tōru, "A Military History of the Boshin War," in *The Meiji Restoration: Japan as a Global Nation*, eds. Robert Hellyer and Harald Fuess (Cambridge: Cambridge University Press, 2020), 153–70.

3. Mito shishi hensan iinkai, ed. *Mito shishi*, chū, vol. 4 (Mito: Mito shiyakusho, 1982), 965. (Hereafter cited as *Mito shishi*.)

4. *Mito shishi*, chū, 4:1020–23.

5. Seya Yoshihiko and Suzuki Eiichi, *Ryūsei no gotoku: bakumatsu ishin: Mito-han no eikō to kukyō* (Tokyo: NHK Publishing, 1998), 67.

6. Six orders to local officials, issued between 3/11 and 4/20, underscore the adminstration's desperation (and relative lack of control). See *Ibaraki ken shiryō: kinsei seiji hen*, 1:230–32.

7. Isaka Kiyonobu, *Aizawa Seishisai no bannen to Mito-han: Kokuritsu kokkai toshokan shozō "Aizawa Seishisai shokan"* (Tokyo: Perikan-sha, 2017), 43.

8. *Mito shishi*, chū, 4:1020.

9. *Mito shishi*, chū, 4:1034.

10. This paragraph draws on Laura Nenzi's marvelous biography, *The Chaos and Cosmos of Kurosawa Tokiko* (Honolulu: University of Hawai'i Press, 2015). After the Meiji Restoration, Kurosawa became the first woman primary school teacher in Ibaraki Prefecture.

11. *Mito shishi*, chū, 4:1050–76.

12. *Mito shishi*, chū, 4:1155–56.

13. Ōuchi Jisan, *Takeda Kōunsai shōden: ichimei Mito-han bakumatsu shi* (Mito: Hitachi shobō, 1979 [1936]), 1:178–79.

14. Ōuchi, *Takeda Kōunsai shōden*, 1:215.

15. Quoted in J. Victory Koschmann, *The Mito Ideology: Discourse, Reform, and Insurrection in Late Tokugawa Japan, 1790–1864* (Berkeley: University of California Press, 1987), 151. The rural samurai were a mix of samurai relocated as part of the Tenpō reforms, as well as wealthy farmers who had received samurai status in exchange for monetary contributions to the domain.

16. Ōuchi, *Takeda Kōunsai shōden*, 1:319–22.

17. *Ibaraki ken shiryō: kinsei seiji hen*, 1:234.

18. *Mito shishi*, chū, vol. 5 (Mito: Mito shiyakusho, 1990), 34–36.

19. *Mito shishi*, chū, 5:70–71.

20. For a discussion of the revival of Mito's villages, particularly those in southern Mito, see Yoshida Toshizumi, *Meiji ishin to Mito nōson* (Tokyo: Dōjidaisha, 1995), 20–43.

21. *Mito shishi*, chū, 4:857–62.

22. See, for example, "Urushi hashu hōhō oyobi hanshoku kata shōrei," 1858/3, in *Ibaraki ken shiryō: kinsei seiji hen*, 1:225.

23. Yoshida, *Meiji ishin to Mito nōson*, 20–43.

24. For a detailed discussion of growing instability across a dozen villages in southern Mito, see Yoshida, *Meiji ishin to Mito nōson*, 44–94.

25. Takahashi Hirobumi, *Bakumatsu Mito-han to minshū undo: sonnō jōi undō to yonaoshi* (Tokyo: Seishi shuppan, 2005), 146–54.

26. Koschmann, *The Mito Ideology*, 130–49.

27. "Kannō narabini setsuen tōshin kanchō sasshi oyobi chinbu no ken," 1859/4/10, in *Ibaraki ken shiryō: kinsei seiji hen*, 1:231 and "Gojōkyō zuijū no ninpu fuzaichū nōji hojo oyobi gōchū chinbu nado," 1863/3/26, in *Ibaraki ken shiryō: kinsei seiji hen*, 1:247.

28. *Mito shishi*, chū, 5:119–20.

29. Ōuchi, *Takeda kōunsai shōden*, 1:459.

30. David Howell, "The Social Life of Firearms in Tokugawa Japan," *Journal of Japanese Studies* 29, no. 1 (2009): 65–80.

31. "Jōi no sōkō seigan oyobi muramura mōshiawasegaki," 1863/10, in *Ibaraki ken shiryō: kinsei seiji hen*, 1:249.

32. For discussions of the violence of the Tengutō men, see Takahashi, *Bakumatsu Mitohan to minshū undō*, 117–19, 174–77 and Howell, "The Social Life of Firearms in Tokugawa Japan."

33. Translated by Koschmann, *The Mito Ideology*, 176.

34. *Mito shishi*, chū, 5:282.

35. Conrad Totman, *The Collapse of the Tokugawa Bakufu, 1862–1868* (Honolulu: University of Hawai'i Press), 110–11. Some farmers were conscripted by the rebels, but others joined willingly, hinting at the diversity of political beliefs among Mito's commoners.

36. *Mito shishi*, chū, 5:311.

37. *Mito shishi*, chū, 5:338–40.

38. Totman, *The Collapse of the Tokugawa Bakufu*, 114.

39. Letter from Yorinori to Ikeda Shigemasa, daimyo of Okayama, 1864/7/26; quoted in *Mito shishi*, chū, 5:340.

40. *Mito shishi*, chū, 5:485–89.

41. Takahashi, *Bakumatsu Mito-han to minshū undō*, 175–78.

42. *Mito shishi*, chū, 5:503–6.

43. Takahashi, *Bakumatsu Mito-han to minshū undō*, 187–88.

44. For an overview of the Tengutō Rebellion, see Totman, *The Collapse of the Tokugawa Bakufu*, 108–22 and Koschmann, *The Mito Ideology*, 152–72. For a more detailed account, see *Mito shishi*, chū, 5:185–508.

45. For a study of how one community, Ōno Domain, perceived the Tengutō band, see Maren Ehlers, "Mountain Demons from Mito: The Arrival of Civil War in Echizen," in Hellyer and Fuess, *The Meiji Restoration: Japan as a Global Nation*, 113–36.

46. Yamakawa Kikue, *Women of the Mito Domain*, transl. Kate Wildman Nakai (Tokyo: University of Tokyo Press, 1992), 120–21.

47. *Mito shishi*, chū, 5:385.

48. Yamakawa, *Women of the Mito Domain*, 123.

49. *Mito shishi*, chū, 5:512–16, 520–21.

50. "Gōson shoseido henkaku," 1865/1, in *Ibaraki ken shiryō: kinsei seiji hen*, 1:268.

51. "Senrō shōshi oyobi nanpatsu kison no mono kyōwa narabini ikushi no ken," 1865/5/19, in *Ibaraki ken shiryō: kinsei seiji hen*, 1:271.

52. "Hatto kakushu kagyō reisei chinsei kyōwa no ken," 1865/8/13, in *Ibaraki ken shiryō: kinsei seiji hen*, 1:273.

53. *Mito shishi*, chū, 5:531–38.

54. Takahashi, *Bakumatsu Mito-han to minshū undō*, 225–27.

55. Yoshida, *Meiji ishin to Mito nōson*, 71.

56. For a detailed account of the Nakaminato uprising, see Takahashi, *Bakumatsu Mito-han to minshū undō*, 228–42.

57. *Mito shishi*, chū, 5:547–51.

58. *Mito shishi*, chū, 5:712–35.

59. Yamakawa, *The Women of Mito Domain*, 128–39.

60. *Mito shishi*, chū, 5:771–88.

61. Seya and Suzuki, *Ryūsei no gotoku*, 212–15.

62. "Ansatsu datsuzai nado genkin no ken," 1868/8/20, in *Ibaraki-ken shiryō: kinsei seiji hen*, 1:284.

63. *Mito shishi*, chū, 5:789–814.

64. Akitake to Benkan [Dajōkan], 1869/7/18, in *Ibaraki-ken shiryō: ishin hen,* ed. Ibaraki kenshi hensan bakumatsu ishin bukai (Mito: Ibaraki-ken, 1969), 292.

65. Takahashi, *Bakumatsu Mito-han to minshū undō*, 247.

66. Yasu Norihisa, "Kindai Mito no kōhai to hen'yō," *Rekishi kōron* 9, no. 5 (May 1983): 75.

Conclusion

Mito and Modern Japan

MITO IN THE MEIJI PERIOD

After Tokugawa Yoshinobu surrendered his titles and authority to the emperor in late 1867, the leaders of Satsuma and Chōshū seized the reins of national government in the name of the young Meiji emperor and embarked on a civil war to consolidate control of Japan. The former allies of the shogunate resisted the new imperial army for just over a year, but by the summer of 1869 the civil war had ended, and Japan was unified under imperial rule. The emperor moved to Edo, which was renamed Tokyo, or "eastern capital," and his government embarked on a dizzying series of reforms to continue the late-Tokugawa project of building a "rich nation, strong army." The ideas of Yoshinobu, Nariaki, and Mito's scholars played out in many of these reforms, including military modernization, the colonization of Ezochi (now renamed Hokkaido), the establishment of Shintō as a state religion, and the creation of a centralized national government under the emperor.

Soon, though, the government departed from the more traditionalist and anti-foreign elements of Mito thought, openly embracing Western culture and ideas to promote "civilization and enlightenment," a popular slogan for its program of modernization. The domains of the Tokugawa era were disestablished in 1869, and over the next few years the government abolished the status system, ending samurai privileges and liberalizing the economy to allow for the expansion of capitalist enterprise and state-led industrial growth. This led to dissent within the new regime, most notably from Saigō Takamori, the Satsuma samurai and devoted follower of Fujita Tōko. Since Tōko's death in 1855, Saigō had continued to support Mito's "revere the emperor, expel the barbarian" ideology, but gradually he became convinced that revering the emperor meant overthrowing the shogunate. Ultimately, he led the imperial armies against Tokugawa Yoshinobu and the shogunate, securing victory for the court. But, despite overthrowing the shogunate, he maintained an almost idealistic belief in the samurai morals, including loyalty, virtue, and education in the civil and military arts, that Tōko had emphasized. Throughout the early Meiji period, Saigō hoped to reform (rather than replace) samurai society, and he never fully accepted the move to Westernize Japan by dismantling the social hierarchy of the past or turning to industrialization. He preferred a more traditional vision, one that devoted resources to farmers, banned Buddhism and Christianity, and promised support to the former samurai class.[1] His debt to Tōko's vision of reform was evident. In 1873, he left the government in part to protest its willingness to ignore widespread samurai discontent at the loss of their hereditary status, and, in 1877, he started the Seinan War (Satsuma Rebellion), the last major samurai challenge to the Meiji state.

Saigō's defeat in the Seinan War marked the successful consolidation of power by the Meiji regime and the defeat of the more traditional vision for reform focused on the reinvigoration of samurai morals and the traditional social order. It also marked the restriction of government power to a narrower group of oligarchs. Despite early efforts to create a council of former daimyo to make decisions, the government quickly turned into an institution dominated by the "cliques" of men from former Satsuma and Chōshū domains. Although the cliques included many former supporters of Mito's radicals, such as Ōkubo Toshimichi and Yamagata Aritomo, they made no effort to include Mito men in government. Mito, by virtue of its status as a Tokugawa branch family, was kept at arm's length by the new regime.

While the Meiji leaders embarked on their modernization program, Mito struggled with the aftermath of factionalism and violence. To combat the widespread resentment toward the new government, Ibaraki's governors embarked on a program to win over the hearts and minds of Mito's people by forging a new basis of local identity. They turned to the legacies of Mitsukuni and Nariaki, the two "enlightened rulers" of Mito's history. In 1873, they built Tokiwa Shrine to honor the two daimyo, who were deified there the following year.[2] The Kōdōkan campus and Kairakuen gardens, the defining physical legacies of Nariaki's reign, were preserved as a public park. In 1879, Akitake rebuilt the Shōkōkan historical institute, first founded by Mitsukuni, and encouraged Mito's scholars to resume work on the *Dai Nihon shi*, which—nearly two hundred years after the end of Mitsukuni's reign—was still unfinished.

Mito's new leaders gingerly took steps toward healing its factional divides, but its former samurai continued to resist many of the modernizing changes underway. They tended to stay out of the wave of popular political organizing that swept Ibaraki, like the rest of Japan, during the 1870s. Many ignored the introduction of standardized, compulsory education, and opted for their own academies that offered a traditional Mito-style education in Chinese and Japanese classics.[3] Some criticized the Westernization of Japanese society, while others simply struggled to make ends meet. Farmers and other commoners also struggled, and many resisted the land reforms, new taxes, and other centralizing reforms. Of course, Mito's villagers had spent the last forty years dealing with disruptive reforms imposed from above. For them, the challenges of the Meiji period were not entirely new.

Slowly, though, life began to change in Mito. The establishment of newspapers helped inform the public of new policies and fostered popular discussions and debates about politics and society. As Ibaraki's prefectural capital, Mito hosted a rotating cast of politicians and reporters, allowing it to hold on to its central role in the wider region. Over time, this enabled the recovery of commerce in the city, aided by the relaxation of rules on entertainment in town: Mito gained an official brothel in 1873 for the first time in two hundred years.[4] This took place mostly in the Upper Town, where the government had placed a new hospital, teacher's college, court, and police station, many in Western architectural styles. Mito also flourished as a cultural center, home to many popular and fine arts. In 1889 the railway arrived, breathing new life into the town, which began to grow in size, reversing nearly two centuries of steady population loss.

THE RESURGENCE OF MITO SCHOLARSHIP

In the years after abolishing Mito Domain, Mito's new leaders focused their efforts on celebrating the achievements of Mitsukuni and Nariaki in part because the legacies of Mito's scholars were a lot more contentious. Aizawa Seishisai, for instance, was particularly divisive. Descendants of the radical faction felt that he had betrayed their fathers and brothers. It was not until 1890, when the Meiji emperor and empress made a visit to Mito, that Seishisai was granted posthumous court rank in recognition of his services to the nation. Even then, with memories of the political chaos of the 1860s not yet gone, few people in Mito celebrated his legacy.[5]

The 1890 imperial visit did mark a turning point, however, in boosting the reputation of Mito's nineteenth-century scholarship. Shortly after visiting Mito, the Meiji emperor issued the Imperial Rescript on Education, which outlined the principles of education for Japan's schoolchildren, which was memorized and recited by schoolchildren until the end of World War II. The Rescript is full of phrases drawn from the writings of both Tōko and Seishisai, beginning with the mythic ancestry of the emperor, the importance of loyalty and duty, the unity of the masses, and the role of education in inculcating reverence for the emperor and ethical behavior in subjects. Although we have little evidence that the government referred to specific Mito writings, contemporaries in Mito widely celebrated the rescript as a vindication of Mito ideas, and particularly those of Tōko.[6] Tōko's fame even reached Western audiences. James Morris, who wrote a series of biographical sketches called *Makers of Japan* in 1906, described Tōko's enduring legacy as a man "in advance of his age," whose "steadfast, unwearying inculcation of the doctrines of loyalty to the real sovereign and constant preparation for national defense" inspired the leaders of the Meiji government and paved the way for Japan's strength. "There is little likelihood," Morris concluded, "that Japan will ever forget those who aided in the past to bring about her emancipation from a feudal system which sapped her energies and blighted her prospects of advancement. Fujita Toko lives in the hearts of his countrymen."[7] Finally, in the same year that Morris published *Makers of Japan*, Mito's scholars completed the *Dai Nihon shi*, concluding a project started nearly two hundred and fifty years earlier by Mitsukuni. In the years that followed, Mito's scholars emphasized the significance of Mitsukuni's role as the proponent of an emperor-centered view of Japanese history. They extolled Tōko for his view that the unbroken imperial line was Japan's defining characteristic, the feature that distinguished the country from other nations.

The completion of the *Dai Nihon shi* coincided with the onset of a new era of Japanese society: the era of imperial democracy. Political activists around Japan clamored for a greater popular role in government, while simultaneously supporting the expansion of Japan's empire in the aftermath of the 1904–1905 Russo-Japanese War. Mito's scholars were no fans of democracy—more than a little of Seishisai's dismissive attitude toward "stupid commoners" lingered among the descendants of Mito's samurai-scholars—but they were not unified in their view of how to accommodate this new social movement. Kikuchi Kenjirō, headmaster of Mito Middle School and a prominent scholar of Tōko's work, emphasized the reform spirit of Mito's nineteenth-century scholars, and advocated for teaching *individuals* how to carry that reformist spirit forward as they developed their own sense of morality and action. More conservative scholars like Amagai Takeshi took a stronger monarchist view, arguing that "revering the emperor" and popular mobilization went hand in hand. "'Revering the emperor' gain life only when it is backed by the popular will; and the popular will only gain its strength when combined with reverence for the emperor," he wrote in 1921.[8] It was only as subjects of the emperor that individuals could participate in a democracy. As these examples show, Mito's scholarship continued to generate debate.

Over the next twenty years, the rise of socialism and communism, the spread of Western culture, and, ultimately, the perceived threat to the security of Japan's empire led conservative intellectuals and political leaders to call for a new "Shōwa Restoration," named after the reign of Emperor Hirohito (r. 1926–1989), to strengthen Japan. Tōko's writings about Japanese uniqueness, the sacred inviolability of the emperor, and the threat posed by the West proved fertile fodder for the ultranationalists of the mid-twentieth century. Even more than to Tōko, however, scholars and politicians turned to Seishisai for inspiration in this new moment of national crisis. *Shinron* proved an easy source to mine for concepts and values that conveyed Japan's uniqueness and strength, undergirding Japan's own imperial expansion and rallying the nation in the name of preserving its national essence.[9] Of course, within a few years, defending the nation had turned into a brutal and disastrous imperialist war across Asia and the Pacific.

The violence and brutality of wartime Japan and its imperial conquests provoked a swift backlash against its supporting ideologies soon after the guns stopped in August 1945. The Allied occupation government banned the teaching of Mito scholarship.[10] In 1948, the Japanese Diet formally repealed the 1890 Imperial Rescript. Fujita Tōko and Aizawa Seishisai were struck from school curricula. Prominent liberal intellectuals, freed from wartime censorship, attacked Mito's scholarship as the wellspring of militarism and the authoritarian "emperor system." Ironically, after sixty years of being overlooked and downplayed, the brief revival of enthusiasm for Seishisai, and particularly *Shinron*, came to stand in for all that was wrong about Mito's teachings: its most extreme, xenophobic, and authoritarian tendencies. Seishisai was portrayed as the originator of ultranationalism and emperor worship, a symbol of the latent authoritarianism in Japanese society that had never been fully stamped out by modernizing reforms.[11] The postwar backlash against prewar authoritarianism dealt another blow to Mito's reputation, not long after it had recovered from its post-1868 slump. But it also opened up new directions in studies of Mito's history, and, in the decades since the war, traditional scholarship has been joined by more critical academic studies that have taken a wider view of Mito's social, economic, and cultural history, in turn inspiring new forms of local history that look beyond Mito's scholarly elite.

THE MITO DIASPORA

Many people fled the violence and devastation of Mito in the early years of the Meiji period. Some had lost their families, while others went in search of new careers. Echoing the divide between Edo and Mito during the Tokugawa period, many of modern Mito's most famous figures spent much of their lives and careers in Tokyo or elsewhere. Asahina Chisen, the son of an establishment family, became a prominent reporter in Tokyo. The reformist scholar Aoyama En'u, director of the Shōkōkan until 1869, took his family to Tokyo in 1871 and devoted his scholarly skills to the national government's historical institute. Yokoyama Taikan, a founding figure of modern Japanese art, left Mito as a child in 1878 and spent his career promoting Japanese art and displaying his work around the world.

One particularly influential Mito émigré was Toyoda Fuyu (1845–1941), who became Japan's first kindergarten teacher and a pioneer in women's education. Her mother, Setsuko, was Fujita Tōko's sister and passed on the Fujita family passion for education. In true Mito fashion, Fuyu studied both poetry

Figure C.1. Portrait of Toyoda Fuyu
(On loan to Ibaraki Prefectural Archives and Museum)

and literature as well as martial arts, including three years of *naginata* sword-fighting.[12] In 1862, Fuyu married Toyoda Kotarō, son of the military scholar Toyoda Tenkō, but, sadly, the political activities of her husband and family exposed Fuyu to the turmoil of the mid-1860s. In 1866, radicals assassinated Kotarō as he tried to reconcile Mito's warring factions.[13] With few prospects for remarriage in war-torn Mito, she turned to education to secure her future. She began studying Chinese classics, making sure to carry a short sword—but no lantern—as she walked to and from her lessons every night, the threat of violence still laying heavily across the castle town. To make ends meet, Fuyu taught neighborhood children Japanese and Chinese literature. In 1873, Ibaraki Prefecture established its first school for girls, Hatsuō Girls School, and hired Fuyu as only the second female teacher in the prefecture, after Kurosawa Toki. Fuyu wrote a set of school rules for Hatsuō that reflected the educational philosophy of Mito scholars before her, including the importance of devoting oneself to education and moral development. Unlike most of those scholars, however, she argued that girls should have an education, too.[14]

In 1875, Fuyu got a job at the newly established Tokyo Women's Teachers College. The next year, the Teachers College opened Japan's first kindergarten (*yōchien*) and Fuyu became Japan's first kindergarten teacher. At the Teacher's College, Fuyu encountered a radically new educational environment. During the 1870s, Japanese educational reformers embraced humanistic and liberal educational principles from the United States and Europe, eagerly translating texts and inviting experts from abroad. For Fuyu this meant studying the work of German pedagogue Friedrich Fröbel (1782–1852), the inventor of kindergarten and a proponent of play and imagination in early childhood education. Over the next two years, Fuyu became an expert in his pedagogy and adapted it for a Japanese audience. She became a leading voice in early childhood and women's education. Alongside her kindergarten work, she helped establish the Women's Professional School, which trained women to become economically self-sufficient by teaching them a variety of technical skills alongside English, classical Chinese, mathematics, and morals. But Fuyu did not stay long at the Professional School. In 1887, she was asked to accompany Tokugawa Atsuyoshi, the twelfth head of the Mito Tokugawa household (and Yoshinobu's nephew), to Italy, where he had been sent as ambassador. While in Italy, she visited numerous schools for women, including technical schools, professional schools, and teacher colleges. She also visited schools for blind and deaf women and women in poverty. These institutions had no counterpart in Japan, where women's education was very much targeted at the upper classes. She admired the independence that these institutions fostered and came to believe that women should play a greater role in Japanese society by entering professions still dominated by men.[15]

Fuyu continued teaching after returning to Japan in 1889. Throughout her career, she embodied many of Mito's traditional values, such as the importance of learning both academic and practical arts, the importance of education and also of putting education into practice, and a pragmatic willingness to adopt ideas from abroad to strengthen Japan. But she also developed a new, decidedly modern vision of society, one that cultivated children's sense of play and wonder in kindergarten and that gave women the tools to live independently. Over time, and particularly after she returned to Mito in 1903, she drifted away from the bolder vision of female self-sufficiency of her earlier work, emphasizing instead the importance of teaching women how to be "good wives, wise mothers" (*ryōsai kenbo*). In this regard, she reflected a nationwide trend toward more rigid and conservative gender roles around the turn of the twentieth century.[16] Fuyu continued to teach until 1935, the year she turned ninety-one. She died in 1941 at the age of ninety-seven.

Perhaps the most famous Meiji-era person with Mito ties was Shibusawa Eiichi. Born the son of a wealthy farmer in the hinterlands of Edo in 1840, he studied Mito scholarship under his cousin, who had attended one of Tokugawa Nariaki's hunting parties in 1844 and came away impressed. Shibusawa, coming of age during the tumultuous 1850s, became obsessed with Mito's call to protect Japan, reading Tōko's essays over and over again and even plotting to assassinate foreigners in Yokohama. He ended up in Kyoto instead, where he met Tōko's son, Koshirō, and other Mito reformers, who were accompanying Yoshiatsu and Yoshinobu in the imperial capital. Through these connections, he became one of Yoshinobu's retainers in 1864. His radical sensibilities began to shift once Yoshinobu became shogun, and, in 1867, he accompanied Yoshinobu's brother Akitake to Paris for the World Exposition, eager to learn about the West.

Paris opened Shibusawa's eyes to the brave new world of Western capitalism. After returning to Japan following news of the shogunate's collapse, Shibusawa continued to work for Yoshinobu during his retirement in Shizuoka, but Yoshinobu soon told him to go make a name for himself, releasing him from service. Thereafter, Shibusawa joined the imperial government, helping to establish a modern financial system. Based on his experience in France, he went on to found five hundred companies, including the Tomioka Silk Mill, Japan's first modern silk reeling factory, in 1872. He is known to this day as a father of Japanese capitalism. Throughout his life, Shibusawa maintained his interest in Mito's teachings. In 1922, at the age of eighty-two, he took the occasion of a public lecture to the Fujita Tōko Society—of which he had just become chair—to demonstrate that he could recite Fujita Tōko's poetry by heart.[17] A loyalist to Tokugawa Yoshinobu through and through, Shibusawa spent the last years of his life compiling a massive biography of the last shogun, which helped rehabilitate Yoshinobu's image.[18] In his life and writings, Shibusawa demonstrated the importance of Mito's ideas to his efforts to modernize Japan.

The Meiji era saw the introduction and emulation of all things Western to Japan—even, despite longstanding suspicion and persecution, Christianity. Given the strident opposition of Mito's scholars and politicians to Christianity, it is ironic that two of the most famous modern Japanese Christians had great respect for Mito and its teachings. Nitobe Inazō (1862–1933), son of a samurai from Nanbu Domain in far northern Japan, studied at the American-run Sapporo Agricultural College in Hokkaido, where he converted to Christianity. He then travelled to the United States where he earned a degree in agricultural economics from Johns Hopkins University. After returning to Japan, he served as a colonial administrator in Taiwan and taught colonial studies at Kyoto University. A true cosmopolitan, he became the Japanese representative to the League of Nations and served as one of its under-secretaries-general from 1920 to 1926. He wrote prolifically in Japanese and English and published his most famous book, *Bushido: The Soul of Japan*, in 1900. In *Bushido*, Nitobe introduced samurai ethics and traditional Japanese culture to the outside world, holding up Tokugawa Mitsukuni and Tokugawa Nariaki as exemplars of the "way of the samurai." Critics accused Nitobe of romanticizing and oversimplifying samurai life, but his work captured the imagination of generations of Japanophiles around the world, and—in the heady days of the 1980s, "Japan Studies" boom—a new generation of Japanese, keen to promote their country's uniqueness and samurai identity.[19] Nitobe's ties to Mito were not just abstract. As a young samurai in Nanbu, he encountered the teachings of Nariaki through Nariaki's daughter, Matsuhime, who married the lord of Nanbu in 1857. She brought with her some of the small dolls of farmers that her father used to teach his wives and children to respect the hard work of agriculture. Nitobe, whose family had been assigned to reclaim barren land in Nanbu, was moved by Nariaki's commitment to farmers, and in later years he used the dolls in his lectures to agricultural societies. He created replicas of the dolls and distributed them, even taking some to the United States along with explanatory notes in English.

Uchimura Kanzō (1861–1930) followed a similar path as his close friend Nitobe. He too studied at Sapporo Agricultural College, where he converted to Christianity, and also studied abroad in the United States. In 1894, upon the outbreak of the First Sino-Japanese War (1894–1895), Uchimura published *Japan and the Japanese* (later reissued as *Representative Men of Japan*). In this work, which sought to explain Japan's position (and justify its war effort) through the biographies of five key individuals in Japanese history, Uchimura included a chapter on Saigō Takamori, "a founder of new Japan." The greatest influence on Saigō, in Uchimura's view, was Fujita Tōko, whom he described as "Japan etherealized into a soul."[20] For Uchimura, Tōko played a decisive role in driving the revolution of 1868. Ironically, however, Uchimura is perhaps most famous for losing his job as a teacher at the First Higher School in Tokyo after refusing to bow to a portrait of the emperor during the recitation of the Imperial Rescript on Education—a document that, as we have seen, was celebrated as a vindication of Tōko's political philosophy. Uchimura's Christian beliefs prevented him from worshipping the emperor as a deity, although he avoided this delicate topic in his celebration of Tōko. Both Nitobe and Uchimura embody the struggles many Japanese Christians faced as they tried to reconcile their religious beliefs with their national identity in late nineteenth-century Japan, when the anti-foreign, anti-Christian elements of Mito's ideas continued to echo alongside Westernizing reforms.

Mitsukuni and the reformist scholars of the Late Mito School have gotten the lion's share of attention in tellings of the history of Mito's samurai. But in the twentieth century, Aoyama En'u's granddaughter Yamakawa Kikue (1890–1980) turned to a forgotten half of the samurai past: the women of Mito Domain. A feminist, socialist, and, later, the first director of the Bureau of Children and Women in the postwar Ministry of Labor, Yamakawa introduced a critical perspective to scholarship on Mito, pushing it away from a narrow focus on the elite samurai and scholars toward a broader view of the dynamics of gender and class that shaped life and society.[21] It is thanks to her oral history work that we know so much about Toyoda Fuyu's childhood, for instance. Yamakawa modeled a more inclusive and diverse approach to telling Mito's history. Writing about the turmoil of 1860s Mito while living through the terror of the Pacific War, she often drew parallels between the extremism and bloodshed of those two eras, implicitly criticizing the corrosive effects of "ideological rigidity" on the lives of ordinary people.[22] And indeed, in her own political activism—notably her focus on women's rights and political enfranchisement—she often adopted pragmatic rather than ideological stances. As a result, in part, she became an effective director of the Bureau of Children and Women, outliving the socialist prime minister who appointed her and maintaining her position under the two conservative prime ministers who followed.[23] Yamakawa took, from the history of ordinary people in Mito, the dangers of extremism and applied it to her activism, political work, and academic writing.[24]

LEGACIES

In this book, I have drawn on recent scholarship to introduce some of the complexities of Mito's history, situating the lives of several of its most famous and influential people alongside the social, political, and intellectual context of their times. In so doing, I have tried not to shy away from the uglier sides of Mito's history: the undeniable failures of governance, the xenophobia and bellicosity of its "expel the barbarian" radicals, and the domain's deep and corrosive factionalism. Many of the Mito scholars' writings are undeniably incendiary, and some advocate a doctrine of militarism and emperor-worship that is at odds with modern values. But, for Japanese in the nineteenth century, watching Western empires humiliate China, colonize peoples across the globe, and threaten war on Japan, all in the name of the superiority of Christianity and capitalism, generating an equal and opposite force to preserve their culture and sovereignty did not seem out of the ordinary. I have tried to present Mito's samurai and scholars in the context of their times, not through the lens of postwar Japanese society or present-day values. Their lives are a window into a place that shaped Japan, for better and for worse, more than almost any other part of the archipelago.

But decades have passed since the end of the war, and even more since Mito played its most important role in Japanese history. In light of that, why turn to Mito's history today? What does the city's past teach us?

First, Mito illustrates how history can shape a place and give it an identity. Mito's people are undeniably proud of their city's historical importance. They have preserved the grounds of the castle, turning them over to public schools, and the Kōdōkan looks much as it did in the time of Nariaki. The Kairakuen welcomes hordes of tourists from around Japan to see the plum blossoms in February, while the Kōrakuen in the former Koishikawa estate in Tokyo is one of the rare places in the modern capital that has survived fire, earthquake, and war. The early-Meiji efforts to celebrate Mitsukuni and Nariaki have paid off, with both figures widely celebrated in the city's promotional materials today. Mitsukuni, in particular, has become a much-loved figure around Japan, not least because of his starring role in *Mito Kōmon*. Mito's scholars continue to study the lives and writings of Mito's historical figures. The Tokugawa Museum in town reminds everyone of the family's ties to Mito. In Mito, history is never far from the surface.

Second, Mito's history shows how thinking locally can produce global effects. Tachihara Suiken and his disciples obsessed over infanticide, famine, and other social and political problems affecting their domain in the late eighteenth and early nineteenth century. Their attempts to solve those problems through reform became a model for other domains and the shogunate. This set a template for Aizawa Seishisai and Fujita Tōko, whose response to the Ōtsuhama Incident informed their call to arms for national defense, and Tokugawa Nariaki who urged the shogunate and his fellow daimyo to adopt his reforms to samurai morale and domain government. Through the writings and actions of these leaders, ideas born in Mito made their way across Japan. Many of the most prominent leaders on all sides of the political conflicts leading to the Meiji Restoration were students of Mito, including anti-Tokugawa forces such as the radical young samurai in Chōshū and Saigō Takamori and his fellow Satsuma men, as well as Tokugawa loyalists. The Mito goal of strengthening and protecting an imperial state played out in their actions, as well as Tokugawa Yoshinobu's last-ditch efforts to save the shogunate through robust reform programs.

Third, these ideas from Mito shaped the course of history, often in unpredictable ways. Seishisai and Tōko transformed Japan through their writings and teachings. How many scholars can claim to have influenced so many, and so much? At the same time, their lives are also a warning: powerful ideas have a tendency to take on a life of their own. Even after changing his mind and espousing a new vision for Japan's future, Seishisai found it impossible to rein in the radicals and reformists who had taken his ideas and ran with them in directions he ultimately rejected. Tōko pushed his call for reform to the limits, irrevocably cementing Mito's factional divisions and opening the door to civil war. By assassinating Ii Naosuke, Nariaki's followers triggered a bitter cycle of recriminations between the shogunate and Mito that ultimately led to rebellion and civil war. But even as radicals took the ideas of Tōko and others to an extreme, men like Tokugawa Yoshinobu took from Mito the goal of strengthening Japan by reinventing it as a modern nation. Through his reforms of the shogunate, Yoshinobu demonstrated how the Mito vision of reforming Tokugawa Japan could become the basis for a new political order: a modern nation-state, unified in the face of foreign threats. Yoshinobu remained devoted to the principles he learned as a child in Mito, and they guided him throughout the tumult of the 1860s, but his pragmatism led him down a different path than the Mito radicals whose executions, he allowed at Tsuruga in the winter of 1865.

Finally, Mito's history illustrates the value of starting with a place and exploring the various facets of its history. Mito, during the Tokugawa period, was constantly changing in the face of natural disasters, political crises, reform movements, cultural projects, or warfare. At the same time, the domain's samurai—and eventually a cohort of elite commoners—developed a distinctive identity and reputation, centered on Mito's history, status, and scholarly institutions. The history of Japan's modern transformation looks a bit different from the perspective of Mito: Russia and Ezochi mattered a lot, from as early as the 1780s, and the blend of scholarship and politics was a potent mix that produced devastating results for Mito's people. Ironically, perhaps, given the association between Mito and the formation of national identity, taking a local perspective creates an alternative narrative about the birth of modern Japan, a good reminder of the dynamism and diversity of Japan's many regions in the past, as in the present.

NOTES

1. Stephen Vlastos, "Opposition Movements in Early Meiji, 1868–1885," in *The Cambridge History of Japan*, vol. 5, *The Nineteenth Century,* ed. Marius Jansen (Cambridge: Cambridge University Press, 1988), 386–87. See also Charles L. Yates, *Saigō Takamori: The Man Behind the Myth* (London: Kegan Paul International, 1995) and Mark Ravina, *The Last Samurai: The Life and Battles of Saigō Takamori* (Hoboken, NJ: John Wiley & Sons, 2004).

2. Haga Noboru, *Kindai Mitogaku kenkyū shi* (Tokyo: Kyōiku shuppan sentā, 1996), 298–303.

3. Yasu Norihisa, "Kindai Mito no kōhai to hen'yō," *Rekishi kōron* 9, no. 5 (May 1983): 76.

4. Haga Noboru, *Kindai Mitogaku kenkyū shi*, 289.

5. Kirihara Kenshin, "Aizawa Seishisai to 'Mitogaku' no keifu," *Kinsei kindai ikōki no rekishi ishiki, shisō, yuisho* (Tokyo: Iwata shoin, 2017), 153–58.

6. Yoshida Toshizumi, *Mitogaku to Meiji ishin* (Tokyo: Yoshikawa kōbunkan, 2003), 5–7.

7. James Morris, *The Makers of Japan* (London: Methuen, 1906), 97–113.

8. Amagai Takeshi, *Sonnō minpon shugi* (Mito: Nikakudō, 1921), 10.

9. Kirihara, "Aizawa Seishisai to 'Mitogaku' no keifu," 159–65.

10. Nagoya Tokimasa, *Mitogaku no kenkyū* (Kyoto: Shintōshi gakkai, 1975), preface (n.p.).

11. Maruyama Masao was one of the most notable early postwar critics of Mito scholarship; see *Studies in the Intellectual History of Modern Japan*, trans. Mikiso Hane (Princeton, NJ: Princeton University Press, 1974), 350–67.

12. Maemura Akira et al., *Toyoda Fuyu to sōsōki no yōchien kyōiku* (Tokyo: Kenpakusha, 2010), 10–12.

13. Maemura, *Toyoda Fuyu*, 29–31.

14. Maemura, *Toyoda Fuyu*, 33–36.

15. Maemura, *Toyoda Fuyu*, 321–31.

16. Marnie Anderson, "Critiquing Concubinage: Sumiya Koume and Changing Gender Roles in Modern Japan," *Japanese Studies* 37, no. 3 (2017): 311–29.

17. Shibusawa Eiichi, "Tōko-kai kōenshū," in *Shibusawa Eiichi denki shiryō*, ed. Kawasaki Minotarō (Tokyo: Shibusawa Eiichi denki shiryō kankōkai, 1955–1965), 49:161.

18. Shibusawa Eiichi, *Tokugawa Yoshinobu kō den* (Tokyo: Ryūmonsha, 1918). For a fuller account of Shibusawa and Yoshinobu, see Andō Yūichirō, *Tokugawa Yoshinobu to Shibusawa Eiichi: Saigo no shogun ni tsukaeta saigo no bakushin* (Tokyo: Nihon keizai shinbun shuppansha, 2012).

19. Nitobe Inazō, *Bushidō: The Soul of Japan* (Philadelphia: Leeds and Biddle, 1900).

20. Uchimura Kanzō, *Representative Men of Japan*, in *The Complete Works of Uchimura Kanzō*, vol. 2 (Tokyo: Kyobunkan, 1971–73), 16.

21. Yamakawa Kikue, *Women of the Mito Domain*, transl. Kate Wildman Nakai (Tokyo: University of Tokyo Press, 1992).

22. Kate Wildman Nakai, Introduction, in Yamakawa, *Women of the Mito Domain*, xxiii.

23. Elyssa Faison, "Women's Rights as Proletarian Rights: Yamakawa Kikue, Suffrage, and the 'Dawn of Liberation,'" in *Rethinking Japanese Feminisms*, edited by Julia C. Bullock, Ayako Kano and James Welker (Honolulu: University of Hawai'i Press, 2017), 15–33.

24. There is a small body of work on Mito's women and on gender history in Mito. In addition to work on Kurosawa Toki and Toyoda Fuyu, see Nagahara Kazuko, "Chihōshi no naka no josei o kangaeru," *Ibaraki kenshi kenkyū* 49 (November 1982): 28–31, and also Nagahara's work on prewar women's organizations, "Taishō, Shōwa ki ni okeru fujin dantai no shakaiteki kinō," *Ibaraki kenshi kenkyū* 36 (December 1976): 17–31.

Bibliography

PRIMARY SOURCES AND DOCUMENT COLLECTIONS

Aizawa Seishisai. "Jimusaku." In Imai et al., *Mitogaku*, 361–68.

Aizawa Seishisai. "Kyūmon ihan." In *Nihongaku sōsho*, vol. 8, edited by Nagasaka Kaneo, 38–90. Tokyo: Yūzankaku, 1939.

Aizawa Seishisai. *Rekkō gyōjitsu*. Tokyo: Tokugawa Akitake, 1874 [1861].

Aizawa Seishisai. "Shinron." In Imai et al., *Mitogaku*, 49–160.

Aizawa Seishisai. "Sōen wagen." In *Nihon kyōiku bunko*, shūkyō hen, edited by Kurokawa Mamichi and Dōbunkan henshūkyoku, 372–417. Tokyo: Dōbunkan, 1911–1912.

Aizawa Seishisai. "Sōen wagen." In *Nihon kokusui zensho*, vol. 18. Tokyo: Nihon kokusui zensho kankōkai, 1915–1918.

Aizawa Seishisai. "Tekiihen." In *Shinron, Tekiihen*, translated and edited by Tsukamoto Katsuyoshi, 243–92. Tokyo: Iwanami Bunko, 1942.

Aizawa Seishisai shokan shū. Edited by Osaka Daigaku Aizawa Seishisai shokan kenkyūkai. Kyoto: Shibunkaku, 2016.

Asaka Kaku [Tanpaku] and Imai Kōsai. *Shunsui sensei kōjitsu*. In *Zhu Shunshui ji*, 10–11. Shanghai junxueshe, 1926,. http://www.mgebooks.cn/detail.aspx?id=49391.

Dai Nihon komonjo: bakumatsu gaikoku kankei monjo. 53 vols. Tokyo: Tokyo teikoku daigaku bunka daigaku shiryō hensangakari, 1910–2003.

Fujita Tōko. "Bushi dochaku no gi." In Takasu, *Fujita Tōko zenshū*, 6:259–97.

Fujita Tōko. "Hanhei sankajō (Jinshin fūji)." In *Fujita Tōko zenshū*, 6:124–208.

Fujita Tōko. "Hitachiobi." In *Fujita Tōko zenshū*, 1:249–478.

Fujita Tōko. "Jōge fuyū no gi." In *Fujita Tōko zenshū*, 6:209–39.

Fujita Tōko. "Jōi ni tsuite." In *Fujita Tōko zenshū*, 6:20–44.

Fujita Tōko. "Kaitenshishi." In *Fujita Tōko zenshū*, 1:3–248.

Fujita Tōko. "Kōdōkanki jutsugi." In Imai et al., *Mitogaku*, 259–338.

Fujita Tōko. "Nishiyama tonden." In *Fujita Tōko zenshū*, 6:45–74.

Fujita Tōko. "Seigi no jinbutsu wo suisen suru ni tsuite." In *Fujita Tōko zenshū*, 6:3–19.

Fujita Tōko. "Teishi nichiroku." In *Fujita Tōko zenshū*, 4:317–34.

Fujita Tōko zenshū. Edited by Takasu Yoshijirō. 6 vols. Tokyo: Shōkasha, 1935–1936.

Fujita Yūkoku. *Kannō wakumon*. In Takasu, *Mitogaku taikei*, 3:16–98.

Fujita Yūkoku. "Seimeiron." In Imai et al., *Mitogaku*, 9–14.

Ibaraki-ken shiryō: bakumatsu hen. Edited by Ibaraki kenshi hensan bakumatsu ishin bukai. Mito: Ibaraki-ken, 1971.

Ibaraki-ken shiryō: ishin hen. Edited by Ibaraki kenshi hensan bakumatsu ishin bukai. Mito: Ibaraki-ken, 1969.

Ibaraki-ken shiryō, kinsei seiji hen. Edited by Ibaraki kenshi hensan kinseishi dai 1 bukai. Mito: Ibaraki-ken, 1970-.

Ibaraki-ken shiryō, kinsei shakai keizai hen. Edited by Ibaraki kenshi hensan kinseishi dai 2 bukai. 4 vols. Mito: Ibaraki-ken, 1976–1988.

Kaifūmaru hokai kiji. N.d. Tokyo Daigaku gakujutsu shisan tō Archives. 4:1:28.

Kimura Kenji. *Sokuin goroku*. 1791–1808. Shikyo 32. Hokkaido University Library Northern Studies Collection. Sapporo, Japan.

Kimura Kenji. *Sokuminron*. In *Kinsei chihō keizai shiryō*, vol. 1, edited by Ono Takeo, 2–19. Tokyo: Yoshikawa kōbunkan, 1931.

Komiyama Fūken. *Fūken sensei hiroku*. In *Ibaraki ken shiryō: bakumatsu hen*, vol. 1, 371–478.

Komiyama Fūken. *Tenpō shūhanki*. In *Ibaraki ken shiryō: bakumatsu hen*, vol. 1, 259–330.

Komiyama Masahide, *Fūken gūki*, vol. 5 [1809], MS no. 826-24, National Diet Library Digital Collection, dl.ndl.go.jp/info:ndljp/pid/2560380.

Komiyama Masahide, *Fūken nenroku*, vol. 1 [1807], MS no. 826-27, National Diet Library Digital Collection, dl.ndl.go.jp/info:ndljp/pid/2576962.

Kuno Katsuya, ed. *Tahanshi no mita Mito-han*. Mito: Mito shigakkai, 1991.

Kurita Hiroshi. *Kurisato sensei zatcho*. Tokyo: Yoshikawa Hanshichi, 1901.

Mito-han shiryō. 80 volumes in 3 parts (jō, ge, bekki). Tokyo: Yoshikawa kōbunkan, 1917.

Ōniwa Kunihiko. *Chichi yori Tokugawa Yoshinobu-dono e: Mito Nariaki Hitotsubashi Yoshinobu ate shokanshū*. Tokyo: Shūeisha, 1997.

Shibusawa Eiichi, ed. *Sekimukai hikki: Tokugawa Yoshinobu kō kaisōdan*. Tokyo: Heibonsha, 1966.

Shibusawa Eiichi. "Tōko-kai kōenshū." In *Shibusawa Eiichi denki shiryō*, edited by Kawasaki Minotarō, 49:160–65. Tokyo: Shibusawa Eiichi Denki Shiryō Kankōkai, 1955–1965.

Shibusawa Eiichi. *Tokugawa Yoshinobu kō den*. 8 vols. Tokyo: Ryūmonsha, 1918.

Tachihara Suiken. *Mito Saijiki*. In *Mito Saijiki: Mito-han no shomin shiryō shūsei*, edited by Akiyama Fusako, 5–24. Nagareyama, Chiba: Ron shobō, 1983.

Tachihara Suiken. "Suzuki sōsai ni atau." In Takasu, *Mitogaku taikei*, 4:203–7.

Takakura Taneaki. *Suifu chiri onkoroku*. In *Ibaraki ken shiryō: kinsei chishi hen*, edited by Ibaraki kenshi hensan dai-ichibu iinkai, 31–211. Mito: Ibaraki-ken, 1975.

Takasu Yoshijirō, ed. *Mitogaku taikei.* 5 vols. Tokyo: Mitogaku taikei kankōkai, 1940–1942.

Tokugawa Mitsukuni. *Dai Nihon shi.* 397 vols. Tokyo: 1939.

Tokugawa Mitsukuni. "Seizankō zuihitsu." In *Nihon zuihitsu taisei, dai 2-ki,* edited by Nihon zuihitsu taisei henshūbu, vol. 14, 367–86. Tokyo: Yoshikawa kōbunkan, 1927.

Tokugawa Nariaki. "Hoppō mirai kō." In Takasu, *Mitogaku taikei,* 5:273–308.

Tokugawa Nariaki. "Kōdōkan gakusoku." In Takasu, *Mitogaku taikei,* 5:185–90.

Tokugawa Nariaki. "Kōdōkanki." In Imai et al., *Mitogaku,* 229–32.

Tokugawa Nariaki. "Kokushihen." In Imai et al., *Mitogaku,* 210–27.

Tokugawa Nariaki. "Suifu-kō kensaku." In Takasu, *Mitogaku taikei,* 5:191–272.

Toyoda Tenkō. "Bōkai shinsaku." In Imai et al., *Mitogaku,* 339–52.

PUBLISHED WORKS (INCLUDING PRIMARY SOURCE TRANSLATIONS AND NON-JAPANESE SOURCES)

Aizawa Seishisai. "A Plan for Tasks at Hand." Translated by Donald Keene. *Monumenta Nipponica* 62, no. 1 (Spring 2007): 75–86.

Aizawa Seishisai. *New Theses [Shinron].* In Wakabayashi, *Anti-Foreignism and Western Learning,* 149–277.

Alcock, Rutherford. *The Capital of the Tycoon: A Narrative of A Three Year's Residence in Japan.* New York: Harper & Brothers, 1863.

Amagai Takeshi. *Sonnō minpon shugi: Mitogaku no shinzui.* Mito: Nikakudō, 1921.

Ami Takao. *Aizawa Seishisai no shōgai.* Mito no jinbutsu series 10. Tokyo: Kinseisha, 2016.

Anderson, Marnie. "Critiquing Concubinage: Sumiya Koume and Changing Gender Roles in Modern Japan." *Japanese Studies* 37, no. 3 (2017): 311–29.

Andō Yūichirō. *Tokugawa Yoshinobu to Shibusawa Eiichi: Saigo no shogun ni tsukaeta saigo no bakushin.* Tokyo: Nihon keizai shinbun shuppansha, 2012.

Arakawa Kusuo. *Mito shigaku no gendaiteki igi.* Mito: Mito shigakkai, 1987.

Baxter, James, and Joshua Fogel, eds. *Writing Histories in Japan: Texts and their Transformations from Ancient Times through the Meiji Era.* Kyoto: International Research Center for Japanese Studies, 2007.

Beasley, W. G. *The Meiji Restoration.* Stanford, CA: Stanford University Press, 1972.

Beasley, W. G. *Select Documents on Japanese Foreign Policy.* London: Oxford University Press, 1960.

Bitō Masahide. "Mitogaku no tokushitsu." *Mitogaku.* Nihon Shisō taikei 53. Edited by Imai Usaburō, Seya Yoshihiko, and Bitō Masahide. Tokyo: Iwanami shoten, 1973. 556–82.

Bitō Masahide. "Tokugawa Mitsukuni no 'Dai Nihon shi.'" In *Genroku jidai,* 186–213. Nihon no rekishi 19. Tokyo: Shōgakkan, 1975.

Bolitho, Harold. "The Tenpō Crisis." In Jansen, *The Nineteenth Century,* 116–67.

Brownlee, John. *Japanese Historians and the National Myths, 1600–1945: The Age of the Gods and Emperor Jinmu.* Vancouver: University of British Columbia Press, 1997.

Chang, Richard. *From Prejudice to Tolerance: A Study of the Japanese Image of the West, 1826–1864.* Tokyo: Sophia University, 1970.

Chang, Richard. "Fujita Tōko's View of the West." *Journal of Asian Studies* 2, no. 2 (1968): 130–40.

Ching, Julia. "Chu Shun-Shui, 1600–1682: A Chinese Confucian Scholar in Tokugawa Japan." *Monumenta Nipponica* 30, no. 2 (Summer 1970): 177–91.

Clement, Ernest. "The Boston of Feudal Japan." *The Open Court* 21, no. 8 (August 1907): 485–91.

Clement, Ernest. "Instructions of a Mito Prince to His Retainers." *Transactions of the Asiatic Society of Japan* 26 (1898): 115–53.

Clement, Ernest. "The Mito Civil War." *Transactions of the Asiatic Society of Japan* 19 (1891): 393–418.

Clement, Ernest. "Mito Samurai and British Sailors in 1824." *Transactions of the Asiatic Society of Japan* 33, Part 1 (1905): 86–131.

Clement, Ernest. "The Tokugawa Princes of Mito." *Transactions of the Asiatic Society of Japan* 18 (1889): 2–24.

Clements, Rebekah. "Speaking in Tongues? Daimyo, Zen Monks, and Spoken Chinese in Japan, 1661–1711." *Journal of Asian Studies* 76, no. 3 (August 2017): 603–26.

Craig, Albert. *Chōshū in the Meiji Restoration.* Cambridge, MA: Harvard University Press, 1961.

Drixler, Fabian. "The Discourse of the Louse: Regional Pride and Conflicting Cultures of Parenthood in mid-Tokugawa Japan." In *Kindheit in der Japanische geschichte*, edited by Michael Kinski, Elike Großmann, and Harald Salomon, 159–90. Wiesbaden: Harrassowitz Verlag, 2016.

Drixler, Fabian. *Mabiki: Infanticide and Population Growth in Eastern Japan, 1660–1950.* Berkeley: University of California Press, 2013.

Ehlers, Maren. *Give and Take: Poverty and the Status Order in Early Modern Japan.* Cambridge, MA: Harvard University Asia Center, 2018.

Ehlers, Maren. "Mountain Demons from Mito: The Arrival of Civil War in Echizen." In *The Meiji Restoration*, edited by Robert Hellyer and Harald Fuess, 113–36. Cambridge: Cambridge University Press, 2020.

Faison, Elyssa. "Women's Rights as Proletarian Rights: Yamakawa Kikue, Suffrage, and the 'Dawn of Liberation.'" *Rethinking Japanese Feminisms.* Edited by Julia C. Bullock, Ayako Kano and James Welker. Honolulu: University of Hawai'i Press, 2017. 15–33.

Fraleigh, Matthew. "Songs of the Righteous Spirit: the 'Men of High Purpose' and Their Chinese Poetry in Modern Japan." *Harvard Journal of Asiatic Studies* 69, no. 1 (June 2009): 109–71.

Gordon, Andrew. *A Modern History of Japan: From Tokugawa Times to the Present.* 3rd Edition. Oxford: Oxford University Press, 2014.

Haga Noboru. *Kindai Mitogaku kenkyū shi.* Tokyo: Kyōiku shuppan sentā, 1996.

Hammitzsch, Horst. "Die Mito-Schule und ihre programmatischen Schriften Bairi Sensei Hiin, Kodokanki, Kodokangakusoku und Seiki no Uta in Übersetzung. Ein Beitrag zur Geistesgeschichte der Tokugawa-Zeit." *Mitteilungen der Gesellschaft für Natur- und Völkerkunde Ostasiens (MOAG)* 31, Teil B (1939): 1–95.

Hara Yūichi. "Mito-han Komagome-tei no kenkyū." *Tokyo Daigaku shi kiyō* 28 (March 2010): 41–63.

Harootunian, H. D. "Late Tokugawa Culture and Thought." In *Uneven Moments: Reflections on Japan's Modern History*, 95–176. New York: Columbia University Press, 2019.

Harootunian, H. D. *Toward Restoration: The Growth of Political Consciousness in Tokugawa Japan*. Berkeley: University of California Press, 1970.

Hellyer, Robert, and Harald Fuess, eds. *The Meiji Restoration: Japan as a Global Nation*. Cambridge: Cambridge University Press, 2020.

Howell, David. "Foreign Encounters and Informal Diplomacy in Early Modern Japan, *Journal of Japanese Studies* 40, no. 2 (Summer 2014): 295–327.

Howell, David. "The Social Life of Firearms in Tokugawa Japan," *Journal of Japanese Studies* 29, no. 1 (2009): 65–80.

Hōya Tōru. "A Military History of the Boshin War." In Hellyer and Fuess, *The Meiji Restoration*, 153–70.

Huber, Thomas. "Men of High Purpose and the Politics of Direct Action, 1862–1864." In *Conflict in Modern Japanese History: The Neglected Tradition*, edited by Tetsuo Najita and Victor Koschmann, 107–27. Princeton, NJ: Princeton University Press, 1982.

Ibaraki kenshi: shichōson hen. Edited by Ibaraki kenshi hensan sōgō bukai. 3 vols. Mito: Ibaraki-ken, 1972–1981.

Iechika Yoshiki. *Tokugawa Yoshinobu*. Tokyo: Yoshikawa kōbunkan, 2014.

Imai Usaburō, Seya Yoshihiko, and Bito Masahide, eds. *Mitogaku*. Nihon shisō taikei 53. Tokyo: Iwanami shoten, 1973.

Inui Hiromi. *Mito-han Tenpō kaikaku to gōnō*. Osaka: Seibundō, 2006.

Isaka Kiyonobu. *Aizawa Seishisai no bannen to Mito-han*. Tokyo: Perikansha, 2017.

Isaka Kiyonobu. *Edo jidai kōki no Mito hanju: sono katsudō to tenbyō*. Tokyo: Kyūko shoin, 2013.

Isoda Michifumi. "Hansei kaikaku no denpa: Kumamoto-han Hōreki kaikaku to Mito-han Kansei kaikaku." *Nihon kenkyū* 40 (November 2009): 13–42.

Isoda Michifumi. "Mito-han Tenpō kaikaku no dōjidaiteki hyōka to eikyō: shin shiryō 'Mito kenbunroku ron' no bunseki." *Ibaraki kenshi kenkyū* 95 (March 2011): 31–50.

Jansen, Marius, ed. *The Nineteenth Century*. Vol. 5 of *The Cambridge History of Japan*. Cambridge: Cambridge University Press, 1989.

Jansen, Marius. *Sakamoto Ryōma and the Meiji Restoration*. Princeton, NJ: Princeton University Press, 1961.

Kajiyama Takao. *Fujita Yūkoku no monogatari*. 3 vols. Tokyo: Kinseisha, 2014.

Kajiyama Takao. *Gendai Mitogakuron hihan*. Tokyo: Kinseisha, 2007.

Kajiyama Takao. *Mito no kokugaku: Yoshida Kōdō o chūshin toshite*. Mito: Mito Shigakkai, 1997.

Kirihara Kenshin. "Aizawa Seishisai to 'Mitogaku' no keifu." In *Kinsei kindai ikōki no rekishi ishiki, shisō, yuisho*, edited by Kindai Ibaraki chiikishi kenkyūkai, 147–72. Tokyo: Iwata shoin, 2017.

Kirihara Kenshin. "*Shinron* juyō no ichikeitai: Yoshida Shōin o chūshin ni." In *Kokumin kokka keisei ki no chiiki shakai: kindai Ibaraki chiiki shi no shosō*, edited by Sasaki Hiroshi, 61–90. Tokyo: Iwata shoin, 2004.

Kobayashi Noriyoshi. "Tokyo Gakuin no shiteizō: E. W. Clement to Sakata Tasuku." *Eigakushi kenkyū* 26 (1993): 137–47.

Komuro Masamichi. *Sōmō no keizai shisō.* Tokyo: Ochanomizu shobō, 1999.

Koschmann, J. Victor. *The Mito Ideology: Discourse, Reform, and Insurrection in Late Tokugawa Japan, 1790–1864.* Berkeley: University of California Press, 1987.

Koseki Yūichirō. "*Meikun*" *no kinsei.* Tokyo: Yoshikawa kōbunkan, 2011.

Kracht, Klaus. *Das Kōdōkanki des Fujita Tōkō (1806–1855): Ein Beitrag zum politischen Denken der Späten Mito-Schule.* Wiesbaden: Otto Harrassowitz, 1975.

Kracht, Klaus. *Japanese Thought in the Tokugawa Era: A Bibliography of Western-language Materials.* Wiesbaden: O. Harrassowitz, 2000.

Kuno Katsuya. "*Mito kōmon* to Matsushita Kōnosuke," *Kore ga Mito kōmon da.* Tokyo: Hinode shuppan, 2003.

Kurihara Shigeyuki. "*Chishima ibun kō.*" *Nihon rekishi* 469 (June 1987): 44–62.

Kurihara Shigeyuki. "*Shinron* izen no Aizawa Seishisai: chūkai *An'i mondō.*" *Tokyo Toritsu Daigaku Hōgakkai zasshi* 30, no. 1 (1989): 181–231.

Kurihara Shigeyuki. "*Shinron* izen no Aizawa Seishisai o megutte." *Nihon rekishi* 506 (July 1990): 84–88.

Kurihara Shigeyuki. "Tokugawa Mitsukuni no seiji shisō." *Toritsu Daigaku hōgakkai zasshi* 18, nos. 1–2 (1978): 547–628.

Lamberti, Matthew. *A Political Study of Tokugawa Nariaki of Mito, 1800–1860.* PhD Diss, Columbia University, 1968.

Lamberti, Matthew. "Tokugawa Nariaki and the Japanese Imperial Institution, 1853–1858." *Harvard Journal of Asiatic Studies* 32 (1972): 97–123.

Lukacs, Gabor. "Chikyū bankoku sankai yochi zenzu setsu: The First Japanese World Map with Latitudes and Longitudes and with an Extensive Japanese Explanatory Note." *The Cartographic Journal* 53, no. 2 (May 2016): 49–157.

Maeda Kōkyō. *Tachihara Suiken.* Mito: Tachihara Yoshishige, 1963.

Maemura Akira et al. *Toyoda Fuyu to sōsōki no yōchien kyōiku.* Tokyo: Kenpakusha, 2010.

Maruyama Masao. *Studies in the Intellectual History of Modern Japan.* Translated by Mikiso Hane. Princeton, NJ: Princeton University Press, 1974.

Matsuura Akira. "The Trade in Dried Marine Products from Nagasaki to China during the Edo Period." In *Copper in the Early-Modern Sino-Japanese Trade*, edited by Keiko Nagase-Reimer, 118–56. Leiden: Brill, 2016.

Matsuura Rei. *Tokugawa Yoshinobu: Shōgunke no Meiji ishin.* Tokyo: Chūō kōronsha, 1975.

McNally, Mark Thomas. *Like No Other: Exceptionalism and Nativism in Early Modern Japan.* Honolulu: University of Hawai'i Press, 2016.

Mitani Hiroshi. *Ishin shi saikō: kōgi, ōsei kara shūken, datsu mibun ka e.* Tokyo: NHK Books, 2017.

Mito shishi hensan iinkai, ed. *Mito shishi.* 9 volumes in 3 parts (Jō, chū 1–5, ge 1–3). Mito: Mito shiyakusho, 1963–1998.

Monma Takeshi. "Tokugawa Nariaki no meiyo kaifuku o meguru dōkō." In *Kinsei kindai ikōki no rekishi ishiki, shisō, yuisho,* edited by Kindai Ibaraki chiikishi kenkyūkai, 21–51. Tokyo: Iwata shoin, 2017.

Morris, J. *The Makers of Japan.* London: Methuen, 1906.

Nagahara Kazuko. "Chihōshi no naka no josei o kangaeru." *Ibaraki kenshi kenkyū* 49 (December 1982): 28–33.

Nagahara Kazuko. "Taishō, Shōwa ki ni okeru fujin dantai no shakaiteki kinō." *Ibaraki kenshi kenkyū* 36 (December 1976): 17–31.

Nagai Hiroshi. *Tokugawa Nariaki: Fukakujitsu na jidai ni ikite.* Tokyo: Yamakawa shuppansha, 2019.

Nagoya Tokimasa. *Mito Mitsukuni to sono yokō.* Mito: Mito shigakkai, 1985.

Nagoya Tokimasa. *Mitogaku no kenkyū.* Kyoto: Shintōshi gakkai, 1975.

Nagoya Tokimasa. *Mitogaku no tassei to tenkai.* Tokyo: Kinseisha, 1992.

Nakai, Kate Wildman. "'The Age of the Gods' in Medieval and Early-Modern Historiography." In *Writing Histories in Japan,* edited by James Baxter and Joshua Fogel, 11–39. Kyoto: International Research Center for Japanese Studies, 2007.

Nakai, Kate Wildman. Review of *The Mito Ideology* by J. Victor Koschmann. *The Journal of Japanese Studies* 14, no. 2 (Summer 1988): 526–34.

Nakai, Kate Wildman. "Tokugawa Confucian Historiography: The Hayashi, Early Mito School, and Arai Hakuseki." In *Confucianism in Tokugawa Culture,* edited by Peter Nosco, 62–91. Princeteon, NJ: Princeton University Press, 1984.

Nakata Shōichi. *Mito-han to ryōmin.* Tokyo: Kinseisha, 2008.

Nakata Shōichi. *Yoshida Shōin to Mito.* Tokyo: Kinseisha, 2015.

Nenzi, Laura. *The Chaos and Cosmos of Kurosawa Tokiko.* Honolulu: University of Hawai'i Press, 2015.

Nishimura Fuminori. *Aizawa Hakumin.* Tokyo: Shōkasha, 1936.

Nitobe Inazō. *Bushidō: The Soul of Japan.* Philadelphia: Leeds and Biddle, 1900.

Nogami Taira. *Mito-han nōson no kenkyū.* Tokyo: Fūtōsha, 1997.

Ōishi Shinzaburō. "Matsunami Kanjūrō to Tokugawa Mitsukuni." In *Edo to chihō bunka,* edited by Ōishi Shinzaburō, vol. 1, 85–106. Tokyo: Bun'ichi sōgō shuppan, 1977.

Opitz, Fritz. "Die Lehensreformen des Tokugawa Nariaki nach dem 'Hitachi-Obi' des Fujita Tōko (Ein Beitrag zur Lehensgeschichte der Tokugawa-Zeit)." PhD Diss., Ludwig-Maximilians-Universität zu München, 1965.

Ōuchi Jisan. *Takeda Kōunsai shōden: ichimei Mito-han bakumatsu shi.* 2 vols. Mito: Hitachi shobō, 1979 [1936].

Paramore, Kiri. "Political Modernity and Secularization: Thoughts from the Japanese Eighteenth and Nineteenth Centuries." *Journal of Religious History* 36, no. 1 (March 2012): 19–30.

Ravina, Mark. "Kindaika, kindaisei to meikunzō no saikentō." *Rekishi hyōron* 717 (January 2010): 37–50.

Ravina, Mark. *Land and Lordship in Early-Modern Japan.* Stanford, CA: Stanford University Press, 1999.

Ravina, Mark. *The Last Samurai: The Life and Battles of Saigō Takamori.* Hoboken, NJ: John Wiley & Sons, 2004.

Ravina, Mark. *To Stand with the Nations of the World: Japan's Meiji Restoration in World History.* Oxford: Oxford University Press, 2017.

Roberts, Luke. "The Diverse Political Languages of Edo-Period Histories." In *Writing Histories in Japan*, edited by James Baxter and Joshua Fogel, 223–52. Kyoto: International Research Center for Japanese Studies, 2007.

Roberts, Luke. *Mercantilism in a Japanese Domain: The Merchant Origins of Economic Nationalism in 18th-Century Tosa.* Cambridge: Cambridge University Press, 1998.

Sapporo-shi kyōiku iinkai, ed. *Shin Sapporo shishi.* 8 vols. Sapporo: Sapporo-shi, 1986–2003.

Seya Yoshihiko. *Aizawa Seishisai.* Tokyo: Bunkyō shoin, 1942.

Seya Yoshihiko. *Ibaraki no shiwa.* Mito: Ibaraki shinbunsha, 2000.

Seya Yoshihiko. "Kaidai." In *Mitogaku*, edited by Imai Usaburō, Seya Yoshihiko, and Bito Masahide, 473–506. Tokyo: Iwanami shoten, 1973.

Seya Yoshihiko. *Mito no Nariaki.* Mito: Ibaraki shinbunsha, 2000.

Seya Yoshihiko and Suzuki Eiichi. *Ryūsei no gotoku: Bakumatsu ishin: Mito-han no eikō to kukyō.* Tokyo: NHK Publishing, 1998.

Shinozaki Yūta. "Ka'ei-ki ni okeru Tokugawa Nariaki 'san'yo' no jittai to eikyō." *Meiji ishin shi kenkyū* 15 (March 2018): 1–21.

Suzuki Eiichi. *Fujita Tōko,* Tokyo: Yoshikawa kōbunkan, 1998.

Suzuki Eiichi. *Mito-han gakumon kyōiku shi no kenkyū.* Tokyo: Yoshikawa kōbunkan, 1987.

Suzuki Eiichi. *Tokugawa Mitsukuni.* Tokyo: Yoshikawa kōbunkan, 2006.

Suzuki Fusako. "Mito-han Tenpō kaikaku no ichi kōsatsu: Komiyama Fūken to hansei kaikaku." *Ochanomizu shigaku* 15 (1972): 64–83.

Tadano Masahiro. *Fujita Tōko no shōgai.* Mito no jinbutsu series 6. Tokyo: Kinseisha, 1997.

Tadano Masahiro. *Mito shigaku no kakuronteki kenkyū.* Tokyo: Suibunsha, 2006.

Takahashi Bonsen. *Nihon jinkō kenkyū.* Tokyo: San'yūsha, 1941.

Takahashi Hirobumi. *Bakumatsu Mito-han to minshū undō: sonnō jōi undo to yonaoshi.* Tokyo: Seishi shuppan, 2005.

Terakado Morio. "Mito hanryō Hōei rokunen no zenpan ikki." In *Ibaraki hyakushō ikki*, edited by Ueda Toshio, 13–48. Tokyo: Fūtōsha, 1974.

Terunuma Yoshibumi. "Ihōjin no Gikō kan" In Terunuma, *Mito no gakufū*, 190–203.

Terunuma Yoshibumi. *Mito no gakufū: toku ni Kurita Hiroshi hakase wo chūshin toshite.* Mito: Mito shigakkai, 1998.

Terunuma Yoshibumi. "Ponsonby-hakase to *Eiyaku Kōdōkanki*." In Terunuma, *Mito no gakufū*, 166–89.

Toby, Ronald. *State and Diplomacy in Early Modern Japan.* Princeton, NJ: Princeton University Press, 1984.

Totman, Conrad. "Political Reconciliation in the Tokugawa Bakufu: Abe Masahiro and Tokugawa Nariaki, 1844–1852." *Personality in Japanese History*, edited by

Albert Craig and Donald Shively, 180–208. Berkeley: University of California Press, 1970.

Totman, Conrad. *The Collapse of the Tokugawa Bakufu, 1862–1868.* Honolulu: University of Hawai'i Press, 1980.

Totman, Conrad. "Tokugawa Yoshinobu and Kōbugattai: A Study of Political Inadequacy." *Monumenta Nipponica* 30, no. 4 (Winter 1975): 393–403.

Uchimura Kanzō. *Representative Men of Japan.* Vol. 2 of *The Complete Works of Uchimura Kanzō,* edited by Yamamoto Taijirō and Mutō Yōichi. Tokyo: Kyobunkan, 1971–1973.

Vlastos, Stephen. "Opposition Movements in Early Meiji, 1868–1885." In *The Nineteenth Century,* edited by Marius Jansen, 367–431. Cambridge: Cambridge University Press, 1989.

Wakabayashi, Bob Tadashi. *Anti-Foreignism and Western Learning in Early-Modern Japan: The "New Theses" of 1825* (Cambridge, MA: Council on East Asian Studies, Harvard University, 1986).

Walker, Brett. *The Conquest of Ainu Lands: Ecology and Culture in Japanese Expansionism, 1590–1800.* Berkeley: University of California Press, 2001.

Webb, Herschel. "The Mito Theory of the State." In *Researches in the Social Sciences on Japan: Essays and Abstracts by Graduates of the East Asian Institute, Columbia University,* edited by John E. Lane, 33–52. East Asia Institute of Columbia University, 1957.

Webb, Herschel. "What Is the *Dai Nihon Shi?*" *Journal of Asian Studies* 19 (1960): 135–49.

Xu Xingqing. "'Seizan inshi' 70-nen no saigetsu: Tokugawa Mitsukuni no gakumon, shisō keisei oyobi sono bunka isan." *Nihon shisō shi* 81 (2014): 8–25.

Yamakawa Kikue. *Buke no josei.* Tokyo: Iwanami shoten, 1983.

Yamakawa Kikue. *Women of the Mito Domain.* Trans. Kate Wildman Nakai. Tokyo: University of Tokyo Press, 1992.

Yasu Norihisa. "Kindai Mito no kōhai to hen'yō." *Rekishi kōron* 9, no. 5 (May 1983): 72–79.

Yates, Charles L. *Saigō Takamori: The Man Behind the Myth.* London: Kegan Paul International, 1995

Yokoyama Yoshinori. *Kaikoku zenya no sekai.* Nihon kinsei no rekishi 5. Tokyo: Yoshikawa kōbunkan, 2013.

Yonemoto, Marcia. *Mapping Early Modern Japan.* Berkeley: University of California Press, 2003.

Yoshida Kazunori. *Dai Nihon shi kiden shihyō sensha kō.* Tokyo: Kazama shobō, 1965.

Yoshida Toshizumi. *Meiji ishin to Mito nōson.* Tokyo: Dōjidaisha, 1995.

Yoshida Toshizumi. *Mito Mitsukuni no jidai: Mitogaku no genryū.* Tokyo: Azekura shobō, 2000.

Yoshida Toshizumi. *Mitogaku to Meiji Ishin.* Tokyo: Yoshikawa Kōbunkan, 2003.

Yoshida Toshizumi. *Kansei-ki Mitogaku no kenkyū.* Tokyo: Yoshikawa kōbunkan, 2011.

Yoshikawa, Lisa. *Making History Matter: Kuroita Katsumi and the Construction of Imperial Japan.* Cambridge, MA: Harvard University Asia Center, 2017.

Yoshizawa Giichi. *Hoppō ryōdo tankenshi no shin kenkyū: sono Mito-han to no kakawari.* Tokyo: Kinseisha, 2003.

Index

Shintō priests, 99, 142, 146, 191–94, 197, 202
Shintō: in Mito scholarship, 24, 28, 35, 71, 82–83, 94–95, 104–5, 122, 140; and religious reforms in Mito, 41–42, 126–27, 142, 147; as state religion, 82–83, 95, 105, 112, 217, 219–221
shishi, 82, 103–4 105, 109–12, 157, 164, 170–71, 192
Shōkōkan, 29–30, 35–36, 41, 51, 56; Aizawa Seishisai and, 87–89, 96, 98; Fujita Tōko and, 124, 130; Fujita Yūkoku and, 70, 74–75, 123; Harumori's downsizing of, 73; Komiyama Fūken and, 130–31; Tachihara Suiken and, 57–59, 69, 73; in the Meiji era, 218, 222
Shōwa Restoration, 221
shrines. *See* Shintō
spiritual history, 10, 13n20, 26, 52, 72, 75, 77n6
status order, 18, 21, 64, 208, 217–18; as idealized in Mito scholarship, 32, 70, 76
Student Faction, 203

Tachihara Suiken, 5, 51–52, *58*, 76, 148; birth and upbringing, 57; and *Dai Nihon shi*, 73–75; and Ezochi, 68, 84–85; Fujita Yūkoku and, 69–70, 73–76, 130; historiography of, 52; infanticide policy of, 65, 128; Komiyama Fūken and, 130–31; local scholarship of, 59–60; moderate reformers and, 75, 127; and Nagakubo Sekisui, 65; Neo-Confucian education of, 47; and shogunal reforms, 68–69; and Shōkōkan, 57–59, 69, 73; social observations of, 64–67, 134; and Tokugawa Harumori, 62–64, 67–69, 76; Takakura Taneaki, 16, 22, 59, 63–64
Takasai, Battle of, 204
Takasugi Shinsaku, 163–64

Takeda Kanejirō, 210
Takeda Kōunsai, *196*, 196–99, 202–7, 210
Tamazukuri, 197–98, 202
Tanaka Kōnan, 58–59
Tanuma Okitsugu, 67–68
taxation, 16, 19–22, 24, 36, 38–39, 41–42, 44–45, 53–56, 63–64, 125–26, 131–32, 136, 138–40, 145, 199, 219
temples. *See* Buddhism
tengu (as epithet), 129
Tengutō, 202–7. *See also* civil war
Tenpō Famine, 136–38
Tenpō Reforms, 5, 97–101, 119–21, 125–38; factionalism in, 130–32, 139–42, 148; as national model, 142–44, 149; reception in other domains, 144–45; resistance to, 127–30, 134, 139, 141–42; revival in the 1850s, 147–48
Three Houses (*gosanke*), 1, 4, 15, 17, 105, 143, 161, 166
Toba-Fushimi, Battle of, 156, 183–84
Tokiwa Shrine, 218
Tokugawa Akitake, 161, 211, 218, 224
Tokugawa Harumori, 52, 62–69, 72–76, 84–85, 176
Tokugawa Harutoshi, 75, 89, 122–23
Tokugawa Iemochi, 167, 178–80, 208
Tokugawa Iesada, 155, 166–67, 190
Tokugawa Ieyasu, 15–17, 26–27, 140
Tokugawa Ieyoshi, 143, 157, 160–61, 166
Tokugawa Mitsukuni, 3, 5, *25*; birth and upbringing 26–28; Confucianism and, 28–29; *Dai Nihon shi* and, 7, 26, 28–35, 45, 52, 56, 71, 74–75, 87, 220; death of, 44; domain crises and, 43, 53, 55; emulation of, 68, 132; "enlightened rule" of, 36–38, 45–46; Ezochi and, 39–40; imperial court and, 42, 44, 164; imperial loyalism of; 30–33; and Mito's "Golden Age," 15–17; murder of Fujii Mondayū,

About the Author

Michael Alan Thornton is a historian of early modern and modern Japan, with a particular interest in urban history. His work focuses on the transformation of Japanese cities between the Tokugawa and Meiji periods, including the development of new forms of social and political organization and municipal administration, with an eye to lessons that the rest of the world might learn from one of the planet's most urbanized societies. He is currently writing a book about Sapporo, Japan's first colonial capital, and co-editing a new historical guidebook to Tokyo with colleagues in the United States and Japan. After growing up in Kobe and Tokyo, he moved to the United States, where he received a BA in history from Yale University followed by a PhD in history from Harvard University. He is currently a postdoctoral associate at the Council of East Asian Studies at Yale.